REVOLUTION IN THE CLASSROOM

The inspired educational ideas of Maria Montessori have taken root all over the world—in Europe, the Americas, Russia, India, China, Japan. Through the Montessori method even the physical aspects of elementary schoolrooms have changed from dull regimentation to colorful informality.

Maria Montessori's first observations came from an Italian classroom of retarded children; she found that even these unfortunates, when encouraged, had a *spontaneous* interest in learning, and a *spontaneous* self-discipline. Applying her discovery to normal children, allowing her students to progress in an atmosphere of freedom, Dr. Montessori found that they paced their own development through a series of sensitive periods during which they became acutely aware of language, order, their own senses, society. Her method encouraged these periods to *explode* into bursts of creativity—reading, writing, passionate curiosity—thereby freeing the mind of even the apparent dullard and giving new scope to education and new breadth to the mind and spirit of the child.

E. M. STANDING was born of Quaker missionaries in Madagascar in 1887 and was educated in England in Quaker schools and at Cambridge University. A student of philosophy and a teacher of wide experience, he became a Catholic in 1923. Mr. Standing first met Maria Montessori in 1921, and for the next thirty years worked in close collaboration with her. This book was written in response to her urging that he prepare a systematic presentation of her principles and practice.

E. M. Standing

MARIA MONTESSORI

Her Life and Work

With an Introduction by
John J. McDermott

Ⓟ
A PLUME BOOK

TO
MARIA
MONTESSORI

PLUME
Published by the Penguin Group
Penguin Books USA Inc., 375 Hudson Street,
New York, New York 10014, U.S.A.
Penguin Books Ltd, 27 Wrights Lane,
London W8 5TZ, England
Penguin Books Australia Ltd, Ringwood,
Victoria, Australia
Penguin Books Canada Ltd, 10 Alcorn Avenue,
Toronto, Ontario, Canada, M4V 3B2
Penguin Books (N.Z.) Ltd, 182-190 Wairau Road,
Auckland 10, New Zealand

Penguin Books Ltd, Registered Offices:
Harmondsworth, Middlesex, England

Published by Plume, an imprint of Dutton Signet, a division of
Penguin Books USA Inc. *Maria Montessori: Her Life and Work* originally appeared
in a Mentor edition. Published by arrangement with the Estate of Edwin M. Standing

First Plume Printing, September, 1984
16 15 14 13 12

 REGISTERED TRADEMARK—MARCA REGISTRADA

LIBRARY OF CONGRESS CATALOG CARD NUMBER: 84-60705

PRINTED IN THE UNITED STATES

Caro Benedetto Sta..dic? .

   Era una meraviglia quello scritto sulla
mia vita – bellissimo come arte di scrittore! (non
faccio commenti sulla sostanza, perché è un
aspetto ora esprime le sue impressioni a traverso
le sua propria esaltazione.) Ho fatto alcune piccole
correzioni da dettagli storici... Sono impaziente
d'vedere tutto il libro... ... .
Grazie tanto e tanto delle sue lettere e d' quelle
fedele Benedette – che rende prezioso il suo cuore.
   Coraggio.....! coraggio per il raccolto —
Sua sempre affma
       Mem...molina

Author's Note

DR. MONTESSORI promised to write an introduction to this book, but she died before she was able to fulfil her promise. She did, however, at one time or another read a large part of the manuscript and expressed her warm approval of it. Below is part of one of her letters referring to it (Benedetto was the Dottoressa's name for the author):

Dear Benedetto Standing,

What you have written on my life is a wonder—and beautiful as a piece of writing! (I am not making any comments on the substance of it because here is an apostle who is voicing his own enthusiastic impressions.) I have, however, made some minor corrections in matters of "historical" detail. I am impatient to see the whole book . . .

Thank you again and again for your letters and for that blessed loyalty—which makes your friendship so precious.

Courage . . .! Courage for the harvest—

Yours always most affectionately,

MAMMOLINA

Contents

LIST OF ILLUSTRATIONS
(BETWEEN PAGES 192-193)

1   Maria Montessori. A portrait by Sir Frank Salisbury.

2   Maria Montessori as a university lecturer and practising physician in Rome (*circa* 1905).

3   Above. Exercises of practical life. "Washing day" in a Montessori school in Berlin.

4   Below. A room in a Montessori school in Rotterdam, showing a part of the carefully prepared environment.

5   Above. Indirect preparation for writing: the sandpaper touchboards, "Rough and Smooth."

6   Below. Indirect preparation for writing: composing words and sentences with the movable letters (Denmark).

7   Writing has now come of itself, and the big words come pouring easily out of the small head (Acton School, England).

8   Above. First steps in addition with number rods. "Steps," be it noted, in a literal as well as a metaphysical sense.

9   Below. History Time-Line from 2000 B.C. (Abraham) to A.D. 2000. It is divided into centuries.

10   Working out, by means of coloured symbolical pegs, the square of a trinomial (Athens).

11   Dr. Montessori at the age of eighty, at the Gatehouse Montessori School, St. Bartholomew the Great, London. This was during her last visit to England (1951).

Introduction

Unfortunately, except when it is centered on a notable and precocious performance here or there, the media's attention to children is generally focused on the heinous crime of child abuse. For those of us for whom children are a sacred trust, the increase of such abuse is bewildering. Part of the cause of such social violence is that as a society we have not sufficiently articulated both the fragility and the potentialities of the child. The moguls of national education seem to be of little help on this matter, for they concentrate on quantitative scores in their evaulation of children, as though preparing little creatures for a fattening, for entrance into the churning and anomic gears of postindustrial society.

In all seriousness, though many of our children suffer from the deep maladies of inner loneliness, alienation, cultural sadness, and the confusion that often results from broken families—many educators now think that the number-one priority for a child in our society is the attainment of computer literacy. Surely by now, in the penultimate decade of the twentieth century, we should realize that mere technological gimmicks do not address the needs of the inner life of the child. Maria Montessori (1870–1952), for one, knew better. It was she, more than any other person in our century, who realized that the life of the child demanded an education that was ordered, creative, and distinctively personal.

Maria Montessori had great hope that ours would be the century of the child. For that hope to be realized, one thing above all was necessary— that Western civilization cease viewing the human situation as hierarchical, as a ladder on which our first steps take meaning only from the last. Within such a conceptual framework, the child was required to become an adult as quickly as possible, and the education of children was characterized by the imposition on the child of the needs and the frame of reference of the adult world.

Freud, by proving that the phenomena of childhood pervade the human situation, demonstrated the inadequacy of such a viewpoint. He held that adult life could be understood only as a continuance of phases and tensions at work not only in the child but in the infant as well. Unfortunately, the original power of this insight has not been sustained; contemporary psychiatry, occupied with easing the plight of the beleaguered modern adult, has failed to make a breakthrough on the problems posed when Freud's view of the child is placed within the total fabric of society, particularly as related to elementary education. Instead, what were originally placeholders in a fascinating descriptive analysis of infantile and child psychic life have tended to become doctrine closed to experimental reworking; open terms have become locked categories which cut us off from the freeing experiences that should spring from insights as seminal as those of Freud.

Now the biology that informs Maria Montessori's view of the child is of a different cast. She shares with William James, Henri Bergson, and John Dewey the late nineteenth-century awareness of the developmental nature of humankind in an evolutionary context. The theory of evolution caused most people to look behind them toward the origins of humankind; but the more explosive insight—to use Montessori's metaphor—was achieved by those who took seriously the fact that matter had a history and then boldly affirmed that it must also have a future. An understanding of human life, they held, depends on a new formulation of the unique way in which we live through matter while not equivalent to it. This tradition, central to contemporary thought, offers a series of insights and methods that assume a developmental framework and simultaneously point the way to sustenance of those values central to the genuine growth of personal life. It seeks in addition to create new values capable of moving the human situation to the "unheard-of-heights" dreamed of by Thoreau.

Though Americans have begun to realize it only within the last two decades, the work of Maria Montessori is in the forefront of such efforts. It is a unique contribution to a distinctly modern movement. She began her work with mentally retarded children and thus, in a sense, shares a point of departure with Freud, who started with people suffering aberrant personality problems. Yet Montessori soon became far more concerned with the wider possibilities offered by the application of these new scientific methods of inquiry to the normal personality, particularly that of the child. She shares with Dewey an evolutionary and experimental pedagogy; yet she is far more willing than he to submit religious and spiritual qualities to the rigorous demands of concrete educational processes. Deeply committed to Catholicism, Montessori nevertheless opposes that type of religiously oriented school which is characterized by an educational theory outmoded in language and insight and negligent of empirical data about the human personality. Montessori demands that the data of anthropology and the natural sciences take their place at the base of educational practices, including those of a religious nature. By comparison, then, with other modern efforts, Montessori's view of the child is perhaps the most comprehensive available. And for this reason: she does not see children as an element in a series of overarching concerns; she sees them as an experimental touchstone of both educational methods and the human experience as a whole.

Not the least merit of Mr. Standing's book is this, that it is permeated by love of Maria Montessori and her work. Standing writes simply. Without distortion, he brings together the main lines of her thought and places them in the context of their concrete application in the Montessori schools. After a discussion of her early career as a pioneer woman physician in Italy, he turns to an analysis of her remarkably successful work with slum children in 1907. Mr. Standing rightly holds that the search for the "normalized child" is at the heart of the Montessori approach and is the catalyst that allowed her so many fruitful insights to the genuine situation of childhood. Reversing the usual approach that considers the child a fertile field in which the adult plants the seeds of sound development, or a formless being awaiting the molding of the educator, Montessori "discovered that children possess different and higher qualities than those we usually attribute to them. It was as if a higher form of personality had been liberated and a new child had come into being."

Just as the liberation of the inner life of the child is the point of origin for Montessori's work, so too is liberty the atmosphere in which the life of the child is to develop. She then offers us a truly amazing set of interdisciplinary elements as necessary to pedagogy. Her basic atmosphere for the educational process is freedom; her basic methodology is experimental. Montessori seeks as the goal of freedom the ordering of the inner life of the child as well as the ordering of the relationship existing between the highest activities of the mind and those fundamental sense activities so brilliantly described and analyzed by her under the name of "sensorial foundations." Montessori is also profoundly aware of the necessary communal setting for all individual life; she has bequeathed to us some remarkable instances of successful miniature life communities carried on in her schools, better known as "prepared environments." So intriguing is her notion of freedom that she claims as a result of its proper nourishment, children prefer "work" to "play," or at least the distinction is rendered as not to the point.

If we are given a new set of perspectives for viewing human life, a new set of values and relationships emerges. What has been said of William James by Bergson is certainly true of Montessori; with her "the whole man [woman] counts." And she shares with James the belief that religious experience is a legitimate and indeed, a profound aspect of the philosophy of the person. In the same decade that Montessori makes her discovery of the "normalized child" and attempts in her *Casa dei Bambini* to realize experimentally each heretofore hidden dimension of the child's life, James tells us in the conclusion to his *Varieties of Religious Experience* that "so long as we deal with the cosmic and the general, we deal only with the symbols of reality, but *as soon as we deal with private and personal phenomena as such, we deal with realities in the completest sense of the term*.'' Maria Montessori was fascinated by such private and personal phenomena, particularly as found in the child, and she utilized all the available empirical data and experimental techniques. But her insights into the child soon outstripped the techniques she inherited. She was now forced to couple her vision with technical innovations in materials and methods. Only these would enable her to solve the educational problems she clearly diagnosed.

With regard to the book in hand by E. M. Standing, I offer praise and some caution. Mr. Standing is an enthusiastic disciple of Maria Montessori. In fact, this book is almost hagiographic—that is, Montessori is presented as virtually without fault. In a time when we are hypercritical of the efforts of our peers, this attitude of Standing is refreshing. She is worthy of his praise, and her work stands as a monument to our efforts to understand and educate our children. He is right in concentrating on her accomplishments, for they are many and important. Yet the readers who find themselves enthusiastic about Montessori and her achievements as a result of Standing's exposition should not allow their enthusiasm to flower in a cultural vacuum. Rather they should acquaint themselves with the intentions, accomplishments, and weaknesses of the American educational establishment. It makes no sense to adhere to Montessori's program at the expense of that of John Dewey and other pioneers in early childhood education, most of whose vision has been distorted in the competitive atmosphere so characteristic of early-learning centers. To do so would be the height of irony, since one reason why the Montessori method did not take root earlier in America, despite its effort to do so, was the fact that it was too often seen as an antidote to American educational practice and values when, in fact, Montessori schools can be structured to sustain those values that are worthy. The gap between the philosophical, psychological, and social perception of the child as held by Montessori and that held by John and Alice Dewey and their followers is small and not significant. Montessori had a richer grasp of the life of the child, whereas the Deweys knew more of the social and environmental context in which children come to consciousness and learn.

A second problem with Standing's approach, which can be infectious, is the temptation to accept the Montessori system whole and entire rather than as one set of seminal insights among several, all of which can be used to formulate an expandable educational theory. (The adherents of Freud face this difficulty; so do the adherents of Montessori.) Certainly, the varied exercises of Montessori's pedagogy form a remarkably coherent and unified latticework of theory and practice. Yet she herself regarded that splendid creation as *un tentativo*: the person who ceases to be experimental ceases to follow Montessori's example. The cultish atmosphere that at times surrounds her followers does violence to her basic concerns. For example, the famous Montessori materials used for teaching reading and mathematics lack modern aesthetic qualities; there is no reason why they cannot and should not be radically improved through experiment. Some followers, however, consider them sacrosanct, an indication perhaps that they have lost Montessori's commitment to scientific inquiry. Rigid devotion to the details of her method might permit Montessori schools to spread; but they would do so as a parallel system—something foreign, something that did not penetrate to the heart of the contemporary scene. It would, I feel, be far wiser for the reader of this book to come away from it an advocate of those elements essential to Montessori's view of the child, for they can stand not only the test of time but the fluid nature of the society in which we live.

The most striking feature of Montessori's work is that her method, her teachers, and the learning children in her programs are to be found throughout the world. No other educator has such global influence, for although Pestalozzi, Rousseau, Herbart, and Piaget have each made their contributions, they are restricted for the most part to Western culture. John Dewey, it is true, has had enormous influence in the Orient but not in Western Europe nor the third world. Montessori, to the contrary, has struck a universal chord in the lives of children wherever they are found. I trace this important fact to three sources. First, she wisely believed that children of very early age had an ability to learn—independent of their peer group cultures—that was rarely tapped in any formal way. Second, it was not necessary to import teachers who had a secret message to deliver. Indeed, teachers in the usual sense were not part of the Montessori picture. What was important was the presence of Montessori directresses and later directors, who could be either imported or homegrown so long as they honored the autodidactic activities of the children. It was the children, after all, who taught themselves, so long as the environment was prepared, the materials utilized, and the goals or directions made clear. In very young children this could take place, and *has* taken place, in a wide variety of cultures throughout the world. Third, The Montessori children were not class-structured. From the first days of the Casa dei Bambini, Montessori was convinced that children of all backgrounds and all cultural limitations were capable of self-learning. Indeed, it is often characteristic of a Montessori program that the children are representative of a far wider range of cultural and economic advantages than is true in the more traditional programs.

The global influence of Montessori was not an accident of history. Long before our own awareness of the inextricability of our lives on this planet, she saw the need for the recognition and development of the abilities of children throughout the world. As early as 1910, she resigned her lectureship at the University of Rome, struck her name from the list of practicing physicians, and committed herself to "all the children in the world, born and as yet unborn." She then began a lifelong journey on behalf of children's rights and of their liberation from the darkness of unknowing. Her work was to take her beyond Italy to the United States, Latin America, India, Ceylon, France, Germany, Holland, Ireland, Spain, Austria, and Pakistan. Unesco had its spiritual if unsung founder, and the global consciousness of our time can be traced back to its remarkable anticipation by this extraordinary woman educator.

When Maria Montessori died in 1952, she was all but unknown in the United States. But her view of education can contribute to the solution of problems facing contemporary America. At this time, in 1984, there are close to one thousand Montessori schools in the United States. Further, there is increasing evidence of the influence of the Montessori method on early-learning programs of every persuasion. To those concerned with religious education she speaks in this book of the role that experiment and awareness of the child's developmental nature must play if true religious education is to be achieved. For those concerned with public and secular education, she cuts through the peculiar dilemma that arises from the affirmation of the continuity of school and society and the simultaneous denial of the teaching of values central to that very same continuity. To all, the work of Maria Montessori proclaims that the role of the spirit in the development of the child—a role that experimental methods help us define—can be wedded to a methodology harmonious with the nature of the child and pointing toward the direction modern pedagogy must take. In this way, the work of Maria Montessori presents a vigorous challenge to American thought and culture, particularly as ramified in education. After all, if we are to have a future, every century should be the century of the child.

John J. McDermott
Distinguished Professor of Philosophy
Texas A&M University

Preface

With Dr. Maria Montessori there came into the sphere of education a new and vital impulse. There is not a civilized country which has not in some measure felt the impact of her vivifying principles. This was made abundantly clear at the time of her death, in May 1952, when tributes to her life-long labour on behalf of the child appeared in the press in every part of the world.

More than a generation has passed since the year (1907) when the name Montessori flashed like a comet across the sphere of education, and the world read with astonishment of the almost incredible doings of those small slum children in the first Casa dei Bambini in Rome. Yet notwithstanding this considerable passage of time—a period in which two world wars took place—we find the Montessori principle as powerful today as ever it was. Indeed more powerful, for every year it continues to make fresh developments and new conquests. Its conquests are not so sudden and spectacular as in those early years, but they are none the worse for that; for they are more profound, and more permanent. Every year in England,[1] Ireland, Italy, Holland, Denmark, Germany, France, and India (this list is not complete) students congregate at various training centres, to take courses varying from six months to three years in the Montessori method. Furthermore, the demand for such courses greatly exceeds the supply, on account of the insufficiency of trained personnel to give them.

For more than a quarter of a century Montessori principles have worked like a leaven in almost every country, affecting to a greater or lesser degree the spirit of their educational systems, especially Infant and Primary Schools. Sixteen years ago Sir Percy Nunn, Director of the London Day Training College, wrote: "It argues no ingratitude to the great name of Froebel and his thousands of devoted followers to connect the new impulse which is everywhere at work in our schools more

[1] Montessori Training Organization, 1 Park Crescent, London, W.1.

directly with the doctrine and labours of Dr. Maria Montessori than with any other single source."

Dr. P. Ballard, author of many well-known books on education, and for thirty years an L.C.C. Inspector of Schools, stated in a book on Individual Work Methods that "the influence of Dr. Montessori's principles revolutionized the infant schools in the London County Council within a dozen years." In the report of the Consultative Committee on Infant and Nursery Schools, published by the Board of Education in 1933, the authors state that the adoption of Individual Work Methods in L.C.C. schools was largely the result of the impact of Montessori's ideas. In the same way it could be shown how Dr. Montessori's influence has been a vital factor in educational developments in many other countries.

Unfortunately, the beneficial effect of her influence has often been much reduced by those who have only partially grasped her ideas. To take one or two of her principles—as many persons have done—and attempt to put them into practice without regarding their relationship to the whole, is bound to result in something bizarre and lopsided. Such fragmentary applications of Montessori's ideas perfectly exemplify the old motto, *Corruptio optimi pessima*.

One could give numerous examples. Many people, for instance, have seized hold of Dr. Montessori's idea of giving the child liberty without understanding its true nature, nor its relation to the prepared environment, nor to the other children in it. This has resulted in an undisciplined chaos; and explains why one may still hear the criticism that under the Montessori system there is no discipline and the children are allowed to do anything they like. "Nothing," says Father Drinkwater in his *Educational Essays*,[2] "could be more comically untrue; no one who has seen Dr. Montessori for five seconds, even on a film, could seriously believe it; Montessori freedom means *unlimited freedom to do right*."

One could give many more examples of this misapplication of Dr. Montessori's ideas; but it always comes to the same thing. It inevitably brings disaster if one tries to put the Montessori method into practice without a previous grasp of her principles, seen as interrelated parts of a living whole.

A principle—as its very name implies—is something which comes first. A principle is a master key which opens a thousand locks; a compass which will guide you, even on an uncharted sea. To remain on the level of practice, without a grasp of principles, is to be in constant danger of floundering from one error to another.

[2] Burns and Oates, p. 263.

In this book we have not attempted to give a detailed account of how the various school subjects—the three Rs, history, geography, geometry, religion, etc.—are taught under the Montessori method. Our aim, rather, has been to delineate the various psychological and pedagogical principles which underlie Montessori's whole approach to the child. It will be found that—taken as a whole—these principles coincide with the laws of psychophysical development. They are primarily concerned with those mysterious "inner directives" which govern the successive stages of the child's mental growth, as his intelligence—supported by the senses and movement—constructs itself from year to year.

Medieval philosophers were right when they said that education (like medicine) is an art which necessitates the cooperation with nature. In her later years Montessori used to describe the function of education as an "aid to life." And certainly the more deeply one penetrates into her ideas, the more surely does one find oneself in the presence of the mysterious, hidden, creative forces of life itself. This is what made Professor Brooglever-Fortuyn, a Dutch biologist, write nearly twenty years ago: "Those who are not favourable to the Montessori method ask sceptically what will become of the method after a number of years, meaning to imply that before long a new system will have taken its place. It is not difficult to explain to such that the Montessori method is founded on general characteristics of life proper to all organisms; and that it will last as long as life itself. It is not possible to imagine that such a principle having once been introduced into pedagogy could be abandoned."

The author first became acquainted with Maria Montessori in 1921; and from that time, until her death in 1952, was fortunate enough to be in constant touch with her, collaborating in one way or another—through articles, lectures, teaching in Montessori schools, or as her assistant and representative in training courses for teachers.

Dr. Montessori's published writings—many of which are unfortunately out of print in their English translations—do not give an adequate idea of the magnitude and variety of her labours. It is probably no exaggeration to say that less than thirty per cent of her researches have as yet found their way into print.

Though her writings are brilliant and have been translated into over a score of different languages, it was as a lecturer that Montessori expressed herself most fully. It was, in fact, largely through her lectures, especially in her international training courses, that she made known as years passed the results of her latest researches. (Her last book, for instance,

The Absorbent Mind, is an almost verbatim record of a series
of lectures given in her twenty-fourth international course in
Ahmedabad, India, in 1948.)

The materials for the present book have been culled from
many and varied sources; in part from Dr. Montessori's own
published works; but mostly from a collated study of type-
script records of innumerable lectures given at courses and
congresses during the past thirty years; and also from conversations with Dr. Montessori herself. For this reason it has been
found almost impossible to give chapter and verse for the
many quotations from Dr. Montessori which are scattered
copiously throughout the pages of this book. But the reader
may take it for granted that any passage in quotation marks,
not otherwise acknowledged, is a genuine statement by Dr.
Montessori.

Some of Dr. Montessori's ideas, such as valorization of personality, or "education as an armament of peace," have necessarily been left out; others, such as the "absorbent mind" and
the reform of secondary education, only cursorily touched upon. It seemed better—for the time being at any rate—to omit
these in order to make room for that section of this book
which is devoted to a comparison between the ideas and practices of Maria Montessori and those of her great predecessor,
Friedrich Froebel, founder of the Kindergarten. This is an
urgent practical matter on which questions are constantly
being asked by parents and teachers, and upon which, unfortunately, there still exists a good deal of misunderstanding.

The chapters devoted to Dr. Montessori's life make no
claim to be a complete biography. They have been limited to
those aspects of her career which help to illuminate her life-
work.

In conclusion, I would like to record my gratitude to: Miss
Fox, Mrs. Carr, M.D., Rev. Dr. and Mrs. Wallbank, Mrs.
Polak, Mr. A. Goodbody, Mrs. O. Goodbody, Sir Thomas and
Lady Bazley (and many others) who have in one way or an-
other assisted in the production of this book.

E. MORTIMER STANDING

The Feast of the Epiphany, 1957 [3]

---

[3] Exactly fifty years, to the day, from the opening of the first Casa dei Bambini in Rome (see p. 38).

PART ONE

Life of Dr. Maria Montessori

CHAPTER I   PREPARATION

Early Years

When I was at school we had a teacher whose fixed idea was to make us learn by heart the lives of famous women, in order to incite us to imitate them. The exhortation which accompanied these narrations was always the same: "You too should try to become famous. Would you not like to become famous?" "Oh no," I replied drily one day, "I shall never be that. I care too much for the children of the future to add yet another biography to the list."

In spite of this praiseworthy desire, fame did come to that schoolgirl when she grew up, and with it "yet another biography" to add to the list.

Maria Montessori was born at Chiaravalle in the province of Ancona on 31st August in the year 1870—the year in which Italy first became a united nation. Her father, Alessandro Montessori, was descended from a noble family from Bologna. He was a typical conservative of the old school, a military man, who in his time had been commended for bravery in action. To the end of his life he was dignified and soldierly in his bearing, and well known for his punctilious politeness.

Dr. Montessori's mother was Renilde Stoppani, niece of the illustrious Antonio Stoppani, the great philosopher-scientist-priest to whom the University of Milan erected a monument at his death. Renilde Montessori was a lady of singular piety and charm, and between the daughter and the mother—whom she resembled in appearance and temperament—there grew up an affection and understanding which remained unchanged through all the vicissitudes of Maria's life until death separated them in the year 1912.

There are still some people who think that the Montessori method consists in allowing children to do just what they like. This was emphatically not the method employed in Maria's home: her mother believed in discipline, and Maria's life was none the less happy on account of it. One day, on coming back from a month's holiday, little Maria began to complain: "I am hungry; I want something to eat." "You must wait a little while, dear," replied the mother. But the child would not wait, and became so insistent that her mother, opening a cupboard and finding a piece of bread left there from a month before, said, "If you cannot wait, take this!"[1]

Every day Maria had to do a certain amount of knitting for the poor. This certainly could not have been a trial for her, for even as a child she showed an interest in those less fortunate than herself. In her neighbourhood was a hunchbacked girl. Pitying her condition, Maria made special friends with her, and used to take her out for walks as often as possible. This good intention did not however bring equally good results, for the contrast between the two girls was so striking that in the end her mother tactfully suggested that this plan should be dropped and other means found to help the unfortunate girl.[2]

Another incident in her childhood is recorded which also has somewhat of a prophetic note. On one occasion it happened that there was a sharp difference of opinion between her parents. Little Maria took a chair, dragged it to a position between them, climbed up on it, and then joined their hands together as tightly as she could. Just as we shall find her all her life interested in "the underdog," so she has always tended to be a peacemaker. In fact her whole life's work could be summed up as an effort to bring to an end the agelong struggle which has been waged and is still being waged between the Child and the Adult, a struggle which—as we shall see later—is no less real because it is carried on unconsciously.

Maria's childhood was spent in Ancona, where she attended the usual state day school. As a young child it would seem that she was without any special scholastic ambitions. One day she met one of her little companions crying bitterly because she had not been moved up into another class. "I could not understand this," said Montessori, "because—as I told her—one room seemed to me just as good as another!"

Maria must have seemed at times a rather odd and puzzling child not only to her teachers but to her school companions. When playing with these—she was generally the leader—she would sometimes make the most unexpected remarks, as when, to express her disapproval, she would exclaim contemptuously, "You! why you are not even *born* yet." Was she, even at that time, dimly aware of her doctrine that the development of the

[1] *A True Romance*, by Anna Maccheroni, p. 11.
[2] *Op. cit.*

individual can be described as a succession of new births at consecutively higher levels? Anyway, her companions objected to this treatment, complaining to their parents, "She says we are not even born yet!"

Maria herself had a great sense of personal dignity even as a child. One day one of the teachers spoke disparagingly of the expression in her eyes (*quegli occhi*) in her hearing. As a protest Maria never raised "those eyes" in the presence of that teacher again. This incident, trifling in itself, is worth recording in view of the great importance Montessori placed, in her system, of treating even the smallest child with a respect that amounts almost to reverence. It is interesting, too, to note that she found it easier to protest against an infringement of her personal dignity by an adult than by her companion; witness the remark she once made to one of these, "Please remind me that I have made up my mind never to speak to you again!"

Choosing a Career—"Anything but a Teacher"

When Maria was about twelve years old her parents moved to Rome so as to be able to give their only child a better education than Ancona could offer. But even with the educational advantages of the metropolis it was not easy to satisfy the ambitions of this singular child. She already had her own ideas as to her own education. At the age of fourteen she became very interested in mathematics, an interest which she retained all her life. Her parents suggested that she should take up teaching, which was practically the only career open to women at that time. But this she categorically refused even to consider. Anything but this! Since she had an aptitude for mathematics, and was very fond of it, she decided that she would take up the career of engineering. Even at the present day (war emergencies excepted) that would be rather an unusual career for a woman; but in those days it was unthought of. As the "high-class seminaries for young ladies" did not cater for such an unusual ambition, Maria attended classes at a technical school for boys. After a while, her tastes again changing, she felt more strongly the attractions of biology. But in time, the sensitive period [3] for this having passed, she came to the final decision that what she really wanted was to study medicine.

Unfortunately this was a case of jumping out of the frying pan into the fire. A young lady to attend a medical school!! The thing was unheard of, preposterous, impossible. All the Italian Mrs. Grundys raised their hands in pious horror. This

[3] See Chapter VII.

determined young lady cared not a whit; but snapping her fingers at all of them, managed to obtain an interview with Dr. Bacelli, head of the Board of Education. When *he* informed her in quite definite terms that it would be impossible for her to carry out her project, she thanked him politely, shook hands cordially, and quietly remarked, "I *know* I shall become a Doctor of Medicine." Thereupon she bowed and went out.

We cannot follow all the details of her struggle. Suffice it to say that she had her way in the end, and was duly admitted to the medical faculty of the University—the first woman medical student in Italy.

And what is more she won a scholarship—in fact a series of scholarships, year after year. She further augmented her income, whilst a student, by giving private tuition. In fact she very largely paid her own way through her university career, a point which is worth noting in connection with the ideas she was to put forth in later life as to the value of economic independence in adolescent development.

Trials of Student Days

Once admitted to the faculty of medicine, this intrepid girl by no means found herself at the end of her difficulties. The men students, jealous of this intrusion into a sphere hitherto exclusively their own, subjected her to a series of petty persecutions for many months. They soon discovered, however, that she was not to be frightened away. She confronted her tormentors with such pluck that in time persecution was changed to a sort of grudging admiration. Typical of her good-humoured indifference to their attacks was the remark she used to make to some of the students, who—when passing her in the corridors—used always to emit a contemptuous "Pooh!" "Blow away, my friends," she would cheerfully reply, "the harder you blow, the higher up I shall go."

There was a force of character in this girl student—a something or other about her—that impressed even those light-hearted medical students. One of these, who used to sit behind her in the lecture room, had developed a habit of making a kind of trembling movement with his foot, so that Maria felt the vibrations transmitted to her desk. She did not like this, and turning her head round looked angrily at her fellow student. He stopped the movement at once, whispering to his neighbour, "I am immortal." "What makes you say that?" was the whispered reply. "If I weren't I should be dead. Did you see the look she gave me?"

"In those days" (I once heard Montessori remark) "I felt as if I could have done anything"; and certainly it seemed that—for her—difficulties existed simply to be overcome.

When the present writer was in Rome he met an aged professor who had been a lecturer in the medical faculty at the time we are speaking about. This gentleman related an incident which stood out in his memory after many years. It happened one day (he said) when he was due to lecture, that a tremendous snowstorm swept over Rome. It was a blizzard of such exceptional severity that all his students failed to turn up—all except one; and that was his girl student. The latter, finding herself the only person in the auditorium, modestly suggested that the professor should postpone his lecture. He would not hear of it; such zeal should not go unrewarded. So the lecture was given as usual—to an audience of one!

Maria had to face other difficulties at the university of a more terrifying nature than the animosity of the men students. In those days it was not considered proper that a girl should dissect dead bodies in the presence of men students. So her practical work in the dissecting room had to be done by herself; and this meant that she was obliged to pass many hours alone amongst the corpses, very often in the evening after darkness had set in. It needed a good deal of determination to carry on in such a macabre setting. Furthermore, her way was made still more difficult on account of the opposition of her father, who disapproved of the career she had chosen.

A Prophetic Incident

We are not surprised to learn that, under the oppressive burden of these and still other difficulties, the spirit of the young pioneer came almost to breaking point. One day, overwhelmed by a feeling of despair, the young girl student determined to abandon the unequal struggle against this "sea of troubles." She therefore left the dissecting room with her mind quite made up to seek another career less strewn with obstacles.

It happened that her way home led through the Pincio Park, which at that hour was almost empty of people. As she walked along, thinking of her decision, she passed a shabbily dressed woman accompanied by a child of some two years of age. The woman was dishevelled and dirty—a professional beggar—and began at once to beg for alms as Montessori approached. It was not the woman, however, but the child who was destined to alter the course of her life. Whilst the mother tuned up her professional whine the little child, quite unconcerned, continued to sit on the ground playing with a small piece of coloured paper. There was something in the child's expression—so serenely happy in the possession of that worthless scrap of coloured paper, observing it with the full absorption of its little soul—that, suddenly, to the student watching, it brought an inner experience best described in the words of Matthew Arnold's *Buried Life*. It was as though

> A bolt was shot back somewhere in the breast
> And a lost pulse of feeling stirred again.

Moved by emotions she could not herself explain, she turned round, and went straight back to the dissecting room. From that moment her revulsion to the work in those uncongenial surroundings left her, never to return. From that moment, too, she never doubted that she had a vocation. After relating this incident, in a conversation, Montessori went on to say, "I cannot explain it. It just happened like that. You will probably think it a very silly story: and if you told it to others they would probably just laugh at it."

In this we see an example of that mysterious affinity which exists, deep down in the soul of the genius, towards that work which he is destined to perform, and everything connected with it. It was the same with Froebel, as we shall show in a later chapter.[4] Both he and Montessori were sent into the world to shed new light on the unfathomed depths of the child's soul.

At that time, and for many years to come, Montessori had no idea that she would find her life's mission in the sphere of education. Her life, taken as a whole, demonstrates the principle she was to preach in later years, that "the preparations of life are indirect." When she was taken ill about this time and her friends were anxious about her recovery, she said, "Do not be alarmed; I shall not die; I have work to do (*Ho da fare*)."

A Reconciliation

Though her father strongly disapproved of the line she had taken, her mother, Renilde Montessori, never doubted her daughter's ability to make good in the path she had chosen. Renilde was Maria's constant friend and sympathizer and helped her in every way she could.

Happily, too, the estrangement between father and daughter was not destined to last for ever: it was in fact terminated in rather a dramatic manner. It was a tradition in the medical school at that time that every new graduate should deliver a

4Chapter XIX.

public lecture to the Faculty after his first year. This was a sufficiently trying ordeal in any case, but especially so in hers. Prejudice was still running high, and many in the audience had come not only in a spirit of criticism, but prepared to create a disturbance. "I felt like a lion-tamer that day," said Montessori in recalling the occasion.

It happened that on the particular morning—when this lecture was to take place—that a friend of Alessandro Montessori, meeting him in the street, remarked with some surprise, "Aren't you coming to the lecture?" "What lecture?" replied the father, who had lost touch with his daughter's doings. Explanations followed; and the result was that Alessandro was persuaded, rather against his will, to come to the lecture. The young doctor's triumph was as complete as Portia's. Her treatment of her theme was so brilliant, her delivery so faultless, her personality so fascinating, that all opposition was swept away and she received a great ovation. Her father found himself the centre of eager congratulations from all sides at having such a daughter. The ugly duckling had indeed turned out to be a swan.

Maria Montessori thus became the first woman in Italy to take the degree of Doctor of Medicine. The same year (1896) she was chosen to represent the women of Italy at a feminist congress held at Berlin. Here she championed the cause of the working women; and did so with such ardour and efficiency that her portrait appeared in the press of many countries. A few years later (1900) she attended a similar congress in London. Here she attacked the practice of employing child labour in the mines of Sicily; and gave her support to a movement—patronized by Queen Victoria—which was directed against the exploitation of child labour. It is interesting to notice at this point how—right from the beginning—we see the prominence of a certain trait in Montessori, which we might perhaps best describe as fighting on behalf of the underdog. In almost the last conversation I had with Dr. Montessori —she was then over eighty years of age—she happened to mention that upon this, her first visit to England, she was entertained, along with other members of the Congress, by Queen Victoria herself, with whom she had a conversation.

Montessori Comes in Touch With Deficient Children

Another ten years were to elapse before Dr. Montessori was to discover her great mission in life—ten crowded years of the most incessant and varied labours, which we must now briefly outline.

Soon after graduating Dr. Montessori was appointed assistant doctor at the Psychiatric Clinic in the University of Rome. Part of her duty, in this connection, was to visit the asylums for the insane in Rome in order to select suitable subjects for the clinic. It was in this way that she was led to take an interest in idiot children, who, at that period, were classed together with the insane. Here again it was a case of sympathy for the underdog: her generous heart was touched by the piteous condition of these unfortunate children, and she longed to help them.

But with her it was not only a question of sympathy, a question of the heart, she used her head too. She saw these poor creatures and their environment with an eye illuminated by the light of genius. The following anecdote is very revealing.

In one of the lunatic asylums she came across a number of these unhappy children herded together like prisoners in a prisonlike room. The woman who looked after them did not attempt to conceal the disgust with which she regarded them. Montessori asked her why she held them in such contempt. "Because," the woman replied, "as soon as their meals are finished they throw themselves on the floor to search for crumbs." Montessori looked around the room and saw that the children had no toys or materials of any kind—that the room was in fact absolutely bare. There were literally no objects in their environment which the children could hold and manipulate in their fingers. Montessori saw in the children's behaviour a craving of a very different and higher kind than for mere food. There existed for these poor creatures, she realized, one path and one only towards intelligence, and that was through their hands. Instinctively the poor deficient mites had sought after that path by the only means in their reach.

The more Montessori came in contact with these defective children—studying them, meditating over their condition, longing to help them—the more strongly did she come to differ from the generally accepted views with regard to them. It became increasingly apparent to her that mental deficiency was a pedagogical problem rather than a medical one. She came to believe that, with special educational treatment, their mental condition could be immensely ameliorated, a view she found to be shared by the French doctors Jean Itard and Edouard Séguin, and a few others.

She says, "That form of creation which was necessary for these unfortunate beings, so as to enable them to reenter human society, to take their place in the civilized world and render them independent of the help of others—placing human dig-

nity within their grasp—was a work which appealed so
strongly to my heart that I remained in it for years."

Montessori Directress of an Orthophrenic School

It was through her interest in defective children that
Montessori came in contact with the works of Jean Itard and
Edouard Séguin, the two French doctors mentioned above,
who had devoted their lives to the education of defectives.
In this way her own intuitions on the subject were strengthened.
In 1899, at a pedagogical congress in Turin, Montessori delivered an address on Moral Education. In this she expressed
her belief that "defective children were not extrasocial beings,
but were entitled to the benefits of education as much as—if
not more than—normal ones." Such an interest was aroused
in what was then—in Italy—a novel point of view that Dr.
Guido Bacelli, the Minister of Education, invited Dr. Montessori to give a series of lectures in Rome on the education
of the feebleminded. She complied with this request, and, as
a result of this course, which laid the foundation stone of
scientific pedagogy in Italy, there came into being a state
orthophrenic school. This was placed under the direction of
Dr. Montessori, a position which she held for two years,
1899—1901.

To this school were brought, from the various day schools
in Rome, all those children who were regarded as hopelessly
deficient. Later on, to this same institution were transferred
also all the idiot children from the insane asylums in Rome.

During these two years Montessori, with the help of her
colleagues, prepared a group of teachers "in a special method
of observation and in the education of feebleminded children."

She also visited London and Paris with the object of studying all the then-known methods of dealing with such problems. Most important of all, upon her return, she gave herself
up entirely to the actual teaching of the children herself. What
his contemporaries said of Sir Walter Raleigh we can also
say of Dr. Montessori, that she has always shown the capacity
"to toil terribly." All day long from 8 a.m. to 7 p.m. she
would spend with the children; and then at night she would
sit up late to make notes, tabulate, compare, analyze and reflect, and prepare new materials. "Those two years of practice," she remarks quaintly, "are indeed my first and only
true degree in pedagogy."

A Dawning Intuition

From the beginning of her work with defective children Montessori had the feeling that the methods which she was using "had nothing in them peculiarly limited to the instruction of idiots." On the contrary she believed that they contained educational principles "more rational than those generally in use." In fact it was just "because they were more rational that through their means an inferior mentality was enabled to develop."

Under her skilful direction the inferior mentality of these defective children (hitherto classed with the hopeless lunatics) developed to a remarkable and unexpected extent. Such indeed was her success that a number of idiot children from the asylums learned to read and write so well that they were able to present themselves with success at a public examination taken together with normal children.

A chorus of applause greeted this seeming miracle; but Dr. Montessori's reflections took another course. "Whilst everyone was admiring my idiots I was searching for the reasons which could keep back the healthy and happy children of the ordinary schools on so low a plane that they could be equalled in tests of intelligence by my unfortunate pupils."

The more deeply she pondered over this anomalous situation the more strongly did she feel that the cause lay in a difference in educational principles. "This feeling, so deep as to be of the nature of an intuition, became my controlling idea. I became convinced that similar methods applied to normal children would develop and set free their personality in a marvellous and surprising way."

Preparing for an Unknown Future

Thus in 1901, when Montessori gave up her work with the deficients in the orthophrenic school at Rome, she was already contemplating the question of the teaching of normal children. Yet seven years were to pass before her theories were put into practice, and her "intuitions" confirmed.

For this delay there were various reasons. In the first place she felt the need for further study and meditation. Although she was already a lecturer at the University, she registered again *as a student,* and attended courses on philosophy and psychology. We can indeed apply to her own development the words which later on she wrote to a young teacher (who was to become one of her most able and ardent followers), "To collect one's forces, even when they seem to be scattered,

and when one's aim is only dimly perceived—this is a great
action and will sooner or later bring forth fruits."[5] Of this
period she herself writes, "It was almost as if I was keeping
myself for an unknown mission."

Looking back over the first piece of Montessori's career we
can easily see how all that she did turned out to be a preparation, and a most fitting preparation, for the great discovery
she was to make at a later period.

But we must not make the mistake of reading her future
into the past. Before it came it was still the future; and it was
still unknown to her. That she felt she had some sort of special
mission to perform is clear, but exactly what that mission
was, or how she would fulfil it, was still beyond her ken.
She could only see her way a step at a time. The future was
still shrouded in a mist, and would have to reveal itself stage
by stage. Montessori was certain that, if she did *her* part fully
in the present, the future would look after itself.

In spite of Dr. Montessori's rigorously scientific training
and the immensely practical nature of her work, there was
a deeper and mystical side to her personality. To her the art
of life consisted primarily in adjusting oneself to those unseen but beneficent influences which operate through the
lives of men and events. Therefore she never unduly strove
to force events, believing (like Hamlet), as a result of her experience, that "there is a divinity that shapes our ends roughhew them how we will." I once heard her, in a conversation,
expound a theory that the art of life consists in learning how
"to be obedient to events." Superficially this might give the
impression of a fatalistic surrender to an external destiny; but
it meant nothing of the kind. Rightly understood, and illustrated as she gave it by reference to her own career, it signi-
fied rather a life full of generous acceptances of duties, and
of hard achievements leading to unexpected developments
along the line of her genius. Thus it came about that her
life was like a path leading through narrow defiles to sudden
horizons; a series of experiences linking themselves together
to prepare the next step. In fact her theory of "obedience to
events," far from being fatalistic, is much more in line with
what Emerson meant when he said "the way of life is wonderful; it is by abandonment." At the great crises of her life
she was aware of a mysterious urge within her, something
deeper that mere reason, almost as if, like Socrates, she had
a "Daemon" within her that knew more than she did.

[5]Letter to Signorina Maccheroni.

A Second Period of Study

When the moment came which would reveal to her this "unknown mission" she would be ready for it. Meanwhile, as we have said above, she felt the need of a deeper and more complete preparation. During this second period of study Montessori made a much more thoroughgoing study of the works of Itard and Séguin, for whose work she had a deep admiration. Itard, who lived at the time of the French Revolution, made a special study of deaf-mutes. He is perhaps best known for his education of an idiot boy who was found abandoned in the forest of Aveyron. It was an undertaking of almost incredible patience, which he recorded in a book, *The Care and Education of the Wild Boy of Aveyron.*

Dr. Edouard Séguin, who was a student under Itard, later founded a school for deficients in Paris. Here he achieved such brilliant successes that his fame spread far and wide. In fact he received the highest praise from the Academy of France. Séguin wrote an account of his methods in a book entitled *Traitement Moral, Hygiène et Education des Idiots.* This volume embodied his ten years' experience with defectives in his school at Paris. So highly did Montessori value the works of Itard and Séguin that—to use her own words—"I translated into Italian and copied out with my own hand the writing of these two men from beginning to end [Séguin's book alone was 600 pages long], making for myself books as the Benedictines did before the diffusion of the art of printing. I chose to do this by hand in order that I might have time to weigh the sense of each word and read in truth the spirit of the authors."

In later life Séguin emigrated to the United States of America where he founded many institutions for defectives, and where—after the lapse of another twenty years—he published a second account of his educational method under a different title: *Idiocy; and its Treatment by the Physiological Method.* This was published in English in the United States of America in 1866. Montessori had heard of the book; but for a long time was unable to obtain a copy. She describes how, in her search for it—when she visited London—she even went from house to house "to nearly all the English doctors who were known to be specially interested in defective children or who supervised special schools." She had just finished translating and copying the 600 pages of Séguin's French volume when a copy of his second book arrived by post. This volume had been found amongst the books discarded from the private library of a New York physician. (When the parcel was opened the book looked so dusty and dirty that Alessandro Montessori insisted on having it disinfected before letting his daughter read it!)

This new and later volume of Séguin's dealt with the *philosophy* of the experiences described in his previous volume. In it Séguin put forward the view that his "physiological method," which has as its base the individual study of the pupil, forming its educational methods upon the analysis of physiological and psychological phenomena, must come also to be applied to normal children. And when this was done he believed it would "lead the way to a complete human regeneration."

Lecturer and Practising Physician

During the ten years that followed Dr. Montessori's graduation in 1896 her interests were by no means confined to defective children. She also made a special study of the nervous diseases of children; and from time to time published the results of her researches in technical journals.[6]

From 1896 to 1906 she occupied the Chair of Hygiene at the *Magistero Femminile* in Rome, one of the two women's colleges in Italy at that time (the other being in Florence). She was also one of the permanent external examiners in the Faculty of Pedagogy. (It is interesting to note, in passing, that the other external examiner in those years was Luigi Pirandello —later well known as a playwright.) Many of the students who studied under her at this time came to occupy important positions in training colleges all over Italy, carrying with them something of her fire and enthusiasm.

In 1904 Dr. Montessori was made a Professor at the University of Rome where for four years she occupied the Chair of Anthropology. Her first major publication was a large volume entitled *Pedagogical Anthropology*.

Dr. Montessori as a University Lecturer

Anna Maccheroni gives an interesting account of her impressions when she first heard Montessori lecture on this subject at a course for teachers at the University of Rome in 1906. "The hall was crowded with young people of both sexes. The lecturer remained standing during her discourse, and

[6]These include: "The Cephalo-Rachitic Liquid in Paralytic Insanity"; "The Case of a Solitary Tubercle in the Middle Brain"; "The Influence of Culture in Reactions to Psychological Tests"; "The Influence of Social Conditions on the Mental Development of Children in School"; "Anthropological Characters of Children who are Judged as either the Best or Worst in Public Schools."

kept her eyes fixed on her audience with a penetrating look. I found out afterwards that, even with quite a large audience, she was able somehow to be conscious of each one individually with what one might describe as a kind of spiritual contact.

"I noticed at once that she was a very good-looking woman; but what impressed me more was that she did not follow the fashion of so many learned women of that time by dressing in a somewhat masculine style. Her attire, though simple, retained an elegant and feminine touch.

"In that opening lecture she spoke, not so much about anthropology, as about schools—what the function of a school should be. She emphasized two main points: first, that it is the duty of the teacher to help rather than to judge; and second, that true mental work does not exhaust, but rather gives nourishment, food for the spirit.

"She was a most attractive lecturer with a manner that was easy and gracious. Everything that she said had the warmth of life. I remember some of the students saying, 'Her lectures make us want to be good,' which recalls the remark made by another teacher at another of her courses a year or two later, 'We do not understand all that she is trying to teach us; but we all find in it a spiritual stimulus.' "

In addition to her work as a lecturer in the University of Rome and the Women's Training College she also practised in the clinics and hospitals in Rome; and—though it seems hard to believe it—even carried on a private practise of her own as well, for at least part of this period.

Her patients—whether in hospital or in their homes—were never for her just "cases"; for combined with her knowledge and skill, there was always the personal interest. The following anecdote, related to the author by a lady who was then living in Rome, is revealing.

One day Dr. Montessori was called in to attend two small babies—twins—who were so near death's door that their father had said, "Why trouble to get a doctor; they are already dead." The parents were very poor and unable to afford either household help or nursing. On her arrival the young lady doctor took in the whole situation at a glance. Taking off her coat, she lit the fire, sent the mother to bed, heated some water, bathed the two babies, "holding them in a special way," prepared their food, and thus little by little, hour by hour, brought them back to life—servant, cook, nurse and doctor in one. In later years when this same mother with her children met the *Dottoressa* in the street she would push them towards her saying, "Go and salute that lady, my dear, *she* is your real mother, not I; *she* gave you your life." A pretty compliment, and well deserved.

If this was typical of Dr. Montessori's way of treating her indigent private patients (and from other sources one gathers it was) is was certainly a good thing for her that she was not dependent for her livelihood on her private practice. Happily, as we have seen, she had other irons in the fire, such as her appointment at the psychiatric clinic, her lectureship at the training college, and later, her Professorship in Anthropology at the University.

But the time was coming, and coming quite soon—though as yet she did not know it—when she would abandon her private practice, resign all her lectureships, and set forth like Columbus across unknown and uncharted seas to discover a New World.

CHAPTER II   DISCOVERY

A New Columbus

If Montessori had died at the beginning of 1906—she was then thirty-six years of age—she would hardly have been heard of beyond her immediate circle. By 1908—only two years later—her name was known all over the world. In that short interval she had made the discovery for which all her previous life had formed a preparation. It is really no exaggeration to say that, like Columbus, she had discovered a new world.

The world which Columbus discovered was a world *without;* Montessori discovered a world *within*—within the soul of the child. Let us make no mistake about it; it was a genuine discovery of something as objective as America was to Columbus, or the Law of Gravitation to Newton. It is really this discovery which has made her famous, not her method.

Her method is but the consequence of her discovery as she herself makes clear. "It would be a great mistake," she says, "to believe that, by merely observing children, we were led to form such a new idea as that of the existence of a hidden nature in the child, and that such an intuition gave rise to a special school and a special method of education. It is impossible to observe something that is not known; and it is not possible for anyone, all at once, by a vague intuition to im-

agine that a child may have two natures (deviated and normal)
and say, 'Now I will try to prove it by experiment.' Anything
new must emerge, so to speak, by its own energies; it must
spring forth and strike the mind evoked by what we call
chance." [1]

What exactly was this new phenomenon which emerged by
its own energy? And what was the chance which called it into
existence?

The Stage Is Set

To answer this we must go backwards for a moment to
trace briefly the providential chain of circumstances which
brought forth this great and unexpected event.

There existed in Rome at that time a slum district known
as the San Lorenzo quarter. It was an area of squalor, poverty
and crime. In it were to be found a number of large buildings,
put up during a building boom, "with utter disregard for the
laws of hygiene, and rendered still worse by being used as
temporary habitations." They were then occupied by the
poorest class of the whole city. Here flourished unchecked all
the evils of subletting, overcrowding, promiscuous immor-
ality, and other crimes. To form an adequate idea of the
appalling conditions which prevailed in this San Lorenzo
quarter one must read Montessori's own account of it. [2]

At that time there was a building society known as the
Institutio Romano dei Beni Stabili—a well-established concern
backed by the principal banks in Italy. This society constructed
two large adjacent blocks of flats in the heart of the San
Lorenzo quarter. (The intention—never carried out—was
eventually to reform all the houses in that district.) When
all was ready, upwards of a thousand of the poor people from
the district were installed, in families, in these flats—on condition that they would observe certain rules of decency and
clean living.

But very soon a new problem arose. Most of the parents
were away at work during the day, and the older children
absent at school. The younger children, left to their own
devices, played up and down the stairs and corridors, de-
facing the walls and staircases and generally creating disorder
—"like ignorant little vandals."

After some consideration it was decided by the authorities
that it would be more economical in the long run to collect
this rabble of children together in one room and pay someone

[1] *Secret of Childhood* (Longmans).
[2] *Montessori Method*, pp. 50 *et seq.*

to look after them, than to be constantly paying for repainting and repairing the damage they had done.

A room was set apart for this purpose. Then the question arose, to whom could be entrusted the care of these children? One of those responsible, recalling a magazine article by Dr. Montessori, decided that she was the best person to direct the work; and accordingly approached her about it. Dr. Montessori readily consented, for she saw in it the fulfilment of a long-cherished hope—the opportunity to work with normal children. We have already noted that for several years she had a hunch that if one were to apply the methods with which she had been so successful in the teaching of backward children to normal ones good results might follow. But hitherto such an opportunity had been denied her because of the regulation that all children at the age of six should attend the state schools; and it had been difficult for her to interfere in this department.

Having accepted the responsibility for these "little vandals" the next thing was to fit up the room which had been set apart for them. It was not in her power to furnish it with desks like an ordinary schoolroom, because her expenses, being borne by a building society, had to be put down as an indirect item in the general upkeep of the building. For this reason the only expenditure permitted was such as would have been required by an office for furniture and equipment. That is why she had tables made for these small children, with chairs to match, instead of school desks which were universally in use at that time. This turned out, as it happened, to be a fortunate limitation. She also had a number of little armchairs made, presumably under the excuse that, even in an office, people have to rest sometimes. In addition, she had some precise scientific materials prepared, not identical with, but similar to those she had used in the institution for defectives. These, too, "had nothing about them which should be considered as school equipment."

Dramatis Personal

Such then was the not very promising stage setting for the unexpected drama which was to follow: a slum quarter in Rome, and a room in a tenement house. Nor were the actors any more promising. Let us look at them: "Sixty tearful, frightened children, so shy that it was impossible to get them to speak; their faces were expressionless, with bewildered eyes as though they had never seen anything in their lives . . . poor abandoned children who had grown up in dark tumble-

down cottages without anything to stimulate their minds—
dejected, uncared for. It was not necessary to be a doctor to
see that they suffered from malnutrition, lack of fresh air and
sunlight. They were indeed closed flowers, but without the
freshness of buds, souls concealed in a hermetic cell." That
is how Dr. Montessori described them.

Owing to her many other duties Montessori was unable to
look after the children continuously herself, so someone had
to be found to do so. As it was a position which offered no
future prospects—this job of looking after these sixty children,
ages three to six—it was given to the porter's daughter. Later
on it was entrusted to a seamstress who, though somewhat
better educated, was equally without training as a teacher.
"Even in this was heaven ordinant"; [3] for the chances are that
if a teacher trained in the old methods had been employed,
she would have been so wedded to the old system that she
would have found it next to impossible to carry out Montessori's directions. Montessori did not train these girls: "I laid
no restriction on the mistress, gave her no special duties; I
merely taught her how to use the apparatus so that she could
present it accurately to the children." [4]

Prologue

It was decided to have an official opening ceremony,
and Montessori was invited to give the inaugural address. The
porter's daughter, wishing to be equal to the occasion, informed Montessori that she had taught her charges how to
make a military salute. But when the actual day came and
the poor dejected mites appeared in their "stout blue orphan
smocks" they forgot even their one accomplishment, and
were led away in confusion. "I wonder," remarked a Roman
lady who was present, "if there will be any change visible in
these children in a month's time." She did not speak hopefully.

Montessori, however, felt differently. On this opening day—
it was 6th January 1906—there came to her suddenly a mysterious intuition of the immense significance of the enterprise
which was about to begin under those humble circumstances.
"I had," she says, "a strange feeling which made me announce
emphatically that here was the opening of an undertaking of
which the whole world would one day speak." It was the
Feast of the Epiphany; and the words of the Epistle seemed
to her at once "an omen and a prophecy." "For behold darkness shall cover the face of the earth . . . but the Lord shall

[3]*Hamlet.*
[4]*The Secret of Childhood.*

arise upon thee. And the Gentiles shall walk in thy light, and kings in the brightness of thy rising. Lift up thine eyes round about and see . . . Then shalt thou see and abound; and thy heart shall wonder and be enlarged, when the multitude of the sea shall be converted to thee. . . ."

When they heard her read these words and listened to the speech which followed the audience were "stupefied"—"amazed" that she should see in a roomful of sixty poor children a matter of such wonderful significance. Yet the event proved her intuition to be right. Before a year had passed, literally kings were to walk in the brightness of its rising, and a multitude from beyond the seas were to become converted, as they beheld with wonder and reverence this new epiphany.

The Curtain Rises—Living in a Fairy Tale

In the whole history of education, from the time of Plato to the present day, there is no episode more remarkable than the series of happenings which came tumbling into being, one after the other, during the next six months. Nothing that took place in Pestalozzi's school at Iverdun, or in Froebel's Anstalt at Neuheim, or amongst Tolstoy's peasant children can equal it for sheer wonder. It reads like a fairy story.

Everyone who wishes to understand the origin of the Montessori method—and indeed the method itself—should not fail to read the whole of Dr. Montessori's graphic and poignant description in *The Secret of Childhood* (Part II, Chapter II) from which these extracts are taken:

> "I set to work," she says, "like a peasant woman who, having set aside a good store of seed corn, has found a fertile field in which she may freely sow it. But I was wrong. I had hardly turned over the clods of my field, when I found gold instead of wheat: the clods concealed a precious treasure. I was not the peasant I had thought myself. Rather I was like foolish Aladdin, who, without knowing it, had in his hand a key that would open hidden treasures."

What were these hidden treasures which revealed themselves so unexpectedly to Dr. Montessori? Speaking generally, they are the *normal characteristics of childhood* hitherto concealed under a mask of "deviations." *Montessori discovered that children possess different and higher qualities than those we usually attribute to them. It was as if a higher form of personality had been liberated, and a new child had come into being.*

We must now pass briefly in review, as Dr. Montessori has

related them, these new qualities which so unexpectedly made themselves manifest.

Before doing so it may be well to mention the fact that, when she had worked with backward children, she had found that the materials she had made proved useful to *her*—as a means of arousing their interest. At the same time, however, she had been obliged all along to put forth the whole energy of her will to persuade the children to keep on working with them. With the normal children things happened differently. In fact—to continue the simile used by Dr. Montessori above —it was the materials which were to prove the Aladdin's Lamp which opened up to her wondering eyes the concealed treasures within. For the children chose them and worked with them *spontaneously*.

Amazing Mental Concentration

One day Montessori was observing a child of three who was occupying herself with some graded wooden cylinders which had to be slipped in and out of corresponding sockets in a wooden block. She was amazed to find this tiny girl showing such an extraordinary interest: she showed, in fact, a concentration so profound that it seemed to have isolated her mentally from the rest of her environment. To test the intensity of this concentration—which seemed so unusual in a child of three—Montessori asked the teacher to make the other children sing aloud and promenade round her. But the child did not even seem conscious of this disturbance; she went on just as before, mysteriously repeating this same exercise (i.e., taking the cylinders out, mixing them, and replacing them in their sockets). Then Montessori gently picked up the armchair on which the child was sitting, with her in it, and placed her on a table. The child, who had clung on to her precious cylinders during this interruption at once continued her task as if nothing had happened. With her scientific habit of measuring phenomena Montessori counted the number of times the child repeated the exercise; it was forty-two. Then quite suddenly she stopped "as though coming out of a dream." She smiled as if she was very happy; her eyes shone and she looked round about her. And, strangely enough, after all that long concentration she appeared to be rested rather than fatigued.

Here we see the germ of what was later to become one of the fundamental principles of the Montessori method, viz., the reliance, in the schoolroom, on the *spontaneous* interest of children as the mainspring of their work.

Love of Repetition

This display of mental concentration in so young a child seemed to Montessori a new phenomenon—"a first glimpse into the unexplored depths of the child's mind." Accompanying it came another interesting revelation, another characteristic feature of child mentality—viz., the tendency to repeat the same thing over and over again. In time Montessori came to regard this mysterious and apparently meaningless repetition of an exercise *already known* as one of the essential features of the child's manner of working. One of the most valuable fruits of that liberty, which has become an essential part of her method, is that it gives unlimited scope for the carrying out of this repetition—which obviously answers to some profound psychological need.

Love for Order

The love for order is not a characteristic usually associated with small children. Here again a surprise was in store. This characteristic, like many others, was revealed by chance, the result of an indiscretion on the part of the teacher. The materials with which the children worked were kept in a large cupboard—locked—and the teacher kept the key. Contrary to what happens now in a Montessori class, it was she who distributed the materials at the beginning, and it was she who collected them and put them away in the cupboard at the end of the lesson. The teacher noticed that these little children—however often she told them to remain in their places—used to follow her when she went to the cupboard to put the materials away and solemnly stand round her watching whilst she put the various objects back. This seemed to her to be nothing less than deliberate disobedience. It is the genius who sees the significance of small things. Watching the children behaving in this way, Montessori realized that what they really wanted was *to put the things back in their places again themselves*. So she left them free to do it.

Whereupon a new kind of life began for them. They revelled in putting things back in their places, and, in general, in keeping the environment in order. Later on Montessori saw in this love of order in small children (which older children do *not* share) an example of a general law—the "law of sensitive periods in development." This was the sensitive period for order, which lasts from about the age of twelve months to three and a half years. Montessori was quick to realize the practical value of this unexpected trait in small children. Unless this love of order was already innate at that early age it would be impossible to impose it on a whole roomful of small children. And without it, it would be impossible to grant choice of occupation and liberty of movement to a group of forty small children without chaos ensuing.

Freedom of Choice

One day the teacher arrived late. In addition she had forgotten to lock the cupboard the evening before. It turned out to be another of those occasions in life when "our discretions sometimes serve us well where our deep plots do pall." [5] Upon her arrival the teacher found the children had already opened the cupboard doors. Some were standing looking on in a meditative sort of way; others were helping themselves to materials; others still had already done so and were taking them away, whilst a fourth group were already busily at work with materials at their own places. The teacher was angry with the children and wished to punish them for "stealing." Again Montessori saw deeper into their motives. She realized that these children, who already knew how to use the materials, were—just because of that knowledge—in a position to be able to choose *some* materials in preference to *others*. This was in fact what they had done. That they had no intention of "stealing" was evident from the fact that they regarded the putting back of the material chosen into its right place as an essential part of the cycle of activity involved—almost the crowning joy of the whole procedure. This incident was the beginning of that principle of "free choice of activity" which became so vital a factor in the Montessori system. *Here again let us notice that it was the discovery which came first and the method followed after.* Shortly after this Montessori replaced the one big, locked cupboard with a number of little low and attractively painted cupboards, placed round the room at the children's level. In these the materials were so displayed that the children could easily see, choose, take and replace them without the need of any assistance from an adult. This formed an important step towards their more complete independence.

They Preferred Work to Play

We usually think of *play* as the natural spontaneous expression of the child's personality; and of *work*, on the contrary, as something which has to be imposed. But now came another and very astonishing revelation. Some of Dr. Mon-

[5]*Hamlet.*

tessori's rich friends—society ladies in Rome who were interested in her work with these poor children—had presented her with a number of costly toys. These included elegant dolls, a doll's house, doll's crockery and even a doll's kitchen. These toys Montessori placed in the room with the children, making them as easily accessible as the materials for work.

This led to the next surprise. *The children never chose the toys.* Montessori was so astonished at this that she intervened herself, showing them how to play with these toys, how to handle the doll's crockery, how to light the fire in the doll's kitchen, "placing a pretty doll beside it," etc. The children showed an interest for a time; and then went away. "They never made such toys the object of their spontaneous choice." In this way Montessori was led to one of the most revolutionary discoveries of all—a fact which is still unknown to, indeed still beyond the credibility of most persons, viz., *that children prefer work to play*. In later chapters we shall study more deeply the nature of the child's spontaneous work, showing at the same time how it differs in quality and motive from that of the adult. We shall also indicate how this discovery has led to one of the main differences in practice between the Froebel Kindergarten and the Montessori School.

No Need for Rewards and Punishment

The teacher—or rather the girl who was put in charge, for she was not a trained teacher—devised a system of rewards and punishments for the children. One day Montessori came into the room and found a child sitting in one of the little armchairs; and on his breast he wore a "pompous decoration" which the teacher had prepared as a reward for good behaviour. As it turned out, however, this particular child was actually being punished. What had happened was that a few moments before a boy, decorated for his good behaviour, had taken his medal off and pinned it upon the breast of the young malefactor. Apparently the former regarded his decoration as a thing of little worth, apt to get in his way when working. The culprit, for his part, looked round about him complacently without feeling at all disgraced by his punishment. This struck Montessori as an anomalous state of affairs. After making a great number of experiments the teacher, realizing that the children set no store by these rewards and punishments, abandoned the practice. As the Montessori method developed and many Montessori schools came into existence, this same experience was repeated many times. The children became good

⁶Chapter XX.

and orderly as soon as they learned how to work. On the other hand it was found that the naughtiness of others was in almost every case the result of "deviations"–i.c., manifestations of disordered personalities, due to the fact that constructive energies had been diverted from their true channels. Further, it was found that no amount of punishment could set the matter right: but only the sloughing off of these "deviations" by a new orientation of the elements of personality through spontaneously chosen work.[7]

Many years after this, the present writer once spent a morning in a large Montessori school in the Borough of Acton (London). There were over three hundred children in that school, yet the only name in the official punishment register was that of the H.M. Inspector whose duty it was to examine and sign his name therein. One might imagine this was a special case; but it is not so. I once sent a questionnaire round to a number of long-established Montessori schools, and one of the questions in it was this: What use do you make of punishments? One directress wrote: "Work is its own reward. Punishments are rare; a troublesome child might be removed from her companions until she is ready to behave properly." Another said: "With younger children the greatest reward is to be able to pass on to a new stage in each subject. It is a punishment to a young child not to be allowed to use the apparatus, but to sit still and do nothing." Another teacher (with twenty years of Montessori experience behind her) said: "If a warning does not suffice, the offender is separated from other children and made to sit beside the directress. The lessons given by the directress to other children generally arouse interest and the child settles down to work. Either this or she becomes bored and asks to return to her place. This 'punishment' proves quite sufficient."

Lovers of Silence

Most persons are apt to think of children, especially in large numbers, as noisy creatures; indeed delighting in noise. As mothers sometimes say: "He is never quiet unless he is asleep." It was therefore a real revelation when Montessori discovered that, deep down in their souls, children have a great love for silence. We must leave the reader to find out for himself (in *The Secret of Childhood*, pp. 153–5) the manner in which, with the assistance of a baby four months old, Montessori was led to make this discovery. In Chapters XI and XIII we have given descriptions of the famous "silence

[7] See Chapter X, Deviations and Normality.

game" which, developing out of this discovery, has become a typical and charming feature of the Montessori class for younger children.

The Children Refuse Sweets

One day when the children had carried out the "silence game," which involves great patience and self-discipline, Montessori decided to reward them each with a sweet. But to her astonishment the children refused them. It was as though they said, "Don't spoil our lovely experience: we are still filled with delights of the spirit; don't distract us."

This phenomenon seemed to Montessori so unexpected, so extraordinary, that she tested it again and again; for, as she remarks, "everyone knows that children are always greedy for sweets. But repeated experiments only confirmed this extraordinary happening." The sweets remained untouched—sometimes for weeks. "Was it," she asks, "from a feeling like that of monks, who flee from ease and from such outward things as are useless for the true good of life, once they have risen in the ladder of spiritual life?"

In later years this same indifference to the allurements of sweets when placed in conflict with the interests of the mind, was to be verified times without number. The present writer himself witnessed a striking example. It happened in a Montessori school in Barcelona run by the Sisters of Charity in connection with a maternity home. A little girl of about five to five and a half years was doing sums with the help of the number rods on a rug on the floor, recording her operations in chalk on a little blackboard. She was so absorbed in this occupation that she had not even left it (though quite free to do so) to join her companions who were dancing round the room to a musical rhythm. The door opened and some visitors entered. One of these—having more kindness than discretion—began to give a sweet to each marching child as it passed her by.

As was only to be expected, this ill-timed charity disorganized the marching, and the children soon began to cluster round the visitor. The latter, becoming embarrassed by this clamorous attention, quickly handed the bag to the young assistant who had, by this time, left the piano. (The senior directress was not in the room at the time.) At this particular juncture the little girl whom I had been watching—being in some doubt as to the accuracy of her latest sum—had left her work and had come to ask the assistant directress to help her. The latter, seeing her amongst all the other little ones crowding

round her holding their hands up for sweets, and thinking she
had come for the same purpose, placed a bonbon in the child's
hand. The little girl's expression betrayed surprise and disappointment. She looked, in fact, as if she had "asked for
bread and had been given a stone." Without saying a word
she turned round and went straight back to her rug, carrying
the sweet in her hand. There she at once set to work to do the
sum over again by herself. The most astonishing thing about
the whole incident was that—far from eating the sweet or
even thinking about doing so—*the child actually used it as a
sort of pointer*—tapping with it each of the divisions of the
various number rods, placed end to end, until she finally came
to the correct answer, which she duly recorded on her little
blackboard. Then, automatically putting the sweet away in her
pocket, she set to work to compose another sum. It was a
complete triumph of mind over matter.

The emergence in these small children of intellectual interests so strong as to cause a sort of "ligature" of the lower
faculties (as in the ecstasies of the saints) seemed so extraordinary that, upon hearing of it, a number of persons came
especially to verify it. One day a cardinal came to visit the
Casa dei Bambini at San Lorenzo. Beneath the scarlet robes of
his high office there beat a simple and kindly heart; and the old
gentleman brought with him a bag of biscuits. Now it just
happened that these dainties had been manufactured in geometric shapes similar to those with which the children had
been working in the wooden insets. Imagine his astonishment
when, instead of eating them, the little children crowded round
the table eagerly looking at them and, recognizing them, cried
out excitedly—"That's a triangle!" "Mine's a circle!" "Cosmo
has a rectangle!" and so on.

A Sense of Personal Dignity

The next incident has its amusing as well as its pathetic
side. One day, when Montessori came to see how the children
were getting on, she decided to give them what was at that
time a rather unusual lesson—on how to blow one's nose. After
explaining first of all how it should not be done she showed
them how to do it as politely as possible, with as little noise
as one need, and taking out the handkerchief unobtrusively so
that the action remains more or less unnoticed. The children
followed her demonstration with silent interest. When the
lesson was quite finished they all together broke forth into a
burst of genuine and heartfelt applause, clapping their hands
"as when in a theatre a great actress evokes an ovation re-

pressed with difficulty." Montessori was completely amazed at this sudden demonstration of emotion, until all at once its true significance dawned on her. The question she had touched upon—keeping one's nose clean—was one which children too often associate with derision and humiliation. People are perpetually complaining to them on this score, and making disparaging remarks, such as "Blow your nose, Tommy," "Why don't you use your handkerchief, you dirty boy," etc., etc. But no one had ever quietly and calmly taught them *how* to do it, without attacking them or reproving them at the same time.[6]

This was the first of many similar experiences by which Montessori was led to realize that even very small children have a profound sense of personal dignity; and that if adults neglect to respect it "their souls may remain wounded, ulcerated and oppressed in a way adults seldom realize." Later on the inculcation of this respect for their personal dignity—of even the smallest child—became one of the most prominent elements in the training of her teachers.

The "Explosion" into Writing

Perhaps none of the happenings which took place during these wonderful months "when we seemed to be living in a fairy tale," made more impression on those who heard about it than the fact that a number of these children—ages four to five years—*"burst spontaneously into writing"* without having been taught.

When she began Montessori had no intention of tackling the problem of writing with children as young as this. In fact she tells us that at that time she shared the general prejudice that it was necessary to begin writing as late as possible— certainly not before the age of six. But the children themselves thought otherwise: some of them came to her and demanded to be taught to read and write. Even then she did not concede this request but gave in only when the parents added *their* solicitations.

She decided to apply means similar to those which she had used previously with defective children. Accordingly she and her assistants set to work to make some sets of alphabets. These were of two different kinds. In one the letters were cut out of cardboard; in the other out of sandpaper—each sandpaper letter being mounted on a little wooden board. Both kinds of alphabets were made in cursive style, i.e., as used for writing, not for printing. The children were not taught the

[6]Here we see a good example of Montessori's maxim, "Teach teaching, not correcting" and also of a "Lesson in Grace and Courtesy." See Chapter XIII.

names of the letters, but only the sounds they represent. Further, they were encouraged to trace the forms of the sandpaper letters with their "writing fingers," i.e., the first and second fingers of the right hand. That was all. They were not taught to write.

One day a little fellow of five made a great discovery. Montessori heard him going around saying to himself, "To make 'Sofia' you need S, O, F, I and A." He had in fact discovered that one can analyze spoken words into their component sounds; and that those sounds were the ones he had already learned in connection with the symbols. Thereupon he, and others with him, began to compose various words with the movable cardboard letters, spreading them out on rugs on the floor.

But still this was not *Writing*.

What happened next was so extraordinary, and so unexpected, that we must give the account of it in Montessori's own words:

One December day when the sun shone and the air was like spring, I went up on the roof with the children. They were playing freely about and a number of them were gathered about me. I was sitting near a chimney, and said to a five year old boy who sat next to me: "Draw me a picture of this chimney," giving him a piece of chalk. He got down obediently and made a rough sketch of the chimney on the tiles which formed the floor of this roof terrace. As is my custom with the littler children I encouraged him, praising his work. The child looked at me, smiled, remained for a moment as if on the point of bursting into some joyous act, and then cried out: "I can write, I can write," and kneeling down again he wrote on the pavement the word "hand" (*mano*). Then full of enthusiasm, he wrote also "chimney, roof," (*camino, tetto*). As he wrote he continued to cry out "I can write: I know how to write." His cries of joy brought the other children, who formed a circle about him, looking down at his work in stupefied amazement. Two or three of them said to me, trembling with excitement, "Give me the chalk. I can write too." And indeed they began to write various words: MAMA, HAND, JOHN, CHIMNEY, ADA [in Italian of course]. Not one of them had ever taken chalk or any other instrument in hand for the purpose of writing. It was the *first time* they had ever written, and they traced an entire word, as a child when speaking for the first time speaks an entire word.

The first word written by my little ones aroused within themselves an indescribable emotion of joy. Not being able to adjust in their minds the connection between the preparation and the act, they were possessed by the illusion that, having now grown to proper size, they knew how to write. In fact they seemed to think that writing was but one of the many gifts of nature; and that at the proper time it would come to them, just as later on, a moustache would appear at the proper age.

The child who wrote a word for the first time was full of excited joy. He might be compared to a hen who has just laid an egg. Indeed no one could escape from his noisy manifestations. In general, after the first word the children, with a species of frenzied joy, continued to write everywhere. I saw children crowding about one another at the blackboard; and behind those who were standing on the floor another line would form consisting of children mounted upon chairs so that they might write above the heads of their fellows.

Others ran to the window shutters or the door covering them with writing. In these first days we walked upon a carpet of written signs. Daily accounts showed us that the same thing was going on at home; and some of the mothers, in order to save the floors of their houses, and even the crust of their loaves upon which they found words written, made their children presents of paper and pencil.

Later experience came to control the exuberance of this phenomenon, keeping it within reasonable bounds, so that now the moment of "explosion" does not come to all the children at the same time. Nevertheless in a well-run Montessori school the rapturous moment of "explosion into writing" still comes for many children. It comes when certain inner elements of preparation, having been completed, fuse together in a psychic synthesis.[9]

The writer knew one little boy who—on the day of *his* "explosion"—went round saying excitedly to everyone, "I can write, I can write," adding quickly and emphatically: "But nobody told me how! nobody told me how!"

The Discovery of Reading

One might very naturally conclude that because these children had learned to write they had also acquired the art of reading. But here again another surprise was in store. Montessori found that writing came before reading; came in fact several months before. "Their tireless activity in writing was like a torrent—six months of continuous and unlimited exer-

[9] See illustrations 5–7.

cise. All their energy, all their forces were given to writing—but not to reading."

One day towards the end of this period Montessori, without saying anything, wrote on the blackboard some little sentences such as "If you love me, give me a kiss." "If you can read this, come to me." For several days she did this, but nothing happened. "They thought"—says Montessori—"that I was just writing on the blackboard for *my* own amusement as they themselves were writing for *their* own joy and edification. However on the fourth day a tiny mite of a girl came up to me and said *eccomi* (here I am) and a short time after another came up and gave me a kiss."

And so the secret was out! One human being can communicate with another in this new and mysterious way *without a word being spoken*. It was a thrilling experience. "And so they watched with silent eagerness as I wrote sentence after sentence—little commands for them to carry out. They read and responded and carried them out with an intense and secret joy.

"In this way they discovered the essence of writing—that it transmits human thought. Whenever I began to write they fairly trembled in their eagerness to understand what I was thus about to communicate to them—without a word spoken." In this way were born those reading commands which have now passed into general use.

Spontaneous Self-Discipline

When one remembers that the very reason why this first Casa dei Bambini came into existence was *just because these children were so disorderly*, their next "revelation" seems all the more astonishing. As the weeks went by and the children became accustomed to this new mode of life, a happy and extraordinary change came over them. From being unruly they became just the opposite. It seemed as though a new form of goodness had developed inside them, which—as it grew—caused their disorderly habits to fall away, as the opening flower causes the leaf scales to fall off. They began to exhibit an extraordinary self-discipline; and with it a serenity of spirit, and a great respect for the rights of others.

It was a *spontaneous* self-discipline coming from within. (We have already seen that rewards and punishments were done away with.) These transformed children moved about their little world in a quiet and orderly manner, each getting on with his own business. They selected their materials for work; settled down at their tables and got on with their affairs, without disturbing their companions; and afterwards quietly replaced the materials when finished with. Their bodily movements became more harmonious; their very expressions serene and joyful. Everything about them betokened a heightened interest in life, and with it a new form of dignity. They looked —as indeed they had become—independent personalities with power to choose and to carry out their own acts. They did not abuse the liberty which had been granted them. Rather this liberty was the very means through which they were able to reveal this new self-discipline.

This independence which they had acquired did not in any way diminish their respect for authority. In fact they became so obedient that the woman in charge of them said one day to Dr. Montessori: "These children are so ready to do what I say that I begin to feel a sense of responsibility for every word I utter." This statement recalls a remark made to the writer, some twenty years later, by an experienced Montessori directress in a school in London.[10]

She said, speaking of the children in her class, "Their docility is so great that when one wishes an individual or a group to do something *at a given moment* one has to take care to explain first *when* to do it before *what* to do: otherwise the children will carry out the order instantaneously."

In after years, when Montessori schools came to be set up in all the countries of Europe and beyond, this same phenomenon of self-discipline regularly appeared. And so it has remained to the present day. Many teachers who still teach the old collective method find it hard to believe that such *spontaneous* self-discipline is possible in a class of forty children under six. They think such descriptions as are given here, and elsewhere, *must* be exaggerations—until they enter a well-run Montessori class and see for themselves. Even then it has sometimes remained beyond belief to some observers. I knew one man, a lecturer on education too, who, rather than believe it, fell back on the theory that somehow or other all these children who appeared free *had really been hypnotized.*[11]

Cosmic Discipline

When Montessori beheld for the first time this self-discipline in such small children—a sight so touching in its simplicity, and as beautiful as unexpected—she was deeply moved. It roused in her a feeling akin to awe. "Where did it

[10]Rev. Mother Isabel Eugénie, now Principal of the Maria Assumpta Training College, Kensington Square, London, W.8.
[11]It reminds one of the man at the Zoo who saw a giraffe for the first time and said, "I don't believe it!"

come from?" she asked herself. "Who was the author of it?"
The more she pondered over it and marvelled at it, the more
clearly was it borne in upon her that it was a part of that
universal discipline which holds the atoms to their affinities and
keeps the stars in their courses.

In a passage of great beauty (even in its translation) she
expressed herself as follows:

> The quiet in the class when the children were at work was
> complete and moving. No one had enforced it; and what
> is more, one one could have obtained it by external means.
> Had these children, maybe, found the orbit of their cycle,
> like the stars that circle unwearying and which, without
> departing from their order, shine through eternity? Of these
> the Bible speaks, in words that could be applied to such
> children, "And the stars have given light in their watches
> and rejoiced: They were called, and they said: Here we
> are, and with cheerfulness have shined forth to Him that
> made them." [12]
>
> A natural discipline of this kind seems to transcend its
> immediate environment, and to show itself as part of a
> universal discipline ruling the world. It is of such discipline
> that the prophet speaks as something men have lost, "Young
> men have seen the light and dwelt upon the earth, but the
> way of discipline they have not known!" [13]

Even at that time—a generation ago—Montessori had the
feeling that the beneficial effect of this revelation would extend beyond the classroom. This is apparent from the rest of
the passage quoted above, which goes on: "One has the impression that this natural discipline must provide the foundation for all other forms of discipline, determined—like that of
social life, for instance—by outward and immediate considerations. One of the things, indeed, which aroused the greatest
interest and gave greatest food for thought, seeming as it did
to hold something mysterious, was precisely this fact of order
and discipline being so closely united as to result in freedom."

"Of Such Is the Kingdom of Heaven"

These then are some of the revelations which were
manifested to Montessori and her assistants by the poor children of San Lorenzo during those extraordinary months in
1907. Not that they complete the tale. Others—like the law of
sensitive periods—were still to come, but for these it was

[12]Baruch iii.
[13]Ibid.

necessary that a longer period of time should elapse before
they could show themselves completely. Nevertheless, this San
Lorenzo experiment, taken as a whole, resulted in an epoch-
making discovery with regard to the nature and capability of
young children.

We can readily sympathize with any reader who finds the
record of these events hard to believe. It was exactly the same
with Montessori herself at the time, as she herself freely admits:

It took time for me to convince myself that all this was not
an illusion. After each new experience proving such a truth
I said to myself, "I won't believe yet; I'll believe in it next
time." Thus for a long time I remained incredulous, and
at the same time deeply stirred and trepident. How many
times did I not reprove the children's teacher when she told
me what the children had done of themselves! "The only
thing which impresses me is truth," I would reply severely.
And I remember that the teacher would answer, without
taking offence, and often moved to tears: "You are right!
When I see such things I think it must be the holy angels
who are inspiring these children."

One day, in great emotion, I took my heart in my two
hands as though to encourage it to rise to the heights of
faith, and I stood respectfully before the children, saying
to myself: "Who are you then? Have I perhaps met with
the children who were held in Christ's arms and to whom
the divine words were spoken? I will follow you, to enter
with you into the Kingdom of Heaven."

And holding in my hands the torch of faith I went on
my way.

CHAPTER III   DEVELOPMENT

Widening Circles

So great a wonder could not remain long hid. The
strange happenings in the heart of the slum quarter of San
Lorenzo began to be talked about. A second "Children's
House" was set up in another tenement building; and there
too the same wonders began to reveal themselves. Soon visitors
of all sorts were to be seen making their way through the drab
streets of San Lorenzo to see these astonishing children for
themselves, and went away marvelling, to relate what they
had seen to their friends.

Not only teachers and others connected with the profession of education came, but persons of all kinds and degrees, from the royal family downwards. Queen Margherita of Savoy was one of the earliest to show her interest, and spent many hours observing the children.

From the very beginning it is noteworthy that people of discernment recognized in Montessori's experiment an event of great significance. Queen Margherita said—"I prophesy that a new philosophy of life will arise from what we are learning from these little children." The head of a religious order, after visiting the schools, said, "This is a discovery which is even more important than Marconi's."

Such expressions may strike one as exaggerated; yet it is an undeniable fact that the majority of those who visited the schools seemed unable to express what they had seen and felt except in some such terms. Nor did the wonder diminish with time. It is interesting to note that those who came in touch with the movement at a later period felt the same urgency to speak in superlative language, as the following incident shows.

In 1918, the Educational Committee of the London County Council, having heard something of this new educational movement in Italy, decided to send one of their teachers to find out more about it. Accordingly a L.C.C. school headmistress, Mrs. Hutchinson, was sent to Rome to take a course under Montessori, visit the schools, and send in a report. When in due time Mrs. Hutchinson's report was read to the Educational Committee of the London County Council, one of those present—Sir Edward Garnett, I think—rose at its conclusion and quizzically remarked: "Gentlemen, this is not a report, it is a rhapsody!"

But Mrs. Hutchinson did more than rhapsodize. At great trouble and at her own expense she fitted up a Montessori classroom in her own school at Hornsey Road. And lo! in due course the same miracles appeared in London. The elderly gentlemen on the Committee could not deny them now, nor banter them away. In time they were convinced and converted; so that when—later on—Montessori herself came to London, Sir John Gilbert, chairman of the L.C.C., said publicly from the platform in the Dottoressa's own presence: "I desire to tender the thanks of London for the far-reaching influence Dr. Montessori has exercised through the Infant Departments on the whole educational system of London."

We are, however, anticipating. Let us go back to those first Case dei Bambini in Rome. The press soon discovered that, hidden in the slums of San Lorenzo, something was happening that was "news." Before long tidings of these wonderful children took wings in print and flew, first over all Italy and then all over the world. Articles on the Children's Houses appeared in various well-known magazines in different countries—*The World's Work* and *The Fortnightly Review* in England, and *McClure's Magazine* in the United States. So great was the interest aroused that second editions of two of these magazines had to be printed, an almost unprecedented event in journalism.

As a result of these widespread reports visitors began to arrive, not only from other parts of Italy, but indeed "a great multitude from across the seas." From the four quarters of the globe they came to observe these phenomenal children "so frank and free, and able to write at four without any forcing or fatigue." In a number of cases these pilgrims were so impressed by what they saw that it changed the course of their lives. Thus, for example, an Englishman, Mr. Bertram Hawker, was visiting Rome on his way to Australia to see his estates there. Happening to hear of these Children's Houses he paid one a visit. So impressed was he by what he saw that he postponed his sailing in order to have the opportunity of talking to Dr. Montessori herself. A second time he postponed his sailing because the more he learned the more he felt there was to learn. Finally he cancelled his journey altogether and returned to England to propagate Montessori's ideas. He was instrumental in founding the Montessori Society in England; and the first Montessori class in that country was set up in his own house.[1] In the same way, two sisters—teachers in Australia—having read about this new method, were so filled with enthusiasm that they sold their house and furniture to pay their expenses to go to Rome and study it. As an indirect result of this act of faith, years later the government of New South Wales sent a letter to Dr. Montessori stating that they had transformed all their kindergartens into Montessori classes; and enclosed an album of photographs showing the schools "before and after." Among the pilgrims who came to Rome at this time especially to see these schools was Tolstoy's daughter.

The Astonished Diplomat

The Argentine ambassador in Rome at that time had heard a great deal about the wonderful behaviour of Dr. Montessori's slum children, and was determined to go and see things for himself. As he was sceptical about the whole busi-

[1] The Old Hall, Runton, near Cromer.

ness he decided to arrive unexpectedly, in order to be sure that no special preparation had been made on his account. The day on which he arrived happened to be a Thursday, and the school was not in session on Thursdays. Whilst this was being explained to him by the hall porter, a little child in passing overheard their conversation, and at once said, "Oh, that's all right. You've got the key (addressing the hall porter) and all the children live here (in the tenement house.)" So the porter opened the door, and the little child went round and collected his comrades. Then they all went into their classroom and did honours to the ambassador by carrying on with "business as usual."

Many of those who came to observe what was going on at the Children's Houses wrote books on what they had seen. Amongst those written in English we may mention *A Montessori Mother* by D. C. Fisher; *New Examples and New Works; A Miracle in Education; The Discovery of the Human Soul.* The general drift of these, and other volumes which appeared at that time, was that the Montessori method had revealed a "New Child." In fact one of these books was actually called *The New Children.*[2] In this book the author went so far as to maintain that the manner of life revealed by these "New Children" disproved the doctrine of original sin.[3] "The children," she wrote, "do not want to be naughty. It tires and bores them to be idle. Of their own accord they work hard, seek after knowledge, cooperate with their elders, and dwell in helpful harmony with one another."

A Universal Appeal

From the very beginning, as soon as the visitors began to appear on the scene, Montessori was impressed by a remarkable fact—the universality of the appeal which was made by the life and behaviour of the New Children. By this we do not mean simply that people of all kinds of views were impressed by what they saw. It was much more than this. To use Montessori's own words, it was because "each visitor seemed to find there the embodiment of his own ideals." Thus, a famous politician remarked: "Here we see discipline through liberty"; a socialist said: "Here we see on a small scale that human society which socialism prophesies—the triumph of individual liberty with perfect organization"; a lady from the Roman aristocracy maintained that, "Here is a form of

[2]By Mrs. Sheila Radice—then assistant editor of *The Times Educational Supplement.*
[3]See pp. 181–182.

education which our children need because it enables them to overcome awkwardness and at the same time conquer timidity."

At a Socialist Congress in Berne it was proclaimed that "to be educated according to Dr. Montessori's method is one of the social rights of man"; a Catholic priest wrote, "The humility and the patience of the mistress in the Children's House, the superior value of deeds over words; the sensorial environment as the beginning of the life of the soul; the silence and recollection obtained from the children; the liberty left to the child soul in striving after perfection; the minute care in preventing and correcting all that is evil, even simple error, or slight imperfection; the control of error by means within the very material for development; the respect shown for the interior life of the child—all these were pedagogical principles which to him seemed to emanate from, and to be directly inspired by Catholicism." [4]

Nor did this universality of appeal lessen as time went on and the method became still more widely known. During the past forty years Montessori principles have been applied by persons of all kinds of religious beliefs, and of none—by Catholics, Protestants, Jews, Hindus, Mahommedans, Buddhists—and atheists; and by persons of all kinds of political creeds—yet always with beneficial results. From this it is quite clear that Montessori principles are based on fundamental characteristics common to all types of humanity.

Struck by the universality of its appeal a Dutch psychologist, Professor Godefroy from Amsterdam, expressed the matter in the following terms: "The Montessori doctrine has awakened in man sentiments which have always existed in a subconscious and latent manner in people's hearts, awaiting only the necessary stimulus to become rapidly and vividly conscious."

Montessori's First Book on Her Method

Montessori's Children's Houses and the principles that lay behind them impressed her friends so strongly "as having an importance for the whole of humanity" that they urged her to write an account of them without delay. "It is your duty," insisted Baron Franchetti, with whose family she was staying as a guest in the summer of 1909. "You might suddenly die; and then nothing of it would remain." Montessori herself was rather amused at this, because, as she says, "I was in excellent health at the time." However, she yielded to their

[4] *The Child in the Church* by Montessori (Sands and Co.)

persuasion and set to work. In less than a month a manuscript was ready which was published the same year under the title: *The Method of Scientific Pedagogy as Applied to Infant Education and the Children's Houses.*[5] The book had an instant and wide circulation. It has since been translated into over twenty different languages. This publication brought Montessori correspondence from all parts of the world—so much, in fact, that she was quite unable to cope with all of it.

One day (as if in confirmation of the words quoted above by Professor Godefroy) a thin, quite ordinary looking envelope arrived, with a Chinese stamp on it, all "puffed out like a pin-cushion." On opening it Montessori found a beautiful piece of silk embroidery and a letter from a Chinese woman in the heart of China. The letter was to the following effect:

> Dear Dr. Montessori,
> I cannot tell you what a joy it has been to me to read your book. I have always felt that children should be treated as you treat them—with respect and reverence—and that they should be allowed to do things for themselves. Everyone told me I was mad because I was always hoping that a new kind of school would be born; and now I know that I was right.
> I beg to enclose a little gift in token of my gratitude and esteem. . . .

Roots Deep in History

One of the most astonishing things about this new kind of school which Montessori had discovered—especially to those in the teaching profession—was the sudden and unforeseen way it seemed to have come into existence, as it were in a moment from nowhere. Her method in fact seemed to have sprung forth from her brain, fully formed and complete, as Minerva is said to have issued forth fully armed from the head of Zeus. What made it still more astonishing was the fact that Montessori herself was a member of the *medical* profession and not a trained teacher at all in the usual sense.

But the great creations of genius do not spring up out of the void, however much they may appear to do so. "The greatest genius," says Emerson somewhere, "is the most indebted man"; and so in fact was it the case also with Montessori. The reason why her method *seemed* to most persons to have come so suddenly from nowhere—"out of the blue" without any antecedent developments—was because the roots from which it

[5]Subtitle: *Auto-Education in Elementary Schools.*

sprang, and of which it was the final flower and fruit, though going deep into the past, were quite unknown to most students of education.

With Friedrich Froebel, for instance, the founder of the Kindergarten, the case was quite different. Every student of the history of education then (as now) was well aware of Froebel's intellectual ancestry. In every textbook it was pointed out that Froebel had been a disciple of the great Pestalozzi and had in fact worked with him at Yverdun. Similarly it was pointed out how Pestalozzi himself, in his turn, had been profoundly influenced by the writings of Jean Jacques Rousseau. Going back further still, it was shown that the author of *Émile* had, for his part, come under the influence of the English philosopher John Locke.[6]

So that if one were to attempt to write down a sort of intellectual genealogical tree for Friedrich Froebel, it would (too simplified of course) look like this:

> Locke (1632—1704)
> Rousseau (1712—1778)
> Pestalozzi (1746—1827)
> Froebel (1783—1852)

On the other hand, were one to attempt to do the same thing for Montessori it would take on a very different form—as follows:

> Pereira (1715—1780)
> Itard (1775—1838)
> Séguin (1812—1880)
> Montessori (1870—1952)

This would of course also be too much of a simplification to be wholly accurate. It would be absurd to suppose that Montessori, who was for ten years a lecturer at the women's training college at Rome, was ignorant of that other—that mainstream of educational development—which flowed through Rousseau, Pestalozzi, Herbart and Froebel. She could not have read through, as one of the examiners, "all those 150 theses on all possible pedagogical authors from the best known to the most forgotten," without becoming acquainted with their ideas. Yet the fact remains that the foundation on which her work was based was not the usual one. It rested on three almost entirely unknown men. Indeed it was not until the educational world beheld with astonishment this new method rise suddenly in the firmament that the ordinary student of pedagogy ever heard of Pereira, the Spaniard, or of the two great French doctors, Itard and Séguin. Nor was this to be wondered at

[6] I heard Montessori remark once that Rousseau was inspired to write his *Émile* through the influence of Pereira, the famous educator of deaf-mutes.

really, because, as we have seen, the work of these men was almost entirely confined to the education of deaf-mutes (Pereira) and mentally deficients (Itard and Séguin).

Montessori generously admits her great indebtedness to these pioneers; and regards herself as one who carried on their work—especially Séguin's—by developing what was potential in it. Far from trying to take all the glory for herself she makes it clear, again and again, how these men had laboured and how she had entered into the fruits of their labour. As she succinctly puts it "Underlying those two years of experiment—in the San Lorenzo schools—there was a basis of experiment which went back to the French Revolution."

An Objection Answered

It might be well at this point—*en passant*—to answer an objection which is still sometimes raised against the Montessori method by those who have no real acquaintance with it. Parents especially are sometimes heard to argue as follows: Dr. Montessori's method came into being as a result of her work with defective children; my child is not defective, therefore he cannot benefit by such a method. The logic of this is quite unsound, because it assumes that there can be no principles common to the education of normal and defective intelligences. "You might as well argue," said Montessori, "like this: Many successful cures for diseases were first worked out on monkeys: my child is not a monkey and therefore he cannot benefit by them."

The Montessori "Movement" Comes into Being

The years of the San Lorenzo experiment (1907-8) form a landmark in Montessori's career. At the commencement of these *anni mirabili* she was known to certain circles in Rome. That was all. By the end of this time—or of the year following—her name had travelled all over the civilized world, even beyond it. We might almost say that, like Byron, "she woke up to find herself famous."

For many reasons she would have preferred to go on living as she had been living, directing the work of the Children's Houses; and at the same time carrying on as a lecturer at Rome University; lecturing at the women's training college; and, in addition, doing as much private practice as time allowed. But it was not to be. From various countries, especially from England and America, people wrote, or came to Rome in person, clamouring for further instruction in the principles of this new method. Apart from these requests, as she came to realize more completely the wider significance of her discoveries, she felt increasingly the burden of a responsibility that could not be evaded. Her mission in life was now no longer a vague sense of something to come: it had crystallized out. Into her hands, without her seeking it, had been placed a key which would unlock immense treasures for humanity. Or, to put it without metaphor, she felt the duty of going forth as an apostle on behalf of all the children in the world, born and as yet unborn, to preach for their rights and their liberation.

She was faced therefore with an important decision. As she had no private means of her own, and was entirely dependent for her livelihood on the emoluments derived from her lectureships and what little private practice she was able to fit in, would it be prudent for her to give them all up in order to free herself completely for this new mission? It is all very well having a "mission" if one is backed up by a "missionary society"; but there was no such missionary society behind her. The question was whether, from a purely bread-and-butter point of view, there would be enough in this new movement to keep her alive, and give her the means to carry on still further researches.

Some of her friends and relations counselled prudence. "Prudence," says William Blake, "is an ignorant old maid courted by incapacity"; but incapacity was never a characteristic of Montessori then or at any other time. The spirit of the pioneer was strong in her; and she felt—as the genius generally does—a confidence in her own powers. Like Emerson, she believed that this was a case where "the highest prudence was the lowest prudence." So she resigned her university lectureships; had her name removed from the lists of practising physicians; and set forth on a new way of life. Her mother, Renilde, with a deep intuitive faith in her daughter's mission, approved her decision.

As before, the event justified her intuition. From that time onwards she *was* able to support herself, and those dependent on her; chiefly through the training of teachers in her method, and to some extent also by the royalties on her books.

In Rome a number of influential people who were interested in the method started a Montessori society, *Opera Montessori,* which still exists. The Queen Mother—Margherita—was its patroness. Other schools and branches of the Montessori society were started in Milan, Naples and elsewhere.

In a few years similar Montessori movements began to spring up in various countries of Europe, and also in America.

All of these looked to Montessori for guidance and help. The position in which she now found herself might be compared to that of a person who has unexpectedly inherited a large estate, and whose time and energies must henceforth be devoted to its care and management. The task of keeping in touch with these various movements, of guiding this vast wave of international enthusiasm, and of keeping it true to her principles, required even more patience, industry and tact than that of managing a very large estate.

It would be quite beyond the scope of this book to attempt to give even a brief account of all the various Montessori movements which sprang up in different parts of the world, or to trace Dr. Montessori's connection with them. An example or two, lightly touched on, must suffice.

Montessori in America—A Prophetic Dream

Amongst the many enquirers who had come from all over the world to study this new method a good many were Americans. Several of these had suggested that it would be a good thing if Montessori went to America herself to give courses there, so great was the interest which her ideas had aroused in that country.

One night—it was during her second international course, held at Rome in 1914—Dr. Montessori had an unusually vivid dream. She dreamt that she was in a rowing boat on the Atlantic, and that she was making her way in it to America. In her dream she remarked to herself, "I had no idea it was so easy to get to America!"

The very next morning a stranger called at her house in Rome. He was a representative of Mr. McClure, the owner of *McClure's Magazine*. He had come with an offer, which was, in effect, that if Dr. Montessori would come over and settle in America, he, Mr. McClure, would build her an institution wholly in accordance with her ideas, money being no object, for he was a millionaire. The institution would have a model Montessori school for normal children; other similar departments for defective, deaf, and dumb children—together with lecture rooms, libraries, and so forth.

It was a wonderful offer. For some days Montessori busied herself enthusiastically working out plans for the building and for the general organization of the institution. Then, quite suddenly, she abandoned the whole idea, and declined the offer outright. "That was the only occasion," says Anna Maccheroni, "when I have seen her depressed." It must naturally have cost her a great struggle to turn down so tempting an offer. Nevertheless she did turn it down, led by that obscure but compelling intuition which often came to her at the decisive moments of her career. No doubt, by tying herself down to one set of circumstances, and to one country, she would have hampered her freedom of action and limited the international nature and scope of her future work.

However, as it happened, Montessori did go to America shortly after this, in response to an invitation to give a course there. Her mother, Renilde, in the meanwhile had died, so it was easier for her now to leave Rome. Her deep sense of bereavement at this loss was shown by the fact that for three days after her mother's death she could not be persuaded to take any food. "She seemed like one stunned, and it was not until after the funeral service was over that she was able to begin to return to her normal self." [7]

In America many interesting contacts awaited her. Soon after her arrival she became a guest in the family of Thomas Edison, the famous inventor, who had a great admiration for her work. Before long an American Montessori Society was formed under the presidency of Alexander Graham Bell, the inventor of the telephone. The honorary secretary of this society was Miss Margaret Wilson, daughter of the then President of the U.S.A.

When Montessori arrived in America she was quite overwhelmed by the enthusiastic welcome which awaited her. The first thing she was told, on arrival, was that a lecture had been arranged for her at the Carnegie Hall. Five thousand people attended it, and hundreds were turned away. In the streets were flags bearing the inscription, "Welcome to Dr. Montessori." So great was the number of persons striving to gain admission to her hotel that the only way her former students, who had followed her course in Rome, could gain entry was by a stratagem. They came carrying large boxes, which were supposed to contain hats and dresses, declaring they were milliners and dressmakers. Amongst them was Miss Adelia Pyle, a society lady from New York, who for many years afterwards was Dr. Montessori's inseparable friend and interpreter.

Dr. Montessori gave a course for teachers in California which was attended by teachers from all over the States. It was the year of the San Francisco World Exhibition. Montessori was quick to seize the opportunity this presented for making her method better known; and in doing so provided the exhibition with one of its most striking and original features. For the whole duration of the exhibition a Montessori class, in a specially constructed room with glass walls, was carried

[7] Anna Maccheroni, *op. cit.*

on under the direction of Miss Helen Parkhurst, one of her trainees. This glass room was surrounded by specially arranged seats from which hundreds of people at a time could watch the children at work. At that exhibition only two gold medals were awarded: the "new children" took both of them.

Whilst she was in America Montessori declined many interesting offers. Perhaps the most tempting was to give a six-month training course at Washington under the sponsorship of Miss Margaret Wilson of the White House; but the pull of Europe was too strong for her.

It would be interesting to speculate what might have happened if Montessori had decided to stay and work on the other side of the Atlantic. Certainly the history of the Montessori movement in America would have been very different. As it was, it became more and more cut off from its parent source, and thus lacked the inspiration, which the European movements enjoyed, of keeping in touch with the continual stream of research which Montessori carried on during the rest of her life. It is not surprising therefore that the Montessori movement in America tended to become diluted from its original vintage; or even to go off the lines altogether.

One of her most enthusiastic followers, Miss Parkhurst (mentioned above), soon developed a system of her own which became widely known under the title of The Dalton Plan.[8] As the decades passed the number of American teachers who really understood Montessori's principles and could put them into practice became less and less. It would be interesting to trace the affinities and contrasts between the ideas and practices of Montessori and John Dewey, in the same way as, later on in this book, we have done in the case of Friedrich Froebel. But that would take us too far afield.[9]

A Worldwide Development

Meanwhile Montessori's writings were being rapidly translated into many languages. Five different versions of her book were made in Russia alone, where a Montessori school was opened in what was then St. Petersburg, in the imperial gardens, for the children of the imperial family and court. Before long schools were opened in places as far apart as China, Japan, Canada, and Valparaiso.

With astonishing swiftness Dr. Montessori's ideas "took

[8]The Dalton system, as a whole, is very different from Dr. Montessori's own idea of how secondary education should be carried out.
[9]There is evidence that a renaissance of Montessori activity is beginning in the United States.

root." In certain countries they even led to a new form of architecture. In Germany, Austria, America, Holland, India, and Italy—to mention no others—special "Children's Houses" were built, many of them in collaboration with Dr. Montessori herself. In these buildings everything was constructed in proportion to the dimensions and needs—physical and mental —of children, *not* of adults.

There is no doubt that the modern nursery school building owes much to the influence of Dr. Montessori. In Barcelona a special "Children's Chapel" was fitted up on similar lines. There Montessori supervised a fruitful experiment in which her principles were applied to the religious education of young children. An account of this was published later in an English translation, *The Child in the Church,* by Montessori (Sands and Co.).

Lectures in Many Countries

As a knowledge of the existence of this new method became more and more widely diffused, Montessori received (and continued to receive to the end of her life) many invitations to lecture in different countries, either to give single lectures, or systematic training courses for teachers. Many of these invitations came from ministers of education; others from educational societies, or groups of interested individuals. In almost every case, whenever she did visit a new country, she received an official welcome in recognition of her services to education generally.

In this way arrangements were made for Montessori to give training courses for teachers in Italy, France, Holland, Germany, Spain, England, Austria, India, and Ceylon. Besides the visit to the U.S.A. already referred to, Montessori also visited the Argentine Republic where she lectured in Buenos Aires and other cities in South America.

In 1919 Montessori paid her first official visit to England. Her reception was almost royal. A banquet was held in her honour at the Savoy Hotel, London, at which Mr. H. A. L. Fisher, President of the Board of Education, took the chair. It is outside the aim of these chapters to attempt to follow Montessori in all her wanderings. It is enough to record that wherever she went she seemed to have made the same impression. Her profound insight into the soul of the child; her long and varied experience; her scientific outlook combined with a maternal tenderness and sympathy; the lucidity of her discourses and their originality; her strong yet charming personality, at once humble yet dignified; the passionate sincerity of her devotion to her mission—all these combined to make her the perfect advocate of her cause, which was the cause of the child. In the whole history of education it has been given to few if any other educational reformers to have their work so fully and so widely appreciated during their own lifetime as was the case with her.

Montessori Looks Ahead

Gratifying as it must doubtless have been to the Dottoressa to have felt herself so widely appreciated, so fêted and honoured, she herself had no intention of resting on her laurels. Much more clearly than any of her followers she realized that what she had accomplished was only the first step. There was much more still latent in her "movement" than anyone else realized. People regarded her then (as many do still) simply as the founder of a new method of education for small children, the inventor of a new and glorified form of Kindergarten, and no more. This was true enough as far as it went, but it was only a part of the story, and not even the most important part. *She* knew that she had discovered a key which could unlock immeasurable constructive energies for human development; and that as yet only a small fraction of these latent energies had become actual. Immense potential energies were still waiting to be set free. She saw, with ever-increasing vividness, that her method for *small children* was not the end of the movement, but only its beginning; that the effect of her "discovery" would act like a leaven which would in due time permeate the whole sphere of education right up to university age.

More than this, she saw that, as the decades would pass, its influence would extend beyond the limits of what is technically known as education, and effect changes in the home; and ultimately in human society. This might not be achieved in the span of one, or even two or three generations; and it would require immense labour both on her own part and on that of many others who followed her. But it would come, and would come infallibly, if only the movement remained true to its first principles.

Just here Montessori recognized the greatest danger. She realized that, as her principles went far out into the world to penetrate by their own expansive force into the home, school, and society, there would be always a grave danger that—in the process—they might be misunderstood and misapplied. And just because she had discovered them and knew them most intimately, she felt that *she* was the best qualified to direct their application in these ever-widening spheres. Therefore it was of paramount importance that she should use her time and talents to the best advantage; and not dissipate her energies by too much travel and propaganda. She felt the need of retiring again into herself for study and meditation, to draw thence insight and power to carry her principles into widening applications. For this reason she was obliged to decline hundreds of invitations to travel and lecture. "I, too, have work to do," she remarked to a friend. "I cannot talk all the time."

Inexhaustible Originality

Montessori lived on for over forty years after she made that remark—years in which she laboured incessantly. So vast and varied has been the output of her work, so original its quality, that it will take another forty years or more before it becomes generally known and applied in the sphere of education. And it will take still another fifty, or even a hundred years, before the impact of her ideas will have worked itself out fully in the home and society as well. Some of this vast output of work has been published—in this language or that —but a great part of it has never been published at all.

Her originality seemed inexhaustible. Every year witnessed some new development, either in psychology or in its practical applications, or in both. Even when she was dealing with a subject she had been lecturing on for thirty years she never mechanically repeated a former lecture. If you had already heard her lecture on a subject—say the function of environment, or the incarnation of man—a dozen times, you could confidently go to hear her speak on it again with the certainty that you would hear something fresh. That is why each new lecture was an event in itself; and always threw a fresh and unexpected light on an old subject, as something seen from a new angle. It was as though into each lecture she put a new part of herself. That is why so many of those who had already studied under Montessori at one of her training courses continued to attend her further courses, again and again, if they had the opportunity to do so.

Further Researches

For fully forty years, now in this country, now in that; in favourable circumstances or difficult; in peacetime or in war —ceaselessly, calmly, undeterred by calamities private or national—Dr. Montessori went on steadily with her researches.

There is no single person living who knows the extent of them. They have never been collected together in one place. As we have just remarked, many of her ideas have never been published. They exist, scattered over the world, in the form of lectures, given in Italian, and translated as they were given by an interpreter, and taken down in English, Dutch, French, German, Spanish, or Hindustani. It will take years to gather together and systematize all these ideas (if it is ever possible); and it will take longer still to work out in practice all that is potential in them.

Obviously we can only give here the barest outline of these manifold researches.

Montessori, as we have seen, began her work amongst normal children with a group whose ages varied from three and a half to six years. It was inevitable—her interest being focused on development rather than mere learning—that it did not remain limited to this age. Her researches did, in fact, lead her in two directions: forward towards adolescence; ar.d backward towards the newly born child. As she herself remarked once in a lecture, "Our studies tend along two diverse paths: one, which leads forward, concerns itself largely with the transmission of culture. This is a study which becomes ever more and more complicated until, as we might say, the child almost disappears. [See diagram, The Prepared Paths, p. 275.] The other study leads backward. It concerns itself ever more directly with the child himself, and leads us towards a contemplation of the mysterious origins of conscious life." [10]

By this second path she does not mean the study of child psychology as that term is ordinarily understood. "We have always thought of the child, however small, as a human being (*essere umano*), a mysterious entity not understood. It is in this human being, with the dignity of a human being, that we are interested, not a set of psychological principles."

We may roughly classify the researches which Dr. Montessori carried out during all these years (i.e., since her first discovery in the San Lorenzo School) under the following heads:

(1) The training of teachers.

(2) The gradual but continuous application of her principles to ever more advanced school ages (corresponding to "the forward path" mentioned above). This has involved:

    (*a*) A study of "sensitive periods in development," and the "analysis" of the various subjects of culture in accordance with these sensitive periods.

[10]See Dr. Montessori's last great book, *The Absorbent Mind.*

Consequently—

 (*b*) The creation of a vast quantity of teaching materials for all sorts of subjects suitable for elementary and junior schools.

 (*c*) The working out of a new system of secondary education, based on the psychological and social characteristics of puberty and adolescence.

(3) The study of the preschool child, i.e., "going backwards" from three and a half years to birth. Much of Montessori's work in this sphere has already been recorded in her *Secret of Childhood*. Her latest researches on the child's development in these earliest years have been published under the title of *The Absorbent Mind*.

(4) A study of the constructive *social possibilities latent in the "normalized child."* This has taken the form of a plan for the reconstruction of society and civilization, based on the idea that "true education is the armament of peace."

The Teaching of Religion

 Dr. Montessori was born and brought up a Roman Catholic, and at various periods of her long life she turned her energies to the teaching of religion—especially to young children. We have already referred to the experiment she made in Barcelona. Later she wrote several books for children, including: *The Life in Christ,* a study of the Liturgical Year; *The Mass Explained to Children;* and *The Opened Book*—a brilliant study of the Mass for older children. She also planned a most ingenious and attractive Children's Missal, which has never yet been published on account of its somewhat complicated nature and the consequent difficulties of production.

Just before Dr. Montessori's death in May 1952, a Catholic Montessori Guild was formed in England with the purpose of carrying on and developing this aspect of her work. Dr. Montessori's last public utterance—written the day before her death—was a message to be read at the inaugural meeting of this Guild.

Since this present book is of a general nature, we cannot deal here with this part of her work, striking and original as it is.[11]

Montessori in the Orient

 With the exception of one training course, in 1946, Dr. Montessori spent very little time in England after 1939.

[11]See *The Child in the Church*. A new and enlarged edition of this book is in course of preparation.

Indeed she was so much out of the "news," and for so long a time, that at the mention of her name, it was not uncommon to hear persons in this country expressing surprise that she was still alive! As a matter of fact during those ten years she was as active as ever. Indeed, it is true to say that this astonishing old lady at the age of seventy—when most persons have already been retired for some years—actually began one of the most interesting and important phases of her already remarkable life.

In 1939 she flew to India to give a training course in Madras, which was attended by over 300 teachers and students from all parts of India. She was thus engaged when World War II broke out; and, being an Italian, she was automatically regarded as an enemy alien. However, exception was made in her case, and she was soon allowed to continue her work. During these war years she gave courses in various parts of India—in Ahmedabad, Adyar, Kodaikanal, and Kashmir (under the sponsorship of the Maharaja of Kashmir). In 1944 she gave a course in Ceylon, where—as in so many other places—her work received government recognition.

During these tours about India she met many interesting personalities, including Mahatma Gandhi, Mr. Nehru, and Tagore.

When the war was over she flew back to Europe (1946) to direct another international training course in London. A "parallel course" was held at the same time in Edinburgh, at the termination of which Montessori was entertained by the civic authorities of that city, and given an honorary fellowship in the Educational Institute of Scotland.

In 1947, at the invitation of the Italian government, she returned to Italy to reestablish the *Opera Montessori* which had been suppressed during the Fascist regime.

In 1948—at the age of seventy-eight—we find her flying back again to India to give more courses there—in Poona and Adyar. She stayed for a while with the Maharaja and Maharani of Gwalior, where, under her direction, at the request of Their Highnesses, a model school was established for children up to the age of twelve. In the same year translations of Montessori's books appeared in two more Indian dialects—Tamil and Marathi.

In 1949 she gave her first course in Pakistan. She herself was not able to stay to the end of it, as she was due back again in Europe to preside over the International Montessori Congress which had been arranged in her honour at San Remo, and took place in July. Leaving her course in Karachi to be carried on by her very able assistant (Mr. Joosten, a Dutchman) she flew back to Europe just in time to be present at the Congress, at which were gathered more than two hundred enthusiastic followers from Europe, America, and the Orient.

The International Montessori Congress at San Remo was the eighth congress of its kind. The previous ones—also under the presidency of Dr. Montessori—had taken place at Helsinki (1925), Nice (1932), Amsterdam (1933), Rome (1934), Oxford (1936), Copenhagen (1937), Edinburgh (1938). The next was in London (1951) and it was the last at which Dr. Montessori was personally present, as she died the following year. The tenth International Montessori Congress was held in Paris, a year after Dr. Montessori's death. It was organized by the French Montessori Society[12] and sponsored by the French Government. These international congresses, which lasted from a week to ten days, are not to be confused with the international training courses described in the next chapter.

The Last Years

The last few days of Dr. Montessori's long life were characterized by the same activity and zeal which she had shown through all her previous career. We find her constantly moving from one country to another to give lectures and direct courses. In the autumn of 1949 she was invited to address a gathering of UNESCO. On this occasion she received a great ovation from all present, the whole assembly rising to its feet to acclaim her at the end of her conference. In December of the same year the French nation honoured her by decorating her with the medal of the Legion d'Honneur. This dignity was conferred upon her with great solemnity by the Rector of the Sorbonne in the name of the French Republic.

Early in the next year (1950) we find Dr. Montessori on a lecture tour in Norway and Sweden; and in the summer of the same year she was back again in Italy, in Perugia, directing a training course for teachers. This was given at the International Centre for Educational Studies, which had been recently formed in connection with the University of Perugia, of which she was made Directress. In recognition of her work there, she was made "honorary citizen" of Perugia. When the course was over, a similar honour was paid her by the cities of Ancona (where she was born) and Milan.

On her way back to Holland—which had become her headquarters again on her return from India—she lectured by in-

[12]The honorary secretary of the Society was the late Madame G. Bernard, wife of J. J. Bernard (the well-known French dramatist and essayist) and Principal of the Montessori Training Centre at 22 Rue Eugène Flachat, Paris, 17. Her daughter now carries on her work.

viation of the Tyrolese government at Innsbruck. Soon after her return to Holland she was received by Queen Wilhelmina, who conferred upon her the rank of Officer of the Order of Orange-Nassau. About the same time she received the honorary degree of Doctor of Philosophy from the University of Amsterdam.

In all these "journeyings oft" and endless labours, Dr. Montessori was assisted—with touching fidelity and measureless devotion—by her son Mario. As the decades passed Mr. Mario Montessori, with an inherited ability, shared in an ever-increasing degree the immense burden of her responsibilities. At her death she appointed Mr. Montessori as her successor in the task of directing and coordinating the work of the Association Montessori Internationale—a position he has more than merited by his profound insight into the Montessori method and his lifelong devotion to "Mammolina" and her cause. This responsibility includes the publication of certain researches which he and Dr. Montessori worked out together, especially those dealing with the development and care of children from 0-3 years; and also the application of her principles to secondary education. A still heavier responsibility laid upon Mr. Montessori's shoulders is the delicate task of safeguarding the integrity of the Montessori movement, in the many countries where it is active, by recognizing under the aegis of the Association Montessori, Internationale [18] only such "Montessori" schools and training courses as faithfully interpret, both in spirit and practice, the Montessori principles.

Maria Montessori's long and self-sacrificing labours on behalf of the child—and through him of humanity—ended suddenly on 6th May 1952 at Noordwijk-on-Sea, in Holland. She was then in her eighty-first year. She was buried in the small cemetery of the Catholic church at Noordwijk, where a beautiful monument has been erected by her many admirers. But her most appropriate and we believe most lasting monument is, and always will be, the serene and joyful atmosphere which emanates from thousands of happy children in every part of the world.

[18]Headquarters: 161 Koninginneweg, Amsterdam, Holland.

CHAPTER IV   A GREAT AND "REPRESENTATIVE" PERSONALITY

Many years ago a writer in *The Times* described Dr. Montessori as "the most interesting woman in Europe"; and it is likely that history will endorse that verdict. Montessori was one of those personalities who are able to arouse a great enthusiasm in their followers. This is a great gift, but not without its dangers.

International Training Courses

It was inevitable that those who were carried away by their first enthusiasm for Montessori's ideas should wish to make them more widely known. But, right from the beginning, experience made it clear to Dr. Montessori that mere enthusiasm did not qualify for this apostleship. A true appreciation of the Montessori method can only be obtained after an intimate acquaintance with the various principles underlying it, seen first separately, and then in their right relationship to each other and the whole.

Bearing these things in mind Montessori worked out her own system for the propagation of her ideas and the training of teachers in her method. This was by means of her world-famous "international training courses." These formed so important a feature of her life's work that some account of them must be given.

Each course, which usually lasted about six months, was composed of three main elements. Firstly, Dr. Montessori's own lectures, which were very varied in their subject matter. They included, on the one hand, the psychological principles which lie behind her method (based on her own inimitable observations of children); and on the other, the nature and purpose of the various didactic or teaching materials. They also dealt with practical problems relating to the direction of a Montessori school. In later years Montessori also included some philosophy and sociology in her training course lectures. These were concerned with the wider applications of her principles in the home and in society—in particular with "the cosmic mission of man on earth"; and "education as the armament of peace."

The second element of the course consisted in a more complete and systematic study of the didactic materials than was possible in Montessori's own lectures. The greater part of this work was undertaken by her assistants, who, as the course proceeded, supervised the students while they worked practically with the materials.

The third element consisted in making a series of visits to recognized Montessori Schools. Each student was thus obliged to spend a minimum of fifty hours observing her method in actual practice. Doctor Montessori insisted rigidly on this third feature because—as she often remarked—"It is not really I who propagate my method. It is true I give lectures and write books; but it is the children themselves who finally make people really believe in it. They are the last and incontrovertible argument in favour of it."

At the end of the six months those students who had made a "Book on the Materials" and had also passed their written and oral examinations, were granted a Montessori diploma signed by Montessori herself. This diploma entitled the holder to open a school, and call it a Montessori School. Two years later, if the student had worked in a Montessori class and proved satisfactory as a Montessori directress, her diploma was endorsed to that effect.

On these diplomas there was a clause expressly stating that, though they qualified the holder to open a Montessori School, they did *not* qualify her (or him) to train other people in the method. Many persons objected that this was a shortsighted policy and put an unnecessary brake on the spreading of her ideas; but Montessori had sound reasons for inserting this clause.

The Personal Contact

A larger number of these international training courses were given in London than elsewhere. In fact, from 1919 to 1938 Montessori gave a course in London every alternate year. But other courses were also given at Rome, Milan, Paris, Berlin, Amsterdam, Nice, San Francisco, Innsbruck, Barcelona; and, going further afield, in Ceylon, Madras, Karachi, Ahmedabad, and Kodaikanal in India.

These training courses were justly described as international because they were often attended by representatives of as many as thirty to forty different nationalities. In this way Dr. Montessori must have personally trained some four to five thousand students from every part of the globe. This is in itself an immense achievement. But it must be remembered that at the same time she was unceasingly pursuing those many and varied researches outlined on pp. 68-69.

This six-month course was not long enough for anyone to obtain a full and complete grasp of the principles and practice of the Montessori method. Nevertheless, year after year people came from the ends of the earth, sometimes at the greatest personal sacrifice, to sit at the feet of Dr. Montessori. Practical-minded readers might be inclined to ask, What did these students (I was almost going to say "pilgrims") gain from Dr. Montessori's courses in any way commensurate with the sacrifice of time and expense which they were obliged to make in order to attend them? What indeed, more than a diploma which, in most countries (at first at any rate), was not even recognized by their own educational authorities?

It is worthwhile pausing for a moment to answer this question. First, there was the stimulus which came from being one of a group composed of all creeds, classes, and colours, drawn together by a common ideal—to help the child. Then, there was the inspiration that comes with spending many happy hours observing the children, so free and so frank, as they lived their lives to the full in a Montessori environment.

But these were not the main things. These could have been obtained elsewhere. The really important factor was Dr. Montessori herself. There is something in the direct personal influence of a great genius that defies analysis. The founder of any great school of thought, or new social movement, contains in some inexplicable way, in his own personality, all the developments which derive from him, though it may take generations for it to unfold.

This was undoubtedly the case with Montessori. There was something in the certainty of her vision of the unlimited possibilities, educational and social, of the "liberated child," and most of all in her personality itself which cast a spell upon her students, irrespective of racial and national differences. It was as if in some strange way her spirit was laid upon theirs.

Comparatively short though this course was, there is no doubt that even from a *purely educational point of view* those who attended it went away fully compensated for the time and money expended. So great was Montessori's insight that, in a generation characterized by numberless educational gatherings, is was still the most valuable and rewarding of them all. Nowhere else was it possible to drink at a source of inspiration so crystal clear, or so bounteous in its continual stream of original ideas.

The fact remains, however, that Montessori courses were felt by those who attended them as something much more than just a study of educational method. They *were* that, of course; for, by the end of the six months, the students had indeed become acquainted with many new facts and principles which would help them in teaching and training children. Yet all the students, by the end of the course, became vividly conscious that they had received something else which was worth all the rest put together. Exactly what it was they had received they would have found it difficult to say, just because it was something too subtle to put into words. Yet if one were forced to attempt the description of it, the words that would come most naturally to one's lips would be—faith, hope, and charity; faith in the new vocation they had chosen, a new hope for humanity, and a deeper charity towards the child.

To explain a little more clearly. These students came expecting to learn about child psychology, hygiene, the didactic materials, class management and so forth. They found in the end that they had learnt something new about *themselves,* and the management of their *own* lives! They came hoping to learn how to help the child to develop, and they found that they had been helped in their own development. During those six months fresh horizons had opened up before them. There had been revealed to them a glimpse of a new world, in the soul of the child, of whose existence they had hardly dreamed. It was almost as if they had been shown a "promised land" and had been called upon to go in and possess it. In short, they had experienced a genuine enlargement of mind, and were no longer as they were when they first came.

From the very beginning those who came in contact with the Montessori movement in Rome received a similar impression, viz., that there was something more in it than a mere educational method. It was the same ten years later when Montessori came to England to give her first course in 1919. At the end of that course the students, through a chosen representative, expressed themselves as follows: "At the conclusion of our course under you, Dr. Montessori, we wish to offer you our heartfelt gratitude for the new hope, the new confidence you have inspired in us, that the teacher's work is not only the noblest that man can do, but that it can be achieved with a success measured *not only in the true progress and happiness of the children, but of ourselves also.*" (Italics are ours.)

At every training course the same thing happened. It was as though Montessori communicated a part of herself to her students, and they gradually became aware that something very precious was passing from her to them. As the course drew to its end many of them felt the need of somehow or other expressing their gratitude, which they did by gifts of flowers and in many other little ways.

L'Envoi

This consciousness of becoming more and more united in a great and noble cause became stronger as each training course drew to a close. And for this reason the concluding ceremony—which had the ostensible purpose of the distribution of diplomas—took on a more than academic quality. Here is an extract from an extempore farewell speech at the close of one of these training courses. After the students had presented Dr. Montessori with a gift and a farewell address she replied as follows:

It is difficult for me to express my sentiments and my thanks. We have been together several months and we have become conscious of a bond uniting us, which has grown stronger and which I believe will never break. I am a pilgrim and you are pilgrims towards an idea. I voyage and you voyage and we unite ourselves together, almost as spiritual pilgrims, to work for the triumph of a principle which does not concern ourselves—but the child for whom we are working, and wish to work.

You and I have been, as it were, seduced by something attractive and deep in the child. Not only in those beautiful individual creatures whom we all love, but also in an almost symbolic being—one who holds in himself a secret, a secret we can never wholly fathom, and one which will therefore always attract us.

We began by protecting the child and now we realize that it is we who need protecting. We began with methods of education and culture for the child, and we end by acknowledging that he is our teacher. Not a teacher who gives us culture, but one who can reveal to us, as no other, our own nature and its possibilities. Therefore we are drawn towards the child, as individuals, as members of society, and for the good of the human race as a whole.

The child is an authority: and the adult must make himself in accord with this authority if he wishes to better his conditions. We have been studying the means towards a harmony between the child and the adult; and we have learned many deep things—but there are many more to be learned.

Some of you will go back to your own country and home just to teach. Others will do more: you will go on studying the child. That is why we are all united in this sphere and can never be separated.

This course has not been primarily a course for the study of culture. I myself speak a foreign language you do not understand; and you, young and old, of all nations, races, religions—some of you still seeking a place in the world, others already with honoured names—you all sit, side by side, together and without surprise. We have come together in this way because we have touched a point which is common to all cultures, nations, societies, religions—The Child.

Fourteen years after the speech we have just quoted, Dr. Montessori was making her concluding address to the Ninth International Montessori Congress held in London, May 1951. It was a solemn and memorable occasion, for many of those present had a presentiment that they would never hear her address them again—a presentiment which turned out to be true.

The Congress had been a great success. Dr. Montessori had been honoured by a host of outstanding personalities and representatives of many societies—from the Minister of Education down to the (equally important!) tiny children who presented her with a bouquet.

In her concluding remarks—after having spoken of her gratitude for the many expressions of homage which had been paid her—she went on to this effect:

Your action, ladies and gentlemen, in giving me this honour, has brought to my mind a very simple and homely simile. Have you noticed what happens when you try to point out something to your dog? He does not look in the direction you are pointing, but at your outstretched hand and finger. I cannot help thinking that you are acting in a somewhat similar way in paying so much attention to *me*. I am pointing—as I have never ceased to point for the past forty years—to someone outside myself, and you are saying in effect, "What a handsome finger she has! and what a beautiful ring she is wearing!" The highest honour and the deepest gratitude you can pay me is to turn your attention from me in the direction in which I am pointing— to The Child.

This Congress—arranged by Mrs. Wallbank, a personal friend of Dr. Montessori and Principal of the Gatehouse Montessori School—was a memorable climax to her long and fruitful labours in England. At the age of eighty she lectured on five successive evenings, half in English and half in Italian, holding her audience fascinated both by the charm of her vivacious personality and the inspiration of her ideas.

Montessori the "Representative" of the "Century of the Child"

In every age there are to be found certain "Representative Men" (the phrase is Emerson's)—persons who in a special way express what the Germans call the *Zeitgeist*, the spirit of their age. In such characters, aspirations which are stirring in the hearts of thousands of their contemporaries find articulate expression. What others feel vaguely, or in disconnected fragments, they see steadily and as a whole. The sayings and actions of these persons have more than an individual significance. As a lens gathers together the many separate rays of light, bringing them to one burning focus, so such representative people unite in their individual personality a thousand separate tendencies, and by the fire of their genius start new movements. Such individuals embody what Shakespeare (who himself was one of them) describes as "the prophetic soul of the wide world dreaming on things to come."

To take a few examples. As Aristotle summed up the knowledge of the ancient world, so St. Thomas Aquinas and Dante, each in his own way, the spirit of the Middle Ages. In a different sphere both St. Francis of Assisi and St. Dominic were especially sensitive to the needs of their times, and responded with the creation of the Mendicant Orders; just as St. Benedict, eight centuries before, had founded monasticism. Similarly Francis Bacon, in the sixteenth century, with his emphasis on inductive logic, may be said to be the founder of modern science; whilst the name of Charles Darwin became, in the popular mind, almost synonymous with the idea of evolution which was "in the air" during his lifetime. History has already come to look upon Karl Marx as the founder of communism; as future ages will see in Churchill the embodiment of the spirit of freedom in Europe's darkest hour.

Without doubt Montessori will hold a place amongst these "representative persons" in world history. In fact she may be said to have already secured such a place. No one acquainted with the educational developments which have taken place in this century would deny the paramount influence which Dr. Montessori has already exercised in every country. She is already a fixed star in the firmament of the history of education, where she will shine forever in company with Comenius, Pestalozzi and Froebel and many others.

Nevertheless we do not think that it will be upon her reputation *as an educationist*—i.e., as the founder of the Montessori school and the Montessori method—that her claim to the gratitude of coming generations will chiefly and finally rest. There is something in her message which is deeper, wider, and more important than this.

Montessori as a Social Reformer, and the Problem of Peace

It is not within the scope of this book to enlarge upon these deeper aspects of Dr. Montessori's work. To do so would be like putting the cart before the horse. For no one can be expected to place much faith in Dr. Montessori *as a social reformer* who has not first been convinced with regard to those psychological "discoveries" upon which such a faith must ultimately rest. Nevertheless, in any outline of Dr. Montessori's life and work, some mention of it, however brief, should be made.

The century in which we live—and Montessori lived—has been called "The Century of the Child." And not without justification; for in no previous epoch in history have there come into existence so many organizations all having as their aim some aspect of the welfare of the child.

In Montessori, more than any other, the underlying significance of all these movements became luminously self-conscious. With the extraordinary sensitiveness of genius she was able to discern beneath these manifold expressions the stirring of something deeper—of a great new movement struggling to come to birth from the subconsciousness of the human race.

As long ago as 1926 Dr. Montessori, in a lecture on Education and Peace to the League of Nations in Geneva, said:

> The crisis we are witnessing is not one of those that mark the passage from one era to another: it can only be compared to the opening of a new biological or geological epoch, when new beings come on the scene, more evolved and more perfect, whilst on earth are realized conditions of life which have never existed before. If we lose sight of this situation we shall find ourselves enmeshed in a universal catastrophe. . . . If the sidereal forces are used blindly by men who know nothing about them—with the aim of destroying one another—the attempt will be speedily successful, because the forces at man's disposal are infinite, and accessible to all at all times and in every place.

These prophetic words, uttered many years before the creation of the atomic bomb, were dreadfully and awfully fulfilled in the apocalyptic lightnings of Hiroshima and Nagasaki. "Humanity today," continued Montessori in that same address, "resembles an abandoned child who finds himself lost in a wood at night, and is frightened by the shadows and mysterious noises of the night. Men do not clearly realize what are the forces that draw them into war, and for that reason they are defenceless against them."

There must be something radically wrong with our civilization that it should be threatened in this way *from within.* The vast majority of human beings on this planet do not want war; yet wars come. The causes of war, she would have us believe, are not those which appear on the surface and immediately precipitate its outbreak. They lie deep down in the collective subconscious of humanity.

The real reason—according to Montessori—is that something was wanting in the building up of our civilization. A vital factor has been left out: and that is the child as a creative social factor. Hitherto all civilizations—including our own—have been built on an insufficient foundation. In building them up we have only taken into account "adult values of life": the child has never been given his rightful place.

Hitherto we have regarded childhood merely as a stage through which the individual has to pass in order to become an adult, and only of value from the individual's point of view. But childhood is more than this. It is an entity in itself with an importance of its own. Childhood is in fact, "the other pole" of humanity.

> The child and the adult are two distinct parts of humanity which must work together and interpenetrate with reciprocal aid.
>
> Therefore it is not only the adult who must help the child, but also the child who must help the adult. Nay more! In the critical moment of history through which we are passing the assistance of the child has become a paramount necessity for all men. Hitherto the evolution of human society has come about solely around the wish of the adult. Never with the wish of the child. Thus the figure of the child has remained outside our mind as we have built up the material form of society. And because of this the progress of humanity may be compared to that of a man trying to advance on one leg instead of two.

How is the child to help in the construction of society? By being allowed to bring his contribution, his "Work." And what is the child's "Work"? It is, as we shall see (Chapter VIII), the construction of the adult-that-is-to-be.

Hitherto the child has never been able to fulfill his potentialities, to construct a harmoniously developed adult society. And again, why not? Because he has never had the opportunity, nor the means to do so. And if we ask once more, Why not? the answer is—that hitherto we have not even *realized* the child's possibilities, his potential function as a builder of society.

For an account of the causes which hinder the normal development of children, the reader is referred to later chapters, especially Chapters X and XV. To those who have seen with their own eyes the "normalization of children through work," with all that it implies, there open up vast vistas of possibilities for the amelioration of human society. For, beyond a doubt, these "awakened" children reveal a higher type of personality.

Montessori has seen a vision of something which does not yet exist, *but which is based on something which already does exist*—the characteristics of the normalized child.

We must not be afraid, she says, of this vision of the child and the claims of the unseen. "By changing the centre from the adult—and adult values—to the child, and *his* values we should change the whole path of civilization.

"The fulcrum which today is an external one would become an interior one: and man himself would be the supreme value to which all exterior values would have to be subordinated—such exterior values to be considered only as the necessary means to human life—means above all to the accomplishment of man's cosmic mission on earth.

"Verily I believe [she says, like Nurse Cavell] that laws and treaties are not enough. What we need is a world full of miracles, as it seemed to us miraculous to see the young child spontaneously seeking work and independence and manifesting a wealth of enthusiasm and love."

Like the disciples of old, the nations of the world are quarrelling as to who shall be the greatest; and—as with the disciples of old—Montessori would place the child in their midst to show them the way of peace.

The Deeper the Trough the Higher the Succeeding Wave

It is a striking thing that in this same epoch of history there have been two great revelations, two great discoveries of unsuspected and hidden energies, one in the world of matter, and one in the world of the spirit. Unfortunately the vast energies locked up in the atom have so far been largely directed towards *disorder and death*. In contrast to this, the mental and spiritual energies which Montessori has liberated in children are leading directly towards harmony and order.

Montessori herself believed it is no accident that these two discoveries (one in the realm of matter and one in the realm of spirit) should have been made in the same age. "It is no coincidence, but a direct order of Providence; one of those happenings linked up with that Spirit which ordains and directs events, often in contrast to the ways of logic. Destruction and reconstruction, war and peace, meet each other when one epoch comes to an end and another begins."

Montessori—A Personal Impression

It is difficult to put in a few sentences the impression made by someone whom one has known intimately for thirty years. This is especially true in the case of Dr. Montessori whose personality presented so many and such different facets. Perhaps the feature which stands out most forcibly is that of a massive and unassailable strength of character—like a mountain unmoved by the storms which beat against it. Montessori was one of those rare persons for whom obstacles do not seem to exist. Such people (Napoleon was a good example) seem to their contemporaries to be capable of almost superhuman exertions, and at times elicit a feeling of awe such as we experience in the presence of the great forces of Nature. "Character," says Emerson, "is a reserved force which acts directly by presence and without means." No words could more aptly describe the influence which Montessori exerted simply by her presence.

Her head was large and well shaped, with a massive forehead and intensely penetrating brown eyes. She had a sensitive mouth and mobile features; and displayed a characteristic Italian vivacity of expression. Yet with all this there was no trace of the bluestocking about her. Essentially feminine, she was always elegantly and tastefully dressed; and combined with her great intellectual powers a singular charm of manner and sweetness of disposition, a trait which was specially noticeable, even to a sort of radiancy at times, when she was speaking to little children.

This winning and gracious aspect of her character was in fact as essentially a part of her character as the indomitable strength of will referred to above, and was a trait more endearing. In a marked degree she possessed a maternal tenderness towards the weak, the undeveloped, and the oppressed. In the presence of such, her generous heart was always stirred with the desire to protect and encourage. This is why to those who knew her most intimately she was—as she must always remain in their memory—just "Mammolina," the little mother.

In conversation, and on the platform, her manner was simple and direct, without any striving after effect. Her actions and her sayings fell from her so easily and naturally as to suggest an immense reserve of strength and wisdom never fully put into operation. In all her many travels—under the most diverse circumstances—she always showed herself equal to the occasion, quietly and calmly sure of herself, and master of every situation.

She was a brilliant lecturer, with a style essentially her own. She had a sound sense of the value of words, and faultless and fascinating delivery. Except in French-speaking countries, she usually lectured in Italian, with an interpreter if required. But her Italian was so clear and so beautiful, her style and expression so vivacious, that even those who did not understand that language derived great pleasure from listening to her. Since each part of her discourse was usually translated as she went along, many of those who attended her six-months course found, by the end of the course, that they had picked up a great deal of Italian; and consequently many were inspired to go on and complete their knowledge of the language.

It was not only Dr. Montessori's manner of delivery which was so impressive. No less striking was the way in which she developed her theme. Especially remarkable was the constant flow of similes and metaphors which adorned all her discourses. Her vivid and brilliant imagination spontaneously supplied her with a constant succession of these, as from an infinite reservoir. Like the greatest of all teachers it seemed natural to her—even in an ordinary conversation—to speak in image and parable.

To take an example just at random out of hundreds—even thousands—scattered up and down her lectures. On one occasion she was trying to make the point that the psychological key to the whole problem of autoeducation was *interest*— "Interest, the compeller of spontaneous activity." "It may often happen," she continued, "that a child may have complete comprehension [of what the teacher says] yet without interest." This was her spontaneous illustration:

"A foreigner but slightly acquainted with the language of a country was accosted by a beggar. The foreigner, who was rich but stingy, listened to the beggar's efforts to make himself understood, and it was a long time before he could grasp his meaning. When he did so the foreigner was silent for a while, and then said, 'I understand—but I give nothing!' "

The Appeal to the Spirit

One of the reasons why Dr. Montessori's lectures had such a widespread appeal was that she never treated educational problems on a purely technical or utilitarian level. Her appeal was always to the spirit.

The same characteristic came to light in her dealings with those whom she was training to be directresses. *Always the appeal to the spirit came first.* "A teacher," she said, "must not imagine she can prepare herself for this vocation simply by acquiring knowledge and culture. Above all else she must cultivate a proper attitude to the moral order." This recognition of the importance of spiritual values formed an ever-present background to all her lectures. Not that she ever preached in the narrower sense of the word by obtruding her own particular religious views. Charles Lamb, had he known her, would never have made the same reply to her as he did on one occasion to his friend Coleridge. When the latter enquired: "Charles, did you ever hear me preach?", Lamb promptly replied: "I never heard you do anything else!" So, when we assert, as we do, that even when Montessori was dealing with a subject like arithmetic or grammar the spiritual element was never absent, we do not mean—far from it—that she ever dragged religion into it. We mean rather she saw in every school subject an activity of the human spirit, and therefore treated it with a corresponding dignity and breadth.

Once Montessori had decided on the path she believed she must follow, no amount of criticism, or adversity, would make her change her mind. When the Fascist rule became dominant in Italy, she came to realize that an education which had as its aim the development of a strong and free personality could not thrive in a totalitarian atmosphere. Indeed, the Fascists ordered all her schools to be closed down. In Germany and Austria — then under Nazi rule — things were even more drastic. An effigy of Montessori was burned over a pyre of her own books in a public square both in Berlin and Vienna. So she went to Spain, where she made Barcelona her headquarters, and carried on with her work there. In course of time the Spanish Civil War broke out. As a Roman Catholic, and one who had written books on the teaching of religion, her life and property were in danger. With the assistance of the British Government she managed to get away (at an hour's notice) on a British battleship. Next she settled in Holland, where, at the age of sixty-five, she opened a new school for children and a training college for students at Laren, near Amsterdam. In spite of these vicissitudes she managed to keep on regularly giving her six-months training courses for teachers, at the same time carrying on her psychological researches in this country or that.

Though Dr. Montessori never appeared to be in a hurry she got through an immense amount of work. The day I visited her school at Laren was typical. She happened to be there too that morning. After visiting the classes and discussing problems with the staff, she motored to Amsterdam; had lunch there; flew to Croydon; and by 6:30 p.m. was lecturing to her students in the London training course then in session.

Another example: in 1948 Dr. Montessori flew from Holland to London, had lunch there, and went on the same day to India by air. Pretty good going, one must admit, for a lady of seventy-eight years of age! The writer was present at that lunch, and recalls that, far from being overcome by her journey, Dr. Montessori seemed in great form, and vigorously discussed the subconscious in its relation to education—maintaining that educational systems, as a whole, do not sufficiently realize the nature and the importance of subconscious activities in mental development.

One reason why Montessori accomplished so much is that she never wasted her energies on trying to do too many and useless things. For instance, someone once asked her why she did not reply to a certain professor who had been making violent attacks on her method. "If I am going up a ladder," she replied a flash, "and a dog begins to bite at my ankles, I can do one of two things—either turn round and kick out at it, or simply go on up the ladder. I prefer to go up the ladder!"

Few educationists have combined so perfectly the theoretical with the practical. She was marvellously quick to see the hidden law in a minute particular; and equally capable of applying universal principles to the smallest practical detail. To give an example: She noticed—as everyone has—that little children like to walk along a line on the pavement. But it was only she who saw in this characteristic its psychological significance. She realized that it is related to the greater difficulty children have than adults in keeping their equilibrium because of the proportionately larger size of their heads. So—following nature as always—she invented those "exercises of balance" (walking on the line, etc.) which are a charming part of the daily routine in every Montessori babies' room.

At another time, noticing how little children have a peculiar fondness for standing on the strands of a wire fence or bars of a gate—feet on one, hands on another—she realized that here was a hidden need of the child's development. This led, eventually, to the invention of the well-known jungle-gyms now found in so many nursery and infant schools and parks.

Though, as we have already pointed out (p. 31), she not infrequently set the course of her life by a sort of intuition rather than pure reason, her well-balanced temperament never led her into eccentricities. A sound Latin sense of form pervaded her judgment and gave prudence to her actions. I have known her return home, after giving an inspiring discourse full of high ideals and noble philosophy before a great and learned audience, to cook an excellent omelette for her guests, doing both with the same thoroughness and serenity.

Her consciousness of a great and serious mission in life did not prevent her from possessing a sense of humour. This quality added an extra charm to her lectures, and gave piquancy to her conversation, which was always original without effort and brilliant without affectation. This sense of humour prevented her from taking herself too seriously—always a temptation to those who have the world at their feet and are followed by crowds of ardent admirers whose enthusiasm often exceeds their intelligence. I have indeed heard some of these latter speak of her as "The New Messiah," "The Foundress of a New World Religion," and so forth.[1] She herself was much more diffident, and listened willingly to criticisms and suggestions from others. In fact some of her best work might never have been given to the world but for the persuasion of her friends.

Montessori received a scientific training; and the first period of her life, up to the age of forty, was spent in an atmosphere eminently scientific. She herself never lost the scientific attitude of mind. A large part of her success was in fact due to this capacity of seeing things with the detached spirit of the scientific investigator. All her life she manifested in a high degree that humility which is ready to put aside traditional prejudices and learn from the observed facts. In this sense it is absolutely true—as she herself constantly averred—that the child was her teacher.

Yet Montessori was never a scientist only. She never permitted the scientist in her to go beyond its proper sphere. She always realized that science deals with secondary causes and not with the ultimate mysteries of life, i.e., with the First Cause and *meta*physics. That is why, in spite of her scientific

[1]"Those who were associated with us, in our desire to help the child, became aware that they had much to learn from him, and ended by a veneration verging on idolatry. This caused the question to be raised, 'How far will this enthusiasm of yours carry you? Before long you will be starting a philosophy of the child, a religion of the child.' This is not so, however, for our love of the child has always been tempered by a scientific attitude."

training and outlook, there was never with her—as with many others—a sense of opposition between science and religion.

A scientist, and respected by scientists all over the world, she wrote books on the teaching of religion which have won the admiration of the highest ecclesiastical authorities. It was this twofold preparation, this double background, this happy combination of scientist and mystic which gave to Montessori's personality, and to her achievements, their wholeness and harmony. It is this which has given to her educational method self-consistency, logical coherence, and scientific exactness on the one hand; and moral and spiritual soundness on the other. It is this, too, which has given the movement which she started an appeal as wide as humanity, and as deep as the soul of man.

In conclusion we can say that Maria Montessori was herself the personification of what her own ideal teacher should be— "one who combines the self-sacrificing spirit of the scientist with the love of the disciple of Christ."

PART TWO

The Psychology of Development

CHAPTER V   THE YOUNG EXPLORER

There was a time when meadow, grove and stream,
The earth, and every common sight,
To me did seem
Apparelled in celestial light,
The glory and the freshness of a dream . . .
                                        WORDSWORTH

What struck visitors to the first Montessori schools more than anything else was the fact that the children worked spontaneously, i.e., for the love of work itself. When Montessori schools were set up in London the same thing happened. Dr. Ballard—for thirty years an Inspector of Primary Schools in the L.C.C.—tells us in his book, *The Changing School,* how the Montessori method brought about the miracle of Montessori—i.e., "the miracle of making it possible for private study to take place in an infant school, of making it possible for a number of little children to work independently in the same room at the same time and *without any driving power beyond the impelling force that comes from the work itself."* (Italics ours.)

It is the same at the present day. Accompany anyone who has never seen a Montessori school before on his first visit, and you will usually hear him make some such remark as—"I could never have believed it possible that children would work like that, of their own accord, unless I had seen it with my own eyes."

There have been visitors who have actually seen children at work in a Montessori school, and have *still* been unable to believe that the children were really working *spontaneously.* They have been constrained therefore to invent other reasons to account for it; such as that the children had been subjected to some form of hypnotic influence; or that coercion was being secretly applied behind the scenes when no visitors were present. One Montessori directress related to me how one such incredulous visitor, who had been watching the children work, came up to her and said in an undertone: "Come now, as one teacher to another, tell me where you keep your cane!" And when she assured her that she had none and that the children's concentration was entirely spontaneous she exclaimed "Very well then, if you don't want to tell me, you needn't!" and walked off in high dudgeon.

In spite of this incredulity, it nevertheless remains true that the *Montessori method is based fairly and squarely on the spontaneous activity of the intellect.* In previous methods it was usually taken for granted that it was not natural for children to work for any length of time without the stimulus of some extraneous motive. They would *play* continuously for long periods, but work—no! An important part of the teacher's art, therefore, consisted in knowing how to keep their attention fixed on the matter in hand—sugaring the pill in various ways, which included the use of rewards and punishments.

Montessori's view of the matter is quite different. If children do not reveal a desire to work *spontaneously* the fault lies not in the children but in the manner of presenting the subjects to be studied. She believes that if children are bored, inattentive, and uncomprehending it is because the methods of teaching used present insuperable barriers to the "spontaneous" functioning of the child's mind. It is interesting to note, in passing, that this view is in accord with Aristotle and the Scholastics, who maintained—as a principle—that "all hindrance being removed a faculty must work, this being indeed the very evidence for its existence." It is as natural for the intellect to function spontaneously *all hindrances being removed* as it is for the heart to beat. It is as natural and certain that a child will begin making comparisons and classifications, as it is that—when the right moment comes—he will begin to walk.

The best argument to prove all this, for an open-minded person, would be to show him a Montessori class in action. Unfortunately, this is not always possible. But there is another argument of great cogency which is more accessible. It consists of getting people to *consider the amount of work which has been accomplished spontaneously by the child's intellect (no one teaching him or even directing him) during the first three or four years of his life,* i.e., before he goes to school at all, even to an infant school. Nothing but the blinding effect of custom prevents us from beholding with breathless astonishment the almost miraculous results which are being achieved every day, and all day long under our very noses, by the unaided minds of small children in every walk (or should we say "crawl"!) of life.

"A Big Buzzing Booming Confusion"

Let us carefully compare the mental horizon of a child of three years with that of a newly born infant. To do this successfully, we shall have to make a real effort of imagination; but it is well worth it. As we do so we shall begin to realize something of the stupendous task which is being accomplished spontaneously in this tiny mite of humanity by the luminous power of the intellect.

How does the world present itself to this small creature who, not without suffering and discomfort, has just begun a separate existence? From the stillness and security of its prenatal existence—where everything was done for it by another, even to its eating and digesting—it finds itself suddenly plunged, naked, into a new and strange world. It is a world so new and so strange that there is literally nothing in it that it can recognize, not even itself. It knows nothing, remembers nothing, understands nothing. Yet from this new and unknown world, through all its senses, which have just begun to function, hundreds of bewildering impressions come pouring in. As Professor James well said, its universe is nothing but "a big buzzing booming confusion." Have you ever, reader, had the experience of visiting some huge factory—passing from room to room, each more bewildering than the last—rooms filled with strange whirling, clanking machines, weird beyond description in their form, variety and purpose? You do not know the names of these things, nor their uses, nor can you interpret the strange sounds you hear. Such an experience gives us but a faint idea of the strangeness of its environment to the newborn child. It has no ideas of time, space, form, colour, cause and effect; or the difference between the Self and the Not-Self. Indeed it has no ideas of any kind, for ideas presuppose a sensory experience,[1] and of this it has had none. No memories from the past are there to help it to adjust itself to this bewildering present. The names of things are as unknown as their uses. When it feels discomfort it has no adequate means of expressing its need—it is

> An infant crying in the night,
> An infant crying for the light,
> And with no language but a cry.[2]

[1] See Chapter IX.
[2] *In Memoriam*, Tennyson.

The Immense Jigsaw Puzzzle

From this "big buzzing booming confusion"—mere "thatness"—from all these sensations that come pouring in through all its senses at once, this small mite of humanity has to build up an orderly scheme of things. Immediately, therefore, this tiny philosopher—undaunted by the gigantic task before him—begins the labour of creating a cosmos out of this chaos. To speak more accurately, he sets to work to build up *two* worlds—one without and one within.

When does this great work begin?

At birth. "A baby only a month old had never been out of the house. His nurse was holding him on her lap when his father and an uncle living in the house appeared before him *together*. Both men were more or less the same height and the same age. The baby made a start of intense surprise and almost of fear. The two men stayed in front of him, but separated, one moving to the right and the other to the left. The baby turned to gaze at one of them with plain anxiety, and after a long look at him smiled. But all at once his expression again became anxious, and more than anxious, frightened. With a swift movement he turned his head to stare at the other, and only after gazing at him a long time again smiled. He repeated this passage from anxiety to smiles, and those movements of his head from right to left quite twenty times before light dawned in his little brain, and he realized that there were *two* men. They were the only men he had seen. Both had made a fuss of him, had nursed him, and spoken affectionate words to him, and he had understood the fact that there was a different kind of being from the many women who surrounded him. He had understood that the world held a different kind of human being from his mother, his nurse, and the various women whom he had occasion to notice, but never having seen the two men together he had evidently formed the idea that there was only *one* man. Hence his fright when he suddenly realized that the being he had so laboriously catalogued out of chaos had become double."[8]

In that one phrase "laboriously catalogued out of chaos" we get a perfect description of the nature of the work which is carried on spontaneously by the human intellect right from the beginning.

The universe, as it appears to the child, may be compared to a huge jigsaw puzzle made of an infinite number of separate pieces not one of which, at the beginning, fits into another. Instead they are all jumbled up, higgledy-piggledy, anyhow, in

[8]*The Secret of Childhood.*

an inextricable confusion. It is the office of the intellect to fit the pieces together so as to form one comprehensive, meaningful, harmoniously interrelated whole. To the end of our lives this "fitting in" process continues, and we never complete it. Even after we have lived in this world for half a century we are constantly coming across experiences which seem to us so odd and strange that we find it hard to fit them into our scheme of things—like bits of a jigsaw that seem to have no place. How difficult then must it be for the child! No wonder—as we shall see later when we are dealing with the "sensitive period for order"—no wonder the child clings on desperately to that little oasis of order which he has created for himself amidst the desert of the unclassified which surrounds him!

The Problem of Space

Let us look a little more closely at some of the elements in this great cosmic jigsaw puzzle which confronts the child, and see how his mind—quite unaided—sets to work putting them together. Take the question of space, and the spatial position of things—their sizes, and their relationships one to another. This is a great problem to the small child; and even remains something of a problem for the rest of our lives—as Einstein has shown. Who does not know that odd sensation of sitting in a railway train and thinking we are moving, suddenly to realize that it is not ours but the other train which is moving? The baby's existence must be full of surprises of a similar nature. It has no notion of the distances of objects from itself, and will put out its hand to seize the moon. It is the same with regard to the sizes of things.

My sister was once carrying her little baby in a field when its eyes beheld for the first time a real cow. Up to that time the little one, aged eighteen months, had only seen a tiny model of a cow, with which she played at home. At once, however, she recognized the real cow as of the same category. Jigging herself up and down in her excitement, she put out her little hand—opening and shutting it in anticipation—and cried out imperiously, "Have it! Have it!" Her mother explained that it was impossible for her to give her the cow on account of its size; but the explanation was meaningless to her. Even when my sister carried the little one right up to the cow she still continued to clamour with undiminished vehemence for it to be placed in her chubby little hand. This incident recalls another. The philosopher Helmholtz records that when he was a small boy, walking with his mother near Potsdam, they saw some people moving high up in a church tower. He thought they were as small as they looked, and asked his mother to get one of them down for him to take home; and was very very annoyed when she didn't.

It must indeed be a strange world that children live in. No wonder they readily accept the most impossible stories as true, since they themselves expect the impossible, as the following anecdote makes clear. I was playing once with my young friend Tony—aged two and a half years—in the nursery. We were playing "gardens"; that is, each of us had made an enclosure or garden with wooden rods on the floor. "Tony," I said, "would you like to come into my garden?" He at once consented, and stepped into my enclosure. Not to be outdone in hospitality he then invited me to come into his, which was only about eight inches by four. I accepted the invitation, and he got out of his "garden" to let me in. But, of course, on actually attempting to enter, I could not even get one shoe into his garden—they were much too big. We considered the situation for a few moments during which Tony meditatively got in and out of his garden several times. Then I said, "Tony, shall we change shoes?" to which suggestion he joyfully assented as an excellent solution of the difficulty. It was not until we had both taken our shoes off and I had actually tried in vain to fit my big feet into his tiny shoes that my young friend realized the plan would not work.

When my brother was a little boy, I forget how old, but at any rate old enough to sit at table, someone said to him, "Look out, Bert, or you'll fall into your mug!" For several weeks after nothing would persuade him to drink out of that mug! A little girl I know was simply furious with her doll because, when she put it sitting on a chair, its head and shoulders did not come above the table like a full-sized person. We could multiply such examples indefinitely, and so probably could many readers.

Bearing in mind this ignorance with regard to the sizes of things and their relationships one to another, one can more readily appreciate the intense interest and concentration aroused in the minds of these inexperienced little folk by the Montessori cylinders.[4] One can now understand why they attach themselves with such joy to these rather odd and unromantic looking objects, working with them day after day, and week after week, even month after month. Their satisfaction comes, not from the actual accomplishment of the exercise, but from a growing sense of power which accompanies it—a power or capacity which enables them to recognize and compare with an ever-increasing facility the sizes and dimen-

[4]See page 41.

sions of things. And this, in its turn, gives them a new sense of satisfaction in being able to orient themselves with more certainty in their own environment, becoming masters of it.

The Problem of the Self and Not-Self

To come now to another element in this big jigsaw puzzle—the child's own self—its body first; and then its personality, its "I" or "Ego". How puzzling to the small infant must be its own body and bodily organs, their positions and functions! Sometimes you may see a very small infant lying on its back and waving its arms and legs about in a vague sort of way from sheer *joie de vivre*. Then, by pure accident, its hand will get hold of a foot. At once there seems to come a change in its expression; a look of definite interest, not to say surprise—which, being interpreted, would run as follows: "Hullo, what's this! What *ever* is this! most intriguing! I can feel it both ends! How strange! Let's do it again!"

I recall a lecture in which Montessori gave a description of a baby of six months who was in its pram, and holding an object. With a fixed expression of attention and concentration directed to its own hand, the baby slowly opened its fingers, one by one, beginning with the first until the object (a rattle) fell to the ground. When it was replaced in the child's hand, it repeated the process—many times. Evidently, said Montessori, it was not the object or its falling which fascinated the child, but the discovery of its own fingers and the fact of prehension.

If the existence of its own body is a mystery and a problem to the infant, how much more its own existence as an individual human entity! At first the child knows no distinction between itself and its environment. It is the work of the intellect—ever making distinctions by its very nature—which enables it to come gradually to the consciousness of itself as a separate individuality—a thing no animal is ever able to accomplish.

> The baby new to earth and sky,
> What time its tender palm is prest
> Against the circle of the breast,
> Has never thought that "This is I."
>
> But as he grows he gathers much,
> And learns the use of "I" and "me,"
> And finds "I am not what I see
> And other than the things I touch."
> *In Memoriam*—TENNYSON

More Jigsaw Fragments—Imagination, Dreams, Reality

Montessori remarks somewhere that the usual books on child psychology begin at volume X! No one has ever written the first nine volumes, and probably no one ever will. They would deal with those first mysterious operations of the dawning intellect before the child can speak; those marvellous inner creations by which the child's mind passed as it were from nothingness to something. We cannot tell what is going on in his mind; we can only make faint guesses based on deductions from his actions and expressions. By the time he is old enough to speak, he will have forgotten those experiences, just as we ourselves have forgotten them. But the wonderful inner construction remains, foundation of all that is to be built later.

How interesting it would be if we could read those "first nine volumes," but they remain his secret; for truly every infant is, in a sense, a Newton "voyaging through strange seas of thought—alone" (Wordsworth).

Let us return to our consideration of the various problems which our young philosopher has to solve—unaided. How and when, for instance, does he come to realize clearly the distinction between an experience, and a vivid recollection of that experience? Or between real and imaginary experiences? At a certain stage, children tend to muddle up the real and the imaginary. And how often do grown-ups make it more difficult for them by telling them imaginary stories as real! And, how often do these same grown-ups punish these same children for "telling fibs." Sometimes the foundation of a child's lie is a remembered experience in a very vivid dream, which he has not yet learned to distinguish clearly from the experiences of waking life. Even grown-ups sometimes exclaim "Now did I dream that, or did it really happen?"

Yet somehow or other the mind of the child does eventually come to make these distinctions, between the dream world, the real world, and the world of imagination. Who knows what puzzling, not to say distressing moments children may pass through on their way, like the little girl in *Punch* who—crying in the night—sobbed out "Mummy, Mummy, I dreamt I swallowed myself—have I?" The child's constant query from about six to seven—"Is it true?"—gives us another glimpse into this process of inner construction which may take months to complete. The beginnings are lost in mystery (in those first nine volumes). As Wordsworth says:

Who knows the individual hour in which
The habits were first sown, even as a seed?

Who shall point as with a wand and say
"This portion of the river of my mind
Came from yon fountain"?

Montessori asserts that it is unwise at this stage to confuse the
child's immature mind with stories of fabulous beings—
witches, fairies, gnomes and the like—for he accepts them as
realities, a point to which we shall return in a later chapter (XX).

The Problem of Cause and Effect

Young children have the vaguest ideas about cause and
effect. "Look out," said a jovial uncle to his small nephew who
was peering up a big old-fashioned chimney, "look out, or you
will fall up that chimney." For some days after the young
gentleman in question would not go near that chimney, though
it was summertime and there was no fire in it.

The commonest properties of things in the way of cause and
effect are matters of interest and surprise to small children. At
some moment or other it must have dawned on each of us for
the first time—no doubt very vaguely at first, but with increasing certainty—that objects fall; that water wets; that fire burns;
that smoke rises; that sounds travel; that mirrors reflect; that
sponges absorb water; that the wind moves objects with an
unseen hand; that another hand as mysteriously removes pud-
dles from the street; that water turns into ice; that snow turns
into water; that rain and snow come from the sky; that the
sun (and other lights) make shadows; and so on through an
immense range of phenomena. These, and hundreds of other
such relations of cause and effect, which we adults take for
granted without a thought, are for these young scientists matters of the deepest import, calling for genuine investigation.
Constantly they seek for the inner relationships between things
—what Froebel used to call "inner connexions." My young
nephew came running in to his mother one day to announce
with great excitement, "Mummy, I sneezed and the clock
struck!" I can remember as vividly as yesterday, though it is
more than half a century ago, my excitement as a boy of six,
when—playing in the sand at the seashore—I thought I had
discovered a way of changing stones into bits of leather!

The more one considers the matter the more clearly must
one realize the fact that the small child lives in a world where
the most ordinary things fill him with astonishment and delight.
Get a newspaper and roll it up so as to make a long thin tunnel. Then blow a puff of smoke through it, in front of a child

of two or three years, and you will see him go into an ecstasy of delight as he watches the smoke issue from the far end. I would wager the reader a hundred to one that as soon as he has performed this rite, the child will ask him to do it again. And not only once more, but possibly a dozen times. Indeed the chances are the adult's patience will wear out before the child's. I suppose the fascination lies in the fact that the smoke passes *invisibly* (and thereby mysteriously) all along inside the tunnel and then suddenly seems to materialize itself in a new and different place.

It is just because the small child is ignorant of the *ordinary* behaviour of things that he will often pass by the really unusual without comment. It is for this reason too that the conjuror's art is lost on *very* young children. Let the magician with never so much skill produce a rabbit out of a top hat and the child will not bat an eyelid. His experience is so limited that, for all he knows, such may be the natural habitat of the animal. He is far more interested in the rabbit itself with its long ears and nobbly nose, which perhaps he sees for the first time. And in a way he is right. To produce a rabbit (in the way God does) is a much more amazing feat than merely to produce one out of a top hat!

The Mystery of Time

No less a mystery than space is time and its divisions. The capacity "to look before and after" is essentially a human attribute; but in the beginning it is only there potentially. For a long period the child has only vague notions on this subject. Thus, for instance, to Tony (two and a half) every event in the past—whether it happened only yesterday or six months ago—took place "last night." And similarly for him all future events were to happen in one vast undivided "tomorrow." (like Macbeth with his "yesterdays"). To the child, as to most of us, the smaller divisions of time make themselves felt first as practical emergencies; time to get up, time for lunch, time for bed, etc. Even then children are very vague about it, and sometimes you may hear a child in the afternoon suddenly ask "Have we had lunch yet?" Learning to tell the time is a matter of great interest to most children; so are the days of the week, the names of the months and the seasons.

To the end of our lives the essential nature of time remains a mystery, but most people do not bother about it—agreeing with Polonius that "to expostulate why day is day, night night and time is time were nothing but to waste day, night and time!"

The Order of Creation

This first rough dividing of time into past, present, and future, without any subdivisions (as shown by my young friend Tony) is a very significant phenomenon. It illustrates, in fact, an interesting law with regard to the way in which the mind creates itself. When Michelangelo set out to create a statue he would first of all roughhew the block of marble into the general form of the figure to be. So was it also with the Master Mind in the beginning of the world, as we find it in the account of the creation in Genesis. First, there was primordial chaos "without form and void." Then the Spirit moved upon the face of the waters, and there came the first great subdivision—light and darkness. Then came another great division, "the waters under the firmament from the waters above the firmament." Next land was separated from sea. *It was only afterwards, and on the basis of these first great divisions, that God proceeded to the creation of the finer details—plants, animals, and finally man.*

In the creation of the mind by itself this same phenomenon is repeated—the microcosm reflects in its creation the method of the macrocosm. We see how the child's mind *first creates the general divisions* and then goes on later to create the details.

Take colours, for instance. Long before the child is able to identify and name each colour, his mind has already—working quite spontaneously—created a general category for colour. And similarly, though he may not be able to count properly, and has as yet no clear idea of what the names stand for, already he had created a "number department" in his mind. Thus for example you may ask a child what colour a particular object is and he may answer "blue" instead of "red" *but he will not answer "six."* You may ask another how many cherry stones there are on his plate and he may say six instead of four, *but he will not say "pink" or "yesterday."* This may appear a trivial matter but it is really very significant. For it means that the mind has already been at work making broad, general divisions; and it is on the basis of these that the finer work of creation can and will proceed later on. This is a matter of practical importance to us as teachers, for (as we shall see in Chapter VIII) it indicates the path we must follow in assisting the child's intellect at its mysterious task of self-creation. In this connection I might relate an illuminating anecdote about my same young friend Tony. He had learned by himself to count (verbally) as follows—always in the same order— 1, 2, 3, 4, 5, 6, **9, 14.** I often used to ask him to go on after 14, but he always stopped there and began *da capo.* One

day I pressed him to tell me what came after 14; in fact I kept
on urging him to do so quite unwarrantably, even to the point
of annoying him. At last in a vexed tone, as if he were being
forced to do violence to his nature (and clearly in order to
get rid of me) he suddenly blurted out "1, 2, 3, 4, 5, 6, **9, 14—**
Thursday, Friday and Saturday!" and walked off in a huff.

The Mystery of Language

Time, space, causality, the properties and reactions of
the "four elements," the existence of the self and not-self—
are, as we have seen, some of the great problems which con-
front the tiny child in his strange voyage from nothingness
to something. One would think that they would be enough to
exhaust his mental activity. Not a bit of it! As if these were
not sufficient he has to grapple, during the same period, with
the enormous problem of language.

Think what that means. We know from experience what
a business it is learning a foreign language, even if we live
in a foreign country. The child not only has to learn a new
language, *but he has to learn at the same time what language
is, its very nature, possibilities, and purposes.* For instance,
he not only has to learn the names of things, but that things
have names. There must have been a certain period in his
life when this astonishing fact revealed itself—that everything
has a name.

When *we* learn a foreign language we have therefore one
great advantage over the child. Before he can properly learn
a word he has to go through a corresponding experience of
reality. Thus, for example, before he can know what "up" or
"down" means he must first have the experience of "upness"
and "downness" himself. And not only that, but he must be
lucky enough to hear someone as it were label this experience
at the right moment by sticking the appropriate word on it.
It is rather as though (if I were learning French) in order to
know what "falling in love" was in that language, I should
have first to fall in love myself, and then be lucky enough to
hear someone name my experience in my hearing.

These are only a few of the difficulties connected with
language which the child has to surmount. Think how incessantly active his mind must have been—quite spontaneously—during all those months, in order for him to become as
proficient, in speaking and understanding, as he is when he
arrives at three or four years of age. Think of the infinite and
unbridgeable gulf between such a mind and that of the most
educated chimpanzee. Nor must we forget the actual mus-

cular triumphs involved in learning to pronounce so accurately. It is just here that the child, with his "sensitive period" for language, beats us adults out of hand (or rather "out of mouth"!).

The Mental Horizon of the Three-Year-Old

That the child, after measuring himself successfully against these colossal tasks, comes out of the experience fresh and smiling, and ready for more, is, could we read it aright, the clearest and most incontrovertible proof of the tremendous spontaneous power of the human intellect. In its way it is just as wonderful—even more wonderful—than what Dr. Ballard calls the miracle of Montessori, as quoted above. The success of the child's mental efforts during these first three years in building up an orderly world system is as undeniable as it is worthy of admiration. His intelligence *has* succeeded, quite by itself, in fitting together an immense number of the disconnected pieces of that higgledy-piggledy jigsaw puzzle in which he found himself—willy-nilly—immersed at birth.

His mental horizon is still very limited, it is true, but within those limits his mind is stable and orderly; and his relations to it crystallized into a tolerably successful daily adjustment.

We may compare this young three-year-old to an explorer who has mapped out great tracts of an unknown country—although still greater regions of undiscovered land await him. His world may be compared to one of those quaint maps drawn up by medieval geographers. In the centre one sees an area in which the outlines of the countries are fairly clearly marked out and the details and nomenclature fairly accurate. Around this central area there extends a zone of countries and oceans whose boundaries are vague and indeterminate. Beyond this again is a vast illimitable ocean—the rest of the world—in which fabulous monsters can be seen sporting by the shores of frankly mythological islands. For as Montessori puts it, "the child of three still carries within him a heavy chaos."

The Young Explorer

The astonishing thing is that in spite of the immense work achieved in so short a time the child's mind shows not the least sign of being overcome by such Herculean labours. True, he falls to sleep suddenly at the end of the day; and no wonder; but next day finds our young explorer up and out with the dawn and ready for more adventures. He assaults the most mountainous obstacles with buoyant determination, greeting all experience with the joyful and undaunted spirit of an explorer.

Indeed we may say that, from the very nature of the human intellect, every child is a born explorer. From the first moment he opens his eyes they are wide with wonder. G. K. Chesterton says somewhere: "When we are very young we do not need fairy tales: we need only tales. A child of seven is excited by being told that Tommy opened the door and saw a dragon. But a child of three is excited by being told that Tommy opened the door. Boys like romantic tales but babies like realistic tales —because they find them romantic." It is only by an effort that we can recapture something of the spirit of wonder and adventure with which every small child encounters life. "Even nursery tales," goes on G. K. Chesterton, "only echo an almost prenatal leap of interest and amazement. These tales say that apples were golden only to refresh the forgotten moment when we found they were green. They make rivers run with wine only to make us remember, for one wild moment, that they run with water."

Watch carefully the spontaneous activities of any small child of two or three years of age, and you will see what we mean. You will be impressed how much of his time is spent in exploring, experimenting, dissecting, examining. His little hands are nearly always clasped round some precious treasure which he has picked up—the latest object of his unremitting research. Everything in the environment is of interest to him—even the smallest and most insignificant objects—things one would imagine too small to catch his attention. A piece of wood that floats on the water, water itself (surely one of God's masterpieces), a pebble, a shell, an empty tin, or a tin with a stone in it; a piece of coal (can't you hear the nursemaid shouting "Put that down at once: dirty!"—smack!), a bit of coloured paper,[5] or a flower; or a beetle ("Alexander"),[6] a bit of string or leather, a nut or a nutshell—in fact anything and everything.

Whatever he can grasp in his tiny hands he tries to grasp with his mind! It all comes as grist to the mill.

The Philosopher in the Pram

It is not only the toddler who is an explorer. The child is a philosopher before he can talk, an explorer before he can walk. Look at that baby left in its pram outside a shop and you will see that it, too, is busy doing a bit of research on its own—unless it is so firmly pinioned down by its straps that it

[5] Cf. anecdote, Chapter I, p. 26.
[6] *When We Were Very Young,* by A. A. Milne.

cannot even move—in which case it gives up the struggle and goes to sleep, making the best of it, like Kent in the stocks. You will see those tiny fingers, tentacles of the opening mind, seizing whatever they can. Perhaps it is a leather strap, or its mother's handbag, or maybe a bit of paper, or the edge of the pram coverlet, in fact anything within reach. The baby will seize it, examine it, turn it about, taste it, pull it to pieces if possible; and always with that same intent expression on its tiny face.

In some such way it profits by every passing moment of its waking life. Every second of its time is precious to the baby, and no wonder. How else could it hope to accomplish those marvels of mental construction in so short of time. The mothers may stand and dawdle, wasting the precious morning hours in idle gossip, but the babies never. Nature sees to that, she hates to see them idle; never lets them lose a moment, but whispers in their tiny ears, "Do something, my child, do something! Here, take this scrap of paper, look at it, feel it, crumple it, hear it crackle, see it change its shape!," or "Take that bit of stick, and hit it rhythmically against the side of the pram, and you will hear a corresponding rhythm of sound—fascinating, isn't it? Do it again! Now hit the woollen coverlet and you will find it makes no noise. Very odd! Do it again to make sure! Now hit one and then the other and notice the difference —again, again, and yet again. No my dear, it is no accident; whatever the reason there is a real difference!" Or again, "Take up that little box your mummy left and have a good look at it, string and all. Now put it under the coverlet. Gone! out of sight, out of mind! Lift up the coverlet again. Golly, it's still there! was there, in fact, all the time, though invisible! Who would have thought that, now?" Or to another child, "If you've nothing else to get hold of, my child, then get hold of your own foot, nose, finger, hair. Even that will teach you something—teach you a lot; teach you in fact the first steps towards the understanding of a great mystery, that 'I am I'—which is the queerest thing of all." Or again—"Look, my young philosopher, here now is a great chance! Someone has moved another pram alongside o' yours. Whatever is that quaint looking creature in it, bobbing up and down in his straps, fit to break them, all excitement and all eyes and hands directed towards you? Why is he so excited? Because he's seen you! You're as big a wonder to him as he to you. Up then and doing (as far as those plaguey straps will permit), lean over and have a crack with him; examine him, touch him, stroke him." "Wonder of wonders, he's smiling at me! No one shall say I'm not a good mixer—I'll smile back. Heavens, do I look like that! all head and hardly any feet!"

What experiences could they relate, these young explorers, if only they had language! How little do their mothers realize the intense drama that is going on in their lives, compared with which their own bargains and gossip are as water to champagne.

Helping the Philosopher in the Pram

Most grown-ups—including the child's parents—are unaware of this immense work of exploration, and the continuous self-creation which goes with it; for it takes place silently, like all the great creative processes of nature. But all the time exploration and inner growth go on together; they are in fact different aspects of a single process. Every child at this stage, if he could speak, could truly say, like that other great explorer, Ulysses—"I am become a part of all that I have seen."

"God's Spies"

The young explorer is never idle, because he is looking in the world to find *himself*—reflected in a mirror with a thousand facets. That is why everything attracts him. Whilst he is examining the objects in the world around him, he is—as it were—stealing from them their qualities—their shapes, surfaces, textures, their colours, weight, sizes, uses, composition, and so forth.[7] These he mysteriously builds into himself (like a spiritual caddisworm) and with them constructs his mental being.

Thus—touching, handling, moving, comparing, contrasting, arranging, rearranging, opening and shutting, breaking asunder and putting together—the work goes on. These miniature scientists are forever prying into everything, "taking upon themselves the mystery of things, as if they were God's spies."[8] To them every passage is a secret passage, every carpet a magic carpet, every animal a fabulous monster, every walk a South Sea voyage of discovery.

We miss the whole significance and drama of the child's existence if we forget this—forget that for him each morning is as fresh and as wonderful as that first morning in which the stars shouted for joy at the creation of the world. Every time we see a small child standing at the prow of his pram, sailing along

[7] See Chapter IX.
[8] *King Lear*.

the pavement, gazing at the world before him, we see a new Columbus setting forth to discover a new world. It is he, this child of Man, this joyous explorer—and not any sceptical twentieth-century philosopher—who has the right to quote Miranda's beautiful words, *"O brave new world that has such people in it!"*

Every child should be called Miranda, for its eyes are bright with wonder. "Admired Miranda" they should be called, for our own wonder at the child's wonder should keep alive in us this precious quality, without which spiritual life atrophies. As a modern writer says, "To admire something is like a stream of fresh water, flowing over the soul's surface. Children are so happy, because for them, there is so much to wonder at. The deep solemnity of their untarnished eyes is the solemnity of wonderment. Woe to the man who has nothing to wonder at!" [9]

Sail on, thou tiny explorer, "whose exterior semblance doth belie thy soul's immensity." Sail on in your wonderful barque with its five senses—and its intrepid captain—the intellect. The whole world lies before you; "your business everything"; and all that can be known is on "the list of your voyage." [10] From the bottom of our hearts we adults of a different world wish you Godspeed—for you carry—literally you carry—in your frail barque, the hopes of humanity and the destinies of the human race.

CHAPTER VI   STAGES OF DEVELOPMENT OR GROWTH AND METAMORPHOSIS

The Master Principle

In giving an account of the Montessori system it is difficult to know where to begin, because it is hard to single out one principle as more important than the others. In an organism all organs are essential, for each plays a necessary part in the whole. And so it is in the Montessori system, and for much the same reason; because it is a *living* system. It displays that multiplicity in unity which is characteristic of all organisms. What would be the value, for instance, of the "prepared environment" without the "directress" as the link between it and the children? Of what avail the principle of

[9] *The Personality of Christ,* by Vonier.
[10] *Twelfth Night.*

nonintervention of the teacher without at the same time giving the children liberty? Or again how would it be possible to give this liberty without the prepared environment? and so on.

There is, however, one principle which—according to Montessori herself—may be regarded as more fundamental than any other; probably because, in a sense, it includes all the rest. It is this: that *we must constantly bear in mind the fundamental difference between the child and the adult.*

But what is the fundamental—the essential difference? Is it that the child is small and the adult large? Or that he is weak whereas the adult is strong? Or is it that the children are ignorant whilst we are rich in experience? Or is it, perhaps, that children live largely in a world of concrete things, and we in a world of ideas? Or shall we say that it lies in the fact that the child is all activity—"perpetual motion"—whereas we adults, by comparison, are sedate (which means seated)? Not in these, nor in many other points one could mention, does Montessori find the fundamental difference, but in this, that *"the child is in a continual state of growth and metamorphosis, whereas the adult has reached the norm of the species."*

Metamorphosis

Here, as so often, we find Montessori speaking in biological terms. The *fact* of metamorphosis, if not the name, is familiar to all. Everyone is at least superficially acquainted with the changes which take place in the life history of the frog and the butterfly. The latter, as we know, hatches from the egg into a minute grub which immediately begins to grow. The important thing (from the point of view of our discussion) is that, as it grows, it retains for a long period the same form (i.e., a caterpillar); and with it a whole group of characteristics which remain constant for a definite epoch. Its colour, form, means of locomotion, diet, manner of eating and so forth remain unchanged during a period in which it continues to grow steadily and uniformly.

But only for a time. Then, quite unexpectedly, and without any external cause—when the destined moment arrives—it begins to undergo a profound change. It ceases its voracious feeding, and begins to do something which it has never shown any sign of doing before; it spins for itself a sort of silken hammock, or cocoon. This done it sinks into a profound slumber, during which it undergoes a series of changes which seem to go almost to the root of its being. On this plane it remains for another epoch of its life, during which growth proceeds but on entirely different lines. Old organs disappear and new ones take

their place (e.g., wings). Then comes a period of transition—
brief, critical, and dangerous—and out comes the butterfly.
It has at last attained "the norm of the species," the adult.

Now, says Montessori, the important thing for us to realize,
as educators, is that in a similar (though less strikingly visible
manner) the child in his development passes through different
epochs of more or less uniform growth, which alternate with
periods of transition or metamorphosis. These latter are real
"transformations," "since nor th' exterior nor the inward man
resembles what it was."[1] They relate to the physical, mental,
and social aspects of development.

Bodily Metamorphosis

Though we are primarily concerned in this book with
the stages of *mental* development through which the child
passes, we must not forget that he undergoes a bodily metamorphosis also. Quite literally so; since the proportions of the
body of a newly born child are completely different from those
of an adult. In one of her training courses (in Barcelona) Dr.
Montessori had a model made of a newly born infant which
was as large as an adult. When placed on the platform side
by side with an adult it appeared a very monster of deformity.
The creature's head was so huge that its chin came right down
to the breast of the adult; and other parts of the body looked
equally disproportionate.

This physical transformation through which the child passes
before he reaches adult proportions, throws a light on certain
characteristics of children; as for example their imperfect
equilibrium long after they have learnt to walk. (This is because their heads are too big and their feet too small.) Who
has not noticed the delight with which children will walk along
a line, or a plank, or a wall, like miniature tightrope walkers?
It was, I believe, Dr. Montessori who first realized the significance of this; and here, as always, seconded the child's
natural tendencies. Thus there came into being those "Exercises of Balance and Rhythm" which form a regular feature of
every Casa dei Bambini. In connection with this bodily metamorphosis we may mention here, *en passant,* the value of those
"Exercises in Practical Life" which are dealt with more fully
in a later chapter (XIII).

[1] *Hamlet.*

Mental Metamorphosis and Stages of Development

Of equal, or even greater, importance to parent and teacher is a knowledge of the various stages which occur in the child's *mental* development. For convenience' sake we shall discuss them separately, though in actual life, of course, they are intimately bound up with the corresponding physical changes which are taking place at the same time.

We must, then, constantly bear in mind this fact that the growth of the child, from birth to maturity, is not like that of an oak tree which grows by simply getting bigger, but is rather to be compared with that of the butterfly; for *we have to do with different types of mind at different periods.*

These periods indeed differ so greatly one from another that some psychologists, including Montessori, have compared the development of the human being to a succession of new births. This is of course an exaggeration; but nevertheless it does almost *seem* as though, at some periods of life, "one psychic individual ceases and another is born."

First Stage: 0-6 *years*
A Period of Transformation—divided into:
(*a*) 0-3 years: The Absorbent Mind (unconscious)
(*b*) 3-6 years: The Absorbent Mind (conscious)
Second Stage: 6-12 *years*
A Period of Uniform Growth, an intermediate period—or—the second stage of childhood.
Third Stage: 12-18 *years*
A Period of Transformation—subdivided, as in stage one, into:
(*a*) 12-15 years: Puberty
(*b*) 15-18 years: Adolescence

After about eighteen years of age there is no longer any transformation. The individual simply becomes older.

First Epoch of Development (0–6 Years)

The Absorbent Mind. This first period, taken as a whole, makes a complete life in itself. There are in it, as we shall see, definite changes forming subdivisions; but the whole period is characterized by the same type of mind. It is a form of mind which is quite different from that of the adult, which Montessori describes as The Absorbent Mind. The nature and workings of the absorbent mind are full of mystery, and the further we go back to the beginnings of life the more mysterious do they become.

We cannot hope in our limited space to give a full and complete account of Montessori's doctrine of the absorbent mind, but it would be unfair to Dr. Montessori not to attempt to give a brief description of it—hoping that any readers who feel unsatisfied will turn to Dr. Montessori's own book on the subject.[2] So—continuing our description of the characteristics of the first stage of childhood (0–6 years)—we come to:

Subdivision A: 0–3 *years. The Unconscious Mind.* In this first subdivision, 0–3 years, we have to do with a mind that is constantly absorbing impressions from the environment; and yet does this without knowing that it is doing so, and without willing it. When you come to think of it, how could the mind of a child in the first year be conscious of what it is doing, or what it is learning, since he has not yet achieved self-consciousness? That is why Montessori says that, at this stage—strange though it may sound—we are dealing with an *unconscious mind.* The researches of modern psychologists have familiarized us with the idea that self-consciousness— speaking biologically—is a later development. "Experience shows us," says Jung, "that the sense of 'I'—*the ego,* consciousness—grows out of unconscious life. The small child has psychic life without any demonstrable ego-consciousness; for which reason the earliest years leave hardly any traces in memory." [3]

It may seem illogical to suppose that there can be a *sub*-conscious activity before there exists a conscious one: for that reason we prefer to use the term *un*conscious mind.

It is in this First Stage of Childhood (0–6 years)—especially the first part of it (0–3 years)—that intelligence, the great instrument of man, is being formed. And not only the intelligence, but other psychic faculties also are being constructed. "It is therefore a period of creation; because, before, nothing existed; since the individuality starts from zero. Here we are confronted then not only with something which is developing, but with a creation that starts from nothing (except of course a potentiality). To accomplish this miracle, the newly born infant *must* possess a different type of mind from ours, endowed with different powers."

To continue (in Montessori's own words): "This is not done with the conscious mind. We adults are conscious that we have a will; and when we want to learn something we deliberately

[2]*The Absorbent Mind.*
[3]Jung, *Modern Man in Search of a Soul,* p. 212.

set about it. But there is no consciousness in the small child, no will: both have yet to be created. That is why I say that if we call *our* type of mind a conscious type, then we must describe that of the child as an unconscious one.

"Now an unconscious mind does not mean an inferior mind. You will find this type of intelligence everywhere at work in nature. Every insect has it, for instance; but theirs is not a conscious intelligence; even though sometimes it appears to be so."

Montessori goes so far as to assert that, in those first months of the child's life *before he is able to move*, he takes in *the whole of his environment* by means of the absorbent power of the unconscious mind. The child seems to take in these things *"not with his mind but with his life."*

As an example of the workings of this unconscious mind Montessori points to the way in which the child absorbs its mother tongue, simply by living in the environment where it is spoken. During one of her lectures—given at a course in Ahmedabad, India, in 1947—a simile suddenly occurred to her as she was lecturing, which with characteristic genius she developed—extemporally—as she went along.

"There has just come to my mind," she said, "a sort of simile to explain the contrast between this taking in of language by the small child, and the effort required, by the adult, in learning a new language. If for instance we wish to *draw* something we take pencil or colours and draw it; but we could also use a camera and take a photograph of it. Then, however, the mechanism would be different. If we had to draw one man it would take some time; but if we had to draw ten men it would take a much longer time still, and demand a correspondingly greater effort. Whereas if we were to take a photo of a group of ten men the film would have no more work to do than if it were only of one; for the mechanism works instantaneously. In fact it would be just as easy for the film to take in a thousand people, if the machine were large enough.

"It is similar with the absorbent mind. It works rapidly, taking in everything without effort and without will." Enlarging on this comparison (as she went along) Montessori then pointed out how a photograph is taken in darkness; and—still in darkness—undergoes a process of development. Then, still in darkness, it is fixed. Finally it is brought up to the light, where it remains fixed and unalterable. So too with the absorbent mind; it begins deep down in the darkness of the subconscious; it is developed and "fixed" there; and finally emerges into consciousness, where it remains a fixed and permanent possession.

From the Unconscious to the Conscious

In the first year of its life, then, a child takes in the whole of his environment unconsciously. In this way he accumulates the materials from which he will later build up his conscious life. It is an immense operation, the every existence of which was, until quite recently, almost unknown. Even now the majority of people still think of the baby during the first six months of his life as being almost without mental activity; more like "a little animal," concerned only with eating, drinking, and sleeping, etc. Instead, Montessori presents us with this surprising picture of an infant who acquires "the whole world" unconsciously; and then passes gradually from the unconscious to the conscious.

How is this passage from the unconscious to the conscious accomplished? *"It is through movement which follows the path of pleasure and love."* "When the child begins to move, his absorbent mind has already taken in the world unconsciously. Now, as he starts to move, he becomes conscious. If you watch a small child of two, or even one, he is always manipulating something. This means that—while he is manipulating with his hands—he is bringing into consciousness what his subconscious mind had already taken in before. It is through this experience of objects in his environment, in the guise of playing, that he goes over again the impressions that he has already taken in with his unconscious mind. It is by means of this "work"—for it is as much work as play—that he becomes conscious, and constructs himself. He develops himself by means of his hands, using them as the instruments of human intelligence."

We Cannot Help Directly

When we understand the powers which belong to such an unconscious mind—a mind, that is, which must achieve consciousness through work and experience carried out with objects in its environment—it makes us realize that *we cannot reach it to teach it directly*. We cannot intervene in this mysterious process of passing from the unconscious to the conscious, i.e., of constructing the human faculties. It is a process which goes on independently of us, and we can only help by providing the best conditions.

Speaking generally with regard to this first period of child-hood (0–6 years) we can say that (*a*) in the first three years there is a creation of faculties; and (*b*) during the *next* three years there is a further development of the faculties so created. The second subperiod—from three to six years of age—is also a period of construction, but it is a conscious one, for the child now takes in *consciously* from the environment. He has forgotten the events and experiences of the preceding epoch (0–3 years); but, using the faculties he created then, he can now will, think, and remember. For memory itself is one of the faculties which has been created. Therefore, *now*, when the things he had acquired unconsciously in the first stage are brought to the surface (through the work of his hands) they are remembered; for memory is now there to receive them.

So too is it with the will. If in the first period (0–3) the child was a sort of "contemplative," observing the environment and taking in from it without effort what he needed for his growth, *now*, in the second period (3–6), he still continues this process of self-construction, but in so doing he is using his own will. For that, too, has come into being. Before, it was as if a force outside him moved him; now, it is the child's own ego which guides and directs.

Takes in Through His Hands

To sum up then. In this second subperiod (3–6 years) the child still retains that sort of embryonic power of absorbing without fatigue which Montessori calls the absorbent mind. But there is this important difference. Whereas in the first stage the child absorbed the world through his unconscious intelligence, merely by being moved about in it, now he takes in consciously, using his hands. The hand has now become the instrument of the brain; and it is through the activity of his hands that he enriches his experience, and develops himself at the same time.

We shall return to the significance of this twofold creative activity of hand and brain in a subsequent chapter.[4]

The Construction of Individuality

Of the first stage of development *taken as a whole* (i.e., from 0–6 years) we can say that it is primarily concerned with the construction of the human individual. The child is not yet

[4] The Significance of Movement, Section III, Chapter XIV.

a *social* being in the full sense of the word; the individual's energies being still largely directed to the acquisition and perfection of new functions.

In our dealings with the child at this stage we are confronted with a simple but important fact. It is not direct help the child needs: indeed, to attempt to do this would impede his growth. What he needs most of all is the possibility of acting freely on his own initiative without intervention of the adult. To obtain this result most satisfactorily we have found it best to place the child in a specially prepared environment (Chapter XVI) in which he can choose his own actions and make his own social contacts. Set free to live his own independent life in this prepared environment he not only learns to do things by himself and acquire new moral and social aptitudes, but also makes swift and surprising progress in the elements of culture. Because he still possesses "the absorbent mind" (though now working, with his hands) he learns writing, reading, fundamental ideas of number, and many other things besides, *spontaneously and without fatigue.*

In this first epoch if the child is given the opportunity to construct his individuality through independent "work" [5] we see the emergence of a higher type of normality, a process which has often been described by observers as the "revelation of the new child." [6]

The Second Epoch of Development (6–12 Years)

Compared with the epoch preceding it, and that which follows it, the second stage of development (6–12) is one of great stability. By this we mean that growth continues for a long period along the same lines, preserving the same type of mind, the same group of psychological characteristics. In other words it is a period of growth *without much transformation,* whereas the other two periods are more aptly described as growth *with* transformation.

The epoch we are now considering (6–12) is one of great strength and robustness of body and mind; a fact indicated by a distinct falling off in the incidence of sickness and mortality. It is a period of comparative calmness and serenity. During these years children are capable of accomplishing a great deal of mental work. It is their "years of plenty"; and, if given the right opportunity and the right means, they will lay up a great store of cultural information.

[5] Cf. Chapter VIII.
[6] Chapter X.

Transition from First to Second Stage of Childhood

The transition from the first to the second stage of childhood is marked by certain physical and mental changes. The rounded contours of childhood disappear, and the boy becomes thinner and more bony. His milk teeth begin to fall out, and he begins growing his second set. In character he becomes stronger and more self-conscious, a fact which shows itself in a tendency to boast. ("I can throw a stone further than you!") In fact his mother wakes up one day to find that her "child" has disappeared, and a regular "tough guy" has taken his place.

The Herd Instinct

Socially, this period is characterized by a marked development of the herd instinct. As through drawn together by some irresistible power boys at this stage seek one another's company and form themselves into "gangs" of all kinds. In fact they possess at this stage characteristics so clear and definite that they seem almost like a race apart. They are so sure of themselves, so precise in their interests, so happy in one another's company, so busy with their own affairs, so unconcerned as to the fate of the rest of mankind, that they might almost be denizens from another planet. Of all their characteristics the herd instinct is one of the most dominant. Whatever they do at this stage they tend to do it in groups. A friend of mine suggests that this collective activity is the means by which they are able, unconsciously, to wean themselves from maternal domination. Be this as it may, this group instinct is there, and it is of prime importance that we should recognize it and make use of it. In what ways Montessori would have us harness the herd instinct to help on the boy's (or the girl's) social and moral development we must leave to a later chapter (Chapter XXI).

Development of the Reasoning Faculty

Mentally, this second stage of childhood (6–12) is marked by a great strengthening of the reasoning faculty; which shows itself in many ways. On the moral plane it shows itself in a marked tendency to examine the rightness and wrongness of actions. Only the other day a lady said to me, "My little girl (aged ten) keeps on repeating the same question, day after day: 'Is it fair, Mummy? Is it fair?' She will, for instance, make some such remark as this: 'A lot of the girls in my class weren't allowed to go bathing today, because yesterday they went out without permission.' Then follows the inevitable 'Is it fair, Mummy?' " This indicates a quickening of the conscience. An awareness of this characteristic on our part can help us in dealing with children at this stage.

We need not follow Montessori into a more detailed description of the special features of this "gangster age," for they can be found in other psychological textbooks. Where Montessori shows her originality is in the suggestions she puts forward as to how we can best respond to these new developments.

Different Stages—Different Principles

Because the child is almost a different being at different stages of life we cannot have just one set of education principles for every period. We cannot expect that those methods which were used with success in the first stage—i.e., the age which most people would think of in connection with the name Montessori school—could be applied, without modification, in the next.

The Montessori method for the junior stage of education differs from that used in the Montessori Kindergarten just as much as the mental and social characteristics of the second stage of childhood differ from those of the first. (Again see Chapter XXI.)

Third Epoch: Adolescence (12–18 Years)

It does not really come within the scope of this volume to discuss secondary education and its problems; but it will not be out of place, just to round off this chapter on stages of development, to say a few words about the adolescent (12–18).

The first period of adolescence (12–15) resembles the first epoch in childhood (0–3) in that it is one of great transformation, both physical and mental. The advent of puberty marks the end of childhood, nature itself making it evident that a new stage of development has begun by the profound physical changes which take place.

It is a great mistake to think that because the child is getting older he must therefore be getting correspondingly stronger, both in mind and body. In fact to some extent it is just the reverse. "That period of life in which physical maturity is reached is a dangerous and difficult time because of its rapid development and the changes which take place in the organism as a consequence. In fact the organism becomes so delicate that doctors consider this epoch comparable, in respect of health, to that of birth and the rapid development immediately succeeding it. There often occurs at this period a special liability to certain weaknesses and diseases, sometimes called 'adolescent complaints'—predisposition to tuberculosis being one of them."

The word *neonato* (newly born) which Montessori applies to the individual who has entered the first stages of adolescence has a wider significance than just its application to the new physical characteristics just mentioned. With even more justice can it be applied when we take into account the new *psychological* characteristics of this fresh epoch. Amongst these Montessori mentions "doubts, hesitations, violent emotions, discouragement and an unexpected decrease in intellectual capacity." Other traits in the adolescent she mentions are "a state of expectation, the tendency towards creative work, and a need for the strengthening of self-confidence. This is sometimes accompanied by a tendency to indiscipline and revolt against authority, especially if the latter lacks sympathy and understanding.

"Whereas in the preceding epoch the individual tended to be an extrovert, the adolescent tends to look inward. It is one of those mysterious periods when something is being formed which does not yet exist; a "mystery of creation" which is taking place within him independently of his own will—the creation of the *socially conscious individual*."

Just here—according to Montessori—is the crux of the whole matter, the most essential feature of adolescence, and therefore the most important for all those who have to do with the training of adolescents. There is being born in him a new "sensitive period" which reveals itself in a *greatly increased sensitiveness to all facts and experiences which relate to his life as a social being*. For the first time he becomes clearly conscious of himself, not simply as an individual— i.e., a member of a herd or gang—but as a separate member of human society with all that it implies. He feels, for instance, the need of being treated with a new kind of dignity and respect. Similarly he becomes acutely sensitive to all forms of criticism; and is quick to imagine he is being ridiculed. He feels himself observed; and is anxious to cut an equal figure with those around him. He begins to be acutely conscious of differences in social status. Such matters as clothes, pocket money, personal appearance become of great importance to him—things which did not bother him so much in the earlier period.

Compared with the "tough guy" of the preceding period (8–12) he is like a crab which has just cast its old strong shell, while the new one is still soft and sensitive—a dangerous condition. "It is just because this is the time when the social man is being created—but has not yet reached his full development—that many defects in adjustment to social life take their origin. For example, a feeling of inferiority at this period may give rise to an 'inferiority complex'; and there may arise a repugnance to social life which may endure for years. Such defects in social adjustment may have dangerous consequences for the individual, resulting in timidity, anxiety, depression, as well as the inferiority complex just mentioned. Bad results may follow for society, too, in the form of incapacity for work, laziness, dependence on others, a cynical outlook, and even 'criminality.' Here—in the problem of social adjustment—lies the really vital problem of education for the adolescents, far more so than in the passing of examinations."

How would Dr. Montessori have us organize the life of the adolescent so as best to respond to his dominant need of right social adjustment? This cannot be fully treated here in this volume. We have no space to describe the Dottoressa's plans for youth settlements (*Erde-Kinder*) in country districts. It must suffice here to note that she would have the whole life of the adolescent revolve round this idea of society, its structure, and its obligation. In these "land settlements" for youths the life of the adolescent would be so arranged that, through his participation in a special form of social life (the new "prepared environment" which corresponds to this stage), he would be made ready for his participation in the great world of adult society. Through his studies, which would be related to practical activities, he would become acquainted with the structure of society—its very ligaments—which are production and exchange; because, says Montessori, "the basis of all civilization rests on the products of the earth."

As each previous stage of development was marked by the acquisition of new forms of independence, so should and would it be in this. The form of independence which it is most necessary for the adolescent to acquire, according to Montessori, is *economic independence*. Exactly what she means by this, and how all this is to be worked out in practice, cannot be gone into here. We can only lay down the general aim—that "the whole life of the adolescent should be organized in such a way that it will enable him, when the time comes, to make a triumphal entry into social life—not entering it debilitated, isolated, or humiliated, but with head high, sure of himself. Success in life depends on a self-confidence born of a true knowledge of one's own capacities; combined with many-sided powers of adaptation—in fact on what we have called 'valorization of personality.' "

"There are two faiths which uphold a man; faith in God and faith in himself. And these two faiths exist side by side: the first belongs to the inner life of man; the second to his life in society."

CHAPTER VII   "SENSITIVE PERIODS" IN DEVELOPMENT

A Law of Development

The definition of a school, according to Montessori, is a "prepared environment in which the child, set free from undue adult intervention, can live its life according to the laws of its development." In the foregoing chapters we have already dwelt on some of these laws of development. We shall now consider another—what Montessori calls the law of sensitive periods. No part of her teaching is more important and none more original.

Sensitive Periods in Biology

The phrase, "sensitive periods in development" was first used by a famous Dutch biologist, Hugo de Vries, in connection with his researches in the development of certain animals. Later it was applied by Montessori to human development. We might note again, in passing, that here, as so often, we find an underlying affinity between Montessori's system and biology. Indeed it is true to say that her whole system—in theory and practice—has a biological foundation.

It will be a help to the understanding of our subject if we first consider some examples of sensitive periods taken from the sphere of animal life; in particular from the life history of certain insects which pass through metamorphosis. There is a certain butterfly (Porthesia) which lays its eggs on the bark of a tree, in the forks where the branches come off from the central trunk. From these eggs emerge small and tender caterpillars.

Their mouth parts are so small and delicate that they can only manage to eat the youngest and most tender leaves. But such leaves are just the ones furthest removed from the baby caterpillars, being naturally at the very tips of the branches. Who is going to show them the way to these tender leaves? De Vries discovered that these newly hatched larvae have a special sensibility towards light, which causes them to move towards it with an irresistible impulse. Consequently, they make their way to the tips of the branches, where they regale themselves on the tender green shoots. After a while, however —when they have grown bigger and stronger—they lose this special sensibility to light, with the result that they now make their way indifferently to all parts of the tree. This is a good thing for them, as they are now sufficiently developed to avail themselves of the ample stores of fully grown leaves. These latter, though tougher in texture, are now no longer inedible, since by this time the caterpillars have developed stronger jaws.

It is interesting to observe that the *dis*appearance of this sensibility to light—when it has served its purpose—is as important, for the insect, as was its presence in the earliest period. For—as Montessori says—"conditions, extremely favourable to development at one stage, may become ineffective or even unfavourable at a later period."

Definition of a Sensitive Period

How then shall we define a sensitive period? We may say that during the development of certain organisms there come periods of special sensibility. These periods of sensibility are related to certain elements in the environment towards which the organism is directed with an irresistible impulse and a well-defined activity. These periods are transitory; and serve the purpose of helping the organism to acquire certain functions, or determined characteristics. This aim accomplished, the special sensibility dies away, often to be replaced by another and quite different one.

In all forms of growth the organism develops at the expense of certain elements in the environment; but the distinguishing feature of growth during a sensitive period is that an irresistible impulse urges the organism to select only certain elements in its environment, and for a definite and limited time, i.e., only for as long as the sensibility is present.

Sensitive Periods in Human Development

Her long experience with children convinced Montessori that similar phenomena are to be found in their development. "Children pass through definite periods in which they reveal psychic aptitudes and possibilities which afterwards disappear. That is why, at particular epochs of their life, they reveal an intense and extraordinary interest in certain objects and exercises, which one might look for in vain at a later age. During such a period the child is endowed with a special sensibility which urges him to focus his attention on certain aspects of his environment to the exclusion of others. Such attention is not the result of mere curiosity; it is more like a burning passion. A keen emotion first rises from the depths of the unconscious, and sets in motion a marvellous creative activity in contact with the outside world, thus building up consciousness."

When a sensitive period is at its height we may compare it to a searchlight—coming from within the mind—illuminating certain parts of the environment, leaving the rest in comparative obscurity. The effect of this luminous and selective ray of attention is such that, where before there was confusion and chaos, there now comes into being order and distinction.

A Flame Which Burns Without Consuming

The intense and prolonged activity aroused and sustained by a sensitive period does not cause fatigue; rather the reverse. After a spell of work done at the imperious bidding of this inner urge the child feels better, stronger, calmer. Why? Because by means of such "work" (see Chapter VIII) he has been creating himself. Hence Montessori compares a sensitive period to a flame which burns brightly but does not consume—like that flame which Moses beheld in the burning bush on the Arabian desert. "Such instincts," she says, "are not so much reactions to the environment as delicate inner sensibilities, *intrinsic to life*—just as pure thought is an entirely intrinsic quality of the mind. We might continue the comparison and look on them as 'divine thoughts' working in the inmost centres of living creatures, leading them subsequently to action on the outer world in realization of the divine plan." (*Secret of Childhood*, p. 252.)

The Sensitive Period for Language

In each sensitive period, then, the child is endowed with special powers which help it to construct its personality through the acquisition of some well-defined characteristic or function. These generalities will become clearer as we come to examine some examples. One of the earliest and at the same time the most wonderful of the sensitive periods in the child's development, is that which is concerned with the acquisition of spoken language. Any adult who has tried to learn a new language (even when he is living in the land where it is spoken) realizes how hard a task it is. Indeed one might say it is almost an impossible task; for, however great his efforts and however good his teachers, he is almost bound to reveal the fact that he is a foreigner. Contrast with this the capabilities of the baby. Without the help of reason, without lessons, and without conscious effort he learns to pronounce the language he hears around him with perfection. In common parlance we say that a child can "pick up" a language just by hearing it. This fact is so well known that many families engage foreign governesses in order that their children will grow up bilingual.

The inner significance of this well-known fact has been largely overlooked. The more one thinks about it the more wonderful does it become. What does it mean except that, for a period of its life, the child is endowed with a special sensibility towards a certain element (language) in its environment, which enables it to establish a new function— speech. Furthermore, this sensibility is transitory, and once gone never returns. It was Dr. Montessori who first saw this phenomenon as one of a series of such transient sensibilities, each with a constructive and developmental aim.

The sensitive period for language has already begun in the child long before it can speak or walk. At four months a baby may be seen intently watching the mouth of the speaker and making "vague soundless words." It is as though the muscles of his mouth and lips, hitherto used only for sucking and crying, now begin to vibrate in harmony with the spoken sounds he hears. At six months the baby will begin to make real sounds. Everyone must have heard a baby "practising" sounds—the elements of the words to come; and have noticed the joy with which it carries out these exercises that prepare and animate the organs of speech.

We observe too that it is not a parrotlike imitation of *all* the sounds which come to it from his environment. It is more particularly to the human sounds that the child seems so irresistibly drawn. It is language that exercises the potent spell. "When the child is born the sounds in its environment form a confusion, a jumble, a chaos. Then suddenly this mysterious urge begins in its soul, this inner flame of interest is lit up, and is turned outward as a light upon this dark exterior confusion. Under its influence sounds separate themselves, though as yet language is not understood. Nonetheless these sounds have become distinct, fascinating, alluring." The child's mind now listens voluntarily to the spoken language; which becomes as "a kind of music that fills the soul." Witness the rapturous smile with which the baby listens to words slowly and clearly pronounced.

So first we have the psychic factor, as in all sensitive periods; and then the corresponding activity, as the fibres of the vocal muscles begin to vibrate in harmony to a new order and a new rhythm. "The sensitive period is at work like divine command; the child imitates and does not know why; the words penetrate as if drawn by a secret magnetism. They put themselves in order. All seems so clear and simple, and all happens in such a way that the mind does not work at all; for it is not a question of reason or judgment or conscious effort. It seems like a reaction between this creature, who must conquer his instrument for the expression of his intellect, and this language, which is in his environment" *(Secret of Childhood).*

Of all the processes of "animating the flesh" [1] this is the hardest and most intricate; and therefore the sensitive period for language is one that lasts longer than any other. Anyone who has tried to teach the deaf and dumb how to speak has realized how numerous and varied are the muscles employed in speech; how complicated their movements; and how painful are the efforts required to learn them when nature's normal means of development are lacking. We adults get some idea of it when we try to learn a new language. "Which of us could command our muscular fibres to vibrate, now, in such an exact way?" Yet, on the full tide of this sensitive period, the child beats us out of hand (or perhaps we ought to say "out of mouth!") accomplishing his difficult task eagerly, joyously, triumphantly—*simply by living.*

It is interesting to reflect, in passing, that this sensitive period for the acquisition of language has a national as well as an individual significance. It is by means of it that the children of any country preserve intact the continuity of their nation's language. Let us put it this way: suppose it were possible to remove all English babies as soon as they were born, and transplant them—say to France—and allow them to return only when the sensitive period for language had passed, what havoc it would work with our language! Thus, as Montessori says, "The adult is capable of defending his country and guarding its frontier, but it is the child who maintains its spiritual unity through its language."

[1] See Chapter XII.

Sensitive Period for Order

One of the most interesting "sensitive periods," through which the child passes, is that which Dr. Montessori describes as the sensitive period for order. The Dottoressa was, I believe, the first to have drawn attention to this fascinating and rather mysterious phenomenon. But like the continent of America —once discovered—it can be easily verified by anyone in daily contact with very young children.

This sensitive period for order begins to reveal itself as the child reaches his second year; and lasts for about two years, being most marked in the child's third year. During all this period the child displays an almost passionate interest in the order of things both in time and space. It seems to him, at this stage, a particularly vital matter that everything in his environment should be kept in its accustomed place; and that the actions of the day should be carried out in their accustomed routine. In fact he becomes a positive ritualist in such matters, appearing almost tyrannous in his demands. Let an armchair, or any other piece of furniture, be removed from its usual position; or the corner of a rug turned up; or let a member of the family sit at his "wrong" place at the table; or let a cupboard door be left opened, or some object be put away in a new place; or an umbrella carelessly left on the table; or let the child be given a small spoon instead of the usual larger one for his sweet course: let any of these or a hundred other such deviations be made from the *status quo* and you will find, in the vast majority of cases, it is the small child of two and a half years, or thereabouts, who will immediately become aware of these irregularities, and be upset by them; and not the older children of nine or ten.

It frequently happens that small children are driven almost frantic by such small infringements of the established order of things; and register their protests in despairing cries and so-called tantrums. In a great number of cases the adult in charge has not the faintest idea what the child is crying about; and if she has, as like as not regards it as "a much ado about nothing"—a meaningless caprice which should be sternly overridden. In her book *The Secret of Childhood* Montessori gives a number of illuminating examples of the way in which children protest, in their own particular manner, against such things. Here is one:

I found myself one day with a group of people going through Nero's grotto at Naples. With us was a young mother with a child—about one and a half years old—too small to be able to walk the whole length of the way. In fact after a time the child grew tired and his mother picked him up, but she had overestimated her strength. She was hot and stopped to take off her coat to carry it on her arm, and with this impediment once more picked up the child, who began to cry, his screams growing louder and louder.

His mother strove in vain to quiet him, she was plainly tired out and began to grow cross. Indeed the noise was getting on the nerves of all, and naturally others offered to carry him. He passed from arm to arm, struggling and screaming, and everyone talked to him and scolded, but he only grew worse.

I thought of the enigma of infancy, of how reactions must always have a cause: and going up to the mother I said, "Will you allow me to help put on your coat?" She looked at me in amazement, for she was still hot; but in her confusion she consented and allowed me to help her on with it.

At once the baby quieted down, his tears and struggles stopped, and he said, "Mamma, coat on." It was as if he wanted to say, "Yes, Mamma, a coat is meant to be worn"; as though he thought, "At last you have understood me," and stretching out his arms to his mother he came back to her all smiles. The expedition ended in complete tranquillity. A coat is meant to be worn, and not to hang like a rag over one arm; and this disorder in his mother's person had affected the child as a jarring disturbance.

Even more interesting, perhaps, is the incident related on pages 66 and 67 in the same book.

Here is another story which was related to me by a Norland nurse who had been looking after a little girl about three years old. She had been away for a three-weeks holiday, and during her absence there had been a temporary nanny in her place. "Well, and how did you like your new nanny?" said the Norland nurse on her return. "She was very naughty," replied the little girl in all seriousness. "Why, what did she do?" "She barfed me at the wrong end of the barf!"

One could give endless examples; but one more must suffice. I was visiting a house once where there was a little girl just turned two. After tea Audrey—for that was her name—was allowed into the drawing room. Shortly after we had been introduced she came up to me carrying a large book with illustrations. Then she began turning over the pages intently as though she was anxious to show me a particular picture. She found it at last. It represented a man lying on the ground who had obviously fallen off his horse, which was standing patiently by, with bridle and empty saddle, waiting for his master to remount. As soon as she came to the picture, Audrey, after pointing out the man to me, at once began to belabour him with evident displeasure. The poor fellow looked pretty shaken up with his fall as it was, and struck me as more deserving of pity than castigation. At that moment her mother coming into the room, I enquired if she could enlighten me as to what crime this fallen knight had committed. "I can't make it out at all," she replied. "Audrey is extraordinarily interested in that picture, though I don't know why. She is always turning to it; and yet it seems to annoy her in some way."

Then suddenly remembering Dr. Montessori's teaching, a light dawned. Here was something in Audrey's little world out of its proper place. The man lying on the ground ought to have been *on* the horse (even the horse knew that!) and this disorder was worrying her deeply. So I took out a pencil and drew in a man sitting on the saddle of the waiting horse. He was not half so handsome as the other fellow, but he had this supreme merit in Audrey's eyes: *he was in his right place.* She surveyed my handiwork with great joy; and, after looking at it for a few moments, heaved a sigh of contentment. Some weeks later I met the mother again; and she informed me that Audrey had never again been worried by the picture. She also informed me that Audrey gets very upset if she sees a fashion advertisement for a lady's hat *without a face under it,* her motto evidently being the same at Hamlet's "Your bonnet to his right use; it is for the *head*."

The Psychological Significance of the Sensitive Period for Order

It would have been a valuable contribution to child psychology simply to have been the first to draw our attention to this mysterious trait in small children. But Montessori goes much further: she explains the cause of it. The adult's love of order in his environment (when it exists!) is of a different nature from that which possesses the soul of the small child; and springs from a different motive. *We* like to live in an orderly environment because it ministers to a sense of comfort in us, and aids our efficiency. "The housewife who says, ' I must have my house in order,' is by comparison only talking; but the small child *cannot live in disorder*. Order is for him a need of life; and if this order is upset it disturbs him to the point of illness. His protests, which seem like mere caprices, are really vital acts of defence."

It is necessary for the child to have this order and stability in his environment *because he is constructing himself out of the elements of the environment*. His mind is not a mere mirror reflecting the outside world. From the very beginning there is selection in the formation of his store of images. The principle of order is there from the start; and is the foundation of the work of collecting further images. But this principle of order within requires as a help—as a kind of support—a stability of order in things without.

This is the reason why the child, at this stage, so passionately desires to have an environment in which things keep their accustomed places and preserve their proper uses. The child, we must remember, starts from nothing; and at two years he has not travelled very far in comparison with us. We are rich in experience; he is poor, and therefore much more dependent on his environment. Our experience is already ordered, with pigeonholed memories and reasoned principles. Not so his. The order which he is able to find in the environment is almost his all; it is his foundation. Even we grown-ups, after having lived in this world for half a century, may at any moment run into some strange experience, which we find hard enough to fit into our established philosophy of life. How much more bewildering must life be for the small child, to whom, as we have seen, space, time, number, causation, and many of the commonest facts of our experience, are still unknown. He is striving incessantly to bring this bewildering universe, as he knows it, into some sort of order. No wonder it upsets him when that minimum of order which he *has* discovered becomes destroyed.

Suppose a surveyor is sent out to make a map of a new country, say in central Africa. How would he feel, if—after weeks of work—the mountain and the river which he had taken as a fixed basis for further research suddenly changed places? He would feel as though the construction he had been at such pains to create was tumbling back into chaos.

The Sensitive Period for Order and the Game of "Hide and Find"

This passion for order in small children is manifested in certain of their games. Many a grown-up has discovered, not without surprise, that you cannot play at hide-and-seek with *very* small children. The game always seems to go off the lines; and always in the same way. Tommy goes and hides, shall we say, behind the curtain. As you approach him he squeals with joy, making no effort to conceal his presence.

Then he will go and hide in the same place, time after time. "Now you hide," he will say, indicating the same hiding place. So you "hide" there in your turn. He knows quite well you are behind the curtain; and yet he will come and find you there with the greatest excitement. If you have other small children with you, they will all take turns "hiding" in the same place, one after the other. It seems to us adults an extremely futile sort of game, making such a fuss about finding a person in the place where you know he is. Yet actually, for these little people, that is the whole point of the game. It is not really for them a game of hide-and-seek; they do not want to have *any* real hiding. The whole zest of the business lies in *finding a person, or thing, in its right and accustomed place, even though he or it is out of sight.* If they come to "seek" you in the place tacitly agreed upon, and you are in another, they are obviously disappointed. It is just the same if you play with them a game like hunt-the-thimble. The important thing is not the hiding of the object but *seeing that it returns every time to its proper place* and the joy of finding it there. (See *Secret of Childhood*.)

How We Can Help the "Baby" Through the Sensitive Period for Order

From what has been said above about the child's need for order in his life, as a basis for the construction of his mind, it is clear that we can help small children—even before they can walk or talk—by trying to preserve as far as possible a stability in their environment; and in the general rhythm of their lives. As an example, Montessori shows how the nurse-maid who takes the child for its daily walk in the pram can really help it by taking the same route each day; and she should choose a route with well-defined landmarks. The child will soon learn to recognize these with great joy, especially if the nursemaid does not rush by those objects which particularly interest him.

When Sir Walter Raleigh was having his last cup of sack, on the morning of his execution, someone asked him how he was enjoying it, and he replied, "It is a good drink *if a man might tarry by it.*" So it is with these tiny mites. We are so apt to forget that the rhythm of their lives is much slower than ours: and therefore we should learn to put the brake on our adult tempo, so that the child "may tarry by" his experiences. In our haste we may easily cancel impressions that are being made on the soft wax of the child's soul, causing them to be washed out, like footprints in the incoming tide.

Sensitive Period for Order and the Montessori School

This sensitive period for order is a matter of great practical significance in the running of a Montessori school. Sometimes people say: "But how can you possibly give freedom to forty small children at once, allowing each to choose his occupation? What immense confusion and disorder it must lead to!" But in fact it does not. These tiny children, just because of this sensitive period for order, very quickly get a sort of mental photographic impression of the position of everything in the classroom; and furthermore they take an exquisite delight (especially the very small ones) in seeing that everything returns to its proper place. One of the reasons why children feel a sense of calm and repose (spiritually) in the Montessori school is just because it is an environment where everything *has* its proper place and must keep to it. If it were necessary for the teacher to impose this respect for order on all these thirty to forty little ones at once it would be impossible, especially as they are free to choose their own occupations.

Generally speaking, as the child passes into his third year, the sensitive period for order becomes calmer; and his reactions against disorder are not so violent and disturbing. It is then that it becomes of such value in education, "merging into an active, tranquil period of application in the school."

The Small Child's Interest in Small Objects

Somewhat allied to this sensitive period for order, and coming at the same time, is another characteristic revealed by small children, which begins in their second year. This, too, is not one that is generally known, even less so perhaps than the sensitive period for order. It is a curious but indubitable fact that children, at this age, are drawn by a peculiar fascination to tiny objects in their environment, objects so small that they are often missed by adults in their company. It is as though what interests them is "the invisible; or that which lies on the very edge of consciousness."

I noticed this sensibility for the first time in a little girl of fifteen months old. I heard her laugh out loud in the garden, in a way unusual in such small children. She had gone out there alone and was sitting on the paving stones of the terrace. Near her was a bed of magnificent geraniums, flowering under an almost tropical sun. But the child was not looking at them; her eyes were fixed on the ground, where there was nothing to be seen.

Here then was another of the enigmas of infancy. I crept up and looked where she was looking, but saw nothing. It was she who explained to me, in words that were hardly words, "There is something tiny moving down there." With this guidance, I was able to see a tiny, almost invisible insect, the colour of the stone, moving very quickly. What had struck the child was that such a tiny creature could exist, and could move, could run. *(Secret of Childhood.)*

We adults miss many such things in our environment because, the contents of our minds being immeasurably richer, we tend to project our own synthesis into what we see. The above trait in children so young may surprise some people, for it is commonly supposed that chldren under two are attracted only by rather violent stimuli such as flags, bells, gay colours, singing, bright lights, and so forth. Certainly it is true that they *are* attracted by these things; but Montessori maintains that these are not the characteristic objects of their interest. Supposing, she says, by way of an illustration, that a man was sitting absorbed in reading a book, and then a band went by in the street, or a voice began shouting, and the man looked out of the window. You might argue that he was more attracted to such sounds than his book, whereas in reality he is more interested in the latter less obvious and less violent stimulus. Similarly with these small children, the deep formative current of their mental life is not so easily discernible as their reactions to more obvious stimuli "which shows that they have risen from the mere sensorial impression of baubles to the intelligence of love."

Sensitive Period for Refinement of Senses

It must be borne in mind that a sensitive period not only puts the child's mind in relation to certain selected elements in his environment; but it *also establishes and perfects a function in development*. It is a well-known fact that the child, before the age of reason sets in, has a special interest in sensorial impressions of all kinds—in colour, sound, shape, texture, and so forth. What is perhaps *not* so universally recognized is that this age is also one in which there is a sensitive period for refining the senses. This is the period in which Montessori gives the children the sensorial materials. These not only respond to the child's natural interest in sensorial impressions, but—by the activity which they stimulate—refine the senses, perfecting their functions.

It is quite astonishing the degree of sensitiveness which can be attained in this way. Take for instance the sense of colour. Children who have worked with the colour tablets develop a discrimination in delicate shades of colour which many grown-ups have never reached, and will never reach, because their sensitive period for such a development has passed. One of the games commonly played in a Montessori schoolroom is to place the sixty-three shades of colours, from the colour box, all out on a table. A child is shown a particular shade; and then he has to go into the next room (where the same sixty-three colours are spread out on another table) and match it *from memory,* by bringing back the corresponding colour tablet. It is also at this stage that the sense of touch is trained and made practical use of in the learning of the shapes of the letters of the alphabet, and of the geometric forms.

There are amongst the sensory apparatus various materials —such as the cylinders, long stair, pink tower, etc.—which, being carefully and scientifically graded, give accurate impressions of the dimensions of things. Through working with these, the children often develop a sensibility in comparing the dimensions of things by sight which is more perfect than that of any adults. A workman who was once bringing a piece of wood to fit into a window frame in a Montessori classroom, was told by a passing child that it was too short; but he was not convinced. The child—who had already learnt to tell the various number-rods with her eyes shut, just by the feel— turned out to be right, and the man wrong.

This is the period, too, when the children should be given "The Bells." Not at first with the purpose of playing tunes on them (which comes later) but simply as a sensorial exercise in matching and grading the notes *by pitch,* just as they match the colour tablets by colour. It is beyond question that many adults who cannot tell one note from another *could* have developed their musical capacity, and a sense of pitch, if they had only had the means to lay the right sensorial foundation at this critical and creative period.

Montessori points out how important it is in adult life— especially in some vocations—to possess delicate and discriminating senses. How valuable to a doctor, for instance, is a keen sense of colour or a delicate touch, and a good sense of smell. (I know a doctor who tells me she is able to diagnose many diseases the moment she enters the patient's room simply by the smell; and affirms that "most diseases have an odour peculiar to themselves.")

Montessori lays such emphasis on the training of the senses that many writers have maintained that this is the distinguishing feature of her system. This is not true, as will be seen from the other chapters of this book. Nevertheless, it is true that she regarded the training of the senses as very important. Indeed it was for this purpose that she devised the well-known sensorial materials used in all her schools. But these she regards as forming a foundation upon which the child will later build more accurate imaginative creations and clearer abstract ideas.

Sensitive Period for Learning Good Manners

The period we have just been discussing (2½–6 years) is sometimes referred to by Dr. Montessori as the special epoch for sensation. But the child is not only interested in external sensory impressions; his attention is also directed by nature at this stage to his own bodily actions.[2] This is why this period is so perfectly adapted to the learning of "good manners," i.e., the practising of a great number of such actions as opening and shutting a door, handing a sharp instrument to another person, eating correctly, saluting, taking one's leave, and so forth. This is why the "lessons of grace and courtesy" described on page 215 should be given at this psychological moment. It is also the age in which children will learn most easily and perfectly what one might describe as the "good manners" required in assisting at Divine Service—how to walk quietly, make the sign of the Cross, genuflect, light a votive candle and carry it without spilling grease, etc. All these and much besides can be learnt, and best learnt, long before the child is old enough to begin his catechism or follow a reasoned discourse.[3]

Anyone who has had to do with small children around the ages of two and a half to four, must often have been surprised by the firmness with which they insist on doing things in the accustomed—and therefore to them right—way. As Montessori often remarked, "a master of ceremonies at a big court or an ecclesiastical function could not be more exact, and exacting." If we leave these things to be taught at a later age, the special and spontaneous interest in them will not be there, having vanished to give way to other interests of a more intellectual nature.

Later Sensitive Periods

A sensitive period dawns, waxes stronger, attains its zenith, and eventually fades away, giving place to others, "so ever on its heel a new perfection treads" (Keats). In Chap-

[2] See Chapter XIII.
[3] See *The Child in the Church*, by Montessori.

ter XXI we shall deal at length with some of the characteristic mental traits which reveal themselves in the second stage of childhood—that of the junior schoolchild. We have also briefly touched on some of the sensitive periods which come with adolescence. But—as this book is primarily concerned with the first stage of childhood—we shall not attempt here to carry on this description of sensitive periods to later ages of development. Of more practical importance is the consideration of:

The Educational Value of Sensitive Periods

Many people think that Montessori's most valuable and original contribution to education is this doctrine of sensitive periods, because of the practical results that have come with it and from it. It has, of course, been recognized for centuries that the aptitudes and capacities of children are different from those of adults; and also that children at different ages display different interests. But Montessori's study of sensitive periods in human development, her recognition of their biological purpose, her descriptions of the successive phases through which the child passes from birth to adolescence, and—above all—the practical light which this knowledge sheds on the whole problem of education—all these have opened up a new chapter on education.

Before going on to discuss the practical applications of sensitive periods in the schoolroom it will be necessary to add a few more paragraphs concerning their nature in specifically human development.

The Sensitive Period a Burning Intellectual Love

The sensitive period of the caterpillar towards light mentioned at the beginning of this chapter is an instinct pure and simple. But the sensitive periods in human development are not mere instincts; indeed, one sometimes wonder if they should be put down under this category at all. According to Montessori "the essence" of a sensitive period in human development is a "burning intellectual love"—it is a "drama of love between the child and its environment." As such, "it is an animating psychic factor leading to an immense mental activity. Starting from nothing, from the depths of the unconscious, there arises a new interest which illumines the mind, stirring it as it were to new vibrations. This new sensibility is attuned selectively to only certain elements in the environment—even as a radio set selects certain vibrations and is indifferent to the rest."

But we must not let this metaphor run away with the bit

in its teeth. There is really *nothing mechanical about the selective affinities of the sensitive period*; "it is the choice of a keen intellectual love." In fact, on one occasion, by way of illustrating this point, Montessori did actually use the simile of a person in love. "Such a one in the midst of a crowd will at once be able to single out the face of his beloved, or distinguish her voice amongst a medley of others."

School Work and Sensitive Periods

When the education of children is organized in relation to their sensitive periods, they work with a sustained enthusiasm which has to be seen in order to be believed. Then "all is easy, all is eagerness, all is life; and every effort brings an increase of power. How different from our adult work with its external motive, our cold effort and wearisome labour! Urged on by this 'intellectual love,' in a joyful simplicity of soul, a child can make enormous progress." That is why children, in the freedom of a Montessori school, often accomplish in a few weeks, in some particular subject, what would have taken months to learn at the tempo of ordinary class teaching.

When I was lecturer at a government training college, one of my students happened to do her teaching practice at one of the primary schools in the Borough of Acton, run on Montessori principles. At the end of the first day she reported that one of the boys in the class had begun working at his multiplication tables at 9.30 a.m.; and had gone on doing it all the morning. Furthermore, as soon as he came into school after lunch, he immediately went straight to the cupboard, got out the same materials, and continued his researches until it was time to go home. The student was astonished: but I was not; nor was the Montessori teacher in whose class she had been assisting.

When persons unacquainted with the Montessori system hear of these prodigious labours, or see them with their own eyes, they are so astonished that they sometimes change their tune altogether and go to the opposite extreme. They say, "I think it must be dangerous to push the children on to these precocious efforts." Such a criticism is of course unfounded; because no one is "pushing" the children at all. They are quite free to stop at any moment and change their occupation; or just take a rest if they feel like it. Such critics do not realize that working under the urge of a sensitive period is a vital function, and therefore does not tire one any more than does one's breathing, or the beating of one's heart.

We might mention, in passing, that many of the primary

schools in the Borough of Acton (London, W.5) are run on Montessori lines, and have been for many years. This is partly due to the original enthusiasm of a group of Acton primary teachers who years ago studied under Dr. Montessori—thereby setting an example which most subsequent infant teachers followed. But it is also due to the sympathetic interest and encouragement of Dr. Ewart Smart, o.b.e., who has been Borough Officer for Education in Acton for the past twenty-five years. No one in authority in this country has done more towards making the Montessori system appreciated in official circles than Dr. Smart, who for a great part of this time has been—in a private capacity—chairman of the English Montessori Society. In 1954 Dr. Smart received a medal of honour from the Italian Government in recognition of the work he has done on behalf of their great contemporary.

It was Dr. Smart who related to me the following anecdote which bears on the subject of this chapter. One day he was accompanying a newly elected Mayor of Acton on his official visit to one of the primary schools. At the conclusion of his tour of inspection the Mayor made a short speech to the assembled children, at the end of which he said with expansive geniality—"And now, children, I suppose you would like me to ask Dr. Smart to give you a holiday this afternoon." Imagine his surprise when his suggestion was met with a polite chorus of "No, thank you!" Some readers might be inclined to exclaim, "Little prigs!"; but they would be wrong. For, to these children, work—as they do it, or rather as they *live* it, under the guidance of these sensitive periods—is as natural as play and fills them with an even deeper joy.

Let us hope that the Mayor, and the cardinal mentioned on page 46, went away not sadder but wiser men, to use their influence to promote the study and adoption of Montessori principles. Whether they did so or not, a day is surely coming when educationists all over the world will realize the criminal folly of not availing ourselves of these formidable natural energies—these "periods of power." When that day comes our present methods will be seen to resemble those of the ancient Roman architects who—at tremendous labour and expense—constructed immense aqueducts to carry water from one side of a valley to the other—an end which was later achieved with infinitely less labour and expense by simply following more closely the laws of hydrostatics (in particular the law that water always rises to it own level). When that day comes many of us modern teachers might justly be compared to the natives of Madagascar who, on being supplied with wheel-

‘Dr. Smart has just retired.

barrows, filled them with earth and carried them on their heads, being as ignorant of the principle of the wheel as we of sensitive periods.

Taking the Tide at the Flood

Because sensitive periods do not last for ever, but are *by their very nature* transitory phenomena, it is very important that we should be able to recognize them in order to profit by them to the fullest extent. In fact—adapting Shakespeare a little—we might say of these creative epochs: There is a tide in the affairs of children, which, taken at the flood, leads on to fortune . . . omitted, all the voyage of their lives is spent—if not in "shallows and in miseries" at least in a less perfect condition.

Take for example the refinement of movement. There is, as we said above, a period in which children are interested in learning how to perform precise movements, and in the "logical analysis of movements" (see page 222): at this stage they delight in carrying out such actions with an incre'sing perfection. "If," says Montessori, "this perfecting of movement is introduced at *the creative moment* (2½–4) it not only tends to the normal development of mind but also affects the whole personality, bringing contentment, concentration, and inner nourishment. Whereas if these exercises are not given, and the perfection of movement is lacking by consequence, the personality develops out of balance, less happy, not so sure of itself, bearing defects which may increase in successive stages of growth."

"Dropped Stitches in Our Mental Life"

It is true, of course, that a child will nevertheless grow up even without having made use of this or that sensitive period in his development; but he will be a "diminished individual" by comparison with what he might have been, and should have been. With each sensitive period that we miss, we lose an opportunity of perfecting ourselves in some particular way—often for ever.

To illustrate this point Montessori had recourse to a simple and homely simile. "Granny is sitting by the fireside knitting a stocking. She is very old, and her eyesight is failing; and every now and then she drops a stitch without noticing it. But she goes on knitting just the same; and in due course the stocking is finished. But, on account of the dropped stitches, it is not so strong or so perfect a garment as it might have been.

Similarly, if the child misses some of his sensitive periods during his development, he will still grow up into an adult. But that adult will not be so strong nor so perfect an individual as he would have been if he had been able to avail himself of their constructive power."

Most of us grown-ups are painfully aware that there have been many "dropped stitches" in our physical, mental, and social makeup. If only the right means had been forthcoming in our environment at the right time we feel that we might not have grown up so awkward in our movements, or so bad at games, so unappreciative of music, so lacking in colour sense, so ignorant of art, so bad at figures, so atrocious in our accent, so illegible in our handwriting, so shy in company, so dependent on others, so vacillating in our decisions, etc., etc. One could continue the list through a host of other possible dropped stitches.

Missing the Bus

It is useless to try to catch the sensitive period after it has passed. We have missed the bus—the last and only bus for that particular destination. To take an example. It would be useless to expect a child of seven or eight years to be enthusiastic about learning his letters by feeling round the contours of the sandpaper letters; for—by that time—his special interest in tactile experiences would have vanished. Similarly, we could not expect a child of the same age to work with the geometric insets with as much eagerness and profit as would a child of 4–4½. It may seem strange to the reader that a child can recognize (and name) the various regular polygons—pentagon, hexagon, octagon, etc.—*before he can count properly*. The reason is because, *at that age,* he recognizes these figures sensorially, by their look, without counting their sides or angles at all. In fact as soon as the child *can* count, and becomes interested in counting and comparing the number of sides, he has passed beyond the purely sensorial stage: and—says Montessori—"when we have passed to a higher stage we are no longer able to take what was accessible in an earlier."

"Difficulty Not a Question of Age"

The more closely we study the sensitive periods, the more clearly do we see how unfounded are some of the commonest assumptions which underlie our ideas of mental development and educational procedure. For instance, it is usually taken for granted that a thing is more easy or more difficult to learn according to the age of the pupil—i.e., more difficult for the younger, easier for the older. Yet this is by no means always true. "The question of whether a thing is easy or difficult can only be defined in relation to the possibilities of the individual"—and this holds good for any age and any work.

We have already noticed how easy it is for small children to learn to speak a new language and how difficult for adults. In a similar way it has been found that progress in sensorial discrimination is easier for children than for adults. Much the same is true with regard to the faculty of memory. Years ago at a certain school I once had a weekly class in poetry with a group of eight-year-olds. One day—when I gave them some verses to learn by heart during the lesson—just for the fun of the thing I learnt them myself at the same time. At the end of the period we—they and I—had all memorized them. When the same period came round next week, the children remembered the verses perfectly, whereas I had forgotten them almost completely!

Montessori discovered—or rather the children showed her —that the *best age to learn to write* is from three and a half to four and a half. The child, at the beginning of this period, is not interested in writing sentences, or even words. As a matter of fact, paradoxical as it may seem, he is not interested in writing at all. What interests him are certain purely sensorial aspects of the matter—the *shape* of the sandpaper letters (especially when he feels the contours with his two writing fingers). He is also interested by the fact—again a purely sensorial one—that each letter has a corresponding sound. He is at a stage when the world of touch means enormously more to him than to us. Indeed, it commonly happens that a child at this age who cannot recall the phonetic sound of a letter by *looking* at it, will at once remember if he runs the tips of his fingers over it, touch conveying more to him than sight.

People who maintain that children should not be taught to write till they are six or seven years old have not realized that there exists this purely sensorial aspect of language. They are thinking of it rather in terms of writing and reading whole words or sentences, or even of the ideas they represent. That is why they are so astonished when they see children of 4½–5½ composing long words like "Panama" or "Atlantic" with the movable letters, even before they can read. It was the children who had had the opportunity of learning the shapes of the individual letters by *feeling* them, and who knew their corresponding sounds, who "exploded" with such a dramatic suddenness into writing (see Chapter II) and still do when the right circumstances are present at the right age.

Whilst on this question of sensitive periods in connection with learning to write and read we might mention that this interest in the sensorial aspect of language gives place to a more intellectual one which Montessori calls the *"second sensitive period for language."* It is now the *construction* of language which fascinates the child, and his interest now becomes focused on the *relationship* between words. "His intelligence wishes to see this wonderful gift of language as it were spread out before him in its true nature and composition." In other words this means that the child from seven to nine is passing through a sensitive period for grammar.

In the Montessori school this second sensitive period for language is satisfied by a great variety of the most ingenious and fascinating teaching materials. Some of these deal with word classifications such as suffixes, prefixes, singulars and plurals, gender, and so on; others with the relationships between different kinds of words, as classified according to function (parts of speech); whilst a third set of more advanced materials teaches the analysis of sentences—simple and compound. Montessori goes so far as to say that even if the study of grammar had no practical utility (which of course it has) we should still nevertheless be obliged to present it to children at this epoch as a "mental necessity," i.e., as something required to satisfy the needs of development.

A Redistribution of the Elements of Culture Necessary in Accordance with the Sensitive Periods

A curious and interesting thing has happened quite spontaneously, again and again, in the history of Montessori schools all over the world. Children of a younger age—from a younger class altogether—have come in and watched older children at work with various teaching materials. Then, when the opportunity has presented itself, they have calmly walked off with these materials to their own room and worked at them themselves. As a consequence, there has been a general sifting down of the materials to an earlier age. This has happened so often that Montessori actually says: "When we find a piece of work is difficult for a child at a certain age, we often present it to children of an earlier age."

Hitherto it has been generally taken for granted that many subjects, such as geometry, grammar, geography, biology, are not suited to children under six or seven, but should be introduced a good deal later. Montessori has found that "the children have revealed to us that there exists an early epoch of fundamental importance for mental culture in which many cognitions can penetrate through the senses and through movement in a most efficacious way, and can be stored in the memory in a wonderful manner, remaining there to a later stage. So that, when the moment comes for reasoning on these images, they already form a part of their mental equipment, almost as if they were innate ideas. This leads, at this later stage, to a quicker and more accurate comprehension on the more abstract level."

What Montessori has been describing here is really only a more detailed application of the principle—stated in many educational textbooks—viz., that the subject to be taught should be analyzed and presented to the children in a psychological, rather than a logical manner. But the difference lies in the fact that the genius of Montessori has seen so many applications of this principle that have not occurred to others. It sounds absurd on the face of it to talk of presenting the Continental metric system of measurement to children *before they can count.* Yet this is exactly what she does. The child of two and a half who is working with the sensorial materials is in fact making a firsthand acquaintance with the facts of the metric system. For instance, the long rod is exactly one metre in length, the shortest 10 cm. The smallest cube in the pink tower is a cubic centimetre, the largest exactly one litre in volume. Of course, one does not mention these facts at the time; but, years later, when the children come to learn about these measurements, and calculate with them, they will do so with greater interest and comprehension because, as sensorial facts, they have already been a part of their life for years. It is as though a child might say to himself, "These are old friends of mine, I have known them since I was so high; but I never knew they were so important." Similarly, the various sensorial materials are all based on the number *ten.* "The child cannot yet count and you might say, 'Why then this number?' True, actual counting has not arrived yet; but we can well understand how these items of knowledge can be given in an experimental manner, even if they are not consciously in a mind able to realize their significance. Do you think that doing the same action always ten times does not leave any trace on the motor system of the child? Or that the notions of number, form, weight, volume cannot exist in a fundamental form in the body, in its movement, in a subconscious way before the light of intelligence can recognize and determine them exactly?"

Living in the Present

Another common assumption which is disproved by a study of sensitive periods is that the child learns more or less the same amount every day, becoming more intelligent little by little, in small doses, at a regular rate—"passing from the 'known to the unknown' with a uniform progress 'like the hands of a clock.'" This is not the case with the free and normal child: his mental progress tends to go in jumps or "saltations"—which seems the way of life, both in the individual and in the species. (See de Vries' *Mutations*.)

It often happens that, in obedience to a set programme of studies, a teacher is obliged to hustle on his pupils to reach a certain attainment by a certain date. His eyes, and therefore those of his pupils, too, are fixed on the *future*; and the whole atmosphere becomes one of forward-looking tension. This is a mistake: because, though the sensitive period is a "period of power," i.e., the power of acquiring certain cognitions with a special facility, speed, and thoroughness, it is a *present power,* and will not last for ever. Therefore, in order to make the fullest use of it we must let the child *live wholly in the present, using the wonderful gifts of the present.*

The preparations of life are usually indirect. The butterfly does not begin life as a little butterfly who imitates his mother's mode of living. The mother butterfly, flitting from flower to flower to extract its honey, does not say to the caterpillar, "Do as I do." The naturalist who wishes his caterpillar to turn into a perfect butterfly gives it what it needs most *as a caterpillar,* knowing that it is the best means to the end desired.

Similarly we must not be "overanxious about the morrow," nor be worried if the child's present interests and activities do not seem to be a direct preparation for the kind of life and work he will have when grown up. It is in "successive presents" —each lit up by the glow of its sensitive period—that the child will find his most perfect development; and with it the best preparation for the duties of adult life. This is because each sensitive period not only brings certain physical and mental attainments, but also establishes certain functions. "It comes for a moment but its benefits last for a lifetime."

What all this amounts to means that—as far as possible—we should let nature draw up the timetable for us; let her arrange the general programme of the child's studies from year to year. It does not come within the scope of this chapter—or of this book—to discuss in detail how the various elements of culture should be rearranged in accordance with the different sensitive periods.[5] But it is obvious that the same principles apply to every subject—to arithmetic, history, geography, religion, and so on. Here we are concerned only with the general principle of sensitive periods. We neglect it at our peril; and this not only because children will be able to get on better and more quickly if we respect it, but because if we go contrary to it we shall find many children putting up "psychic barriers" [6] to various subjects, which may last for the rest of their lives.

More Study—Not Less

The tendency today, says Montessori, is to try and solve the problem of education by getting the children to study less. But this is only a negative solution: it will only be through the redistribution of the contents of culture, *taking into account the sensitive periods,* that the problem will be solved. If we do this it will bring about, not a diminution of culture, but an intensification of it. To satisfy the needs of the growing individual he needs to study more, but in a new way. This will result, not in a retrogression with the excuse of not tiring the child, but in more brilliant and more joyful results at every stage of development.

CHAPTER VIII   THE "WORK" OF THE CHILD—THE CREATION OF THE ADULT

A Comparison

Let us suppose we are down by the seashore, and we come across a workman filling a cart with sand; and near him is a small boy similarly engaged filling his toy wheelbarrow. Outwardly, both the child and adult are doing the same work. Now suppose I go up to the man and make the suggestion that I should do this work for him, and offer to take over his spade; he will probably think I am a bit eccentric. But if he comes to realize that I am really in earnest (and not a dangerous lunatic) he would probably say, "Okay, guv'nor, if yer really wants to." He would then sit down and smoke a pipe in peace, meditating the while that there is no accounting for tastes. Now if I similarly approached the small boy, and

[5] We shall return to this subect in a general way in Part V of this book.
[6] See *Secret of Childhood,* Part II, Chapter IV.

—offering to take his spade—said, "Let me do that for you," do you think he would let me? The chances are a hundred to one that he would flatly refuse; and if I persisted the young fellow would probably defend himself from my help with great determination.

Furthermore, if we were to watch the small boy continuing at his work we should quite likely see that—when he had filled his wheelbarrow—he would just empty it and begin the process of refilling it all over again; and so on indefinitely. On the other hand, if, having finished filling the man's cart, I were to empty all the sand out again so that he had to begin the job over again from the start, I should probably find our relations would become considerably strained!

External and Internal Aim

Here we discern a great difference between the work of the adult and the work of the child, which we can express thus: the adult works with an external aim, to accomplish some change in his environment—in this case to fill the cart with sand for building purposes. But it is not so with the child's work. If his real aim was to fill his barrow with sand, why does he empty it again as soon as it is filled—to begin the "work" all over again?

Take another example. A lady was watching a small child slowly and laboriously buttoning up a very long pair of gaiters. She longed to help; but remembering Dr. Montessori's admonition to let children help themselves she resisted the impulse. Higher and higher up the legs toiled the little fingers till at last the top buttons were reached, and the lady heaved a sigh of relief. Imagine her astonishment when the child immediately began to undo all the buttons, and started the whole business *decapo*.

The same sort of thing happens every day in a Montessori school. You may see a child of three and a half take all the ten cylinders out of their sockets and replace them a dozen times; and very likely she will do the same thing tomorrow; and perhaps every day for a week. If the aim of her work was to replace the cylinders, doing it once would have sufficed. In a school in Holland I once saw a little queue of children all waiting to polish the *same* brasses! "We adults don't fritter our energies away like that! We work to finish. The best runner is the one who gets there first; the best sempstress who sews most quickly; the best charwoman who gets through her work most speedily. 'She is a quick worker,' we say with praise."

Not so the child. He seems in no hurry to finish his work,

and will repeat it quite uselessly it seems to us. But it only seems useless to us because we are judging the child's work by our adult standards. The aim of the child's work is not external but internal. He works in order to grow. You cannot therefore see visibly the end for which he is expending all these labours. It is something remote, hidden in the obscurity of the future. Indefatigably, irresistibly, unceasingly, joyfully, the child is working to create the adult, the man-that-is-to-be.

This distant end for which the child is working is not of course consciously present to him; but the serene joy which we see in his expression indicates the satisfaction of a profound need of life. The child who is happy filling his bucket, washing a table, working with the cylinders, arranging the colour tablets, counting the number rods—or whatever it may be—is obeying certain laws of growth—"inner directives": hence his contentment. As Montessori says, "Blessed is the child who has the joy of obeying in a manner exact, though unconscious, those divine forces which are in him. His is the joy of the creator. If from the newborn baby, helpless and unconscious, dumb, unable to raise itself, comes forth the individual adult with perfected form, with a mind enriched with all the acquisitions of his psychic life, radiant with the light of the spirit, this is the child's doing. For it is the child who builds the man. Truly, as Wordsworth says, 'The child is father of the man.'"

Work and Environment

The work both of the child and of the adult has a definite relationship to the environment. We may say that the adult works to perfect his environment, whereas the child works to perfect himself, using the environment as the means. The adult—just because he is an adult—is no longer developing; he has reached the norm of the species; but the child is a being in a constant state of transformation. He is progressing, step by step, towards a more advanced state of being; and each new stage of development is marked by a new phase of this inwardly creative commerce with the environment, which we call work.

The Different Rhythm of the Child's Work

The more carefully we study the nature of the child's work the more clearly do we realize how profoundly it differs from that of the adult. So much so indeed that it is only the limitation of language that obliges us to use the same word. On more than one occasion I have heard Montessori complaining that, in order accurately to describe the child's nature and his activities, we need a "new vocabulary," since the accepted meanings of the words we are forced to use are often more of a hindrance than a help. And here we have a case in point.

For this reason we must analyze the matter a little further. As a corollary to the contrast already noted (between the nature of the work of the child and that of the adult) there arises another difference—in the inner rhythm or mental tempo which accompanies the two forms of work. A few examples will make the point clear. It is not uncommon to observe that a child of three and a half who wants to work with the ten cubes of the pink tower on a rug on the floor will make ten separate journeys from the cupboard to the rug— one complete journey all across the room, in and out amongst the little tables, for each separate cube, even for the smallest. He could quite easily have taken two or three cubes together to save time and effort. An adult, or even a boy of seven years, would never act in that way. Or again, if you observe children carrying out the exercises of practical life you will see the same sort of thing. How slow they are, how unreasonable in their expenditure of effort! Take for instance the business of washing their hands. What an unconscionable time they take over it! How they seem to dwell, with a sort of inner relish, over each separate action, each little step in the process! Very slowly and deliberately, they will begin by turning up their sleeves, as if the whole morning was before them. How slowly —how caressingly—they will wash each separate finger— often pausing to look at their hands as though in contemplation —giving to each of the thirty different stages in this action as much interest and attention as a Benedictine monk who is performing a complicated liturgical ceremony.

To us adults it is a torment simply to watch this imperturbable leisureliness. We can hardly refrain from rushing in and taking over the action ourselves in order to get it finished and done with.

Why do we feel like this? Simply because the whole work-rhythm and tempo of our lives is different from theirs. We "gnaw the nail of hurry." [1] All the time we cannot help envisaging in our mind's eye the completed action towards which we are moving. Inevitably we hasten towards this end as quickly and as economically as possible. The future of our day, week, year, lies all mapped out before us with their allotted tasks; whilst we, impelled by an inner tension, press

¹Hassan, by Elroy Flecker.

onward to their fulfillment, our "present" for ever leaning over into an urgent "future."

But it is not so with the child. He lives in a sort of everlasting present. He does not hurry as we do towards the end of the action, because for him the end of the action *is the action itself*. His whole being is expressed in his work; he loves it, lives it, rejoices in it, preserves in it, repeats it—*because it is the means by which he is perfecting himself*.

It requires a real effort of imagination on our part to free ourselves from our own rhythm of work and project ourselves into his. We are always saying to these poor creatures: "Hurry up!" "Dear me, how slow you are!" or (worse still) "Here, let me do that for you!" Yet our efforts are as futile as those of the man on whose tombstone was carved "Here lies the man who tried to hustle the East." It is equally futile to try to hustle the work of the child. "He cannot be twenty before he is twenty." Nature has fixed his programme; and you cannot change it; for, as Montessori says, "He is following the timetable like the most diligent scholar in the world—following it with the unshakable constancy of the stars in their courses."

Respecting the Child's Rhythm of Life

One of the first essentials for any adult who wishes to help small children is to learn to respect the different rhythm of their lives, instead of trying to speed it up, in the vain hope of making it synchronize with ours. To illustrate this point Montessori relates the following anecdote. One day she was watching a child of about five years composing the numbers 1–100 with the number frame. This is a material not unlike those wooden frames one sees put up in churches to indicate the numbers of the hymns to be sung. The child was patiently putting the cards in and taking them out. She had before her the task of separately composing each number from 1–100. To Montessori it seemed a dreadfully slow and long-drawn-out business. So, thinking she could help the child to arrive more quickly at its goal—which she took to be the number 100—she began asking her to compose some numbers further on, skipping out others to accelerate the process. The child submitted to her suggestions for some time with quiet patience, obediently doing what she was asked to do. Then, as if she could stand it no longer, she said, politely but firmly, "Please will you go away and let me do it my own way." Whereupon the little girl went back to the point in the number series where she had been interrupted; and carried on from there at the same tempo as before. "I felt justly rebuked," said Montessori, "for my stupidity. I had made the mistake of thinking the child's interest lay in getting to the end of the process and not in the process itself." This reminds one of R. L. Stevenson's remark: "To travel hopefully is a better thing than to arrive."

The Child, the Mystic, and the Artist

The inner rhythm of the child's life in some ways resembles that of a mystic; for both may be said to live in a sort of "eternal now." The contemplation of the mystic does not produce anything practical outside himself—it is an end in itself—and the end is self-perfection. Having become "as a little child," he is liberated from the hustle and bustle of adult life (this *vorticoso diventare*) with its ever-quickening tempo. The reason why the great liturgical ceremonies of the Church seem to us at times so long-drawn-out and tedious is just the same—i.e., because we are still clinging to the hurrying tempo of our everyday living. We have not been able to live ourselves into the majestic rhythm of those actions which savour more of eternity than of time.

The child resembles the artist, too, as well as the mystic; because he has the task of creating a great masterpiece—which is the man-to-be. That is why you can no more hurry him than you can hurry on the work of an artist. If you think an artist can be hurried, read the story of the impatient Father Prior who tried to hustle on Leonardo da Vinci into finishing the painting of his famous Last Supper.[2]

Distorted Modern Ideas of Work

In the Book of Genesis we read how God created the world from the formless void; and man from the dust of the earth. Something similar happens in the development of every individual. As Margaret Drummond used to say, "In every child the world begins anew."

Our modern industrialized society, according to Montessori, has lost all true sense of the value and meaning of work. This is partly because, in the present state of society, division of labour as we know it rests on false foundations; it is the result of the unchecked possessiveness of whole groups of men. Love of possession and love of power are "deviations"[3] from the normal. It is these which have brought about a social condi-

[2]See Vasari's *Lives of the Painters.*
[3]See Chapter X.

tion in which some do no work at all, or very little, but live parasitically on the labours of others. "Work," says Montessori, "is so truly the natural expression of 'normalized' mankind (each species living on earth has its 'cosmic mission') that man's true name should be *homo laborans* rather than *homo sapiens!* But, alas, as things are at present, most persons have lost this 'instinct of the species.' It is only in persons of exceptional power—the geniuses—that this love of work persists as an irresistible impulse, surviving in spite of the unhappy conditions which have smothered it in the majority. Such are for example the artists, discoverers, explorers, reformers, and so forth who—like children—cannot help working, and have by their heroic efforts rediscovered the instinct of the species."

Montessori believes that if the child, the boy, the youth—at each stage of development—was given the opportunity of doing the special kind of work for which his nature craves, it would lead to a more harmonious humanity, a humanity largely delivered from the love of possession and the love of power.

There exists, in our present society, an unhappy divorce between the "working" classes and the "professional." So we have "hands" without brains, and "brains" without hands. The whole trend of Montessori's influence in the sphere of education is to unite these two elements right from the start; or better still never to allow them to be separated. As she herself says, "What God hath joined let no man put asunder!" If infants, children, and youths were trained on these practical lines at every stage of development, there would come into existence a nobler conception of work—as of something essential to the dignity of every human being.

The Laws Governing the Child's Work and the Adult's Compared

Both the work of the child and that of the adult are subject to certain laws; but since (as we have seen) their work differs in nature, so do the laws which govern them.

Let us look first at the laws which govern the work of an adult.

(1) *Division of Labour.* Since the end of the adult's labour is an external one—to produce something—it is possible to divide up his work, and share it between a number of persons. "Many hands make light work." Also the work can be differentiated according to kind and quality.

(2) *"Maximum Result with Minimum Effort."* Arising out of the external nature of the adult's work comes the fact that he seeks to produce as much as he can with the least amount of effort. This does not, in itself, imply any unwillingness to work, but simply means that there exists a nice economy of effort. Hence the adult can use labour-saving devices to shorten his hours of labour.

Now when we come to look at the child's work we find that these two laws simply do not apply. If you come to think of it, there can be no "division of labour" in his case. Since his work is, in essence, to grow, he *must* do it himself; and no one, however willing, can do it for him. In fact "every useless aid arrests development"—and "to become a man of twenty he must take twenty years."

It is the same with the second law—"maximum result with minimum effort." This, too, does not apply to the child's work, "which springs from an internal fount of energy which has no quantitative relation to the external end."

The Joy of Work

Because the child's work springs from this "internal fount of energy" it is no burden to him—any more than we feel the beating of the heart to be a burden. They are both vital functions. But the work of the child is on a higher plane than the beating of the heart—a mental plane; hence he consciously rejoices in it, "as a strong man to run a race."

Work is for him a necessary form of life, a vital instinct without which his personality cannot organize itself. So essential is it for the child to have the opportunity and means for this creative "work" that if it is denied him his deviated energies will result in all sorts of abnormalities. Conversely, there is one thing, and one only, which will cure the child of his abnormalities—and that is work. This is Dr. Montessori's doctrine of "normalization through work" which we have developed in Chapter X.

Many adults look upon work as a disagreeable necessity—the "Curse of Adam." Very different is the child's attitude, which is much more in line with Elizabeth Browning's couplet:

> Dear work! if thou wert God's curse
> What must His blessings be?

It is this joy which the children manifest in their work which makes the Montessori school so indefinably attractive. Theirs is indeed a cosmic joy, which springs from the very heart of being, because it is the joy that comes through acting in accordance with the laws of one's nature. It is akin to that of which another poet speaks, when he says:

> With joy the stars perform their shining,
> And the sea its long moon-silvered roll.
>
> "Duty," by M. ARNOLD

The Meaning of Repetition in Childhood

As soon as one understands Montessori's idea of the nature of the child's work, many mystifying phenomena become clearer. Chief amongst these is the well-known and remarkable tendency of children to repeat the same thing over and over again.

A two-year-old boy of my acquaintenance removed and replaced the lid of the little box in which I kept my shaving soap forty-two times in succession—quite spontaneously. Preyer relates how his little boy did the same thing with the stopper of a bottle fifty-four times. A Dutch friend of mine watched—unseen—while a little girl traced her fingers over a single sandpaper letter more than 100 times! I knew a nurse who told the same story to a little girl twenty-five times—at the child's own request.

What drives children to this apparently meaningless repetition? In one of her training courses Dr. Montessori forced a group of her students to repeat the exercise of taking out and replacing the wooden cylinders for twenty minutes, without stopping, till they were heartily sick of it! At the end of this she remarked with one of her illuminating smiles, "Now by the very boredom you have experienced in this repeating and repeating this same exercise, you will be able to measure that imperious inner urge that drives the children to do the same thing."

G. K. Chesterton writes (in *Orthodoxy*):

All the towering materialism which dominates the modern mind rests on one assumption—a false assumption. It is supposed that if a thing goes on repeating itself it is probably dead. People feel that if the universe was personal it would vary; if the sun were alive it would dance. The sun rises every morning: I do not rise every morning; but the variation is due not to my activity but to my inaction. The thing I mean can be seen for instance in children when they find some game or joke they especially enjoy. A child kicks its legs rhythmically through excess not absence of life. Because children have a bounding vitality—therefore they want things repeated and unchanged.

"This repetition," says Montessori, "is a spontaneous phenomenon due to the child's interior energy—powerful and irresistible. . . . We are here before a reality; and we must respect this energy; help it; and give it the necessary direction to unfold itself."

The Cycle of Work

The adult stops working when he has reached the end for which he set out—i.e., when his job is finished; or when he is too tired to go on. But, as we have seen, the child does not stop when the external end has been reached; he very often goes back to the beginning and repeats it, many times. But he does stop in the end—and that quite suddenly. Why does he stop just at that moment? It is because, unconsciously, he feels within himself that he has obtained what he needs from that particular activity—for the time being at any rate. While he has been repeating the exercises, there has been going on inside him a process of psychic maturation, which has now come full circle. A need has been satisfied; and he stops because the "cycle of work" has been completed. (See Chapter XVII.)

Refreshment Through Work

The child does not stop working because he is fatigued. On the contrary, he issues from such a "cycle of work" as one strengthened and refreshed. His whole being manifests a characteristic calmness, almost a radiant serenity. He can be compared, on the psychic plane, "to a man who feels refreshed and content after a good meal." The child who has come out of one of these prolonged periods of concentration feels "at peace with the world." His soul is in a particularly sensitive state. He observes many things in his surroundings that he did not observe before. He experiences a deepening of the social sentiment. "He becomes richer and more openhearted. This is just the moment when he may choose, quite spontaneously, to make some intimate communication, or demonstration of affection to his teacher, or to others; or even experience some new manifestation of the religious sentiment. The diner, who has dined well, will greet a friend affably whom before dinner he might have passed without even a glance. This need not surprise us; before being able to expend our forces we must first collect them."

Some Exceptions Which Prove the Rule

The distinction drawn above between the nature of the child's work and the adult's is not to be taken as absolute and invariable. There are times when the child works like an adult, just because he then has an external aim. At such times he, too, works "economically," that is, with just the expenditure of energy necessary to produce the result required, and no more.

In illustrating this point Montessori uses a simile which is really more than a simile. Babies, at a certain stage, repeat the syllable "da" indefinitely. "Da-da-da-da . . ." they say *ad lib*. This is not speech; only the prelude to it. In making these "noises" the baby is perfecting his powers of articulation by constant repetition. But there comes a moment when he will say less, and mean more. He will confine himself to saying, consciously, "da-da"; and "behold! he summons his father!"

Similarly the child, who—following a kind of instinct—has traced over the sandpaper letters again and again for many days—perfecting something in himself—will one day consciously set out to compose words with the movable letters. First, then, the child creates by repetition a faculty *inside himself*; and then he creates something with it, outside himself. This is an experience which gives him a new kind of joy, the conscious joy of the creator.

Spontaneous Organization of Work by Children

When this unconscious inner preparation, through a process of self-perfection, has created in children the power to work consciously for an external end, there then arises for them the possibility of gaining another new experience, this time on the social plane. For now, since their aim is external, children can unite together on the principle of the division of labour.

So now you will see these small children forming themselves into spontaneous groups to accomplish collectively some definite task. One group, for instance, will lay the tables for lunch; another prepare vases of flowers to adorn them; others again will wait on their companions; and other groups still clear away and wash up afterwards.

At this point Montessori utters a word of practical warning to directresses. If you see this sort of spontaneous organization of work springing up in your class, beware of the temptation to systematize it. A directress might think, "Good! now we must do this systematically; make a programme; draw out a timetable; make lists of children for each job, and so on." "Not" (continues the Dottoressa) "that this would be a crime, but the experienced directress—who seeks always to know the limits of her intervention—will do so here also.

"The instinct towards such organization in children is as irresistible as that which, at other times, drives them to solitary work. Even then it is not the same thing as with adults. For with the latter it is willed and rational; with children, instinctive. Their distribution of the work amongst themselves is not the fruit of reason, but of a harmonious cohesion which arises from that sentiment which the human instinct shows when it is about to produce its greatest work. Beware of crushing this tender thing into an adult mould. The greatest prudence is necessary, if the teacher is going to intervene, lest this graceful and charming scene should lose its character, and its light be put out."

More Exceptions That Prove the Rule—The Sportsman and the Religious

Just as there are these times when the child works like an adult towards an external end, with a minimum expenditure of effort, so there are times when the adult expends a vast amount of energy which appears to have no quantitative relationship to the outward end. Watch a man practising his stroke at golf! He repeats the same action again and again, and yet again, producing nothing new externally. He reminds one of the child doing the cylinders, acting with the same apparently unreasonable repetition. Why does he act thus? Because his real aim—like the child's—is an internal one, to perfect himself. We might in fact apply to him, with absolute justice, the words with which Dr. Montessori describes the child at his typical work: "He wastes an immense amount of energy over an insubstantial end; and he wastes not only driving energy but intensive energy in the exact execution of every detail." ("Shoulder up!" "Keep your eye on the ball!" etc.)

If this is true of the sporting man it is even more so of the spiritual man whose aim is to advance his spiritual growth. He too makes use of external things in his environment with an internal aim—the perfection of his soul.

The Child's "Work" is "Useless"

Looked at from the point of view of the "practical" adult (whose aim is to produce something outside himself) the child's work is quite useless. The work of the adult has a social value; he produces something which is useful to society. In one of her lectures Dr. Montessori drew a striking imaginary picture of the adult workers of the world. There was the blacksmith at his anvil; the builder at his wall; the farmer at his plough; the scientist in his laboratory; the legislator with his new code of laws, and so forth. In and out amongst these busy workers wanders the child. But amongst them there is no place for him, nor his "work." He does not belong there because he is of no "use" there; he is an alien to that society of busy adult workers. He is in fact an "extra-social" being because he cannot adapt himself to the standards and aims of this adult society; and so can take no part in it.

But the Child's Work is not Really Useless

Nevertheless, if we look into the matter more deeply, the child's work is far from being useless. In fact, it is just as important as that of the adult—even more so. It is not we adults who can transform a child into a man, any more than we could transform a man into a baby. That is the child's work—to create the adult!

It is by virtue of the child's incessant activity, as he unconsciously carries out this great aim, that we call him a worker. For he does not "create the man" by meditation or rest, but by unceasing, unwearied activity, carried on, year in and year out, for upwards of twenty years. As Montessori says:

> The child exercises himself, moves himself, makes his own experiments, learns to coordinate his movements, goes hither and thither seizing ideas from the external world. He learns, in what seems a miraculous manner, to speak, to stand upright on his feet, to walk, to run—in all this seeking, little by little, to give precise form to his intelligence—so that we can say: these are the characteristics, and this the intelligence of a child of five: and of eight; and of eighteen respectively; for the child will not disobey the programme drawn up for him by nature. Thus, through indefatigable activity, through efforts, experiments, conquests, and griefs; through harsh trials and wearisome struggles, step by step he fulfils his difficult and glorious task, adding always a new perfection.

Great and important as the child's work is, it has never yet been fully recognized by society—the chief reason being because it does not produce anything visibly useful outside itself, as is the case with adult labour.

The Two Dependencies

If the child cannot do the adult's work it is equally true that the adult cannot do the child's. The perfection of the full-grown man depends—when you come to think of it—on this long-continued work of the child who creates him. The adult, if you look at it in this way, is just as dependent on the child for the richness of his physical, mental, and spiritual endowments as the child, for his part, is dependent on the adult for his many needs. In his own sphere the child is master and can say, "I, too, have a kingdom; and you—adults—are my dependents." Upon the realization of these two dependencies, Montessori sees the only foundation on which to build "the fundamental framework for harmony among mankind."

The Worker and His Workshop

Every adult worker has his workshop, a place dedicated to his productive labour; the blacksmith his forge, the carpenter his bench, the businessman his office, and so forth. *Adults* realize the importance of having such a specially prepared environment where work can go forward under the best conditions—no time wasted, and all the necessary means to hand, etc. For the child, too, it is equally important that he should have a place dedicated to his work. But since the child's work is not yet generally known and appreciated, not many people bother about preparing such a special place for it; and fewer still know how to set about doing it.

Yet more than ever, in these times, is it necessary to have a place especially set apart for the child's work. With the growth of large industrial areas, and the multiplication of mechanical appliances—rail, car, plane, phone, radio, etc.—the rhythm of life has become ever "faster and faster" (as the Red Queen said to Alice). But, as we have seen, it is just in the rhythm of his work that the child so profoundly differs from the adult. In ancient times this contrast was not so acute; for primitive society lived in closer contact with nature, and was more influenced by the unhurried and not-to-be-hurried rhythm of the seasons. The child under these conditions was free to run about field and farm, amongst the birds, beasts, and flowers, making his own discoveries—as "the young explorer" unhindered by adult intervention. The problem of the transmission of culture, too, was also less acute, since the majority of the population were still illiterate.

In place of nature we now have an artificial "supernature," an environment made for adults and to adult proportions. How different now the child's surroundings in a modern flat or a back-to-back house! How often do we read in advertisements —"We do not take in children." This artificial world of adults has engulfed the bewildered child, who is more like an exile or a refugee. One thing only has remained unchanged throughout the changing conditions; that is the child's irresistible urge to activity, to grow through the accomplishment of his work. But alas! how often can he find no place in which the delicate, sensitive, complicated work of total growth can proceed at its own tempo, free from unnecessary (though well-meant) adult intervention.

Better Working Conditions or The Living Environment of the Spiritual Embryo

We have all heard of movements whose aim is to improve the conditions of the working classes. But mention this subject to anyone, and it is certain that your interlocutor will think you are referring to adult workers. But—if we can believe Montessori—the time is coming when the social conscience (which has at last become sensitive to the conditions of the *adult* worker) will be likewise awakened to the even greater importance of giving right working conditions to that "other pole of humanity"—the children. What is needed, and what will surely come, if and when Montessori's ideas have percolated through to the masses, is a vast social movement for the betterment of the working conditions of the child. But this reform will never come until society as a whole understands what *is* the work of the child.

In order that the child may be able to carry out his great work properly, he needs something more vital and dynamic than a workshop. We must accustom our minds to the notion of an environment which will be more akin to that living environment which surrounds the embryo in the maternal womb—something at once protective, sustaining, and above all life-giving. The tissues that are being formed in the physical embryo are infinitely delicate, the process of growth so subtle, that nature has seen to it that the greatest care and protection is forthcoming. So should it be with the "spiritual embryo." Both physically and mentally and spiritually—perhaps most

⁴See *Secret of Childhood*, Chapter II.

of all spiritually—the child requires a life-giving environment of calm and peace, sheltered from the hustling modern world (not to mention the hustling teacher and parent).

A New Conception of Educational Reform

When Montessori says that we adults must take it upon ourselves to create this living environment for the work of the child, she has something in mind much more extensive than the prepared environment of the ordinary Montessori school. What must be done next is to work out, for each succeeding epoch of development, that particular type of environment which corresponds to its particular needs. What people ordinarily think of as the Montessori school is really only the first stage. The same thing must now be done for the junior school or boy scout age, and for the adolescent. This means that we must create, for each of these later stages, an environment in which these developing individuals can live their lives—intellectually, socially, and spiritually, freed from unnecessary adult intervention—according to the laws of growth characteristic of each stage.

To some extent this has already been done with regard to the junior school age (see Chapter XXI); and there exist Montessori schools—so called—in Holland which carry on up to university age. But, so far, Montessori's ideas with regard to junior and secondary education have never yet been fully realized in any country.

It would be a great mistake to think of this tremendous reform in terms of educational ideas and aims as we are accustomed to think of them at the present time. She envisages something on a new and vaster scale than anything we have hitherto even dreamed of; something which would involve a collective effort of the whole adult humanity comparable, in its intensity and sacrifice, to—let us say—the manner in which a modern nation wages total war.

An Example From Nature

If we wish to find something with which we can compare the magnitude of this task which must be undertaken by humanity for the coming generation, we must look outside humanity, for humanity has not yet realized its importance. We must look to nature. We must turn our attention to those "touching and almost miraculous manifestations of the maternal instinct taken in its widest sense." When we look at a hive of bees what do we see? We behold a society in which the whole energies of the adult population are devoted, with unremitting self-sacrifice, to the task of building up a prepared environment for the coming generation, and to the care of that generation as it is developing. "Strange, is it not," ejaculates Montessori, "that man, the architect, the builder, the producer, the transformer of his environment, does less for his offspring than these creatures." But a time is coming (though we shall not live to see it) when mankind—or what is left of it after the "Last War"—will turn it highest constructive energies to this task of creating these "prepared environments" in which the young can grow (as they never have done yet) into their full stature—not into the deviated misfits that most of us are.

The Child's Work and the Problem of Peace

Montessori believes that the problem of world peace can never be satisfactorily solved until we start with the child. "By taking the child into consideration we touch something common to all humanity. We cannot achieve world harmony simply by attempting to unite all these adult people who are so different; but we can achieve it if we begin with the child who is not born with national and racial prejudices."

Our civilization, as Montessori never ceased to tell us, has been built up on adult values. By this she means that, in its creation, no sufficient use has been made of the constructive potentialities of childhood. All civilizations, hitherto, have been constructed by only a half of human life, the adult half. That is why they are so terrible, so hard, and so "unchangeable." But childhood—the other half of humanity—could help if it were only given a chance.

Each of us has not always been a grown-up person: it was the child who constructed our personality. Before we became the important adult personage we are now, the respected member of society, we were another personality— very different, very mysterious—but not considered by the world, at all; not respected; of no importance whatever; with no say in the running of things. Yet all that time we were really a personality capable of doing something that we cannot do now. He who is the constructor of man can never be a person of no importance. He is capable of doing something great, like a seed. It is only when we realize the wonderful way in which the child creates the man that we realize, at the same time, that we hold in our hands a secret by which we can help in the formation of a better humanity. (Just the opposite of a secret weapon to destroy it).

We should be wrong, however, if we were to conclude from this that Montessori is advocating a purely humanitarian doctrine. Religion would still play a major part—in fact *the* major part. But—and this is a very big "but"—Montessori affirms that, up to the present time, even religion has never had the opportunity of exercising its fullest potential influence. This is because hitherto the best—and in fact only—foundation for such a complete development of religion has been wanting. That foundation is—or rather should be—a "normalized" humanity, normalized through work in the sense that we have discussed it in Chapter X. All theologians agree that the best foundation upon which the Christian religion can work for the betterment of humanity is the fullest development of the natural faculties. (That is why missionaries nearly always begin by educating the people they wish to raise up; and, incidentally, why so many missionary orders have adopted the Montessori method.) It is only then, when these two factors come together in the fullest degree—a "normalized humanity" and the Christian religion—each supplementing the other— that we can look for the realization of Montessori's ideal of "A New World for a New Man."

CHAPTER IX   THE SENSORIAL FOUNDATIONS OF INTELLECTUAL LIFE

In a previous chapter we saw how Montessori trusts to the spontaneous working of the child's intellect to provide the power that keeps the Montessori school going, thus combining the acquisition of culture with autoeducation. And in another, we noted that this does not seem such an extraordinary thing to do after all, if one takes into consideration what the child's mind has already achieved *spontaneously*, before he comes to school at three years of age.

But in order to ensure that the child's mind will work effectively and for long periods in this spontaneous manner, it is necessary to know the conditions which are most suited to it.

The first and most important point to realize is that the

child's intellect does not work in isolation, but is everywhere and always intimately bound up with his body, particularly with his nervous and muscular systems.

Theoretically it is of course possible to conceive of intellectual beings whose mental operations are carried on quite independently of matter. (According to theologians this is precisely the nature of the angels, who are "pure intellects" or "pure spirits"—i.e., without any admixture of matter.)

But in the case of us human beings the soul and the body are inextricably woven together in an indissoluble unity. This fact profoundly affects all our manner of thinking, and is a dominant factor in the child's development.

Montessori never commits what Maritain calls the "sin of angelism," that is, the mistake of treating the human being, especially the child, as if he were a pure intellect. On the contrary, more than in any other system of education, her whole method is based on a deep understanding of the relationship between these two elements—mind and body.

It is true that Montessori holds the view that man is distinguished from the lower animals by the possession of the power to reason; but she never forgets that, along with the animals, he possesses a material body with inherited instincts. It is this material body, with its five senses, that connects his inner life—even his highest spiritual experiences—with the physical world outside. There is no more interesting study in psychology than that which deals with the way in which these two parts of our nature react upon each other—i.e., the intellectual part, which is concerned with universal or abstract ideas, pure reason, and free will; and the bodily or material part of us, with its five senses directed towards individual objects in the outside world.

The newborn baby starts life with no more ideas in its head than a newborn puppy. And yet, within the short space of three or four years, every normal child will have in his mind a store of such notions as softness, hardness, height, length, colour, goodness, badness, and so forth—mental concepts which no dog would acquire though it live to be a hundred years old. Yet the child and the dog both live in the same world, touch the same objects, hear the same sounds, are made wet with the same water, warmed with the same fire, and satisfied with the same, or similar, food and shelter. More than this, their sense organs work on the same plan: under the microscope there is not any noticeable difference in the structure of their nervous and muscular systems.

Whence then comes this great difference? The inference is unavoidable. The child must possess within himself, from birth, a capacity—only potential at first—of abstracting or taking off from particular things their essential qualities. If you watch carefully any small child, of one to two years old, you will see that he is not only interested in objects as a whole, but also in their qualities, such as roughness, smoothness, hardness, softness, colour, taste, texture, weight, pliability, and so on.

We grown-ups have an immense store of these abstract ideas in our minds. Where did they come from? How and when did we acquire them? For the most part we do not remember. Nevertheless, one thing is certain: we got our ideas of smoothness from smooth objects; of roughness from rough objects; of squareness from square ones; of length from long ones. Similarly we obtained our notion of naughtiness from naughty actions and goodness from good ones. All this means, when reduced to its essential elements, that we possess within us, as part of our mental makeup, a capacity which in some mysterious way is able to draw off from things outside us certain abstract qualities or ideas, entities which exist only in our minds. Thus, to take a simple example, from five similar objects placed in a group—five apples, five nuts, five pencils—the mind is able to abstract the *idea five* which can be applied universally to any such group of objects thus thought of. This no animal can do.

It was Aristotle who first clearly recognized, and analyzed, this unique capacity of the human mind. He expressed the truth behind it, for all time, in the famous dictum: "There is nothing in the intellect which was not first in the senses," (adding however) "but it exists in the intellect in a different mode from in the senses."

The Sensorial Materials and the Intellect

It is one of Montessori's principles always to follow nature. Wherever she finds that the child tends to act spontaneously and constructively in any particular way—and by "constructively" we mean with an activity which helps the child in his great task of creating himself—she always tries to help him along the same path.

Here we have a case in point. She was well aware—from observation—of this tendency of the child's mind to draw off from material objects their intangible essences, thus building up a store of abstract ideas. These ideas reflect the *essential* nature of the outside world; and, at the same time, raise us above the confused flux of merely sensorial impressions—that "big, booming, buzzing confusion" of which Professor James spoke.

So Montessori deliberately set about trying to help the child to make these abstractions more easily and more accurately. This is, in fact, one of the main purposes of the sensorial materials; each of which is designed to help the child's mind to focus on some particular *quality*. Thus the red rods teach the idea of length; the cubes in the pink tower, of size; whilst the bells teach the notion of musical pitch; and so on with the others. She has been able to do this by making use of the principle of the "isolation of stimulus." Thus, for example, the red rods are all the same colour, the same breadth and width, made of the same kind of wood and *vary only in length*. As a consequence the child's mind becomes psychically "blind" to any other quality except that of length in the rods. Furthermore this quality is brought still more clearly into focus through the fact that the interesting activity of putting them out in their proper order can only be done at all by reference to this quality.

Similarly the colour tablets are all made the same size, the same weight, the same shape and so forth; and differ only in the one quality of colour. This quality therefore at once becomes the centre of the child's attention, and continues to be so as long as he uses the materials in the right manner. Again, the musical bells look all exactly the same (like shining metal mushrooms on a wooden stalk) and the only way of arranging them in their proper order is by striking them with a small hammer which reveals their musical pitch, by which they can be compared with the others. Here the eye cannot help—only the ear; for it is only by using his ears to distinguish the pitch that the child is able to arrange the bells in a musical scale, or pair like with like.

We have already pointed out that the function of the sensorial materials is not to present the child with new impressions (of size, shape, colour, and so forth) but to bring order and system into the myriad impressions he has already received and is still receiving. We can now see more clearly *how* this order—this comparison and classification—is brought about. In one of her discussions on the sensorial materials Montessori —quite casually—makes one of those remarks which show how profound was her insight into psychology. "We have no other possible means," she says, "of distinguishing objects than by their attributes." We have just seen how each of the sensorial materials, rightly used, focuses the child's mind on a particular attribute and by an active manipulation leads to a comparison of these objects along the line of that particular attribute.

In this way—by working with the different sensorial materials—the child is led to study such qualities as length, breadth, height, colour, texture, weight, size, and so forth; and also such geometric forms as squares, triangles, circles, trapeziums and many others. Nor must we forget to note that it is at this stage that the directress gives the children those "naming lessons" (e.g., "This is *long*: this is *short*") which are based upon the sensorial materials. These naming lessons are only given *after* the child has occupied himself with the materials and has gained certain mental experiences through them. Coming when they do, and in the manner they do, they serve to crown the child's experience by giving it a clear and accurate expression. This expression takes the form of a logical judgment, in which subject and predicate are linked together by the directress with an almost ceremonial solemnity.

Children of Promise

All these explorations into the sphere of sensorial attributes, carried on day after day and month after month, collectively form an unusually sure and broad foundation for the child's subsequent higher mental life. It is a real inward preparation.

Those children who have been through it are different from others: "The imagery in their minds is clear. . . . All their impressions are distinct one from another — sorted out — classified, arranged, each in its own place as in a well-ordered house. Every image seen in the world without goes straight to its own place in an orderly mind. Imagine what it means to have, even from childhood, a mind with images not confused, and with ideas not confused! Just think what all this signifies as a foundation for future growth! In short, these are 'children of promise,' for they have taken the first steps in the creation of their own minds."

The preparations for life are usually indirect. Observe the caterpillar voraciously and unceasingly devouring the substance of the leaves, a thing of the earth, earthy, hardly more than a worm. Yet this lowly creature's constant preoccupation with the "base matter" of the leaves is the necessary preparation for a form of life to come—but how different! It will turn into a beautiful winged creature, palpitating with the joy of life, its colours flashing in the sun as it flits through the ethereal medium of the air, sipping nectar now from this flower and now from that.

Similarly with the mental development of the child. That incessant preoccupation which we observe in small children with material objects—all day and every day, devouring (if we may use the word) their attributes such as colour, shape, texture, sound, and so forth—all that is a preparation for a higher and more "ethereal" stage in their mental development. In other words, a full, varied, and ordered sensorial life is the best preparation for the higher life of the intellect in the years to come.

The Origin of Abstract Ideas

Many teachers of the old type, when they visit a Montessori school, are apt to complain that too much emphasis is laid on the use of materials. And they apply this criticism not only to the prominent place given to the sensorial materials in the early stages, but also—and even more so—to the great quantity of materials which are used in connection with the teaching of arithmetic, geometry, algebra, grammar, history, geography, Scripture, and other subjects. "Surely," they object, "this preponderance of material aids is bound to render the children too dependent on such outward supports? When they move on, and up—as they must soon—to higher forms, or different schools, they will then be obliged to do without them. Will they not then always be reaching out for these mental crutches, and feeling helpless without them?" Those who make such criticisms have really no idea of the true nature of the process of abstraction as it takes place in the minds of children. It would do such critics a world of good to take a course in Aristotle; for the great Stagyrite has described the whole process with inimitable insight.

What is most interesting, and most significant, is that Aristotle has described the whole process in terms of a gradual discarding of matter, until only the abstract idea is left, which is a purely *immaterial* entity. Thus, to indicate very briefly, we have the following stages: (1) We start with a material object —say a cup. Then (2) we can have a sensation of that cup, such as you get when you look at a cup; and for just as long as you look at it. Your eye, which gives you this sensation, is also a material thing (like the cup since it is a part of your body. The sensation remains as long as the cup is there, and as long as you look at it. But now take the cup away, what happens? The cup has gone, and with it the sensation of the cup—but something remains. What? We have still remaining (3) the mental image of the cup, which—like Wordsworth's

daffodils—can "flash across our inward eye." Now (according
to Aristotle and modern psychology) this mental image is
also a material thing—insofar as it is dependent for its existence in consciousness on the stimulation of certain nerve cells.
It is just for this reason (i.e., because it is dependent on a
material substratum however fine) that the mental image is
always an individual image—so shaped, so big, so coloured,
etc. A mental image then is always a particular individual
thing, even as the original cup, and the sensation of it, were
individual things.

Finally, from this image, already more mental and less
material than the original cup, or the sensation of it—from
the image of this cup (and others) there is drawn off, or
abstracted (4) the pure idea of a cup—the very essence of
cupness. This is a purely intellectual concept—the universal
idea "cup," which will cover all individual and particular cups
that are, have been, or will ever be. This general notion, this
universal idea cup, *is something entirely removed from matter*.
This is, in fact, the very reason why it will describe the essence
of *all* actual and possible cups; for it is matter which is the
principle of individuation. As soon as matter enters into the
process it becomes at once a particular cup, or a sensation of
a cup, or a mental image—but not the abstract idea "cup."

It is the presence of matter then (either in the image, or
the sensation, or in the cup itself) which makes it a particular
image, sensation, or object—just as it is the absence of matter
which confers upon the idea its universality. In the abstract
idea all the accidental attributes — such as size, shape, big
handle, small handle, etc.—have vanished, leaving only those
qualities which are essential to the existence of any cup at
all.

So much for Aristotle. It is only fair to Montessori to say
that she did not start with this, or any other particular theory
at all. She started with the child, the free child busily working
with material objects. But observing the child and his reactions
she saw this process of spontaneous abstraction taking place
before her eyes. It was the children, aged three to five, who
had been working with the colour tablets who would make
such remarks as "Oh, look, the sky is blue!" or "Your dress
is exactly the same shade of blue as the flowers in the next
room." Similarly it was the children who had been working
with the trays of geometric insets who would suddenly discover
that their environment was full of circles, rectangles, triangles,
and so on. They were able to do this precisely because some
power in their minds (the *"intellectus agens"*) had taken off

from the wooden geometric insets their "essential forms"; and were therefore able to recognize in these other similar, but different, objects the "universal idea." The same thing happens, as we have seen, with the other sensorial materials: they become "Keys to the Universe" revealing to the children a new and deeper kind of knowledge about the objects seen in the outside world.

Here, as usual, Montessori simply followed the way of nature, helping the children's minds to do more efficiently and more easily what they were tending to do in any case.

An Example from Geometry

To return once more, for a moment, to the geometric shapes. The child first meets them in the form of solid wooden insets which can be taken out and fitted into corresponding wooden sockets. Such a triangle (1) is a very material, tangible, movable object, so is the corresponding socket which acts as "control of error." Later (2) the child is given the corresponding forms printed on cards with the shape wholly filled in. Next (3) comes a series of the same forms not filled in now, but drawn with thick outlines; and finally (4) the forms are shown by a thin outline only. Nothing remains to be done now but the last stage (which of course comes a good deal later) which is to arrive at (5) the Euclidean definition of a triangle, i.e., a plane figure enclosed by three straight lines. This last one is a purely intellectual concept and can only be "seen" by the intellect and not by the eye at all.

If anyone doubts whether it is possible to see a thing intellectually and without forming a mental image of it let him consider what a myriagon is. It is a plane figure enclosed by 1,000 equal straight lines. You cannot make a clear visual image of this (as you could of a triangle or a square or a hexagon) but nevertheless you can "see" it, or "conceive" what it is, with your intelligence quite clearly and accurately.

When one looks at these various series of geometric forms (series 1, 2, 3, and 4) and compares one series with the next, one at once sees how Montessori's practice fits in with Aristotle's theory, viz., that the formation of abstract ideas is accompanied by a gradual elimination of matter. One can see how these exercises, taken in their right order, help the child's mind to pass from the consideration of one single material object (the wooden inset) towards an idea from which all that is individual and material has been eliminated—leaving only the universal concept—triangle.

The Use of Concrete Materials in Mathematics

But it is not only with the sensorial materials that Montessori assists the child's mind through individual and concrete things to the abstract idea.

It is a characteristic of her system, all along, in practically every subject. It is specially obvious in the sphere of mathematics. In her lectures on this subject Montessori often used to remark, "I present the children with 'materialized abstractions.' " By this she meant "I present the idea (it might be an operation in arithmetic like long division for instance) in a material or concrete form; and always combined with an activity." As the child (after being initiated) works for a long time with this material, day after day and it may be month after month, working at his own pace, unperturbed, unhurried, gradually there comes off from the material (almost as imperceptibly as a perfume, or exhalation)—the very essence of the operation. This sinks quietly into his mind and becomes a part of him. It is the same with almost any other arithmetical operation—whether addition, subtraction, multiplication, factors, H.C.M., L.C.M., even square- and cube-root. Always the child works these operations in the concrete, first, until the very essence of the "rule" becomes absolutely clear to him.

It is best—indeed necessary—for him that he should work in this way; for this process of abstraction is by its very nature an individual one. No one can do it for another, however much he may wish to do so. Abstraction is an inner illumination; and if the light does not come from within it does not come at all. All we can do is to help the children by giving them the best possible conditions, which include presenting them with external concrete materials. In these materials the abstract idea or mathematical operation which we wish to teach is, as it were, latent. The child works with them for a good while; and —as he does so—his mind rises eventually to a higher level. From this level his intelligence now sees the particular examples of the operation he has been doing as parts of a general law.

There *must* be, first, this ascent of the mind to a higher level; because an abstraction (or idea) can never be seen by the senses however acute; but only by a mind building on a sensory basis. The senses can only inform us of individual men, The eye can see a man, for instance, or a lot of individual men, but it cannot see "humanity." Only the intellect can do that.

Some children (and grown-ups too) are much quicker than others to make the mental leap by which the mind seizes or apprehends an abstract idea, or general law. For these a shorter period of working with the materials will suffice. Other children, on the contrary, take much longer to ascend into the plane of the abstract. These will have to remain much longer in company with the materials: they may also need to occupy themselves with a number of "parallel exercises" [1] before they really understand the general law.

Essential Factors in the Process of Abstraction

The process of abstraction—says Montessori—depends on two factors, both of which must be present. The first is that there must be absolute clarity in the concrete. And the second is that the child must have reached a certain maturity of mind. "One could have a perfectly clear knowledge of the fact and yet not be ready for the abstraction." Thus—in the same class —one child might have reached the point of abstraction, and his neighbour not.

"We arrive at abstraction," says Montessori, "by the law of least resistance and least effort." What does this mean? I can best answer this question by relating an incident that happened to me in one of my first visits to a Montessori school. A little girl of about seven was doing a "long multiplication" sum, 2,436 x 374. Usually the children do such sums on the bead frame, a sort of glorified abacus. But I noticed that the bead frame was standing idly by her on the table. "Why don't you use the frame?" I queried. "Because," she said simply and wisely, "I can do it quicker without!" This means that when a child, having done many examples with the number frame, really understands the innermost essence of the operation, he no longer needs its help. What was an assistance in the first stage may now become an obstacle—and that was why she instinctively discarded it.

The Spontaneous Ascent

Those critics mentioned above, who fear that the children's minds will remain as it were fettered to the materials, misunderstand the very object of the materials—which is, here, there, and always, not primarily to teach something, but to assist the mind's development.

A much more real danger, and alas one that is present in many schools, is that of hustling on the child's mind, and

[1] Parallel exercises are exercises which are different in form but all on the same mental level, dealing with the same essential problem, which is thus approached from different angles.

forcing it to do sums in the abstract before it has formed a clear notion of the operation in the concrete. How many people, to the end of their lives, harbour vague and embarrassingly inaccurate notions about the simplest mathematical operations (getting the right change for instance!) simply because, long ago in their earliest arithmetic lessons, they were dragged incontinently from one exercise to another, before they had clearly understood what it was all about. To their dismay they felt themselves sinking, helplessly and hopelessly, ever more deeply into the ignominious quicksands of ignorance and mortification. Most emphatically the mind of the child who is working with the concrete materials is not like a tethered balloon (as these critics say) unable to rise from the ground. On the contrary, Montessori compares it to an aeroplane which, *in order to rise into the air by itself*, needs first to run for a while along the ground. But, when the right moment comes, the aeroplane will "take off" from the solid ground and rise into the more abstract medium of the air, where it will operate more rapidly and more freely. Exactly so, the child's mind—*in order to rise into the abstract*—needs first to move in contact with the solid and concrete. But when the right moment comes (which is different for each child) it will "take off" from the materials; and will then of its own accord rise into the realm of the abstract, where it will operate more easily, more efficiently. And more quickly too—quicker even than the fastest aeroplane; for it works, quite literally, with the speed of thought.

But the child's mind will not remain perpetually on these high and abstract levels. As the aeroplane has to come down to solid earth, again and again, to refuel and prepare for fresh flights, so too the mind will often come down to earth (to the didactic materials) for fresh experiences in the concrete, in order to enable it to take off again in fresh flights into the abstract.

Thus there is always going on a certain interdependence between the purely intellectual and the purely material. This is true of all of us, all our lives, but it is especially true of children who are still developing; i.e., constructing their personalities by a sort of mental commerce with the outside world. We shall see this more clearly as we come to deal with Montessori's doctrine of the "Centre and the Periphery"—and the "Point of Contact." [8]

[8] Chapter XIV.

We are so accustomed to the fact of growth that famil-
iarity has blinded our eyes to the wonder of it. It seems to us
quite the natural and proper thing that a kitten should grow
up into a cat, a puppy into a dog, and a big-headed baby with
his fascinating gibberish into a sedate and articulate adult. But
supposing inanimate things suddenly took it into their heads
to grow—supposing, for instance, that our egg spoons began
to develop, passing through the successive stages of tea, and
dessert spoons, to finish up as tablespoons. Or supposing—
blessed thought for mothers!—that a child's garments began
to grow with him, in proportion to his own growth, like a cat's
fur or an oyster's shell—then indeed we might begin to "sit up
and take notice," and humble ourselves before the almost incredible mystery of growth.

In this section of the book we are specially concerned with
the problem of development, and attempt to probe a little into
some of its secrets; but in the last analysis growth must always
remain an insoluble mystery, like life itself, of which it is a
unique expression.

But even if we are in the presence of a mystery it does not
mean that we can know *nothing* about it. Montessori holds
that the processes of growth are governed by certain invisible
forces to which she gives the name "inner directives," a term
which of course does not explain the mystery but helps us to
define it.

General Characteristics of Growth—Mental and Physical

Without attempting to dogmatize on the ultimate nature of these "inner directives," we can say that there are certain general characteristics of growth which are universally
recognized:

(1) Every organism develops according to a preordained
pattern.

(2) This development takes place at the expense of matter

169

taken in from the environment by a process of selective activity in the organism itself.

(3) This external matter, so taken in, is assimilated into the organism by another active process—digestion—in such a way that it is made one with it, in the "unity of a living organism."

Further, it is generally conceded that on a different and higher plane—i.e., in the course of mental development—analogous characteristics are to be found. The mind, too, like the body, grows by "taking in" impressions from without. And finally, in order that the process of mental growth should be complete, the knowledge so taken in from without must be digested or assimilated.

Two Streams of Energy

In the growing child there are, according to Montessori, two streams of energy whose balanced interplay is of the utmost importance. One is the physical energy of the body—especially the muscular energy expended in *voluntary* movement; and the other is the mental energy of intelligence and will—which in the last analysis is an immaterial spiritual force. Actually of course these two streams of energy never operate in complete separation. Indeed if anything should stand out clearly in Montessori's view of the child it is just this—that these two aspects of the psyche, mind and body, *should never be thought of as separate.*

If during the child's development these two streams of energy (which working in unison make the complete man) should—instead of being brought more intimately together—become divorced or partially divorced from each other, we should expect to find deviations from the normal. And this—according to Montessori—is exactly what we do find.

Physical and Mental Deviations from Normal Compared

Everyone knows more or less what is meant by a deviation from the normal when it is a question of physical growth—the growth of the body—for everyone has seen such malformations as the harelip, the clubfoot or the hunchback. Physical deviations can generally be traced to some adverse factor in the environment or to some inherited weakness. In any case what happens is that constructive energies of growth have been diverted from their true course, and so, as a consequence, the "pattern of the species" has not been produced properly.

Now if you believe—as Montessori does—that *mental* growth is also determined by inner directives towards the pattern of the species, then similar disasters could take place on the mental plane, resulting there, in just the same way, in deviations from the normal. But here we come across an important difference. Deviations from physical normality are as a rule easy to recognize because they generally result in some visible malformation. In fact we all carry round with us a kind of mental picture of physical normality; and this is the reason why we are struck at once with any marked deviation from it. Deviations from *mental* normality, however, do not advertise their presence so clearly and unmistakably. Their presence can only be inferred by some form of behavior which differs from the normal. But—and this is the crucial point—we do not all carry round with us a clear and uniform picture of mental normality, as we do of physical.

In fact Montessori quite seriously puts this question: Do we really know the characteristics of mental normality, not only of the adult but at each stage of human development? Her answer is rather surprising, for it is in the negative. When the gravedigger was asked why young Hamlet (who was "mad") had been sent to England, his reply was, "It will not be seen in him there; there the men are as mad as he." A race of abnormal people would never have the materials with which to build a true picture of mental normality.

We shall return to this somewhat disquieting thought later on, and endeavour to substantiate Montessori's challenging point of view. In the meantime let us return to the interaction of those two streams of energy—mental and physical—which plays such an important part in the child's development.

Factors Which May Cause Deviations in the Child's Development

The main factors in the child's daily life which may lead towards an unnatural separation of these two streams of energy are: (1) When the child has the will to act but his movements are inhibited; and (2) When the will of the adult is unnecessarily substituted for that of the child. To these factors we may add a third. It often happens that, when children are abandoned to their own devices, they are unable to find the path which brings together these two elements (the psychic and the physical). How often one may hear an impatient adult exclaim, "Oh, be quiet, can't you! Why don't you get something sensible to *do*?"; and the pathetic reply comes, "I don't know *what* to do," or "I haven't *got* anything to do." As Montessori puts it: "The child feels a sense of *mal-essere* (ill-being), conscious of an impulse driving him he knows not where, which must ease itself he knows not how."

Forms of Deviation in Childhood

The forms of deviation in childhood are legion. In fact it is much easier to describe the characteristics of normality than to enumerate all the various possible forms of deviation, just as "it is much easier to describe a jug than all the various bits and pieces into which it breaks on falling."

We may, however, mention two main groups of deviations. In the first we have a series of traits which are generally recognized as abnormal by most writers on child psychology. These include lying, timidity, quarrelsomeness, gluttony, fears of various kinds, stammering, disorderly and destructive movements, continued disobedience, and so on.

Besides these well-known and unpleasing traits Montessori also regards as deviations certain ways of behaving which most people would regard as normal. Amongst these we may mention possessiveness. Another is the excessive development of make-belief—to an extent which causes children to live in a fantastic world of their own—those children, for instance, who are perpetually talking to or about imaginary companions. Then again we have the child who is constantly asking questions without (like Pilate) waiting for the answers; or the child who shows such an extreme attachment to another person that he can hardly exist without him. It may surprise some readers to learn that Montessori also includes in her list of deviations that marked instability of attention which most psychologists regard as an essential feature of childhood.

It is not intended to discuss here the various forms of deviations. Those who wish to study the matter further are recommended to read Montessori's own analysis in her *Secret of Childhood* (pp. 185-225), where, besides those mentioned above, she discusses such topics as "psychic fugues," the power craving, the inferiority complex and various psychic barriers. What concerns us at present is not so much the different forms of deviation as their cure—i.e., the return to normality and how it can be effected.

Normalization Through Work

There is one sovereign cure for all these forms of deviation—one only—says Montessori, and that is *normalization through work*. If we regard the child's work as being what was described in Chapter VIII this must be so logically; for there we spoke of it as being the construction of his own personality.

But it was not as a conclusion drawn from a syllogism that Montessori was led to this point of view. It was in fact just the other way round. She did not start with any theory at all. She started with the children—the free children in the Prepared Environment—and they demonstrated it to her: first in Italy, then in Spain, then in America, and after that in every part of the globe.

The process of normalization is always the same. Into the ordered, tranquil, and harmonious atmosphere of the Montessori class enters the deviated child. It does not matter what his particular form of deviation may be. In some way or other, however, he is a disordered being—that is the essence of it; he is out of harmony; his movements undisciplined, his mind without focus. Very often he is a veritable thorn in the flesh to the directress; a trouble to himself, and a nuisance to his neighbours. He will probably spend a good part of his time pottering around the room trying now this occupation and now that; but he does "everything by fits and starts and nothing long." If he is not watched he may disturb the others, even to the extent of tormenting them. Very likely, too, he is extremely disobedient, and wholly lacking in self-discipline. In short, the elements of his personality are in conflict within himself, as he himself is in conflict with his social environment.

This state of things may last a short or a long time; but short or long it will be terminated in the same way. If the directress has done her duty properly, if she has treated him with a mixture of firmness and respect, if she has been tireless in presenting him with occupations (however indifferent he may seem), if she has encouraged him without coercion, and left him free to wander round at will—provided he disturbs no one—and if she has let him choose his occupations (within the limits described in Chapter XVII), then one day will come the great event. One day—Heaven knows why—he will choose some occupation (very likely one he has trifled with many times before) and settle down seriously to work at it *with the first spontaneous spell of concentration that he has ever shown.*

This is the beginning of his salvation. Though *he* knows it

not, but his directress does, he is now at the beginning of a
new phase of life, almost a new life. His feet are now on the
path which leads to normality.

Concentration Is the Key

Concentration is the key that opens up to the child the
latent treasures within him. We need not repeat here what we
have said elsewhere with regard to the nature of this work:
suffice it to point out that through it those two separated
streams of energy—physical and mental—have been brought
together again. The "point of contact" having been established
at the "periphery," down in the "centre" of the child's personality a mysterious but beneficent change is taking place.
As the scattered elements of his personality come together,
order begins to take the place of disorder, and the work of self-
construction, which had been interrupted, is now taken up
again, as nature had intended all along.

Montessori often compares this inner change which takes
place in the child's whole aspect and behaviour to that re-
orientation of the elements of personality which accompanies
religious conversion—a change which also sometimes takes
place quite suddenly.

It does not matter with what deviation a child may start. A
dozen children may start with a dozen different forms of deviation (like a dozen pieces of the broken jug, mentioned above).
But as each child—individually and in his own time and place
—achieves this experience of spontaneous concentration, until
it has become a habit, each and all will eventually arrive at the
same place, i.e., at normality; so that—to revert to our metaphor—the whole jug will eventually be mirrored in each of
them.

It was thus, through experience, that Montessori discovered
—one might say stumbled upon—the characteristics of the
normal child. She was not looking for them; she was not expecting them; she was not even thinking about them. It was
a genuine and unforeseen revelation. But it did not come only
once, and with one set of children (as with Pestalozzi, who
saw—as in a vision—these same characteristics, but they vanished again.) These normalized children—"the new children"
as they were often called—have appeared again and again in
almost every country in the world for a whole generation.
Race, colour, climate, religion, civilization, all these made no
difference. Everywhere, as soon as hindrances to development
were removed, the same characteristics appeared as if by

magic. And, what is of the greatest practical importance, they are being revealed still whenever and wherever the right circumstances prevail, as anyone can verify for himself if he takes the trouble to do so.

The Characteristics of the Normalized Child

"But what are these wonderful characteristics of normality that you keep talking about?"—we can almost hear the impatient reader exclaim! Most of them have already been mentioned, at least by implication, in previous chapters of this book, especially in Chapter II. But it will be well to summarize them again here. They include:

A Love of Order, which extends down to the most minute particulars; and expresses itself in an intense "love of the environment," and a corresponding desire to preserve the order in it. It is well to remember that the intellect is the principle of order; and that the child seeks and finds order around it— not only in the general aspect of the room, but also in the various occupations which are to be found within it. (See Chapter XVI.) The order which is within the child goes out to meet and illuminate the order without.

Love of Work. Work in this sense means any activity which involves the child's whole personality, and has as its unconscious aim the construction of personality. It is definitely a form of self-expression, and brings the child a corresponding joy in the performance of it. But it is *work* and not play (which satisfies only a part of one's nature). "I have to defend myself," says Montessori, "against those who say that my method is a play-method."

Profound Spontaneous Concentration. This concentration, which is so complete that it often "isolates the child from his environment," is a biological phenomenon. We might call it the attention of life, i.e., of the species, acting through the individual. Or if we put it in another way, we can say that it is a phenomenon of growth. Or again we may compare it to the selective attention, to certain objects in the environment, seen in the instinctive reactions of animals. This is however something on a different and higher plane, for it is the child's intelligence which is concentrating here; constructing itself through commerce with the outside world. Which brings us naturally to the next characteristic, which is

Attachment to Reality. The mind constructs itself through contact with reality, not with the projections of make-believe.[1] The foundation of all is the external world, as taken in first through the senses and movement, and, later, by the reason and imagination. The information so received is worked upon, assimilated and raised to the order of intelligence. So, to function properly and to grow, the intellect must be subject to the discipline of external reality.

Love of Silence and of Working Alone (*"The little hermit"*). This does not mean that the child likes to work in solitude; but rather in that psychological isolation mentioned above which is the result of concentration. At other times—when the aim of the work is more conscious and external—the children frequently work together in spontaneously formed groups ("Society by cohesion").[2]

Sublimation of the Possessive Instinct. The attitude of normalized children to their prepared environment and to all the engaging occupations contained in it, though one of intense love, is not possessive in its nature. It is true that in the first flush of their enthusiasm children may wish to take the materials home with them; but even in these cases, possession as such is not their aim; but only use. I have heard Dr. Montessori remark that members of religious orders and these normalized children might adopt the same motto with regard to property, viz., *Usare sed non possedere"* ("To use and not to possess").

The reason why the normalized child has shed this defect of always wanting to possess things is because he has sublimated his interest in them.

In normalized children the active possibility of interesting themselves in any object leads them to a stage where it *is no longer the object but the knowledge of it which fixes the attention.* So we can say that this possessiveness, because of an intellectual interest, is raised to a superior level. Instead of the instinct of possession we now see on this higher level three things: to know, to love, and to serve. Possession is transformed into love; and when this has come about there is not only the desire to conserve the object but also to serve it. The same children who once tore plants out of the garden, now watch for the plant's growth, count its leaves and measure its sides. It is no longer *my* plant; it is *the* plant..

[1] See Chapter XX.
[2] See *The Absorbent Mind*, by Montessori.

Power to Act From Real Choice and Not From Curiosity.
From what has just been said it will be seen that these
children are now motivated in their actions by real choice and
no longer by mere curiosity.

Obedience. These normalized children are remarkably obedient. *Pari passu* with the process of normalization through work
(indeed it is really a part of the same experience) they pass
through a sort of "novitiate" in this virtue. This involves
progressive degrees of obedience—the last being that in which
they are not only obedient, but *will* to be obedient. To carry
out the command of another has now become a form of self-
expression, just because it involves the joyful exercise of a
newly developed faculty—the will.

This *willing* docility has nothing in common with the blind
obedience of suggestion, nor the ineluctable submission of
the weaker to the stronger will. This is proved by the fact
that it goes hand in hand with a high degree of

Independence and Initiative. The whole aim of the Montessori
system can be summed up as the "valorization of personality"
at each stage. This involves, amongst other things, that the
child should acquire as much independence as is possible for
him to acquire at each stage of development. Or to put it
the other way round, the directress must always seek the limit
of her intervention by giving "the minimum dose"; always acting in accordance with the famous slogan, "Every useless aid
arrests development."

In a class of normalized children *mutual aid naturally takes
the place of competition.* Far from trying to outdo each other,
or displaying any jealousy, these children are always helping
one another. The older and more advanced show a keen interest in the progress of the younger and more backward;
and it is often quite touching to observe the way in which
the former regard the triumphs of the latter with as much
joy as if they had been their own achievements.

Another important point to remember is that Montessori
will have none of that horizontal grading of children according
to age and attainment, or intelligence, which is so common
today. She insists on having, if possible, several age groups
together—for this very reason, viz., that mutual helpfulness
can have full play.

Spontaneous Self-Discipline. This is one of the features that
usually astonishes visitors most when they see a Montessori
school for the first time. This discipline is so complete that

the absence of the directress for quite long periods of time does not affect it. This discipline is one of the fruits of liberty. In fact we might say that such discipline and liberty cannot really be separated: they are like the opposite sides of the same coin.

Joy. The crowning characteristic of a group of normalized children is joy. It pervades the little community like a perfume; and is as hard to describe as it is easy to perceive. This joy which shines in the children's faces, and indeed in their whole demeanour is something more than pleasure or the happiness of being entertained. Like the concentration referred to above it is a deep and mysterious emotion. It is in fact the joy that nature always grants as the accompaniment to the right use of our faculties. It is the joy which comes with acting in obedience to the laws of our nature.

In September 1955, at the opening of the new session of the Montessori Training Course at the Montessori Centre, 22 rue Eugene Flachat, Paris, 18, an address was given by the famous French writer, Gabriel Marcel. In the course of his speech he spoke of "the astonishment which I felt when, for the first time, I visited a small Montessori school at Sévres. What struck me most—it is not too much to say, what caused me a profound emotion—was to see with my own eyes in this school, children not only working with perfect calm, but children who were in the grip of a mysterious happiness. A mysterious happiness—I repeat the words—for I would have them penetrate your souls like a melody. What was it, this happiness? An 'ensemble' of favourable conditions had been realized in conformity with Maria Montessori's ideas, which permitted these children to give themselves without reserve to the miraculous act which we call knowledge." [8]

Normalization the First Step in Education

If one listens to experienced Montessori directresses discussing their pupils together, especially those who have only recently come to school, one does not usually hear them saying, "How is Tommy getting on with his sums?," or "Has Francis begun to read?" but "Is he normalized yet?" For until this has happened his real education has not begun; indeed cannot begin. "Our schools," says Montessori, "may be compared in the first place to sanatoria; for the first thing that happens in them is that the children are restored to mental health."

[8]Bulletin No. 14, October 1955, Association Montessori for France.

Montessori Essentially a Discoverer

If what we have written in this chapter is true—and the facts confirm it—then Montessori's chief claim to our gratitude lies not so much in the fact that she has established a new educational method, as that she has been the means of revealing to us the true characteristics of the normal child —that, "given the right conditions, children change their character, almost their nature, revealing profound qualities in the infant soul which had hitherto remained unknown."

The Discovery Confused With the Method

A question which might legitimately be raised is this: though Montessori's work has been known now for some thirty years, how is it that so few people seem aware of this epoch-making discovery? Montessori herself accounts for it as follows:

It is true that these little children *have* demonstrated to us the interior laws of the formation of man, laws which have given rise to a method of education which has spread all over the earth. Unfortunately the stupendous importance of this revelation has become overlaid and confused by a disproportionate emphasis on the new method which came out of it. For it was not the method which produced the marvellous manifestations, so much as the manifestations which produced the method—or, more accurately, sketched out its general outlines.

A Movement With a Halo

From its very beginning, as we have seen, the Montessori movement seemed to impress many of those who came in contact with it as being something much more than a new method of education. It came enveloped with an unexpected beauty which was the more surprising considering the place of its origin. This is the reason why it inspired, and still inspires, a devoted enthusiasm which is hard to explain if there is nothing more in it than a new method of teaching. From what we have considered above we are now in a better position to understand this enthusiasm. There *is* something wonderful and mysterious about the Montessori movement; but the mystery is not in Dr. Montessori or her followers; it is in the child, that luminous and beautiful creature who has given us these touching and unexpected revelations. It seems almost as though Montessori's discoveries have added a new lustre to the human race. We are better than we thought we were—at least our children are—and if our children, then why not eventually the adolescents, and finally the adults?

A Hope for the Future

To those who see the whole matter in this light—and they are to be found in every civilized country—these normalized children have indeed inspired a new hope for the future of humanity; and the significance of their revelation can be expressed in the following terms.[4] As modern physical science has taught us how to liberate physical energies hitherto unsuspected (which, alas! are being used for the *de*struction of human beings) so Montessori has shown us how to liberate *psychic* energies hitherto unknown, which, *Deo Gratias,* make for *con*struction and the building up of a better and more harmonious type of humanity.

Montessori indeed regards these normalized children not only as a hope but as a promise—almost, one might say, a pledge of better things to come.

The Search for Normality

Here again we are confronted with a similar question to that which we discussed some pages back. Are we acquainted with the real characteristics of the schoolboy, and the adolescent, i.e., their true normality? Or have they, too, been hidden from us under a mask of deviations so universal that their revelation would fill us with the same wonder and surprise as they have already done in the first stage?

The answer to these questions lies in the future. It will render itself up to those who put as their first aim in education the establishment of the "new relationship"[5] at each of these succeeding stages. This would involve, as we shall see, the setting up of the right kind of prepared environments, suited to the needs of each stage, together with the granting of the right kind of liberty to make the best use of them.

"A Utopian dream!" you exclaim. "Wishful thinking!" But is it? The whole argument of this book, *which can be verified,* goes to prove that it is not simply a dream. The first stage of this emancipation is already an established fact, undeniable as the Law of Gravitation or Mendel's Law. These normalized

[4]Cf. p. 82.
[5]See Part IV, Chapters XV–XVIII.

—these "new children" or whatever you may like to call them —cannot be argued away. They can be produced as certainly as you can produce good apples by preparing the right environmental conditions and removing obstacles to growth.

It will be seen from all this how truly prophetic was the remark made to Dr. Montessori as far back as 1907 by Queen Margherita of Italy when she said, "I prophesy that a new philosophy of life will arise from what we are learning from these little children"; or that other comment by the head of a religious order that "this is a discovery which is more important than that of Marconi." It was realized even then, by the discerning, that eventually this movement would have repercussions outside the walls of the schoolroom, and tend towards a general social amelioration.

Note on the "New Children" and the Doctrine of Original Sin

Compared with their deviated prototypes normalized children are "good" children. They have sloughed off their unpleasant and "bad" characteristics, such as lying, tantrums, disobedience, quarrelsomeness, possessiveness—and so forth— as the snake discards its old skin. Indeed so obvious is the change from "bad" to "good" that many persons have argued that Montessori's work, in revealing to us the true nature of the child, has disproved the doctrine of Original Sin and its effects. This is not so, of course. The problem, speaking theologically, is really quite simple and easily cleared up.

To do her justice Montessori did not worry herself a scrap about such questions. She was so anxious to help the children that she had not time to spend on theological controversy. Nevertheless she understood the point at issue—no one better —as the following quotation shows:

When we look at the stars which shine in the firmament, so faithful in following their courses, so mysterious in their manner of keeping to them, we do not exclaim, "How good the stars are!" We say the stars obey the laws which govern the universe; we exclaim how marvellous is the order of creation. In the conduct of our children there is made manifest a form of order in nature.

Order does not necessarily imply goodness. It neither demonstrates that "man is born good" or that "he is born evil." It only demonstrates that nature, in the process of constructing man, passes through an established order. Order is not goodness; but perhaps it is the indispensable road to arrive at it.

The order which is revealed in these children comes from mysterious, hidden "internal directives," which can only reveal themselves through liberty; which permits them to operate.

Before arriving at real goodness (i.e., in the supernatural sense) it is necessary first "to enter into the order of the laws of nature." Afterwards from this plane as a basis, it is possible to elevate oneself and ascend into a supernatural order in which the cooperation of conscience is necessary.

Similarly with regard to "badness," it is also necessary to distinguish *dis*order, in the order of nature, from the deliberate descent into morally inferior planes. To be "disorderly" with respect to the natural laws which direct the normal development of children is not necessarily to be "bad." In fact the English use different terms for the "badness" of children and of adults; they call the first "naughtiness" and the second "evil" or "badness."

Those who believe in original sin, as well as those who do not, should equally rejoice in the manifestation of this unexpected goodness in human nature. The latter, because they recognize no other kind of goodness than that which is inherent in human nature as such; the former because—as every theologian knows—the fullest development of the natural virtues is the best preparation for the development of the supernatural ones, since Grace does not destroy nature but elevates it.

PART THREE

The Significance
of Movement in Education

CHAPTER XI   A VISIT TO LILLIPUT OR AN HOUR
IN A MONTESSORI SCHOOL[1]

If anyone imagines that the age of wonders has passed away let him visit a well-run Montessori school, and he will find plenty to marvel at still.

Our first impression as we enter the building is that we have passed into a different kind of world—a world of new dimensions and new values, where the things that belong to our adult civilization have been left behind. We are dealing here, not simply with rooms for children in an ordinary kind of building, but with a veritable *Casa dei Bambini*, i.e., children's house—rooms, passages, cloakrooms, stairways, all the furniture and appurtenances, the house itself and garden have all been designed to accommodate a Lilliputian order of beings. (I once visited a Montessori school where the doors were so low that the adult had to stoop in order to enter—a circumstance not without its symbolical significance!)

From the garden with its small paths, miniature lake and bridges—in one school in California there was a little Wendy House up in a tree—we pass into a sort of entrance lounge ornamented with palms and flowers. Beside the walls there are tiny armchairs and sofas. On one of the latter two small boys are sitting having a quiet conversation—Heaven knows what about—whilst around a table in the middle of the entrance hall three tiny mites are gazing at the strange creatures in an aquarium.

Through an open door we catch sight of another small inhabitant washing her hands at a row of washbasins so low that a collie dog could easily drink out of them. Another child —aged four—is brushing her hair very slowly and deliberately in front of a large mirror, placed so low that she can see the

[1]Portions of this chapter which were written a good many years ago are now applicable to many primary and nursery schools, i.e., insofar as they describe the general appearance of the rooms, their small furniture, low cupboards, and so forth. But the resemblance is superficial. The Montessori school still stands apart in the quality, quantity, variety and purpose of its didactic materials; and in the kind of life—social and intellectual—which is carried on within it.

whole of her tiny self in it from head to foot. Now she has finished brushing her own hair, and turns her attention to a still younger child whose hair she begins to brush with the same air of unhurried serenity.

As we pass through the hall into one of the schoolrooms this impression—that we are in a Lilliputian world—becomes more vivid. We see some thirty to forty children, aged four to seven, scattered over a large room, all doing different things. Most are working at little tables, but some are on rugs spread out on the floor. It is not in the least like a school such as we knew it in our younger days (at least in *my* young days). Gone are the rows of desks with benches; gone is the teacher's high desk and stool; and—most remarkable of all—it seems at first glance as if the teacher herself has vanished too. We do discover her, eventually, down on her knees at the far end of the room, explaining something to a couple of children who are working with number materials spread out on a rug. The rest of the children in the room (except for two or three who are waiting to speak to her) are all carrying on their own business without taking any notice of the directress whatever. It all fits in with our general impression. This is obviously a kind of school in which the adult has retired into the background, whilst the children are correspondingly more active; one might almost say have taken over the initiative. Even the teacher's blackboard has been transmuted into a long low blackboard built into the wall, at which children are writing, not the teacher.

Gone too—completely—is the stillness of the old-fashioned school (so often a stillness of suppression), and with it that immobility which was the immediate cause of it. Instead we are ware of a bustle of activity. In fact the scene before us resembles more the busy stir that goes on in bank or store than in a schoolroom as we knew it. We see people coming and going, opening and shutting drawers, moving objects here and there, conferring together in low tones, working singly or in groups—in fact anything except all sitting together listening to one person talking.

The most astonishing part about it all is that these persons who are doing all this are not grown-ups at all, but children —and quite small children at that, the eldest being not more than seven or eight. Yet what absorption in their tasks, what seriousness in their expression, what quiet purposefulness in their manner, what precision of movement, and what astonishing self-discipline! They remind us of "little men and women"; yet at the same time they have all the spontaneous charm of childhood.

There are some twenty or so gaily painted little tables with chairs to match, dotted around the room as in a restaurant. The greater part of the children are working individually, but some are in little groups of two or three, or even more. All round the room are long, low brightly coloured cupboards. These house an immense variety of fascinating occupations, the teaching materials, many of which are brightly coloured also. Everywhere there is colour—even the dainty little dusters hanging in a row are all of different shades, as are the children's smocks. On most of the tables are placed vases of flowers. All these things together—as the sun comes shining in through the large and low windows—make a most beautiful and attractive picture.

At one end of the room a wall comes out from the centre, forming a partition, dividing into two alcoves. In one of these is a sink (very low, of course) with hot and cold taps for washing up and other domestic operations. In the same alcove are dustpans, brushes, carpet sweepers, shoe brushes, buckets, scrubbing brushes, etc.—in short, almost every sort of domestic appliance—but all on a miniature scale. The corresponding alcove on the other side is fitted up as a little reading room. Here is a small divan with cushions, and some small armchairs. It forms a quiet recess where children can retire with a book to read as a change from working at their little tables. It contains a small library of carefully chosen books.

We cannot help being impressed with the wealth of detail in the environment, and the care with which everything has been prepared. Whoever made this house, and prepared this environment, never said "Oh, it is only for children—anything will do." Rather their motto was "It is for the children—so we must have the very best of everything." The visitor is astonished at the lavish care and expenditure, the long and patient scientific research which has gone into the creation of this "new world" for the "new children." He is intrigued by the many occupations displayed in the cupboards—by their novelty, variety, ingenuity and even strangeness. Yet nothing is more fascinating, more intriguing than the tiny inhabitants themselves.

Can these be ordinary children? we wonder. Whoever saw forty children so young all in one room together, all free to walk about and talk and choose their occupations, and yet no quarrelling, no tantrums, no shouting, but everything running smoothly and in harmony "as in the Golden Age?"

Activity is the keynote of the life that is going on in this "new world." All the children (except a few who are reading in the "library") are busy doing something with their hands as well as their brains. Knowledge is finding its way into those little heads *via* hands, eyes, ears, and feet. This is obviously a school where "children learn by doing."

"But what *are* they doing?" the reader may ask. A moment's reflection will show the impossibility of giving an adequate reply to this question. Here are some forty children, scattered in different parts of the room, and nearly all of them doing different things. One would need as many eyes as the fabled Argus merely to observe what they are all doing at any given moment, let alone describe it. Even the teacher does not know. But this does not worry her. She is quite content if she knows that they *are* working; for then she knows that they are teaching themselves (through the materials) better than she herself could do.

Even if one did try to describe what they are all doing—before one had finished—or scarcely begun—many of the children would be doing something else. For—when a child has worked himself out at one thing—he goes to the cupboard, puts back the material with which he has been working, and chooses another occupation—all by himself. So all we can do, therefore, is to single out a few children, here and there, and describe what they are doing, taking as it were cross-sections of some of these little lives, much in the same way as the B.B.C. commentator does in *In Town Tonight*.

Let us begin with that chubby little fellow that has just passed by us, and watch what he does. With an air of set purpose he threads his way in and out amongst the little tables to the far end of the room. There on the top of a cupboard he finds a number of coloured rugs, each neatly rolled up. Taking one of these he comes back, and, finding an open space between three tables, spreads it out on the floor. All this is preparation—but for what? No one knows but himself—not even the teacher. We must "wait and see." Now, with the same air of set purpose, he goes off to another part of the room to another cupboard. From this he returns laden with a large flat cardboard box like a tray divided into many partitions. In each of these are cut out wooden script letters, consonants in red, vowels in blue. Placing the box on the floor beside his rug he sets to work with great fervour composing words. He takes his cue as to what words to make from little pictures which he first places, one under the other, down the side of the rug—hat, rug, log, sofa, pond, desk, etc.—all phonetic words. (Spelling vagaries are tackled later in a different way.)

Let us leave the young compositor at this job and turn to someone else. A little girl of six sits at a table just in front of us. She is serenely absorbed in a somewhat mystifying occupation which involves a kind of cycle or rhythm of small activities. First she counts out some red beads from a small box; then she puts them down in a row on a square piece of cardboard with little pits in it; then she moves along a little red disc at the top; after which comes some more counting, and finally she writes something on a piece of paper. This done she repeats the whole process again; and yet again. It appears to be a quiet restful sort of occupation, and the doing of it gives her great satisfaction. Remembering your own childhood, you would hardly guess what she is doing—she is teaching herself the multiplication tables. In point of fact she is actually engaged in a mathematical research, the aim of which is to discover for herself, quite unaided, the seven-times table. She does this first in the concrete—i.e., experimentally on the board, and then records the results of her research on a slip of paper—like this:

$$1 \times 7 = 7$$
$$2 \times 7 = 14$$
$$3 \times 7 = 21$$

We watch (unnoticed) until she has completed her seven-times table—her last recording being $12 \times 7 = 84$.

What will she do now? Quietly she gets up and goes, paper in hand, to find the directress and waits patiently for a few minutes till she is disengaged, and then shows the result of her work. The teacher looks it over, nods her head, and returns it with an approving smile; and back comes our young mathematician towards her table. *Now* what is she going to do? She doesn't seem quite sure of herself, and stands a moment reflecting. Then with the air of one who had made up her mind, she sets off once more to the cupboards, and returns with another prepared slip of paper of the same kind. On the top of it is written "Eight Times Table," and under it—

$$1 \times 8 = \ldots\ldots$$
$$2 \times 8 = \ldots\ldots$$
$$3 \times 8 = \ldots\ldots$$
$$\text{etc.}$$

So now she settles down once more, and in the same manner begins to work out the "Eight Times Table," filling in the blanks on her slip with multiples of eight. Notice it was not the teacher who told her to do the next table: *she* confined herself to correcting what was shown her; the decision was left absolutely to the child. Will she go on to the nine-times after the eight? Who knows? No one as yet. We will leave her, then, to work her way through the eight-times table and turn our attention elsewhere.

Here is a little fellow—he can't be more than four and a half—returning from one of the cupboards (those precious storehouses), carrying a wooden box about four inches wide by ten inches long. Arriving at his table he puts the box down, and draws himself up to the table with the air of a man about to enjoy a good meal. (And so he is, but for his mind not his tummy!)

As soon as he removes the lid we see a bright display of colours: red, blue, green, purple, mauve, etc. These are the colour tablets and very attractive they look when he has spread them all out. There are two of each kind—two reds, two blues, and so on—but they are in no particular order. Now he picks up one tablet—the red—and proceeds to search amongst the others on the table for its fellow. Having found it he places the two reds carefully together, side by side. And so on with the others, choosing one at random and then finding its fellow, thus matching the two reds, two blues, two greens, etc., until there are eleven pairs. Before he began this sorting the colours were all mixed together—higgledy-piggledy; but by the time he has finished they are all in twos—like the animals going into the ark.

After completing this exercise he carefully places all the tablets back in the box. Then away he goes to the cupboard, and exchanges it for another and larger box of colours. In this there are no less than sixty-three colour tablets, all different—seven shades of blue, seven of green, and so on. Here the exercise consists not in pairing the colours, but in grading each set according to their shades—thus all the reds together, from the darkest to the lightest; all the greens ditto, and so forth.

This work appears to be somewhat beyond the capacity of our young friend whose colour sense is not yet sufficiently developed, and he gets many of the colours muddled up. The quick eye of the directress observes this as she passes; and as a consequence a few moments later an older child—a girl of six—appears out of the blue. Sitting down beside the little boy she helps him to sort them, and put them back properly in the box. I notice she carries the colour tablets *by the wooden edges* without touching the coloured part, and insists on the boy doing the same. This is a wise rule, emanating from the teacher, which prevents the colours from getting soiled by little fingers not always too clean.

As our young friend goes back to the cupboard to return the colour box, he nearly runs into a little girl who is carrying a bucket of water. Let us follow her and see what she is going to do. She places the bucket down by an empty table; then goes off to fetch a small scrubbing brush, a soap dish with soap, and a cloth. Having rolled up her sleeves she sets to work to scrub some ink stains off one corner of the table. Not content with removing these she scrubs the whole surface, and then, if you please, the legs. This done she wipes the table with a damp cloth, then a dry one; and now looks eagerly round for further fields to conquer. At the far end of the room she sees another table unoccupied; so she carries her washing paraphernalia thither and sets about scrubbing that. Actually this particular table is quite clean, and has been scrubbed already once that morning: but no matter: some mysterious instinct seems to make scrubbing for the time being the sole aim of life—so ascrubbing she will go. So the second table is duly finished. Just then, at an adjacent table, a boy gets up and goes away leaving it unoccupied. At once Mary swoops down upon it. She is in the full tide of her operations (something more than a metaphor!) when the boy returns carrying a quaint-looking box with small pigeonholes in it, each filled with different coloured cards. Astonishment, not to say disapproval, is written all over his face as he sees the intruder in possession. Even so would an author feel, and look, if on coming back to his sanctum he found the charwoman in possession. An animated conversation ensues. It is too far off for us to hear the words, but clearly the owner of the table is registering protest. The little girl looks apologetic and puzzled. It is no good her going away and leaving him his table all wet. A third person comes on the scene; a boy about seven years old. The case is put before him. He sees the matter with a more detached mind: and, like a little Solomon, settles it by pointing to another table which is empty—it is in fact the table just washed by the little girl. They go over and inspect it, feel its surface. It is still a bit damp here and there; so the little girl runs with great willingness and gets a dry cloth and gives it a rub over. Then the boy gets his box, with the pigeonholes in it, takes it to the new table, and settles down to work. Mary returns to her half-scrubbed table; the little arbitrator goes to his work; and all is well.

How significant is this incident, if we only realized it! What a training in social adjustment! Here we see an important social problem solved by these "little people" *independently of an adult*. Similar incidents are happening all the time in that little society, incidents that give rise to situations which require give and take. In the old-fashioned school, where the children are all acting at the direct command of the teacher—

carrying out her will, not their own—such situations would seldom arise; and if they did *she* would settle them, not the children. But under this system such problems are constantly turning up, the solution of which—by the children themselves —provides as many opportunities for developing the social sentiment. Of course, there is always the directress to act as a court of appeal if necessary. Training in right social adjustment at this age (or in fact any age) is as important as learning to read and write.

But to return to our observations. Let us—since choose we must—try and find out what that little fellow we saw just now is going to do with that box containing the multicoloured pigeonholes. Whatever it is, we can see that it is something which interests him profoundly. You may be surprised when you hear what the box contains: it is an exercise in *grammar*— for teaching the parts of speech. We cannot pause to describe how it works, except to say that on each of the little tickets in the red pigeonhole is written a verb; on the black tickets, a noun; while the adjectives are brown, the prepositions pink— and so forth. Without quite understanding what he is doing we realize, at any rate, that grammar—like every other subject in the room—is being learned through an activity.

Our attention is caught by the sound of musical notes; not a tune—but simply notes—pure in quality and clear in tone. On looking round to find out whence they come we discover that they are floating in through the window from the veran-dah. On going to investigate a pretty picture présents itself. A girl of seven is busying herself with a score or so of bright-looking objects, which look for all the world like silver mush-rooms about four inches high, mounted on wooden stalks. They are in fact little bells, which are all identical in size and ap-pearance, and differ only in their pitch. This is an application of principle of "isolation of stimulus"—pitch being in this case the quality isolated—as is colour in the colour tablets. As the little girl strikes each of them with a small wooden ham-mer it responds with a note of a definite pitch. This one is *re,* that is *do,* that next to it is *fa,* and so on.

She is "pairing" the musical notes just as that other little fellow we saw was "pairing" the colours. Thus, without realiz-ing it, she is sharpening her appreciation of musical pitch; and, in the pleasantest way possible, is laying a sure foundation for later musical training. We stand and watch· her; but she is much too interested in what she is doing to feel any em-barrassment. Indeed, one of the things that strikes the visitors most vividly is the calm way the children get on with their work, undisturbed by the presence of visitors. Some of them may look up from their work when a stranger enters and give a smile of welcome. Sometimes a child will come forward and solemnly shake hands; or another may offer a chair. But as a rule their distraction lasts only a few minutes. Soon the mysterious attraction of their work with the materials re-absorbs their attention so completely that the visitor might be in Timbuktoo for all the further notice that is taken of him.

Coming back from the verandah we pause at a table at which a boy and a girl—both aged about four and a half—are seated. In front of the latter is a rectangular piece of cardboard on which has been pasted a large letter *S* cut out in sandpaper. It is amusing to see how she broods over this letter affectionately, almost as if she were embracing it. Every now and then she places her left hand on the cardboard, and runs the two writing fingers of her right hand very lightly and smoothly along the sandpaper letter, thereby tracing the exact movement necessary for writing it (though observe she is *not* writing). Every time she does this she emits a curious little hissing sound—thus, "SS! SS!" Not content with doing this once or twice she does it again and again, each time making the same sound: so that she reminds one of a little steam engine letting off steam at regular intervals. She has done it ten times now; surely that is enough; she pauses for a few moments to have a word with the little boy sitting next to her—who is doing a number exercise called "Odds and Evens." But it is only a pause—and off she goes again with her "SS! SS!" In an amused astonishment I continue to count this inexplicable repetition, during which she does it another ten times, making twenty in all. What mysterious attraction draws her to this letter? She is quite free to stop running her fingers over it at any moment, yet still she goes on.

At this juncture a small boy—also about four and a half to five—comes up to where she is sitting with the box of sandpaper letters on the table beside her. (She has finished the "SS," by the way, and is now busy with the letter *F*. "Betty," says the newcomer, "have you got *O?*" Betty stops her work for a moment to look through a pile of letters on her desk. "Yes," she replies, "here it is: you can have it."

It is amusing to hear these tiny creatures referring in this serious way to the letters as important entities. Even so might a schoolboy in a grammar school say to another, "I say, will you lend me your algebra book?" At this stage we can, with justice, call these children "men of letters" in a literal sense. For they are not as yet interested in sentences, or even words—*but just in letters*. To them it is a truly astonishing thing that you have but to show a piece of cardboard with a letter on it to another person (e.g., *S*) and the other person will respond as by magic with the correct sound though nothing has been said—"just like a musical box wound up." That this preoccupation with individual letters will bear good fruit in due season is evident from what we can see going on in other parts of the room.

Over there at the blackboard, for instance, three or four children are writing away as hard as they can go. That little fellow, too, we saw earlier on (whom we left composing words on the mat), he also has been through this touching-the-letters stage. Let us go and see, by the way, how he has been progressing. We find he has now completely filled up his mat with the words; and has fetched a small chair from somewhere, and is sitting down on it beside the rug. From this coign of vantage he surveys the plain of words spread out before him with an expression of great satisfaction. Even so—to compare the greater with the less—did the Creator look upon His newly created Universe and see "that it was very good." The little fellow is not idly dreaming, as you might suppose at first glance; his little soul is still in real contact with the work he has created. We know this because, as we watch, another child in passing and by accident has disarranged one of his words. At once he is roused from his motionless position, and—like a spider who has felt a vibration from a distant part of his web —comes quickly out of his isolation to protest against the careless intruder.

Whilst we are back in this part of the room again, let us take another look at our little "multiplication girl," and see how she is going on. Did she go on to the "nine times" when she had finished the eight? No; but a strange and unexpected development has taken place. She is busy putting a floral decoration all round the border of the paper on which she recorded the results of the "eight times." Apparently she has had enough of science; and, to balance things up, her soul has turned to Art. She finds no incongruity in mixing together mathematical science and art. We come back just in time to see the finishing touches put to this decorated border; and to observe the care with which she puts the slip of paper with "eight times" written on it away in her little wallet. When she has reached the "twelve times" she will sew them all together into a little book with a decorated cover—decorated of course by herself. It will then be in a very real sense *her* Table Book, made and printed, decorated and bound all by her own self. She will make constant use of it, later on, both for learning the tables by heart, and also for reference, when she is doing sums with multiplication in them.

1 Maria Montessori. A portrait by Sir Frank Salisbury.

Alle mia cara Anna Maccheroni in segno d'vittoria

Maria Montessori

2 Maria Montessori as a university lecturer and practising physician in Rome (*circa* 1905).

3 Exercises of practical life. "Washing day" in a Montessori school in Berlin.

4 A room in a Montessori school in Rotterdam, showing a part of the carefully prepared environment.

5 Indirect preparation for writing: the sandpaper touchboards, "Rough and Smooth."

6 Indirect preparation for writing: composing words and sentences with the movable letters (Denmark).

7 Writing has now come of itself, and the big words come pouring easily out of the small head (Acton School, England).

8 First steps in addition with number rods. "Steps," be it noted, in a literal as well as a metaphysical sense.

9 History Time-Line from 2000 B.C. (Abraham) to A.D. 2000. It is divided into centuries.

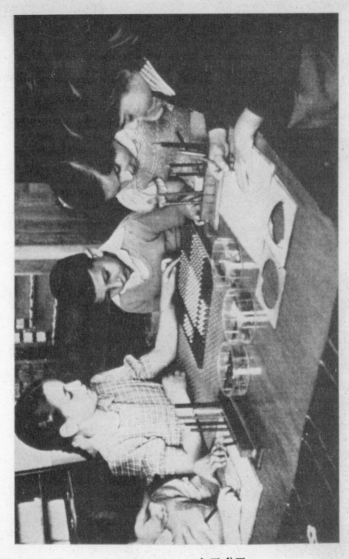

10 Working out, by means of coloured symbolical pegs, the square of a trinomial (Athens).

11 Dr. Montessori at the age of eighty, at the Gatehouse Montessori School, St. Bartholomew the Great, London. This was during her last visit to England (1951).

Free drawing by a boy of 8 years (Rome Montessori School).

A girl at an adjoining table has just finished a number exercise on the numbers 10–19 and has put her materials away. *Now* what is she going to do? There is always this moment of excitement in observing children in a Montessori school, the excitement of the unexpected. Her mind is already made up. She goes to a particular cupboard and returns with a packet of oblong cards fastened together by a rubber band. Sitting down, she draws her chair up to the table, removes the elastic and puts it on one side, takes the top card and places it in front of her, and puts the rest on one side. Then with the whole content of her soul she examines that first card. Some words are written on it; but, from where we are, we cannot read them. Nor does it seem very easy for her to read them either: she is, in fact, only a beginner at reading. I can see her lips forming each letter separately, and then trying to run them together into words, her little head bobbing up and down with each effort. With great perseverance she sticks to the task. Suddenly a light shines in her eyes, a light of joy, triumph, and comprehension. (All this time she has been quite unconscious that anyone is watching her: we feel almost as if we were intruding into something intimate and private.) With a joyful expression, she rises from her chair, places it quietly against the table, and makes straight for the far end of the room, where the domestic appliances are kept. There she procures a glass and pours herself out a glass of water, and drinks it slowly. Whilst she is away we take the opportunity of looking at the card in front of her. On it is written "Go and drink a glass of water."

Soon she is back again. Very soon! for she actually runs in

her eagerness to get on with the next card. Follows the same effort, the same puckering of her little brows, the same sudden flash of illumination. This time—on getting up—she goes to the window, stands on a chair and looks out, and then comes back again. The next card sends her off to pull out some little drawers and push them back again. And so on; each card issues its voiceless command, which she obeys instantly and with an inner joy.

But now it would seem she has come to a card which presents a serious difficulty. She has been right through it two or three times, yet she does not rise, but stays looking at it with a mystified expression. Finally, taking the card with her she goes in search of the teacher. The latter happens to be giving a lesson in division (3263÷3) to a group of six-year-olds on a rug on the floor; and two others are standing patiently by, waiting to consult her also. Our little friend (whose name is Janet) joins up at the end of the queue. She waits for some minutes; but the teacher continues to be busy with the "units, tens, hundreds, thousands" on the floor; and it looks as if that business might go on for some time yet. This is too much for Janet's patience. Leaving the queue, she begins walking round the room as though looking for someone. At last she finds a girl about two years older than herself lost to the world reading a storybook. Janet touches her gently on the shoulder, and the reader turns, rather reluctantly, from her story. Janet then shows her the mysterious card. They are too far off for us to hear the conversation; but there is obviously questioning on the part of Janet, and a good deal of affirmative head-nodding by the elder one; and Janet looks several times at her shoes. The consultation ended, Janet returns to her place—and *then takes off her shoes!*

Putting two and two together we can deduce what has happened. Janet had in fact read the command correctly (it was the same as that which came—even more mysteriously—to Moses from out the Burning Bush: "Take off your shoes"). But this had seemed to her so strange, not to say so unorthodox a proceeding for a schoolroom that she thought she must have made a mistake in the reading of it. Like a scholar faced with a doubtful passage in an ancient manuscript she had felt the need for a more authoritative opinion on it. Again let us notice—in passing—that here we see another problem solved, and quite satisfactorily, *without the help of an adult.* This is the kind of "independence" Montessori encourages, which is a far cry from being allowed to do "anything one likes."

To us adults "reading" has become a familiar and commonplace matter; but to a child at this age—*circa* four to five years, and presented in this way—it is a thrilling and romantic experience. "How wonderful that this insignificant scrap of paper is able to speak to me, like a human being! Though without form or voice, it nevertheless addresses itself just to ME; and so silently, so intimately, that not another soul in the world knows anything about it! It speaks with authority, too; and I love to obey its command." Truly a thing portentous, magical, like a fairy tale—only true. If we pause to think about it, the child's view is the correct one; for the transmission of thought in writing *is* one of the most tremendous achievements of the human race, taking centuries to perfect. But the wonder of it knocks without response at the door of our sophisticated souls.

Let us for a few moments turn now from the children to take a closer look at the gaily painted cupboards placed along the walls. These mean a great deal to the children, for they not only provide them with many interesting things to do, but they are at one and the same time "paths to culture" and the indispensable means to their freedom. Compared with the equipment one usually finds in an ordinary primary school the Montessori teaching materials are simply staggering in their number, variety, scope, and originality. Without instruction, even we grown-ups would be at a loss how to use most of them—how much more so then the children! Therefore one of the main functions of the directress is to initiate her pupils into their right use—and, incidentally—to see that they keep to their right use. As a rule this process of initiation takes place with each child separately, or with a small group who are at the same stage in that subject. It is important that the directress should be able to recognize the psychological moment when any child is in need of a fresh presentation.

It would, as we have insisted, be impossible to describe here these various occupations and what they teach. The task would supply enough materials for a book—indeed for a whole series of books. One would describe all the many and carefully graded occupations that are concerned with learning to write and read; another with arithmetic; a third for grammar, a fourth for music; yet others for geography and history and so forth.[2]

The mention of history reminds us that we ought to say a few words about an activity going on in the hall, which was just beginning as we came through. Three or four children are busy working there with the history time-line. This is a long scroll, made on the plan of those ancient manuscript

[2]See illustration "Prepared paths to culture", p. 275.

books with a roller at each end. When unrolled to its full
length it extends some thirty to forty feet. The time-line is
divided into centuries, beginning at 2000 B.C. and going on
(hopefully!) to A.D. 2000. In the middle of it there is a small
bright golden section; this is the thirty-three years of the life
of Christ—center of all historic reckoning.

Having spread out the time-line along the floor of the hall
(or it might be a corridor, or on the verandah) the children
then set to work placing pictures, with small explanatory
cards to go with them, on the line in their appropriate
centuries. One child is putting down a series of pictures
representing Biblical characters from the Old Testament—
Abraham, Joseph, Moses, David, the Maccabees and so on,
on the B.C. portion. Another, on the A.D. part, is laying out a
series of pictures representing "Transport through the Ages."
This begins with a Roman chariot and finishes up with a
Bentley and a jet engine plane. A third child, on the opposite
side of the A.D. line, is doing a similar bit of work illustrating
different kinds of "Ships through the Ages"—from a Phoeni-
cian galley to the *Queen Elizabeth*.

On the far side of the hall a group of rather younger children are engaged in a research in the nature of numbers, in
particular of the decimal system with its notation. The material they are working with consists of an enormously long
golden chain, made up of a thousand beads, so joined together as to form a chain with a hundred links, each link being
a ten-bead bar. On account of its prodigious length it is quite
a difficult object to cope with. So several children combine
to carry it from the stand where it is kept, and together they
arrange it in a straight line along the floor. It is so long that
it reminds one of the famous Midgard Serpent in the Norse
mythology, which actually went right round the world! Eventually it is laid down in all its shining length, like a golden
railway line. And now the children begin putting down the
hundred cards—100, 200, 300 . . . 900, like stations all along
the line, until they come to the big 1000 card which is the
"terminus." Very imposing it looks in all its glistening perspective, and—as you may well imagine—gives the children
much better understanding of, and respect for, the number
1000 than they could ever have gained by just hearing someone talking about it.

When all the hundred cards have been put down in their
correct places, some of the more advanced children begin a
more difficult exercise. They now place little labels with numbers written on them such as 259, 736, 888, at their appropriate places on the line. When all is finished they go back

into the schoolroom and ask the teacher if she will come
out and check their work. Sometimes, so the teacher informs
us, children will—quite off their own bat—for no one would
dare to suggest such a thing—set off to count, touching with
their fingers, *every* separate bead from the first, to the far-off
1000. It is a colossal task, a veritable pilgrimage. Indeed they
remind one of Elroy Flecker's Pilgrims in *Hassan:*

> Sweet to set off at even from the wells,
> When shadows loom gigantic on the sands.
> And softly through the twilight beat the bells
> Along the Golden Road to Samarkand.

Yes, they too are pilgrims "along the Golden Road"; and like
those others "seeking always to go a little further." Once a
child of five and a half counted as far as 563; and then came
to the teacher and said, "I'm tired" (no wonder!). "May I
put a mark to show where I have got to, and go on again
tomorrow?"

As we return to the classroom where business is going on
as usual we—the teacher and ourselves—are met by two older
boys who have come to show their work to the teacher. They
have been working out the square root of the number 73,441.
It would be a long business to describe the apparatus which
has enabled them to do this, and longer still to describe how
they have been using it. Suffice it to say that they have worked
it out; and what is more, got the correct answer: 271.

It may surprise some readers to find children in the same
room as others who are just learning to read, working out a
problem as complicated at this. But three points should be
noted. First, that this finding of the square root is the term of a
long series of exercises dealing with the squares of numbers
and the facts which underlie binomial expressions in algebra;
secondly, that the actual process of finding the square root
is carried out *in the concrete* by means of movable symbolic
numbers (coloured pegs on a pegboard); and thirdly, that the
Montessori school system does not encourage a horizontal
grading of children, still less classes with "A," "B" or "C"
streams. In fact Montessori insists that, in order to get the
best all-round results, there should be a definite overlap in
age-groups of two or three years.[3]

So far we have said very little about the directress and what
she is doing. She is much less in evidence than the teacher of
the old type of school. That is why the visitor is apt to neglect

[3]The Montessori system—if only authorities would realize it—is the best answer
to the problem of the rural school, where one teacher must, perforce, deal with
three, four, or even five age-groups simultaneously and in the same room.

her, turning his attention to the astonishing and intriguing spontaneous activities of these "free children" with their surprising avidity for work. Nevertheless all the time the directress has been very busy in her own unobtrusive way—helping here, encouraging there, give new "presentations," correcting work which has been brought to her. Or it may be she has been putting something straight in the environment which someone has left out of place; or perhaps checking some as yet not normalized child who is disturbing his neighbour, and trying to interest him in some fresh material. She is in fact never idle. Even when she appears to be doing nothing she is really observing the children at their work to see which ones are in most need of her direction at the next moment. Teaching, under any circumstances, is an art, but nowhere a more delicate one than under the Montessori system; and nowhere a more joyous one. For further information on the art of being a Montessori directress we must refer the reader to Chapter XVIII.

As we wander about the room, realizing with increasing astonishment the immense variety and sheer bulk of work which is being carried on independently of the teacher, two questions keep cropping up in our minds. First, who is making the children work? and second, who is maintaining discipline? and by what means? In the ordinary infant school it is the teacher who does both. She not only decides at what the children shall work, and for how long; but it's also an important part of her job to make them stick to their work. It is her duty—often painful and exhausting—to be constantly rounding up the lagging ones whose attention is wandering, as a sheep dog rounds up the sheep. In a Montessori school this simile would be out of place. Nobody is *making* the children work. This is the discovery which is more and more borne in upon us the longer we wander round and observe. It cannot be the directress, for some of the children have not spoken with her the whole morning, or she with them, save only to salute each other at the beginning of the day. Nor are the children working for marks or fear of punishment, for these are not used.

The discipline, too, does not depend upon the teacher, at least not directly. This has been proved to the writer scores of times by the simple fact that often, when he has been observing in a Montessori class, the directress has gone out of the room and left her class with no one in charge. When this happens the majority of the children are so absorbed in their work that they are not even aware of it.

It is clear therefore that the discipline which reveals itself in the Montessori class is something which comes more from within than from without. But this self-discipline has not come into existence in a day, or a week, or even a month. It is the result of a long inner growth, an achievement won through months of training.

But we must put an end to our meditations and return to the children, for something is happening in the classroom, something unusual, not to say mysterious. An extraordinary change has come over the scene. It is almost as if Perseus had dropped in unexpectedly from the skies, carrying with him the Gorgon's Head, and had turned everyone into stone. After a few moments we discover that it is not the Medusa which has worked this miracle, but a placard unobtrusively hung on the wall with the word "Silence" written on it in large letters. As each child in turn notices it, at once pencils, chalks, letters, rods, counters, beads or whatever it is they are working with are quietly put down; and before long all the little hands have ceased to work, and all the little bodies have become motionless. A calm has spread over the room, as over a pond when the wind has dropped.

As the directress now softly draws the window curtains, the stillness deepens, till a tense mysterious twilight broods over the classroom. When *every* little foot and curly head is quite still the directress begins to walk silently towards the door. She moves mysteriously and solemnly, like a priestess approaching some inner shrine, about to perform a solemn rite. Cautiously she opens the door, not making a sound, and —still on tiptoe—glides out of the room, leaving the door ajar behind her.

The visitor, too, can hardly help himself from being caught up into this mysterious silence. He sits motioness wondering what is going to happen next. For a while nothing happens, except that everyone's attention is drawn automatically to the "sounds of silence" which come stealing out "like mice"— the creaking of a chair, the ticking of a clock, a distant train, the twitter of birds in the garden, a door banging in a remote corridor, far-off strains of music. . . . Then the visitor becomes aware that someone is moving. Through the semidarkness he sees a child rising to his feet. Very slowly and very cautiously he lifts his little chair, and very slowly and very cautiously replaces it on the floor without a sound. Now, with a look of suppressed joy on his face, he begins to thread his way in and out amongst the little tables until he vanishes through the open door. Then another child rises—as softly and cautiously—and he too steals out through the door. Then another; and another. And so, one by one, they all rise and disappear.

At first we wonder why this child rises and not that; and why only one at a time, whilst all the rest remain motionless. The problem solves itself as our ears catch something we did not at first notice. It is the voice of the unseen directress *very softly* calling out the name of each child in turn. Yet it is hardly a voice, scarcely even a whisper; it is more like the ghost of a whisper. In accents hushed and long-drawn-out— like a wisp of smoke drifting through the air, or a floating gossamer thread—mysterious as the voice of a spirit—the voice of the directress comes stealing through the dimlit silence to speak in turn to the heart of each eager and expectant child.

To those who are accustomed to think of small children as mercurial beings "never still unless they are asleep" it comes as a revelation to see a whole roomful of them sitting like statues for ten to fifteen minutes at a stretch without a teacher in the room. But these children have already made great conquests over themselves in many ways (see "The Exercises of Practical Life"—Chapter XII). Furthermore, during the long discipline of silent waiting, each child is sustained by the confident expectation that—if he waits long enough—the call will come to him too; and then with great joy he will arise and obey its summons.

When the last child has vanished from the room the "silence game" is over. The placard with "Silence" on it is turned with its face to the wall; and the children come quietly back to their places; and all the interrupted activities are resumed at the tables or on the rugs on the floor. To revert to our former simile, a wind is once more blowing steadily across the pond and all the little waves are dancing merrily in the sun.

As we turn and take our last look at this new kind of Lilliputian civilization—with standards and values so different from the adult world of competition and struggle in which we live—the words of Miranda spring naturally to our lips:

> O Wonder!
> How many goodly creatures are there here!
> How beauteous mankind is! O brave new world,
> That has such people in't.

CHAPTER XII

MOVEMENT IN RELATION TO IN-
STINCT AND REASON

The Newborn Infant Compared With the Young of Animals

If we compare a newborn child with the newly born young of animals—let us say with a foal, or a chicken just out of the egg—we are struck at once with a marked difference with respect to their capacity for movement. A young chick will run and peck at a grain of corn the moment it is hatched, and a foal will stand up and walk the day it is born. Further-more, the vocal means of expression characteristic of the species is often there from birth in the case of animals. Though their voices are faint and plaintive, puppies emit a real bark, kittens miaow, and lambs bleat: in a word they are endowed with such language as they possess from birth.

With the human child on the other hand when it is born the case is very different. It is less complete physically; and is much slower to develop its powers of movement. The newborn baby has, in fact, very little power of movement: it cannot raise itself, cannot speak, cannot walk. It lies inert and helpless for a long time. Only after long and laborious efforts does it learn to sit up, to crawl, to stand upright and to walk; and does not even walk properly until it is nearly two years old. With its powers of expression it is much the same. For many months it remains: "with no language but a cry." [1]

We should be wrong, however, if we attributed the child's inability to sit up or walk to muscular weakness. Its muscles are strong, as anyone can tell by the force of their muscular thrusts, and the resistance they can maintain. No! the child's backwardness in accomplishing these things comes from a lack of coordination in the muscles—a condition which is due to the fact that the child's nervous system at birth is incom-pletely developed. This does not mean that the child has a *complete* incapacity for coordinated movements. It knows well how to suck, for instance, which is a complicated action re-quiring the accurate coordination of many muscles. But this latter movement is under the direction of instinct, like the movements of newborn animals.

The young of the human species seem, then, at birth, to be inferior to the young of many animals. But it is only *seems*.

[1] *In Memoriam,* by Tennyson.

In point of fact this very helplessness, this incapacity for movement in comparison to animals, is really—when we understand it aright—the very sign of its ultimate superiority.

The Incarnation of Reason

Why, asks Montessori, has the power of instinct which enables the young of animals to stand, walk, run and jump, "speak" etc., almost at birth, deserted the muscles of the baby? She replies, *"Because, in the child, instinct has withdrawn to give place to something higher—to the intelligence and will of man."* These inert muscles are destined to be taken up into a new and higher order than anything in the animal world—into the services of human freedom. They lie there waiting—not the despotic control of unvarying instincts which will move according to the predictable behaviour of the species—but to place themselves eventually at the command of human reason, in the expression of a unique and unpredictable personality.

What it amounts to then is really this, that, in the animal, instinct finds its instrument for movement and expression already formed; whereas *the free soul of man has, in a measure, to create its own instrument*. We may express it thus, that "whereas the animal incarnates an instinct man incarnates intelligence itself."

A Difference in Kind, Not in Degree?

The more deeply we look into Montessori's doctrine of the incarnation of the human soul—this spiritual entity endowed with reason—the more evident does it become that man differs from the animal creation not only in degree but in kind.

It is just here that we find Montessori adopting a different standpoint from many modern psychologists. Take this passage from McDougall, as an example, wherein he describes his own work as an "attempt made to exhibit the continuity of the development of the highest types of human will and character from the primary instinctive disposition that we have in common with animals." (*Social Psychology*, p. 226.)

Psychologists of this school of thought place great emphasis upon the "inherited tendencies to behaviour" which we have in common with animals. Obliterating any sharp distinction between man and the animals, they maintain that everything we do—even our most essentially human acts—is to be explained in terms of instinctive urges. Thus, the love of knowledge is but the sublimated instinct of curiosity; even the worship of God nothing but the instinct of self-abasement raised to the *n*th degree. On the other hand Montessori's prolonged observation of children, carried on through nearly half a century, have led her steadily in the opposite direction. For her, the most significant thing about the child's development —that which dominates and gives it its special form—is *not* these instinctive tendencies which we have in common with the animals, *but that capacity to reason which distinguishes us from them.*

It is not that Montessori denies the instincts, or in any way belittles their significance. Like other modern psychologists she pays her homage to Horme and Mneme. She says, for example—"A vital force is active in every individual and leads it towards its own evolution—it has been called Horme." Or again: "There is a special kind of memory that does not remember consciously, which psychologists call Mneme." Nevertheless, for her, these elementary psychic forces are only a part of the question, and a lesser part. Always "it is the intelligence which distinguishes man from the animals." *"Animals have merely to awaken their instincts towards their specified behaviour—and their psychic life is limited to this. But in man there is this other fact—the creation of human intelligence.* This is the centre which must be taken into consideration when man is studied.

"For man there is no limit. What a man will do in the future no one can foretell—not in the same way, at least, as one can predict the behaviour of animals."

Mysterious Beginnings

Since the psychic life of man is by its nature (i.e., possessing a spiritual or immaterial element) destined to go on for ever, we need not be surprised if we find its beginnings shrouded in mystery. Certain it is that the more intimately one studies the origins of psychic life in the infant, and the building up of human consciousness, the more wonderful and mysterious do they become.

Without doubt it was the Darwinian Theory of the Origin and Descent of Man, expressed in its crudest form, which had the effect of blurring, for a couple of generations, the obvious and time-honoured distinctions between men and animals. Already, however, there are signs that the pendulum is beginning to swing back to a more normal and logical position. And amongst such signs may Montessori's researches be regarded as by no means the least original and important.

Montessori's point of view is not the result of any preconceived theory, still less of theological dogmas, but simply the consequence of a lifetime of scientific observation in the development and behaviour of children. Her researches bear out in a striking manner the dictum of Herbert S. Jennings, in his *Biology in Relation to Education*, that "there is no organism that differs so much from other organisms as do human beings"; and that "the things that are most important about children must be known from a study of children rather than from a study of other organisms." (Quoted by Professor Robert R. Rusk—in his *History of Infant Education*, p. 94.)

Rusk himself, in the same chapter, remarks that:

The adoption of the biological standpoint has adversely affected education through the emphasis which it leads Psychology to place upon the instincts and the subconscious. Psychology is so preoccupied with the least desirable aspects of human nature that it finds no time for the consideration of higher values and the moral order, without which the unconscious would not exist. Instead of the unconscious explaining art, morality or religion, it is the existence of these that create subconsciousness—animals are not afflicted with complexes nor suffer neuroses. The idealistic interpretation of human experience, on the contrary, stresses the higher mental processes peculiar to man —reasoning and intelligence.

Human Reason

Before we return to the study of how the human reason or intelligence "incarnates" itself in the very early stages of human development, it may not be out of place to say a few words—at this juncture—about this august faculty itself. (Those who are not interested in philosophical digressions are recommended to skip at once to page 212.)

More than twenty-five centuries ago Aristotle defined man as a rational animal; and in every subsequent age the generality of men have endorsed this definition. Shakespeare is typical when he exclaims, "What a piece of work is man! how noble in reason, in apprehension how like a God!" So too, when he speaks in the same play (*Hamlet*) of "the beast that lacks discourse of reason." In spite of all efforts to prove the contrary, it still remains true that man alone possesses "that capable and god-like reason."

Reason is the highest human faculty.[2] Theologians and poets agree in pointing out that it is that part of our nature which is most "like to God" in whose image we are made. "The human reason," says Cardinal Manning, "is that part

[2]*Natural* faculty, that is, for we are not here discussing supernatural endowments, such as Faith.

of our nature which is in the most immediate contact with God. It is the light of God in the soul, whereby we are able to know God and ourselves and to judge truth and falsehood, right and wrong."

Let us consider for a moment some of the high consequences which result from our possession of this gift. In the first place it is the intellect or reason which sets us free from the never-ending prison of the present moment in which animals live, dominated entirely from moment to moment by their instincts.[3]

> We look before and after
> And pine for what is not,
> Our sincerest laughter
> With some pain is fraught;
> Our sweetest songs are those
>   that tell of saddest thought.

So said Shelley, and Shakespeare, too, has the same thought— even the same phrase—when he speaks of "God who made us with such large discourse, *looking before and after*." In the same context Shakespeare makes it clear that our power to do this is bound up with reason—which should not "fust in us un-used." Montessori is thinking on similar lines when she writes, "The intelligence of the child will have to take in the present of a life which is in evolution, which goes back hundreds of thousands of years in its civilization; and has also, stretching in front of it, a future of thousands of millions of years— a present that has no limit either in the past or in the future. . . . Its aspects are infinite, whereas for animals there is but one aspect, and that is always fixed."

Again it is this same gift of the intellect which enables us to do what no animal has ever achieved—i.e. to rise to a con-sciousness of our being—i.e. to self-consciousness, to the knowledge that "I am I," with its unique corollary that "You are you."

It is through the reason, too, that man can rise even without revelation to a knowledge of the existence of God, the First Cause, Author and Creator of the Universe."[4]

Of equal importance to the gift of self-consciousness, and resulting, too—like it—from the possession of an intellect, is the gift of freedom. From the time of Aristotle it has been recognized that there can be no real act of free choice unless it has been preceded by an act of judgment. ("The Will takes its root in the circle of thought"—Herbart.) And, since our

[3] Cf. *Montessori Method*. The story of the dog which died of grief at the death of its master.
[4] See Aristotle's four famous "Proofs for the Existence of God."

characters are formed by our decisions, we can say therefore that, without this gift of reason or intellect as a foundation, we could not build up our individual characters. (Montessori defines the intellect somewhere as an activity which enables the mind to construct itself.)

Finally, we can go so far as to say that, without this unique endowment, we should have no hope of entering Heaven. Not that we mean to imply that our meriting Heaven is a matter of the intellect rather than of faith. The point we wish to make, here, is that the gift of grace—which makes faith possible— does not descend upon a soul, as it were, *in vacuo, but only upon intellectual beings,* endowing them with a special kind of illumination. Reason must be there as a foundation in the natural order, before it can be raised by faith to the supernatural. Or to put it the other way round, God does not—we might almost say *could* not in the nature of things—grant the gift of faith to a being like an animal "who lacked discourse of reason."

Theologians tell us that in Heaven, when the human soul is in the enjoyment of the Beatific Vision, even then this highest of human faculties will not have been superseded, but raised to a supernatural way of functioning—in the *Lumen Gloriae.*

The Dawn of Reason in the Infant

Of these high destinies, however, it must be confessed there is little to remind us when we behold the "infant mewling and puking in the nurse's arms." If we put the question: How soon does the child's reason begin to function? Montessori's answer is as definite as it is astonishing—so much so that we must give it in her own words:

> The baby starts from nothing; it is an active being going forward by its own powers. Let us go straight to the point. The axis round which the internal working revolves is *reason.* Such reason must be looked upon as a natural creative function that little by little buds and develops and assumes concrete form from the images it absorbs from the environment. Here is the irresistible force, the primordial energy. Images fall at once into pattern at the service of reason. It is in the service of reason that the child first absorbs such images . . .

In this connection we would remind the reader of the incident so graphically described by Montessori and quoted in Chapter V, pp. 22-23.

A New Chapter in Psychology

In 1944 Montessori gave a course of some thirty lectures,[5] most of which were devoted to the mental development of the child in the first three years of its life. Although delivered in her seventy-fourth year, and under the rigours of an Indian climate, these lectures displayed her characteristic originality and vigour of expression. The conclusion to which her observations led her are so new and unexpected that when one reads them for the first time one feels—as we said in a previous chapter—almost as if one had entered a new and unfamiliar world.

One fact however seems to stand out clearly, viz., that with these researches a new chapter had been added to human psychology—one of those "first ten volumes which had hitherto remained unwritten."

"This vision comes before our minds," says Montessori, summing the matter up, "in which we see the first year of the child's life as that in which the greatest psychic activity is developed by the human being.

"We now know that the one thing which is active during the first year is the brain. So now you will understand," she continues, "why the head of a one-year-old child has doubled in size since it was born. At the third year its brain is already half that of the adult—at four years eight-tenths of its ultimate size."

Montessori even goes so far as to say that, during the first year, the human being grows *principally* in intelligence; the rest of its growth, during this period, being subordinate to this developing psychic life.

These are startling statements; and the reader will doubtless demand evidence before believing them. As this book is primarily concerned with later stages of development (*after* self-consciousness has been built up) we shall not attempt fully to develop this theme here but only add a few considerations to what was said in Chapter VI, again referring those who wish to delve into the matter more deeply to go to Dr. Montessori's own work, *The Absorbent Mind*.

The Child Creates His Own Mind

The *first* thing to be noted here about this epoch (0–3) is that "the child creates his own mind. Intelligence is what distinguishes man from all other animals; therefore the first act of man in this life must be the creation of intelligence.

[5] At Ahmedabad.

"The child is passing from nothing to a beginning. He is bringing into being that most precious gift which gives man his superiority—reason. On this road he goes forward long before his tiny feet can carry his body." *(Secret of Childhood.)*

In an earlier chapter we have very briefly outlined how this mysterious self-creation takes places. First, there is an activity which Montessori calls "the taking in of the whole environment by the unconscious mind." "It is logical that if the psychic life is to construct itself, by incarnating the environment, the intelligence must observe and study it first. It must gather a great quantity of impressions from that environment, just as the physical embryo begins by a great accumulation of cells before starting to build special organs."

(It is well to note, in passing, that *any* argument for the existence of unconscious activities is bound to be deductive, for the simple reason that as soon as one is immediately and directly aware of a mental activity, it is by that very fact no longer in the unconscious.)

What happens next—according to Montessori—is that these multitudinous impressions, thus unconsciously absorbed, are used again by being known again in a different way as the basis on which conscious life is built up. These primordial unconscious impressions are then the stuff out of which is woven consciousness itself, with all that it implies of reason, memory, will and self-knowledge. In this process of building up a conscious intelligence the work of the hands plays an important and essential part, a thesis which will be developed more fully in a later chapter (XIV).

The Intelligence Builds Its Own Instrument

The *second* important fact to notice about this first period of development (0–3) is this—that not only does the intelligence construct itself, but at the same time it begins to construct its own bodily instrument of expression. As a result during this period the whole of the child's powers of movement develop in subordination to this superior aim, i.e., of psychic development. The important consequence of this is that—when the time arrives when the body has developed the power of coordinated movement—its activity will not be confined within the narrow limits of instinctive behaviour. It will function as the instrument of a free moral agent—an immortal soul if you like—a person so free that his own eternal destiny is placed within his own hands.

Marvellous Adaptive Powers of the Child

A *third* characteristic of this period, to which Montessori would draw our attention, is the wonderful adaptive powers possessed by the child, as compared with animals. Whether a cat is born in France, England, or India it will miaow just the same wherever it happens to grow up: but the baby born in France grows up to speak French; in England, English, whilst the brown bambino of India will chatter in Hindustani, Gujerati, or some other Indian dialect. We are so used to this phenomenon that we do not realize how wonderfully significant it is. When we reflect upon it, however, it places in relief the marvellous adaptive powers of the "psychic embryo." For we must remember that the customs, habits, language—in fact the whole civilization of a people—is not something which inevitably belongs to humanity as a whole—in this same sense as barking and wagging its tail are universal canine reactions. Hence we see that if an individual grows up suited to a special country, climate, or civilizaton, it is because of an "inner construction" which has taken place in childhood.

We stand, says Montessori, with wonder before this picture of the infant who comes, sleeping and smiling, into this complicated world—all the time taking in from his environment, adapting himself to the civilization into which he is born. It is all the same whether he is born into the Stone Age, thousands of years ago; or into some quiet epoch like the Middle Ages; or into the midst of a mechanical age like that in which we live. This is the fundamental fact, that he is able to absorb by nature what he finds in his environment. He accepts everything with astonishing ease, and in every epoch reveals himself truly "The Son of Man." This is his work—to accept all. If it were not for this, there could be no continuity or progress in "civilization."

Montessori sees a definite relationship between the newborn child's incompleteness, his incapacity to move and speak, etc., and this function of childhood as the means by which the continuity of civilization is effected, from generation to generation. It helps us to understand why the child is born so undeveloped in movement, including the complicated movement of speech.

It is not generally realized how physically incomplete the child is at birth, still less the psychological reasons for this incompletion. "Everything is unfinished. The feet destined to walk upon the ground and invade the whole world are without bones: they are cartilaginous. The same is true of the cranium that encloses the brain—only a few of its bones are developed. But what is more significant is the fact that the nerves themselves are not completed; so that there is a lack of central direction, and therefore a lack of unification between the organs. The consequence of this is that this being, whose bones are not yet developed, is at the same time unable to obey the urge to move, because every urge is transmitted by the nerves, and these nerves are not yet fully developed."

The Psychic Embryo

"Why is it then that in the newly born human there is no movement, as in the case of animals, amongst whom the newly born walk almost at once?" The answer is that the child even after birth is still in an "embryonic" stage. This statement by no means minimizes the importance of the great crisis of birth—often spoken of by psychologists as the great trauma, or shock of birth. Montessori herself describes this somewhere as a change so "terrific" as to be comparable to that of "passing from the earth to the moon." It is none the less true, however, that the child after birth still remains so incomplete that we can describe him as still being in a sort of embryonic state. Whilst this is true, physically, it is much more true when we consider mental development; for it is a period in which "those human faculties which do not exist must be created."

The important thing for us to realize says Montessori, is that in the twofold development which now takes place (the completion of the body on the one hand, and the creation of the mental faculties on the other) it is the mind rather than the body which sets the tune. The human soul is not united to its physical vehicle in a ready-made relationship which exists at birth, as in the case of animals who merely "incarnate the instincts of their species." Hence the whole drama of these early years, in human development, lies in the effort to achieve what Montessori calls a "progressive incarnation" in which spirit and flesh are brought into an ever more perfect harmony.

Because the infant will grow up into a man who will be a free agent the soul must create its own special individual instrument as the means of expressing that freedom. That is why in man "it is the psychic development which creates movement," whereas with animals the instincts seem to awaken at birth, as soon as contact is made with the environment. In man the psyche must first construct the human faculties, which are not there (except potentially) at birth; and develop, too, those movements that serve these faculties. That is why the human embryo is born incomplete, physically, because the individual must wait, before beginning its movements, until the psyche has constructed itself, so that the body may develop as servant to the spirit.

How wonderful is the economy of means manifested in this period of the development of the psychic embryo! At one and the same time—in one and the same life process—the psyche constructs its faculties; creates its bodily instrument of expression; and, further, carries out that marvellous process of adaptation to the particular civilization and language into which it is born.

Spirit and "Flesh"

It is because this process of "progressive incarnation" does not complete itself for the several years that Montessori sees in the helpless baby "a state of dualism or dissidence" between the purely psychic part and its instrument of expression. We have therefore a powerful soul which has no means of expression—"*a being whose exterior semblance/Doth belie its soul's immensity*" (Wordsworth).

It is as though a great soul was imprisoned in a semi-inert body without the possibility of manifesting its needs. This is a condition "which should arouse our pity and stimulate in us the wish to help this imprisoned soul, striving to come to light, to be born." At this stage the infant *wills* to do many things without the power to do them; "the spirit is willing but the flesh is weak." In this sense the word "flesh" stands for the almost infinite complexity of *voluntary* muscles with which we are endowed. They are the materials out of which the child will have to create his instrument. At birth, and for a long time after, they lack coordination, due—as said above—first to the incomplete development of the nervous system, and secondly, to lack of practice.

These voluntary muscles are so numerous that it is a saying amongst medical students that "you have to forget them seven times before you can remember them!" It is the task of the animating spirit to build up a coordinated system out of these voluntary muscles; or rather a whole complex of coordinating systems—for these muscles do not work separately but in combinations, "whole armies collaborating." They have many different functions. Some are used for moving forward; some backward; some for expressing impulses; others for inhibiting them: and all these functions may vary with different movements. The whole system is capable of an almost limitless refinement. One has only to think of the hand of a surgeon, or a musician, or an artist, or the feet of a dancer, to bring to mind the marvellous perfection which can be achieved.

This simplicity and grace of movement, this perfection of detail does not come by instinct (as with animals when they have it). It is an achievement which results from a long-continued voluntary effort, under the *conscious* direction of the mind, which works upon the dull flesh, animating it to a perfection that is individual and personal.

Unity of Soul and Body

There is just one more point to be made clear to avoid misapprehension. Though we have spoken of the soul "building up its instrument of expression through the voluntary muscular system" we must not let this metaphor run away with us with the bit in its teeth. When the process of progressive incarnation has been completed, we may, by way of illustration if we like, think of the soul as a musician playing upon an instrument. But actually a musician's instrument (unless it be his voice) is something external to him. The soul with its perfected instrument *forms one complete and indivisible whole*. Or to put it in another way, we may say that when "functional incarnation" has been achieved, we must think of it as an indissoluble welding together of two separate elements to form a new thing; just as oxygen and hydrogen combine to form a new thing—water.

Here, as in many other respects, Montessori's ideas—though arrived at as a result of observation—show an unexpected affinity with Aristotelian philosophy. "Any theory which supposes a separation between man's physical life and his spiritual life is artificial and unreal. Philosophically, it is inaccurate to speak of soul *and* body, still less accurate to point a relation between soul and body in any sense which would imply that there is a third entity joining two distinct beings: for man is *one* being not two" (*Man*, by Reys).

We must now abandon the sphere of theory to consider some of its practical applications in the realm of practice.

CHAPTER XIII   THE EXERCISES OF PRACTICAL LIFE

Visitors to Montessori schools are often surprised to see children engaged in occupations which sometimes strike them as being out of place in a schoolroom. Thus they may see one child sweeping the floor with a diminutive but real brush, another polishing brasses, a third putting fresh water in flower vases. Other children, armed with dusters, hot water, soap, and scrubbing brushes are carrying out what seems a veritable spring cleaning of the cupboards. Yet another group may be laying the table for lunch, or perhaps washing up after it. These, and a great many similar tasks which may be going on, strike some visitors as a waste of time—time which could be more profitably devoted to definite school subjects such as The Three Rs.

Yet, in point of fact, no other occupations which could be undertaken by the children *at this stage* (3–5) could be more important for their whole development—physical, mental, and moral—than these "exercises of practical life" as they are called.

The custom of providing such domestic occupation for young children is much more prevalent now than it was a generation ago. It forms a part of the daily programme of many nursery and "activity" schools. Unfortunately, however, many teachers still introduce these exercises of practical life to the children without any true understanding of their real purpose or psychological significance. Consequently much of their value is lost through lack of proper technique.

"Synthetic" Movements a Biological Need

The first thing to realize about these exercises of practical life is that their aim is *not* a practical one. Emphasis should be laid not on the word "practical" but the word *life*. Their aim (as of all the other occupations presented to the children in the prepared environment) is to assist development.

The discerning visitor who observes the children at work on these activities cannot fail to be impressed, as much by the *way* they are doing them, as by *what* they are doing. Their profound concentration, the serious joy with which they carry out their work, the expenditure of energy out of all proportion to the external end in view as revealed in their unreasoning repetition (I once saw in a Dutch school a little queue of children waiting to polish the *same* brasses)—all these suggest that the children are rivetted to this sort of activity by some strange, one might almost say occult, fascination. This is in fact truly the case. Theirs is more than a conscious interest; their whole demeanour reveals the fact that they are fulfilling a biological need; and that it is the interest of life—Horme—which is working in and through them as they carry out these occupations.

Recalling the matters discussed in the last chapter, under the title of "The Progressive Incarnation of Man," it is evident what that need is. All these occupations come under the heading of what Montessori calls "synthetic movement," that is, *movement ordered and directed by the mind to an intelligible purpose.* As such they help the child in his great task of "progressive incarnation," i.e., of building up the physical instrument which is to be used for the expression of his personality.

It is characteristic of all children at this stage of development that they derive immense satisfaction from any use of their voluntary muscles, that is of "the flesh." [1] Here, as always, Montessori's aim is to help the child to do, in a more perfect and orderly manner, what he strives to do in any case by his own natural impulses, but not so perfectly. Our help consists of placing within the prepared environment "motives of activity" designed specially to answer the needs of this "sensitive period" through which he is passing. The child not only has an intense interest in these "synthetic movements" but is endowed with a special capacity for fixing them, i.e., making them habitual, with an ease and spontaneity which never recurs.

Real, Not Make-Believe Activities

It is important to notice, in passing, that these are real, not make-believe activities and that they are carried out in a real and not make-believe environment. The child who is washing dusters is washing real dusters because they are dirty; the children who are laying the table are laying a real table with real knives and forks and plates, etc., for a real meal—not a doll's table in a doll's house for a doll's tea party. Where you see a child swabbing up the water spilt on the floor there has been a real accident, and she is reestablishing order in a real world. This is a matter of great importance to which we shall return in a later chapter. [2]

Some grown-ups, parents especially, are almost incredibly ignorant, not to say stupid, with regard to these exercises for practical life, missing their significance completely. I knew one father, a wealthy man with a large domestic staff, who was quite angry when he heard that his boy of four years of age had been cleaning his own shoes in a Montessori class. "It is not necessary for my boy to do such menial work," he said. "I have plenty of servants to do it for him." The poor man was quite unable to distinguish between an economic necessity and a psychological one.

[1] See above, p. 211.
[2] Montessori and Froebel, Chapter XX.

Classification of Exercises of Practical Life

The particular exercises of practical life which we should present to the children will vary according to circumstances, local and national. Whatever they may be, however, we can classify them broadly speaking under two heads: (*a*) those which have to do with the care of the child's own person; and (*b*) those which are concerned with the care of the environment. Under the former we include such activities as dressing and undressing, brushing one's hair, cleaning one's teeth, washing hands and face, brushing one's clothes, polishing shoes, and so forth. We would include also in this section the various buttoning and lacing frames which Montessori has devised to help children to dress and undress themselves independently of adults.

Under the heading "Care of Environment" we would include such occupations as: sweeping the floor, dusting the furniture, scrubbing tables and chairs, washing and ironing clothes, polishing door handles, arranging flowers, watering plants, tidying out cupboards, laying tables for meals, waiting at tables, washing up afterwards; and a great many more similar occupations. To these we may add such jobs as peeling potatoes, shelling peas, preparing sandwiches; and also many outdoor tasks, such as digging, planting, weeding, watering, sweeping up leaves, and so forth.

Nothing much would be gained by extending the list of possible occupations, for they are almost innumerable; and, as mentioned above, largely depend upon the particular circumstances of each school. It will be more useful to discuss the technique which should be used in presenting these exercises, and the psychological principles underlying it.

Lessons of Grace and Courtesy

If one is starting a Montessori class right from the beginning, it is best to concentrate at first almost entirely on the exercises of practical life (together with lessons of grace and courtesy) and postpone the bringing out of any specialized didactic materials until there has been established what Montessori calls the "right rapport" between the children and the environment.

The lessons of grace and courtesy, just mentioned, are so akin to the exercises of practical life that they can be treated together, just as they should be presented to the children in the same epoch of development (i.e., the period when the child has a special interest in learning precise movements and a

correspondingly special capacity for fixing them). It is therefore an important part of the directress's duty to give definite
and precise lessons on how to behave with "grace and courtesy." That is to say she will instruct them, over a considerable
period of time, how to carry out all the many external actions
which, as it were, lubricate social life, and make it run smoothly
along the road of established custom. This will include such
matters as how to sit down and stand up properly—and *when*
to do so; how to salute persons according to the various
degrees of intimacy; how to beg pardon for small offences, as
for instance in passing in front of another person, or interrupting them in what they are doing; how to open and shut a
door quietly; how to hand objects to another person, especially
sharp ones like a pair of scissors or a knife, and so forth. "In a
word, there is no action which we do not try and teach so as
to approach perfection. We leave nothing to chance."

How to Present the Exercises of Practical Life and Lessons of Grace and Courtesy

One rather obvious preliminary to be noted is that,
before beginning at all, the directress should not only have
prepared the means for carrying out these exercises, but
should also have arranged them—in her mind—in a graded
sequence, commencing with the more simple.

With regard to the actual manner of presenting them Montessori lays down a simple but profound maxim: "Our task is
to show how the action is done, and at the same time destroy
the possibility of imitation." At first sight this appears paradoxical, but, Montessori continues: "What we have to consider is how we can present this action to the small child and
at the same time disturb as little as possible the creative
impulse." "The action must speak for itself, e.g., 'one dusts.'
We do not want this child to do this action because *we* are
doing it, or *as* we do it, or because we have commanded it to
be done. There are, therefore, these two elements to be considered: first, we must show the details of the action as objectively as possible. And secondly, it should so happen that when
the action does come to be carried out by the child, it must
be done *as part of a life that unfolds itself* (*una vita che si
svolge*)."

Here, as always, we should aim at helping the children to
help themselves; enabling them in every emergency to act
independently of the adult—thus becoming masters of their
environment and conscious of their power over it. Supposing
someone has upset a vase of flowers, a child (not necessarily

the one who has done it) already prepared for such an emergency, will go and fetch a pail and cloth and mop up the water, whilst another with equal spontaneity will go and refill the vase and rearrange the flowers in it. Thus everything happens spontaneously from moment to moment. This is what Montessori means by being "part" of a life which unfolds itself.

It will be seen that this way of using the exercises of practical life is not the same thing as is done in many schools—even Montessori schools so called—where they are limited to a certain period only—e.g., the first half hour in the morning, before "work" begins. Such a practice tends to make a "subject" out of them; and—although it is better than not having them at all—it is by no means the same thing. It is just the *spontaneous* use of these exercises of practical life and lessons of courtesy, as the natural expressions of a communal life, which is so important. Without this freedom to use them at any time, it would be almost impossible to bring into being that living "rapport" between the children and their beloved environment which is so essential for their character, and so charming to witness.

The same principles apply to the presentation of the actions of grace and courtesy. We must teach the children the elements of social behaviour so that their interest is aroused; and as a consequence their attention directed to these aspects of life. In this way these little people who, before, only knew vaguely and half consciously what to do in any particular social situation, now have a clear and vivid idea how to react when the particular occasion arises. "But this does not mean," adds Montessori, "that we should follow these children round 'persecuting them in every action.' What is necessary is that we should give them the means to be master of their own actions, and of the situation when, and as it occurs. Thus, if an important person comes to visit the school, they will know how to greet him, if they remember to do so. The teacher should not make a speech and say 'Children, an important person is coming today; you must greet him thus and thus.' It is of no importance in the world if no one greets him(!); but what is important is that the child should not be left in the lurch. He must be given a guide and not abandoned in his rude and uninstructed condition, but rather his individuality should be awakened. The important thing, therefore, is that he should know how to perform these greetings to parents, relations, friends, or strangers, if it comes into his mind to do so. But it is in his mind, and upon his own reflection, that the action should have its origin. Or again, a child may leave school without greeting his teacher. No matter—he should not be reprimanded for so doing; the essential thing is that he should know how to perform these actions of courtesy when his little heart prompts him to do so, as part of a social life which develops naturally from moment to moment."

Children in Montessori schools are usually exceptionally well behaved (though under no coercion to be so), as countless visitors have testified. Their hospitality is so charming just because it is so spontaneous. But without these lessons of grace and courtesy given previously, and without the freedom to express themselves spontaneously, most of these little flowers of courtesy would never have blossomed at all.

Why Imitation Is To Be Avoided

Our aim then must be "to teach the action and at the same time destroy the possibility of imitation." How profound is this maxim when one ponders over it! What respect it shows for the personality of the child!

If the teacher, in presenting the action, does it too forcibly, what will happen? She will attach the child's attention to herself, and not to the action. In fact under such circumstances the child might easily copy unessential peculiarities in the teacher's way of doing it with a slavish imitation (as indeed has often happened).

Again imitation may be a danger just because adults in general do not act in the same way as children. "I dust and it is finished," but not so with a child. He dusts again and again —over, under, around, along—and again once more—because his whole attitude towards dusting is different. As we have seen (Chapter VIII, p. 142), his aim in dusting is really an internal one. So we do not say to him "You like dusting—here is something to dust." What matters is that a mysterious inner force should rise in the child and impel him to do this. So we must be guided by his inner need rather than a present object. The teacher must therefore indicate the action, but leave it to the child to do it in his own way. In one of her lectures on this subject Montessori said it was the difference between *indicare* (to indicate) and *insegnare* (to teach).

In taking this line of approach we are following the method of nature. For instance, contrary to what many people say, the child does not learn to speak by imitation. It is of course true that he would not learn to speak if speech were not in his environment. But when the child does speak he speaks from an inner impulse. In a similar way then we must prepare what is necessary for these actions, indicate how they are done, and leave the occasions for carrying them out to the child to do them when he wants to. Everything necessary, therefore, should always be ready and in its right place. The child who wants to dust should not have to waste any time hunting for the duster, or the psychological moment may pass, and the precious creative energy be squandered, losing itself "like water from a leaky kettle."

Teach, Teaching, Not . . .

In the course of one of her lectures on the exercises of practical life, during an international training course in London, Montessori—speaking in Italian as was her wont—said that we should always *"insegnare, insegnando"* which means "teach, teaching"! Her interpreter paused, and looked up at Montessori with a puzzled expression. It seemed a meaningless remark, as if one had said—one should always eat eating, or run running. But Montessori nodded and smiled and repeated the phrase. Still the interpreter hesitated. At the third repetition, still not without misgivings, she translated the phrase into English, "We must teach, teaching." Then Montessori, with another smile, went on *"non corrigendo"* (not correcting). So we must *"teach, teaching, not correcting."* That is, we should not, for instance, brusquely interfere if we see a child carrying out an action imperfectly, correcting him in the middle of it. His natural reaction, then, would be a defensive one; and in most cases we should probably do more harm than good. But whatever the action was that was being imperfectly done—it might be handing a pair of scissors the wrong way round, for instance—the teacher should make a mental note of it. Then, on another day and without any reference to this particular child's imperfections, at a suitable moment she would give a bright and interesting lesson on how to hand a pair of scissors to another person.

Teach Him! Teach Him!

On the other hand we must not go to the opposite extreme. I have known persons, with a smattering of Montessori ideas, who seem to imagine it is quite enough to place the child in the prepared environment and leave him there—like a horse in a meadow—under the mistaken impression that he will feed his mind on what he finds there, without instruction, as the horse would feed himself on grass. This is a travesty of the doctrine of nonintervention. Whenever the child is not concentrated on some creative activity the teacher need have no scruples about breaking into his life, and presenting him some of the exercises of practical life or any other lesson, always remembering, however, to obtain the child's consent. (See Chapter XVIII.) "One thing," says Montessori, "we should remember. It is never a danger to teach. You ask, 'Am I to teach him or not?' I say, 'Teach him, teach him.'" The problem is not in the act of teaching but in the child's learning. Maybe he has understood; maybe not. No matter if he does it wrong—do not correct him or he will retire into his shell. We must not insist if he makes mistakes. We have taught and it has failed. Leave it at that and turn to someone else.

"Let us suppose, by way of an illustration, that the directress is trying to teach a very small child how to fold a duster, and that the latter finds it too hard. In that case she should not insist. If she likes, the directress could try making a line across the middle of the duster [how like Montessori to think of that!]. Now the little one reacts! That is easy and fascinating. What joy! Now I will go and find all the other dusters and fold them; and then any other cloths I can get, and fold them all. It is a conquest over the world and over myself."

The Motive of Perfection

What distinguishes Montessori's method from many of the other "activity methods" in vogue today is her emphasis on precision, order, and discipline. But in order to achieve this order and discipline the child needs our assistance—in fact he could not attain it without our help. Here, as always, our cue is to provide him with the means to help himself. Very characteristic, therefore, of the spirit of the Montessori method is the next point we have to mention in connection with the carrying out of the exercises of practical life. When these exercises have been presented to the children, in the manner indicated above, the directress should, after a while, wherever possible, introduce into the action what Montessori calls "a motive of perfection." To take an illustration. The directress has already taught the children how to lay a table, putting out plates, cups and saucers, etc.; and they have done this a number of times, and enjoyed doing it. Now she can add a little complication to the action, something which—without making it too hard—makes it more interesting. Thus, at a suitable moment, the directress, taking a cup in her hand, attracts the attention of a child or a group of children; "Look, children, I am going to try and put this cup down on the saucer *without making a noise*." Then she does so, or tries to, for perhaps she has not *quite* succeeded and a slight sound is heard. No matter! A great interest has been roused, and the children are longing to do it themselves. "Softly! softly! no noise! Ah! that is better!" So now the ear enters into the action as a guide, as a monitor, as a new "control of error"; and thus a new interest is added to the joy of laying the table. The child tries to put each cup down on its saucer *without making a noise*. The ear now becomes the "teacher" and does not allow the smallest sound to pass uncriticized.

The impersonal nature of this criticism is very important; for, if it were a grown-up that criticized the child so often and so severely, he would feel oppressed, and his defences would be roused. As the control is in the environment, it does not bring with it to the child a sense of inferiority. Nevertheless it is an implacable critic and overlooks nothing. "But"—as the child might say if he could express himself—"instead of making me feel depressed it acts as a challenge. I must be careful. I have learnt something by myself and no teacher told me. All by myself I have learnt to do it; and I do it a little better every time. I have made an immense effort, but I am satisfied. So great is my joy, in fact, that before coming to the next cup and saucer after such a great effort, I will relax a little and take a little hop and a skip."

The directress will endeavor to introduce similar motives of perfection into as many other exercises as lend themselves to it. For example, when the child goes through the long ritual of washing his hands, he should try and do so without spilling a drop on the floor; or when he puts down his chair on the floor, to do so without making a noise.

This last action is particularly important. If children are taught this practice at the right period, so that it grips their spontaneous interest, before long it will become automatic. It is surprising what an enormous difference this little matter will make in the smooth and orderly conduct of the whole life of the schoolroom.

We repeat once more: it must be borne in mind that it is only at this epoch—during which the child has a sensitive period for perfecting muscular coordination—that the best and most permanent results will be obtained with the exercises of practical life and the lessons of grace and courtesy. If we wait until the children are over seven years of age we shall have "missed the tide."

The Logical Analysis of Movement

Some teachers think (or behave as if they thought) that so long as the children are "active"—"expressing themselves" as they are pleased to put it—it does not much matter what they are doing, short of actually murdering each other! When I visit schools of this type a remark of the German sage Goethe comes into my mind: "There is nothing worse than an unknowing activity."[8] What we have described above as "synthetic movement" is, by its very essence, a "knowing" activity, i.e., directed by the intelligence to a reasonable end. All the exercises of practical life and lessons of grace and courtesy are such; for each has a well-understood purpose which has to be carried out as part of a real social life in a real world. Along this path of "knowing activities" Montessori would have us lead the child still further. She would have us direct the child's intelligence to bear not only on the *end,* but the *means.* The more perfectly the intelligence enters into the child's actions, penetrating them through and through with the light of reason (without of course diminishing their spontaneity) the better. For by this means the child's development is approaching more nearly to nature's aim, which is the "functional incarnation of man," the welding together of the soul with its motor instrument of expression in the unity of personality. This increased penetration of the child's action by his understanding is obtained through a form of instruction known as "the logical analysis of movement."

In every complex action directed towards a single end, such as pouring out a glass of water or opening and shutting a door, there are to be found a number of component actions each directed to a particular and intermediate end. All these subsidiary actions collectively make up the whole. If the whole action is done properly, these subsidiary actions follow one another—as the action proceeds—in a logical sequence. But if, in performing the action, this logical order is not adhered to confusion arises, and there results an unnecessary expenditure of energy combined with a lack of grace. Take, for instance, the opening and shutting of a door. The logical sequence of the subsidiary actions involved is: (1) approach the door, (2) raise the arm and (3) turn the handle, (4) pull the door a *little* way out, (5) let the handle go back, (6) pull the door well out. In closing the door we have the same series of actions in the reverse order. It is a common mistake with children (and with grown-ups too for that matter when they are in a flurry) to commence action (4), that is, pulling out the door, before action (3), turning the handle, has been completed—a proceeding which results in an ineffectual fiddling with the door handle. "To do an action gracefully," says Montessori, "it is not sufficient to do it with a smile on your face!" No action can look graceful if there is a disturb-

[8] Es gibt nichts schlimmer wie eine unwissende Tätigkeit.

ance of this logical order. Supposing you trip on your way upstairs, what has hapepned? You have begun the forward movement of your foot before the upward one has been completed.[4]

We do not mean, of course, that the directress should attempt to explain all this to the children in so many words. What she should do is to go through the whole action herself, indicating as she does so, by her actions, the main subdivisions into which it is broken up. Thus she will take a jug of water and show the children that it would be stupid to tilt the jug until the action of bringing it over the glass has been completed. Otherwise water will be spilt on the table. Or again, in pulling out a drawer she would point out how important it is to keep the drawer at the same level all the way out, and not pull more at one side than the other. If these precautions are neglected the drawer may stick and we shall waste time and energy struggling with it in an unreasonable manner. Locking and unlocking a box with a key, opening and shutting a gate, lacing up one's shoes, tying a bow, even so simple a matter as pulling off a jersey—all these and scores of other such actions can be analyzed in this way. This breaking up of movements into their component parts will arouse a great interest in the children, and invest the actions with a new fascination. It acts as a "little guide," and brings mind and muscle into more intimate association. "I have analyzed a movement: I have had to be attentive; to reason, to direct my movements according to reason. This interests me more than if I had learnt a new action. I have discovered a new world."

In this way we have raised the movement to a higher level. It is as though the "logos," the imminent reason, has incarnated itself in this action, giving it a new significance. "Thus our actions acquire a certain grace, as it were a spiritual perfection."

Little Marionettes?

The objection has sometimes been raised that, if we were to analyze these actions in this way into their separate elements, the children would perform them disconnectedly "like marionettes." But this is a groundless fear; the child at this stage is not a reasoner in the same sense that we are. He sees in this analysis simply a kind of guide and feels in it the satisfaction of a need. It is the same thing with language. An

[4] Cf. Mr. Pooter's remark, "I left the room with great dignity, but tripped on the mat." *Diary of a Nobody,* by Grossmith.

adult learning a foreign language tends to pronounce the syllables artificially; but not so the child at this stage. Whatever may be the number of syllables, the child learns to pronounce the words smoothly. So it is with his actions. Those who have done this, in practice, with small children will agree with Montessori's statement that "he enjoys this revelation and feels the attraction of a demonstration which is more interesting than a fairy tale."

Balancing Exercises

In every country children reveal a spontaneous impulse towards balancing exercises. You will see them walking along a board, or the edge of a pavement, or the top of a wall. Without doubt they feel the need of such exercises as a preparation, albeit unconscious, for the future. If we respond to this need by giving special exercises in balancing we shall find they enter into them with zest. Of all animals man is the only one with an erect posture. But he is not born to it; it is a conquest to be won. Correct balance is difficult for the child for two reasons: first, because his muscular system is not yet perfectly coordinated; and secondly, because the weight of his head and body, in proportion to his legs, is much heavier than in the adult. In the acquisition of a graceful carriage good balance is the first thing to aim at; given this the rest will naturally follow. Therefore in every infant school graded exercises in balance should form a regular part of the children's life. For small children it is quite difficult enough to attempt to walk along a line on the floor (with older children this could be raised a few inches from the ground on a wooden board to make it more difficult). So, in some large room or hall, a line—generally in the form of an ellipse—is painted on the floor. If the number of children is very large there can be *two* concentric ellipses. Since the greatest difficulty in balancing lies in placing one foot in front of the other, children must be instructed how to walk on the line, that is heel to toe, heel to toe, like a tightrope walker. The effort to walk in this way at once arouses the child's interest.

To begin with, just learning to walk on the line in this special way is quite difficult enough for small children; and requires all their attention and effort. When they can do this perfectly little complications can be added, which increase the interest without making it too difficult. Thus, first, we can give a child a small flag to carry in one hand, telling him to hold it well up, keeping the stick vertical. This makes it more difficult

because now his attention is divided between keeping his feet
on the line and holding the flag properly. After this we can
give him a second flag; now he has three things to attend to.
Other interesting complications may be introduced: glasses
filled nearly to the brim with prettily coloured water can be
provided, and the children have to carry them round as they
walk on the line without spilling. Another variation is to have
little bells which the children have to hold vertically and so
steadily that they do not ring. Or a child may carry the blocks
of the Pink Tower, placed one on top of the other, a difficult
feat of balance in itself, and much more so when combined
with walking on the line. Yet another exercise is to carry
something—a basket for instance—balanced on the head.
(It is well known that in those countries where women habi-
tually carry things on their heads they acquire an unusual
grace of deportment.)

In doing these exercises it is a good thing to place the
objects to be carried on a table in the centre of the circle or
ellipse; and let the children help themselves to this or that as
they go round, at times changing one object for another as
desire or opportunity suggests. It is also usual, whilst these
balancing exercises are in progress, for the teacher or her
assistant (or a gramophone) to play slow and quiet music;
not for the children to keep in step to, but to serve as a
"background."

The Silence Game

Spontaneous games of children are valuable indications
of their fundamental needs. Children sometimes seem to enjoy
sitting quite still opposite each other to see who can last out
longest without smiling, or to see who can keep his eyes open
longest without blinking. Again those who are "hiding" remain
a long time quite still. In these games the children almost turn
themselves into statues, and obviously enjoy doing so; as if
this voluntary checking of all movements was a pleasure in
itself. This love of silence and immobility, brought about by
an effort of will, provides then a natural motive, and is doubtless the reason why children so much enjoy the "silence game."
Not that Montessori, in the beginning, deliberately and consciously built up the silence game from the study of these
spontaneous amusements; those who are interested in seeing
how the silence game came into existence should read Montessori's own charming account of it in *The Secret of Childhood*.

We need not describe the silence game here as we have

already done so in Chapter XI, but a few further practical details may not be out of place.

In the first place children should be made to realize, from the beginning, that silence is something which *they make.* It is a collective achievement; something to which each single child contributes. How? By suppressing all his movements. For silence, this mysterious and wonderful thing, cannot be made directly: it is a by-product, and what creates it is immobility.

Listening to the Silence

It is not, of course, possible—even with the inhibition of the voluntary muscles—to obtain absolute immobility. The heart still goes on beating, and respiration continues to function. Therefore the end to be aimed at in the silence game is the maximum silence possible in the circumstances. When all the little hands and feet have stopped moving and the children are quite, quite still, there is always something to be heard, a residue of sound. The silence, to use the poet's words, is always "silence implying sound."[5] This is just what makes it so interesting.

There are grades of silence, each more perfect than the last, until as another poet says:

> The wind has gathered the last leaf,
> And silence has gathered the wind.[6]

Silence and the Soul

Silence predisposes the soul for certain inner experiences. "You are not the same after the silence as you were before it." Great thinkers and mystics have always sought silence for this purpose, as they have also made use of music, incense, and "storied windows richly light, casting a dim religious light." "Silence," says Montessori, "often brings us the knowledge which we had not fully realized, that we possess within ourselves an interior life." The child by means of it sometimes becomes aware of this "Buried Life" (as Matthew Arnold calls it) for the first time.

One day a directress of my acquaintance asked the children to say what they had heard in the silence. Besides the usual sounds such as mentioned in Chapter XI, one child said she heard "the Spring coming"; and another, "the voice of God speaking inside me." It is one of the tragedies of our mechani-

[5]Elizabeth Browning.
[6]Robert Bridges.

cal age that so many people grow up without ever having discovered the beauty of silence. The other day I read in a newspaper of an enterprising American in New York who had fitted up a Hall of Silence, and was selling this rare commodity to all and sundry at fifty cents an hour! In the Montessori classrooms, however, the children do not have to pay for it, not at least in cash. But nevertheless they do have to pay a price for it all the same—in the big effort of sitting so still for so long a time.

The Voice of the Silence

That they do this so willingly indicates that there is in the child's soul a natural affinity for this experience. With unerring instinct Montessori has found how to bring it to expression. In Chapter XI we have described how the directress, having darkened the room, summons each child, separately, to her by calling his or her name in a whisper. To do this successfully requires a definite technique. In order that the child's attention should be fixed only on sounds the directress should stand behind the children, or better still, if possible, out of sight in an adjoining room or corridor.

So, first the silence. Then the voice of the silence. The children, who do not know exactly when the voice is going to begin, are now all waiting for it with a tense inner expectancy. Every scrap of willpower is being put into the inhibition of all movements so that they will be able to hear and respond to the call when it comes stealing through "this silence which they have willed."

To hear himself called and to respond to the summons fulfills the cycle of satisfaction. That is why "*every* child should be called by name however long it takes." For in this game there is a strong emotional element corresponding to the great effort made. The longer the child has to wait the more bitterly would he feel the disappointment if—after all his effort—he did not experience the joy of responding to this mysterious summons. It requires a great deal of patience for a child of that age to keep still for so long—sometimes a quarter of an hour—and if the children felt there was a chance of their not being called their patience would diminish, and with it the silence.

One word about the teacher's voice. It is of absolute importance that it should not disturb the silence. It should seem rather to be its expression. Therefore it should hardly be a voice at all—scarcely a whisper—more like the ghost of a whisper. In accents hushed and long-drawn-out, it comes stealing through the twilight like the voice of a spirit, and speaks in turn directly into the heart of each eagerly listening child. Each name, as it is called, should begin almost insensibly as if it were growing out of nothing and then die away into nothingness again—

> As when, upon a trancèd summer night
> Those green rob'd senators of mighty woods
> Tall oaks, branch charmed by the earnest stars
> Dream, and so dream all night without a stir,
> Save from one gradual solitary gust
> Which comes upon the silence, and dies off . . .
> So came those words and went . . .[7]

Silence Its Own Reward

To experience this mysterious silence and respond to it is the child's reward—a reward so great that Montessori found that, when she gave each child a sweet as he came up he did not eat it, as though a need of the spirit had been satisfied on a higher plane, making the other superfluous.

Looked at from a longer perspective, in time, we may regard the silence game itself as a reward for long-continued efforts in the past. It is the *ultimo passo,* the last step, the consummation of that long process of refinement of movements, achieved through months of practice in the exercises of balance and rhythm. It would be impossible to expect a good silence game from a class composed of unnormalized children who have just come to school. Such children have not yet achieved that functional incarnation of which we spoke in the last chapter. Hence, however much they might wish it, they have not yet the ability to "create" silence by long-continued immobility. The silence game, in fact, represents "a species of triumph," a conquest of the spirit over the "flesh."

CHAPTER XIV   MOVEMENT AND MENTAL ASSIMILATION

The Importance of Movement

When I was living in Rome, working in collaboration with Dr. Montessori, it was my pleasurable duty to accompany visitors to the model Montessori School in Via Spezia. It not infrequently happened that, after watching the children at

[7]*Hyperion,* Keats.

work for some time, a visitor would express himself somewhat as follows: "There is one thing that puzzles me about these children. There they are working away by themselves, some at arithmetic, some at grammar, some at composition, and so forth; and as soon as one has finished a piece of work he quietly puts it away and then chooses another and settles down at that. The enigma to me is, how do they know how to do all these things since nobody seems to be teaching them?"

This is a natural enough question for anyone to ask who does not realize that under the Montessori system there are two distinct stages in learning anything. First, there is a short introductory stage, in which the child is initiated into the use of a new piece of material; and secondly, a much longer and more important one, in which he works with the material, day after day, and often week after week (not all the time, of course, but at chosen intervals). Since the second stage is by far the longer one it follows that, at any particular moment, the majority of the children are engaged in it. Hence it tends to give the casual visitor the impression that the children are not taught at all by the teacher. This of course is quite wrong, since the presence of the directress is as necessary as that of the materials, which would be dead and useless without her vivifying influence.

This second stage, of spontaneous working with the material, always involves movement. Movement is in fact a *sine quâ non* of the Montessori method. From the description given in Chapter XI it will be seen that even those children who are not moving bodily to and from the cupboards but are sitting quietly at their tables, or working upon rugs upon the floor, are all manipulating objects of some kind; all engaged in activities which involve definite and precise movement. It is the teacher's primary aim to set going this "second stage," in which the children *enter into a partnership with the material, live with it, and work with it.*

Simile of the Two Ladies

Montessori maintains that a more profound impression is gained through movement than by any merely visual or auditory aids. Supposing, she says by way of illustration, I wish two ladies to live together in intimate association (as it is our wish that the child should "live" with the materials). Well, first of all I would introduce them to each other (this corresponds to the Herbartian "Presentation"). They are now well able to recognize one another (this we may call the Herbartian "Apperception"). I now go away delighted, thinking that my aim has been accomplished, and that the two ladies will live together.

But I should be wrong; for actually to attain my end something more would be required. Interest would have to be aroused between the ladies, and sympathy, and affection: only then will they live in harmony together; only then could I go away and leave them. Applying this to the learning process, Montessori says, "Let us call 'interest' this union between the child and the object; an interest which brings about an activity prolonged and repeated. When this has been established then the directress can go away and leave the child in the company of the materials."

The Child Constructs Himself Through Movement

The value of movement goes deeper than just helping in the acquisition of knowledge.

It is in fact the basis for the development of personality. The child, who is constructing himself, must always be moving. Not only in those large movements which have an external aim, such as sweeping a room or laying a table or any other of the Exercises of Practical Life, but also when the child merely sees, or thinks, or reasons; or when he understands something in relation to these thoughts and sensations—always he must be moving. *Agire! Agire! Agire!* I would ask you to entertain this idea as a key and a guide: as a key, for it will unlock for you the secret of the child's development; as a guide, because it will point out to you the path you should follow. If you wish to give the means to the child for his development you must give them in such a way that the child can, and must move.

Visual Aids Not Enough

It is not enough then that the child should *see* the things we wish to teach him; we must present them in a form which solicits movement. Neither is it enough for him to *hear* the things which we wish him to learn: our telling is the least important part; it must be followed by a creative movement. "We must give no more to eye and ear than we give to the hand."

Thus, for example, if you wish to teach the child the idea of dimensions, and the grading of dimensions, it is of little avail merely to *show* him diagrams of objects of various sizes. We must give him materials (such as the Cylinders, Pink Tower, Long Stair and so forth) which he can manipulate himself, and compare by manipulating. Or again, take colour; one might perhaps think there could, and should, be no natural connection between learning colour and movement. Yet here, too, Montessori does not merely *show* the colours, but—by means of the colour tablets—presents them with a movement.

So with everything else, whether it be the multiplication tables; the four operations in arithmetic; the parts of speech; or even the theory of Pythagoras—always with a movement.

To take another example—the teaching of the letters of the alphabet. It is often maintained that one should not attempt, at the beginning, to teach small children the *sounds* the letters represent. I have in fact met teachers who actually prided themselves (why I could never understand!) on the fact that their children were ignorant of the particular sounds each letter represents. They maintain that children are not interested in the sounds of the letters, but only in recognizing word or sentence patterns taken as a whole. (At this point the Gestalt Theory is usually trotted out.) The reason why these teachers have failed to arouse a living interest in the separate letters and their sounds is because they have relied solely on visual or auditory aids—and not on a material which solicits an individual *movement*.[1]

If each letter is mounted on a separate card in such a way that it can be treated as an entity in itself, with a sound of its own—something which can be chosen at will, touched and traced, moved about, compared with others, shown to other children (who miraculously respond by making the same sound!)—then there is no question about the interest being forthcoming.[2]

In all her books, lectures, conversations, Montessori incessantly returns to this great theme of the importance of movement. Here are a few more examples taken at random. "The fundamental technique in education is this—that the child should always be active, and allowed to choose his occupations; and thus give form to his actions" . . . "This principle of movement should be carried right through education; so that in all the child's manifestations there should be this union between the ego and its acts" . . . "The organization of movement is not simply the completion of the psychological construction; it is the foundation." And so on.

There Is No Substitute for Movement

It is well known that the child who grows up deprived of any of his senses, who suffers from blindness, for instance,

[1] And also because the children have not begun early enough, say about 3½–4 years.
[2] Cf. the anecdote related by Dr. Montessori in her *Discovery of the Child*, pp. 336–7, Indian edition.

or deafness, tends to be retarded in his mental development. But it is not yet generally realized that the child who grows up deprived of movement (that is, thought realized in action) will also be arrested in his development. In fact, Montessori goes so far as to say that "the man who has developed without practical activity in life is in a worse condition than he who has been deprived of one of his senses. For, deprived of one of his senses, he can to some extent remedy that defect by means of the other senses, but for movement there is no substitute on the same level."

Movement Without Thought

Some may object that Montessori is by no means the first to realize the value of movement in education. Has it not been for a long time the custom in many schools to vary the strain of sitting still at mental work with the movements of gymnastics? True enough! But this, according to Montessori, is by no means the same thing. It is "but to substitute movement without thought, for thought without movement," thus adding one fatigue to another. For "fatigue arises when mental activity and motor activity, which should form a unity, are forced to act separately. If the individual does not act as one whole, mind and body in unison, every effort is resented as a fatigue." (Those hateful school walks in crocodile for instance!) Montessori illustrates this point with one of her simple and telling similes. Persons who try to relieve the fatigue of motionless mental work with the fatigue of set gymnastics can be compared to a man who has been trying to make progress by first hopping along on his left foot, and then trying to rest himself by hopping along on his right. If, however, he puts an end to this artificial divorce and does what nature intended him to do—i.e., use both legs together in walking—then at once progress becomes easy and without fatigue.

Value of Games

A more intelligent alternative to such "thought without movement" is provided by games. Here the movement is more "synthetic," i.e., it is spontaneous and has a definite aim. That is why "sports give better results than gymnastics in the improvement of character and morale. Yet though better in these respects, sports are still an inadequate preparation for life."

In this connection Montessori speaks very highly of eurhythmics. In this we have "a complex activity brought into being by the music; an expression which calls for an exact obedience of the motor organs. It is no longer a question of a contemplative listening to music, but of an interior analysis, with a corresponding external activity. That is why eurhythmics may sometimes bring about something almost resembling a moral transformation of character."

We may note in passing that in Montessori's system (at any rate with the younger children) the place of set gymnastics and drilling is largely taken by the exercises in practical life. In no gymnasium would they have to have such a number of coordinated movements as they do in carrying out all these exercises. In fact, an article appeared recently in a women's journal, analyzing the various movements that the ordinary housewife goes through in the course of her daily duties, and comparing them very favourably with the set exercises she would do if she attended special courses at a gymnasium!

Movement Must Be Synthetic

When Montessori speaks of the educational value of movement we must be on our guard against misinterpretation. "To speak of the value of movement in general would be too vague; and would have no direct bearing on education or development. As everyone knows, the child, unless inhibited, is always moving; but the majority of these movements have no importance for education. There are plenty of people who think that the important thing is that children should have ample space to run about in freely 'like cats and lizards.' But such liberty has little to do with the development of the intelligence. *The educational value of a movement depends on the finality (or end) of the movement; and it must be such that it helps the child to perfect something in himself; either it perfects the voluntary muscular system ('the flesh'); or some mental capacity; or both. Educational movement must always be an activity which builds up and fortifies the personality, giving him a new power and not leaving him where he was. . . .* In this creative, constructive, synthetic movement the intelligence is fixed on the purpose of the movement, not the movement itself. It is the movement as a whole, not the sensorial stimulus, which is the cause of the attention. The movement is only creative when it enables the child to keep united his motor forces and his psychic life."

Another point to bear in mind is that, in order to be effective, synthetic movement must call forth a real effort; since the will like any other organ grows by functioning. To bring about this effort the end to be reached must not be too far off or too difficult: on the other hand it must not be too easy. It must be within measurable distance—"just out of reach, but coming within reach by a 'stretching of the mind'!"

Synthetic Movement and Free Choice

It is not sufficient that the end of the movement must be definite and clearly understood; it must be freely chosen, thus becoming the act of the total personality. In practice, this means that the child's movements should not be just the carrying out of a command by the adult. "When a child, placed in the prepared environment, begins to act freely as his normal routine—washing tables, arranging flowers, doing sums, composing words and so on, *because he himself has chosen to do so,* then his whole ego is active, and his personality functions as a unity. In these circumstances his action will follow the private and intimate rhythm of his own life. When an entire personality is thus acting in a favourable environment we call it *'work.'*"

This question of spontaneity goes right to the root of Montessori's system, but it is often misunderstood even by her own followers. "It is not difficult to get the child to carry out a determined action. The difficult thing (and herein lies the art of the directress) is to draw out this action in such a way as not to influence its spontaneity." "It is easy to substitute our will for that of the child by means of suggestion or coercion; but when we have done this we have robbed him of his greatest right, the right to construct his own personality. If the child is constantly acting at the command of the teacher, or at her suggestion, his own psychic activity may fade away and disappear under the stronger will of another; the personality may become broken and depressed; and abnormal developments will begin to appear. There is here a delicate distinction which it is not easy to grasp in its full significance; yet it represents the most fundamental danger in education. All the psychic future of this individual, for good or ill, depends upon whether—as a child—he has been able to develop keeping united his motive forces and his psychic life."

"The Centre and the Periphery"

The fundamental importance of movement in education is nowhere more clearly seen than in Montessori's doctrine of "The Centre and the Periphery." In most methods of education, she remarks by way of introduction, the would-be teacher is fundamentally preoccupied with a study of the characteristics of the child's mind; how it perceives, remembers, forms new associations, and so forth—in short, with the laws of psychology as applied to the learning process. Great stress is laid on how she should make her lesson notes beforehand—with their "preparation, presentation, development, application, association, etc."—or some modified form of the Herbartian "steps." All this means that the teacher concerns herself very intimately with what goes on in the mind of the child.

Now, says Montessori, our point of view is quite different. We do not deny that there are certain psychological laws which govern the child's apprehension of knowledge, and his mental development. We readily admit that the mind of the learner is something very wonderful, and mysterious, difficult to understand; and requiring great powers of insight in order to penetrate it. In fact, we would even go further and maintain that it is far superior to any conception of it hitherto held. But—and here is the essential difference—Montessori asserts that not only is it difficult to penetrate into these mysteries, but also that, as teachers, we may and even should divest ourselves of the desire to do so. What goes on in this mysterious centre of the child's creative intelligence is his secret, and we must respect that secret. That inner creative "centre" is the part of the individual that belongs entirely to himself; and we need not occupy ourselves with what goes on there.

Let us state this matter more clearly, for it is a basic consideration. The child, as an individual, presents two aspects: a centre, and a periphery. First, the centre. This we may regard as the innermost citadel of the personality from which action proceeds. Montessori insists on this last point. The centre is not merely a sort of mirror or mechanism for returning reflex actions; it is the place from which things start. At this centre the child increases his mental powers by seeking out sensations and movements, which take place at the second part of his personality—i.e., at the periphery.

So we have, secondly, the periphery. This is that part of the child's personality which comes in contact with the external world. It comprises the senses, and movements, and the outward manifestations of his choice. Through the continuous interaction of these two factors, the centre and periphery, the mind of the child develops, unfolds, expands, creates itself in a unity. Sensations are taken in from the outside; and from the centre there comes a corresponding unfolding outwards. It is important to realize that what enters through the senses and muscles does not do so mechanically, automatically, willy-nilly. "No! we *grasp* our sensations; we choose; we act; we are active beings—expressive; and this applies no less to the infant than to the adult. The child chooses something through his senses because he wills it, and we need not be anxious about the reason why." (Cf. that "Inner Sensitiveness" described in Chapter XVII.) In the case of children, this taking in of images through the senses and movement—which is an expression of choice—is "accomplished by the manipulation of objects, by a continuous muscular activity."

We may say that the periphery is that part of the personality which is accessible to us; and it is upon this that Montessori bases her method. However impossible it may be to see what is going on at the invisible centre, it is easy to see what is happening at the periphery—especially when we allow the child freedom of choice in his activities. To be a close observer of the visible, tangible manifestations at the periphery—this is the important thing for the directress. Her commerce is with the periphery; and only through that—*indirectly*—with the centre. Experience will show her how best "to feed the periphery."

The Twofold Rhythm of Growth

We are convinced, says Montessori, through our long experience, that the child grows by a welding together of these two elements of his personality, thereby constructing his own mind and expressing himself at the same time. "Whilst the child is working actively at the periphery with material things, at one and the same time he gathers in sensory experiences and expresses himself. We would go so far as to declare that when the child works thus, in a manner corresponding to the needs of his nature (see Chapter VIII), his work *is* his self-expression." This is a point to which we shall return in a later chapter in a comparison between the ideas of Froebel and Montessori.

This interaction between the visible periphery and invisible centre goes on unceasingly. "It is like the rhythm of the wave that never ceases, the beating of a heart that never stops." In one lecture Montessori compared it to the work of the embryonic heart which, on the one hand, receives nourishing blood from the mother; and in turn passes it on to the other parts of the embryo to build up the organism. It is interesting to note a similar passage from Jung, who describes the work of the psyche as

a diastolic going out and seizing the object, and a systaltic concentration and release of energy from the object seized. Every human being possesses both mechanisms as an expression of his natural life-rhythm—that rhythm which Goethe, surely not by chance, characterized with the physiological concept of cardiac activity. A rhythmic alternation of both forms of psychic activity may correspond with the normal course of life. (*Psychological Types*, pp. 12-13.)

It is not, we repeat, necessary for the directress to know what is going on at the centre so long as she knows that the right kind of activity is taking place at the periphery. For that centre is one of nature's secrets, one of the secret creative laboratories of life.

Serving the Periphery

From this new point of view of mental development and the learning process there arises, as a natural corollary, a new way of teaching. Other methods aim at getting to the centre *directly*, i.e., the teacher applies herself *directly* to the child's intelligence. That is why the teacher strives to make things simple, for she imagines that this immature mind is only capable of making a small effort. It is assumed that the child can only be interested in understanding a thing when it is spoon-fed from another person. Such teachers are not aware (since they have never given the child a chance to reveal it) of that irresistible motor force, coming from the centre outwards; which drives the child to seize (apprehend) things spontaneously for himself through movement, thus developing his mind and constructing his personality.

Our business, then, is to "feed the periphery." This we do by means of occupations so prepared that they meet the child's natural tendency to explore the world about him through material objects, and by doing so to abstract ideas from them. These ideas he spontaneously builds into his own individual mental system. This is the work of the centre.

These materials facilitate the child's spontaneous mental research; for (see Chapter V) the child is by nature an explorer of his environment. By their scientific accuracy, careful grading and the brilliant way in which they "isolate the desired stimulus," these prepared materials reveal with greatest clarity the qualities of objects, their relationship, number, and so forth. The point to emphasize here is that we do not simply *show* him these objects, but we present them in such a way that each material calls forth a visible movement at the periphery. In short, "we never give to the eye more than we give to the hand."

The Teaching Materials

Since our aim therefore is to feed the periphery, the objects which we give to the children, placed at their disposal in the environment, assume a paramount importance in our method. These objects are not chosen at random, or because they happen to arouse a passing interest. Each possesses as it were within it an idea to be realized—not an idea to be announced by the teacher and handed over directly from her to the child. Rather the idea is implicit in, or latent in the material itself. As the material is used, this idea becomes presented—if one might say so—materially and spread out in space. And in time, too, for it is only as the child works with the materials, lives with it (like the two ladies in our simile) hours at a time, and day after day—always active with hand as well as brain—that the idea inherent in the material comes off from it into the child's mind (as a transfer that has been soaking a long time in water comes off on a piece of paper). Or, to vary the metaphor, the idea seems to detach itself from the material, quietly, gently, unobtrusively, as an exhalation or perfume—or even a spiritual emanation—thus entering the child's mind to become part of his very self.

The Successful Directress and the Periphery

This explains why, when the directress sees all her children concentrated on the various occupations—the little hands busy placing and replacing, touching, arranging, feeling, sorting, counting, and comparing, according to the nature and use of each material—she can be well satisfied, and contemplate the busy scene with the deepest joy. For then she knows that, corresponding to all this concentrated "peripheral" activity, development and growth is going on in that inner mysterious "centre." Experience will soon reveal to her that when her children work in this way they are capable of making a mental and moral progress which is truly astonishing.

A New Kind of Teacher Training

It will be readily seen that Montessori's doctrine of the centre and periphery, with its emphasis on freely chosen movement, is bound to have a profound effect on the kind of training given to teachers under the Montessori system. We may say in fact that the training of the Montessori directress is twofold. It consists of:

First. An initiation into a new conception of the dignity of the human personality, which—when understood—leads to the establishment of The New Relationship spoken on in Chapter XV-XVIII.

Second. The acquisition of a certain discipline—simple, exact, and humble—the task of learning how to "serve the periphery." In practice this means that the would-be teacher must spend long hours, day after day, week after week, and even month after month, learning how to use and how to present the immense variety of materials which will surround the growing child in his prepared environment. She will have also to become acquainted with the exercises of practical life and the lessons of grace and courtesy proper to her own country and civilization.

The Point of Contact

The question is sometimes put: suppose you get ready the prepared environment—and present the materials to the children—but there comes no sign of this wonderful twofold activity of periphery and centre, what then? Let Montessori herself reply: "In practice," she says, "you may often see that a teacher has prepared the environment, but the children do not pay any attention, are not interested, and act in a *disorderly* manner. What is the matter? Is it the method, or the environment, or the teacher, or the children? Something evidently has gone wrong." Montessori's answer is clear and unequivocal: what is missing is the "Point of Contact." This may be described as "a psychological bridge which puts the soul of the indiivdual child in contact with some definite, limited piece of external reality."

To illustrate more specifically what is meant by this, let us take an example from the teaching of musical appreciation. Montessori believes that music—like anything else—can best be made comprehensible to the child through movement. With this end in view it forms part of the usual daily programme of the Montessori class that children should spend some time moving freely in response to music. "Now," says Montessori, "we can imagine a case in which the teacher plays music from morning to night (even with a jazz band!) and yet the children continue to move about anyhow, here and there and everywhere, in a disorderly and inharmonious manner. What is lacking here, in order to make possible their musical education, is the Point of Contact. In this particular case it means simply this, that the muscles which move, should move in response to the musical rhythm—thus establishing a psychic bridge between the soul of the child and the external reality of the music. The moment the child understands that there exists this connection (between the music and his movements) then the Point of Contact has been established. *Now,* when the music changes its rhythm, the child becomes aware of it, and changes his movements accordingly; and now he is on the road to the perfecting of himself."

Turning to the mental plane, the plane of the intellect, something analogous must take place if true education is to proceed. In the lecture from which the above paragraphs were taken, Montessori continued her argument in these emphatic words: "This is my Credo! I believe that for mental development to take place it is necessary first to establish this Point of Contact between the soul of the child and an external reality . . .[3] Man develops by putting himself in contact with an external reality, and by continuous exercise with it. This reality may be either material or spiritual; but for the child at any rate it must always be accompanied by movement."

The Point of Contact Brings Precision

Let us return for a moment to our illustration from music. Before the child had established his point of contact with the music his movements had been almost infinite in variety and number, and had been disorderly and chaotic. With the coming of the point of contact, however, we observe two very important changes. *First,* there is a limitation of his movements; and *secondly,* there is exactitude and precision. In the mental sphere an analogous process must take place. Before the establishment of the point of contact the child's mind wanders here and there, turning now to this and now to that, "doing everything by fits and starts and nothing long," his movements being restless and uncoordinated. But with the establishment of the point of contact there results at once a limitation of the mental field, that is, a concentration on a definite aspect of reality; which is accompanied by a movement of exactitude and precision.[4] The point of contact sets going "a movement in consciousness which can be described as the creation of something clear and definite, where before all was vague, formless, without precise outline. Indeed we may characterize it as the construction of consciousness itself, because in the last analysis, consciousness is that part which is—

---

[3]Note that the Point of Contact is with a *reality* and not with a *make-belief,* a point to which we will return in a later chapter (XX).
[4]Cf. the multiplication girl, p. 187.

conscious! i.e., which differs from the subconscious precisely
in the fact that there is this limitation and precision."

How the Point of Contact Helps Development

It will help us to understand the effect of the point of
contact, in the child's mental development, if we recall the subject discussed in Chapter V under the heading of "The Young
Explorer." There we realized the immense task which is spontaneously undertaken by the child's intelligence—nothing less
than the building up of an interior world, a microcosm, corresponding to the external world, the macrocosm. The majority
of impressions have entered, and still enter, his mind without
any system or relationship. What he needs most therefore—to
assist his mental development—is not *more* colours, *more*
sounds, *more* words, *more* information, and in general more
impressions pouring all higgledy-piggledy into his mind without pause; but something which will help him to put in order
the vast heterogeneous collection of impressions already received; something that will enable him to rise above his many
experiences, master them, and organize them into a vital unity.

Now this is just where the point of contact comes in. One of
the commonest misconceptions of the Montessori systems is
that she has devised her materials, especially the sensorial
materials, in order to present the children with new impressions, new sounds, new shapes, etc. This is quite wrong. Their
primary aim is not this, but to bring order into those impressions which the child has already received, and will receive.

Take the colour tablets for instance. Many critics have said:
"Surely these materials are superfluous! Does not the child in
his daily environment—in house, garden, and field—see all
those colours and many more besides?" This is quite true, in
a sense. He sees them, and yet he does not see them—just as
the child heard all that music being played by the teacher (before he made the point of contact) and yet in a sense did not
hear it. The colour tablets, just because they have been created
in such a way that they can be arranged on the principle of
identity, contrast, or gradation; because they call forth a movement limited and precise with a definite aim; because they
isolate the notion of colour to the exclusion of all else; and
because they are limited in number, focus the mind on the very
idea of colours, their gradation, contrast, and identity.

And what is the effect of all this? Is it a limitation because
of the limited number of colour tablets? Exactly the reverse!
It leads to an extension of the child's interest in colours, and
his power to observe them in the world around him. We readily

grant that the manipulation of the colour tablets in itself, while it is going on, brings with it a limitation, a narrowing of attention, a focusing upon a particular aspect of reality—just as the moving of the muscles to the rhythm of the music brought a limitation of movement. But the process does not end there. It is just the child who has been working with the colour tablets who will spontaneously go up to a visitor and solemnly announce, "Your dress is the same shade of blue as the flowers in the next room;" or joyfully proclaim that "John's coat is brown" or that "the sky is blue." Similarly a child of four has seen hundreds of geometric forms in his everyday environment which mean nothing to him. But the same child, after he has been working with the geometric insets, will suddenly discover with a spasm of joy that "the table is a rectangle!" "My plate is a circle!"

"Keys to the Universe"

It is true, then, that the point of contact brings with it a limitation, but it is equally true that it leads to a wider and fuller life. As in the Gospel, "Strait is the gate that leadeth to life"—but not the life to which it leads. Each of the Montessori materials—when properly used—opens up new vistas of experience, revealing new wonders in the world around him, wonders which have always been present but have hitherto remained unnoticed. That is why Montessori calls them "keys to the universe."

"Some persons complain," says Montessori, "that we give too few things to the children. This is because they do not realize that what I do in fact is to give them the means to see better. They confuse the keys to the universe with the universe itself."

"Let us keep, then, constantly before our minds this picture of the child mind, called—through the point of contact—to a small work, limited and exact, 'il piccolo ragionamento' (the little reasoning), but to a real work, i.e., rooted in reality—not a make-belief. As the music summons the child from just making any movements—running, jumping, hopping, somersaults, etc.—to the performance of precise and limited movements in accordance with the reality of the musical rhythm, so the point of contact, in the mental sphere, summons the mind of the child from wandering at large in fantasy to something real, which opens up a new pathway."

Establishing the Point of Contact

As the point of contact is a matter of such importance it may be advisable to mention a few practical rules with regard to how it may be brought about. In the first place: you cannot establish the point of contact with a whole class of children at once. It is essentially an individual process and cannot be mass produced. To be done perfectly, it involves individual initiation, followed by free choice of occupations. Herein, we may note in passing, lies one of the important differences between the Montessori and the Froebel systems. Miss Hume is right in saying that the unit, with Froebel, is the group, whereas with Montessori it is the individual child.[5]

It is no easy or simple matter to bring a class of—say thirty-five—children to a state in which they all can and do work quietly as individuals, revealing that profound attachment to the materials of which we have spoken above. At the beginning it is especially difficult, when a class has been started for the first time. Just because the children are lacking in the point of contact they tend to be restless and disorderly and without concentration. For this reason, says Montessori, in the beginning the directress should deal with the children collectively "like an ordinary teacher," impressing her personality upon them directly in an energetic and striking manner. She might for instance "tell them a story, play games with them, march with them, dance with them, sing to them—in short do anything that fixes the attention of all these tiny beings *on herself,* the normal condition in most schools!"

But this is only at the beginning. Later on she will not do these things, because—as points of contact are set up between individual children and the materials—they will tend to turn more and more to the materials and away from the directress. This is in accordance with the maxim quoted in Chapter XVIII. "He must increase and I must decrease."

There are no particular set rules as to how the directress should establish the required *rapport* between these disorderly children and their environment. With small children, however, we may be certain that the Exercises of Practical Life will play an important part; but in any case—always the point of contact will be established through movement. In one of her lectures Montessori—by way of an example—described how a beginning might be made along the following lines. The directress, who has the attention of the class, might suddenly do something in front of the children which seems quite useless and illogical—e.g., "She gets up from a chair, carries it from

[5] Emily G. Hume, *Learning and Teaching in the Infant School.*

one place, and puts it down in another, and then sits on it."
But mark how she does it!—in a very special way! Seriously,
almost mysteriously, she lifts it, carries it, and sets it down
without a sound! There is no sense apparently in all this! Yet
anyone looking on would be amazed to see what an interest this
simple action, done in this way, will arouse in a class of small
children, especially if they have been told beforehand "to listen
carefully and see if they can detect a sound." They have seen
chairs moved before, and moved them themselves dozens of
times—just taken them up and dumped them down anyhow.
But this is something different. Here is precision, limitation,
movement with a definite aim; and above all (though they do
not realize it consciously) it presents them with a means for
self-perfection. By the expression on their tiny faces you can
see how great is the interest aroused by this action—and—"that
interest is the beginning of a great future." They are all agog
to do the action themselves; and when given the chance to do
so, perform it silently, almost breathlessly, with immense concentration and bright shining eyes. It is as though they were
saying to themselves, "Ah, I have felt something which I have
never felt before, something which corresponds to my soul. I
am '*appassionato*' to do it again, and again."

This is but an example, and the directress might prefer to
approach the problem through some other means. But always
it would involve initiation into some definite and precise movement with a clearly appreciated aim. In this way, as more and
more of the Exercises of Practical Life and the elementary
materials come to be introduced, the directress will find the
children becoming ever more calm and concentrated, carrying
out these occupations "as though deeply touched in spirit." She
will see these neophytes becoming daily more masters of themselves, revealing a higher type of personality than ever she
imagined them to possess; and vindicating the truth of Montessori's maxim that "education begins through movement."

The Point of Contact Established
Through Other Children

Before we leave this subject there is one more point to
mention, and a very practical one. Once a child has really
concentrated on a particular occupation he is not as he was.
He is a changed person; and the more he has concentrated the
greater is the change. A new kind of interest has been aroused
in him; and it is like an appetite which grows by what it feeds
on. We may now see this "awakened child" setting forth deliberately to seek out other children, to find out what they are

doing. This is more than merely giving his consent to an instruction by the teacher; it is an active development. Which means, that the teacher is not the only one who effects the point of contact; it may come through other children.

Every experienced Montessori directress will tell you how often she has been amazed to find out what the children have learned apart from her, even without her knowledge. In the congenial atmosphere of the Montessori school, which allows the children freely to associate with each other, they are always teaching one another. For this reason the directress must learn to distinguish the disciplined "explorer" from the child who is simply a "disturber." Children who have learned how to use the materials very often make excellent teachers. In fact, as Montessori remarks, they are in some cases more successful than adults "who are still too far away from the psychic rhythm of the child's mode of acting." This is especially true in the case of certain older children who may have developed a "psychic barrier" to particular subjects, especially reading and arithmetic. "In vain may a teacher give to such children her best lessons, while a younger child may find the way to infiltrate his knowledge into their closed up minds."

MOVEMENT AND DISCOVERY

Movement and Concentration

It is a common practice in many schools to obtain the attention and concentration of the children in a variety of different ways—such as by visual aids, or a story, or by the vivacity of the teacher's manner, or by some dramatic action; or it may be by offering rewards, or even threatening punishment. With Montessori this interest and concentration is secured through movement.

"Right from the beginning," she says, "this phenomenon of concentration has been our guide in building up our method. Our experience has proved, beyond doubt, that concentration comes when children are occupied with the material, always with the material—never without a material.

"So then it is a material we must have, not a person. And the condition to ensure concentration is as follows: The material must be an object which does not interest in an abstract manner, but because it lends itself to a certain activity, which is such that the child is led to repeat the movement again and again from the beginning." Furthermore, she remarks that this movement must have "an intellectual atmosphere."

Some visitors to Montessori schools, especially those accustomed to the rigid silence of the old order, imagine that it must be very hard—if not impossible—for children to concentrate on their work in the midst of all that coming and going and general stir in a Montessori classroom, which we have compared to the busy hum of a hive of bees. Yet experience shows the contrary. It is movement, through the point of contact, which ensures concentration—not silence. For we must remember that the child is not trying to concentrate on a person; nor yet on an idea in the abstract—which would be difficult. Given the material, however, with the movement it elicits, he can concentrate "even to isolation point" without absolute silence. More necessary to him than silence is that he should be protected from unnecessary adult intervention, once the point of contact has been achieved.[6]

Movement, Repetition, and Discovery

In many methods when a teacher has taught something to a child and the latter understands it, the former thinks his aim has been accomplished; he can now go on to introduce the next step.

But it is not so with us. When the child has come to understand something it is not the end, but only the beginning. For now there comes the "second stage" mentioned above; the more important one, when the child goes on repeating the same exercise again and again for sheer love of it. When I have just been introduced to a person and I find him interesting and attractive, that is not the moment when I turn my back on him and go away!! Rather it is just then that I have the wish to stay in his company and enjoy it.

Sudden Illuminations

This voluntary repetition of movement is of the utmost importance for mental development; for with it there is brought into being a phenomenon which is most characteristic of the Montessori classroom "Very often, when an exercise has been repeated and repeated, out of all logical limits, there will come to the mind of the child—like a sudden light—a mental illumination, as real as it is unexpected, in the form of a new and fecund intuition. It is an experience which may be compared to the sudden turning on of a light which reveals something new, and full of immense possibilities."

[6] Actually the noise is always kept within reasonable limits. Montessori would never tolerate the hideous banging and general pandemonium that one sometimes meets within so-called Activity schools.

Montessori Explosions

It often happens that the outward evidence of this inward mental growth reveals itself with an almost explosive violence. The long, tranquil, unhurried, joyful work with the material; its repeated manipulation, and the deep persuasion that comes with it, result at times in the sudden leap of mind to a new level. (Montessori compares it to the saltations of the species to a new norm.) These experiences are in fact so common that Montessori teachers have given them a sort of nickname: they call them "Montessori explosions." Montessori herself believes that these unexpected intuitions, which are akin to the inspirations of genius, should in fact be the normal accompaniment to mental expansion in *every* individual; and would be, if the right conditions prevailed. Good examples of Montessori explosions are the "exploding" into writing and reading—described in Chapter II; but every Montessori teacher could supply many other examples.

Montessori compares the child who is working with a material, on one level, to someone taking a long run in preparation for a jump to a higher one.

The Materials as the Gateway to New Discoveries

The children are instructed to use each of the materials in a particular way; but very often such instruction does not by any means exhaust their useful possibilities. It therefore often happens that, as a result of this "material—plus—movement," the children themselves discover new ways of using the materials, and in this way are led to the discovery of new facts and new relationships. As a matter of history, many of the exercises now in general use in Montessori schools all over the world, were first discovered by the children themselves in this school or that.

To show how movement with the materials may lead to new discoveries let us take the Number Rods by way of example. Simple and severe as they are in appearance, they often lead individual children to make exciting discoveries for themselves. At the beginning they are used just to teach the numbers 1–10. But by their very nature they are apt to open up other possibilities to any intelligent child. Most children, in fact, *without any suggestion on the part of the teacher*, begin to arrange them in a new way—putting the 1 rod next to the 9, the 2 next to the 8, and so on, until they have turned the Number Stair into a long rectangle with one rod (the 5) left over. So in this way, even before the child properly realizes what he is doing, he has—as it were off his own bat—discovered the various ways of composing the number 10. Having done this it is quite likely that he may begin systematically to undo this pattern, thus working back to the original stair. What he is now doing, in effect, is a series of little sums breaking up the number 10 into various subtraction sums, e.g., 10—1=9, 10—2=8, and so on.

In this way the material forms at one and the same time a mental gymnastic and a ship of discovery. In this connection I might mention a rather interesting incident. I called one day on Dr. Montessori, when she was living in London, to find these same Number Rods spread out on the table in front of her. She was in unusually high spirits because she herself, working with them, had just had a "Montessori explosion"! Though she had been acquainted with this very elementary material for over twenty-five years, she had that very morning discovered that they could be used as a perfect means for demonstrating the algebraical formula:

$$1+2+3+4\ldots.n=\frac{n(n+1)}{2}$$

Incidentally, this illustrates another of the good effects which result from the unhurried manipulation of number materials when they are spread out in space—viz., the manner in which, whilst occupied with numbers, one suddenly finds oneself unexpectedly turning up in the sphere of algebra or geometry, thus discovering, as from a mountaintop, vistas of new territory waiting to be explored.

Movement Perfects Observation

"In order that the child should be able to persist for a long time in ordered observation he must always be moving." Take for instance the idea of height. It is beyond question that the small child in his everyday environment sees many objects of varying height, but his mind is not thereby concentrated on the particular notion of height. In order that this should happen he must see a collection of objects *as a whole* (Gestalt) which vary only in height. It is highly improbable, says Montessori in a rather amusing example, that a child would see going down the street a family of ten persons, father and mother and eight children, all varying in height by an exact and equal gradation from the six-foot father to the tiny toddler. If he did, his interest would certainly be aroused by such an arresting sight. But—and here is the point—even then he would not have the opportunity of moving the members of this family about, mixing them up, and re-arranging them again in their proper order as many times as he liked. This, however, is exactly what he can do with the cylinders (see p. 149). It is, as we have seen in Chapter IX, just in and through this sight, plus touch, plus movement, that there is born in his mind a clear notion of what height is. As Aristotle would say, the idea is abstracted from the "common" sense impression (or "phantasm") by the "active intellect" (*intellectus agens*).

Montessori Principles and the "Activity School" Movement

The widespread development of the "activity school" and similar movements indicates that it is now generally recognized that freedom of movement is the child's right in the infant and primary schools.

Unfortunately it is not so generally realized what kind of movement is essential for the child's physical, mental, and social development. It is just here that Montessori's analysis of the nature and purpose of "synthetic movement" together with her doctrine of the "centre and the periphery" and the "point of contact" are so helpful.

It would be interesting to examine the various "activity" methods now in vogue in the light of Montessori principles, but unfortunately that would take us beyond the scope of this chapter and this book.

PART FOUR

The New Relationship

> The adult has not understood the child or the adolescent, and is therefore in continual strife with him. The remedy is not that the adult should learn something intellectually, or complete a deficient culture. He must find a different starting point. The adult must find, in himself, the hitherto unknown error that prevents him seeing the child as he is. If this preparation is wanting, and if he has not acquired the aptitude that such a preparation entails, he cannot proceed further.
>
> *The Secret of Childhood,* Chapter I.

CHAPTER XV   THE FUNDAMENTAL PROBLEM IN EDUCATION

We live in an age which may be said to be very education-conscious. Not a day passes but one can read in the daily press articles on different aspects of education, not only by those within the profession but by many outside it. It seems generally recognized that—though an immense amount of time, money, and energy is being spent on education—the results are far from being proportionately satisfactory. Many and various are the criticisms put forward; and many and various the suggested reforms. Some, for instance, think that everything will come right if we have bigger and brighter school buildings; others, if we have smaller classes. For such as these it is all a question of organization. Here we might mention, in passing, those who lay a great stress on mental tests and examinations in order to secure a proper segregation of different types of children for different types of schools. Then, again, there are those who affirm that we shall never raise the standard of education until we raise the salaries of the teachers, thus drawing into the profession a better type of citizen.

Those inside the profession—especially in the training colleges—are inclined to see the root problem as a question of

THE FUNDAMENTAL PROBLEM IN EDUCATION

method. Consequently we have advocates of all kinds of panaceas in this direction. We have, for example, on the one hand those who are for free discipline and self-expression; and on the other those who inveigh against "all this modern soft psychology," urging as emphatically a return to the good old principle of spare the rod and spoil the child. Not long ago we had a large and influential group who based everything on the magic word "Activity." Others are equally enthusiastic about centres of interest, projects, environmental studies, and so forth. And of course we have always with us (like the poor!) those who maintain that it doesn't matter two pins what method you use, because, in the long run, everything depends on the personality of the teacher.

Now according to Montessori all these, and similar efforts to improve the situation—many of them very good in themselves—are really beside the point: they do not get down to the root of the matter. Paradoxical as it may seem she says—"the fundamental problem in education is not an educational problem at all: it is a social one. It consists in the establishment of a new and better relationship between the two great sections of society—children and adults." This is the crux of the whole problem; and unless we keep it steadily in front of us, all our endeavours at reform in education are bound to fail, or be merely palliatives. It was doubtless because Montessori was never trained as a teacher along conventional lines, but entered the sphere of education from without—almost, one might say, by accident—that she was able to see the whole problem in this new and unconventional light.

A Universal Oppression

If Montessori affirms so categorically that the real problem consists in establishing a new relationship between children and adults it can only be because she has discovered something radically wrong with that relationship as it is. Put briefly the situation, as she sees it, is as follows: all over the world, in every land—civilized and uncivilized—in every social stratum (not least among the rich) there is going on a disastrous oppression of the weak by the strong—an oppression none the less real and devastating in its effects because it is unconsciously exercised, and therefore unintentional. It is indeed the strangest kind of oppression, because those who exercise it love those whom they oppress, and wish rather to help them than to hinder them. Furthermore the oppressed, for the most part, love their oppressors. Parents, nursemaids, governesses, teachers—in fact all those who have to do with children—are the "guilty" ones. Yet, in a sense, they are not guilty, because it is all a tragedy of misunderstanding.

This may seem to some readers a point of view so extraordinary that they may wonder how a person so eminently endowed with common sense as Montessori should ever have come to adopt it. But it did not come to her suddenly; rather it was borne in upon her as the result of many years of careful observation.

Looking back over her long experience, and taking into account the results which have invariably followed the introduction of her method in a score of different countries during a period of thirty years, Dr. Montessori came to see with a peculiar vividness this picture of the child misunderstood. The rapidity and enthusiasm with which her method was welcomed in every part of the world, and the uniformity of the results obtained, were to her the clearest evidence of the ubiquity of this oppression. Everywhere her ideas, on being put into practice, have acted as a liberating force, setting free a new type of child, in place of the one hitherto oppressed and misunderstood.

This has led her to sum up her work, and the movement connected with her name, as "an active social campaign to make the child understood." "For," she adds, "a multitude of weak creatures living amongst the strong, without being understood, must be an abyss of unsuspected evil." At other times she describes her work as "an effort to bring about a great social revolution on behalf of the 'forgotten citizen' (*il cittadino dimenticato*) whose rights have hitherto never been properly recognized by society."

The Last Revolution

In the past there have been many revolutions on behalf of submerged classes in the social organism—on behalf of slaves, workers, women, peasants, child labourers, and so on. All these movements have been limited to a certain place and period. Never has there been such a universal social problem as this oppression of the child by the adult: it knows no limits of caste, race, country, or epoch. The results of this oppression are so incalculably great that, half in jest and half in earnest, Montessori describes her efforts to remedy it as the "Last Revolution." For, by uprooting this immense and universal social evil, we should at the same time be destroying the seeds of all other forms of injustice which arise out of it.

This does not mean, let us observe in passing, that Montessori does not recognize the importance of religion as a means to social reform. Her point of view is, rather, that as long as this universal oppression of the child continues, religious influences themselves will continue to meet with psychological obstacles which seriously hamper their effect. This is in accordance with the old scholastic maxim that "Grace must build on nature."

The Struggle Between the Child and the Adult

Whenever one section of society is deprived of its rights by another, there always results a tension, which issues in a struggle of reaction against the injustice felt by the oppressed. This oppression of the child, which we are now discussing, is no exception. Hence there has come into existence a discord between the adult and the child which has been going on "undisturbed for thousands of years."

We must now examine more closely the nature of this unique oppression; how it is exercised, and what are its painful results. In order to understand it we must first learn, with Montessori, to look upon childhood in a new and unfamiliar way. For the most part, the average adult tends to look upon the child simply as a miniature adult—of no economic or social value in *himself*. "He is an unproductive member of society, a mere appendage without social functions." His present value to society is nil: his real value, so they believe, lies all in the future, when he shall have become an adult. Worse than that, the child is often looked upon in his present state as "a disturber of the peace" (of the adult of course), one who therefore has to be relegated to the nursery or the school until such time as he is developed enough to take his place as a productive member of society.

But the child is not merely a potential adult; not a being of no constructive social value in himself; not a mere "passage" from nonentity to future citizenship. He is a social entity of the highest constructive value, here and now. Montessori is never tired of pressing home this truth: *"The child is in fact the other pole of humanity."* He is also a producer. He has in fact a constructive part to play in the building up of civilization just as important—if not more so—than that played by the adult. As we have seen (Chapter VIII) this "work" is nothing less than that of creating the adult that is to be.

The Forgotten Citizen

Because of all this, Montessori would have us realize that, just as every adult citizen, *qua* citizen, enjoys certain rights and privileges (such as the right to vote, to a living wage, to a fair trial, and so on) so also the child has certain inalienable rights, also *as a citizen*. Unfortunately these have never been recognized by adults in the past; not through any deliberate wish to deprive him of them, but simply through ignorance. That is why Montessori speaks of the child (as mentioned above) as "the forgotten citizen."

Montessori admits with thankfulness that things are not as bad now as they used to be. During the past fifty to a hundred years there has been a great awakening of the social conscience with regard to children's rights. Many movements have come into being having the child as their centre—such as the N.S.P.C.C.; all sorts of welfare activities; nursery schools; children's clinics; and so forth. In fact society has gone a long way towards recognizing the rights of the child as a *physical* human being. What is still lacking, however, is a corresponding general recognition of the child's rights as a developing human personality—the right to develop a free interior life according to the laws of his mental and spiritual nature. It is ignorance that deprives the child of these more spiritual rights, as it was ignorance a hundred years ago which denied him his rights as a physical organism. The small child, even the infant before he can walk or talk, is not simply a little animal with merely animal needs, but a developing human intelligence who should be treated, from birth, with the reverence due to a creature endowed with reason and an immortal soul.

The Rights of the Child

Anyone who wishes to respect the developing interior life of the child must therefore respect certain elementary rights. Amongst these we may single out the right to independence, the right to activity, and the right to explore the world for himself. To which we may add the right to claim suitable working conditions: i.e., a prepared environment without which his great task of creating the man cannot be satisfactorily accomplished.

Any adult who deprives the child of these elementary rights is laying up trouble for the child (and for himself too). We still read in the press, with alarming frequency, of cases where children have actually been tied up to keep them still, or doped to keep them quiet. Though happily the inhibition of the child's freedom of movement is not usually as drastic as this, yet there are still plenty of adults whose attitude resembles that of the mother in *Punch* who said, "Mary, run upstairs and see what Tommy is doing and *tell him not to.*"

A life tormented by so many inhibitions would be bad enough even for adults; but how much worse are their effects on children, for whom it is not simply a question of feeling irritated or annoyed — as it would be with the adult — but almost a question of life or death—of their very existence as a human being. Independence, activity, free exploration of the world about him through the senses and movement, these form the very essence of his mental life.

The Interrupted Scientist

Perhaps at this point a few examples might help to make clearer what Montessori means by failing to respect the inner life of the child.

I remember standing one day outside a little shop in Salzburg; but it might just as well have been any other town in any other country. A well-dressed lady had gone inside to make some purchases, leaving her little girl, aged about four, on the pavement outside. Close by to where the little girl was standing was a circular trapdoor, set in the pavement, presumably covering a place to put coal in. It consisted of a circular piece of metal covered with a great number of very tiny knobs, causing it to have a rough surface, whereas the surface of the surrounding pavement was smooth. The child bent down, and—with an air of great concentration—began slowly and carefully drawing the tips of her fingers now over the rough surface, now over the smooth. Again and again she repeated this movement. She was in fact making a comparative study of the two kinds of surfaces exactly as the children do in the well-known Montessori tactile exercise called "rough and smooth." [1] She was still absorbed in this genuinely scientific experiment when her mother emerged from the shop. "You dirty little thing!" she exclaimed in a tone of disgust. "Fancy rubbing your hands on the pavement!" Saying which she seized the little girl's hand—that delicate tendril of the opening mind—and gave it a resounding smack; after which she crossly dragged her away from the place, as if from the plague. I shall not readily forget the expression on the little one's face as the mother smacked it. Even so might Pasteur have looked if—while absorbed in the study of his serums—his wife had sud-

[1] A child of three and a half, who was stroking my face one day, suddenly looked very serious and concentrated. Then he began alternatively stroking my chin and forehead saying at the same time—"Rough, smooth; rough, smooth"! —as in the Montessori exercise referred to.

denly entered and whacked him across the head with a rolling pin!

The Miniature Mountaineer

Here is another example—of a more tragic kind, because the trouble in this case actually arose from a praiseworthy desire to help the child instead of thwarting it. A small toddler set out slowly and laboriously to climb up the stairs, an accomplishment she had only very recently acquired. She had succeeded in climbing up three or four steps when her nursemaid seized her and carried her right up to the top. Thereupon the child immediately began to get agitated and to cry loudly. This happened a number of times, always with the same result: the child began to cry when the nursemaid came to its assistance. This latter well-meaning but not very perceptive individual did not realize that what was fascinating the child was not reaching the top of the stairs *but the process of getting there,*[2] the difficult and exciting feat of conquering those—for her—gigantic steps. Deprived of the joy of this effort, she had felt as a rock-climbing mountaineer would feel, if—just after he had set out to ascend the Matterhorn—an angel were to transport him suddenly (like Habbakuk) to the distant summit.

The Jigsaw Puzzle

One more example. A small child had been working for a long time at a jigsaw puzzle, and had finished it all save for one piece. Her aunt who was standing nearby, with the best intentions in the world, took up the last piece and inserted it in its right place thus completing the picture. To her surprise the little one was not only not grateful, but turning on her quickly, with a mixture of reproach and anger, exclaimed, "Oh, Auntie, you've spoilt it all!" Like the nursemaid in the previous story the aunt thought her niece ungrateful and cross-tempered. It was only years afterwards, when she became a student under Dr. Montessori, that the aunt realized how she had infringed one of the great rights of childhood, viz., to be allowed to do things by oneself without adult intervention.

It is a great pity that many adults never realize how profound is this instinct in children—to do things by themselves—or how great is their joy when they have achieved an interior progress through their own efforts. I had once a little fellow —of four and a half—in my class, who discovered, quite off his

[2]"To travel hopefully is a better thing than to arrive!", Robert Louis Stevenson.

own bat, by means of some number-beads, that three sixes made eighteen. He was so elated with this discovery that he went round to every member of the class, solemnly announcing "Do you know? Three sixes make eighteen," adding very quickly and triumphantly each time, "but nobody told me!" Montessori tells a similar story of another little boy, of two and a half years, who had managed quite unaided to undress himself. So great was his joy at this feat that, still in the state of nature, he ran into the drawing room where his mother was having a tea party and exclaimed triumphantly, "I did it all by myself!"

Misinterpretation of Motives

In the majority of cases the friction between children and adults is due to the misinterpretation of each other's motives. This happens because—psychologically speaking—they live in different worlds.

The adult is eminently practical; he wants things finished and done with by a definite time. Not so the child; his business, as we saw in Chapter VIII, is to grow and develop, not only in body but in mind as well. Things are only of "practical" interest to him in so far as they assist him to reach that ever-present but unconscious aim—development. But the average adult sees no reason why the child should not conform to *his* point of view; his plans, his arrangements, his wishes, his environment. He has little or no notion of the laws which govern the child's inner life, nor of the child's "work," nor of the various sensitive periods through which he is passing on his way from infancy to adolescence.

The child, on the other hand, does not understand why he should accept the adult's point of view. Indeed by the very limits of his mental development he is often truly unable to do so. There was a picture in *Punch* of a father with his little girl, standing in front of an ostrich at the zoo. In the caption below the exasperated father is saying "Oh, all right, then, have it your own way! It *is* a hen!" Poor man (and poor child!), he did not realize that the child was doing her best to fit the new bird into her meagre stock of mental categories. It reminds me of the little boy of two who came up to me one day with my tobacco pouch saying, "Here, Mr. Standing, is the *tea* for your pipe!" (Not a bad shot, I thought, for a child of two!) Did not Aristotle say that the mind works by composing and decomposing?

The adult's ignorance of the various sensitive periods is one of the most common causes of misunderstanding. Their urgent and luminous intensity is not easily appreciated by the adult who has already settled down into "the light of common day." For examples of such misinterpretations, and their some-times tragic consequences, we refer the reader to Chapter III in Montessori's own book, *The Secret of Childhood*.

The Child's Reaction Against Oppression

Young children are too undeveloped to realize that their fundamental rights are being denied them, but never-theless they feel the oppression acutely, and—driven by a self-protective instinct—react against this oppression in various ways.

"The child as it were withdraws into himself, dissimulates his powers in order to adapt himself to the adult who lords it over him. He hides his normal self, forgets it and buries in his subconscious a wealth of expanding life."

His legitimate aspirations being frustrated he bears within himself a hidden burden. Very various are the forms which these reactions may take. Sometimes it is crying, disobedience, telling lies, or "tantrums"; at other times they may take the form of various neurotic tendencies such as nightly fears, bed-wetting, timidity, stammering—in short, a whole series of deviations of which we have spoken in the chapter on Normality and Deviation.

A Reformatory for Parents, Nursemaids, Teachers, etc.

To do them justice, most adults do not intentionally infringe the rights of childhood, but do so from ignorance, misapprehension, or lack of patience. Following up a sug-gestion of Montessori [8] I have often indulged in the daydream of a wonderful training college or reformatory (call it what you will) for parents, nursemaids, teachers, and all others who are responsible for the care of children, especially of small children. It being understood that expense would be no object, I would have a whole wing of this institution constructed on a gigantic scale. I do not mean just a very large building, but literally on a scale suitable for giants—i.e., as disproportion-ately large in comparison with ordinary adult dimensions as our adult scale is to the children who have to live in our en-vironment. For example, I would have all the pegs for hang-ing coats and hats placed about eight to ten feet above the floor. We should then witness the edifying spectacle of grave solicitors, stout stockbrokers, and stately dowagers having to

[8] Cf. *The Montessori Method*.

jump to reach their hats and coats. Should one fail in this
attempt he or she would be obliged to drag a very heavy chair
across the hall in order to climb up upon it, thence to reach
his belongings. The washstands would be built into the wall
so high that these adults would only just be able to peer
over the edge of them. Furthermore they would be furnished
with huge, unwieldy angular cubes of soap about the size
of half a loaf of bread. Similarly the chairs would be so high
that these ladies and gentlemen would have great difficulty
in clambering on to them; and when they had succeeded
in doing so their feet would dangle uncomfortably in space.
The chairs and all the rest of the furniture and appurtenances
would be constructed so heavily that my "students" would
only be able to move them about with great difficulty. The
lavatory accommodation would be so enormous that in using
it the adults would be afraid of falling in! To elaborate this
idea still further the reader has only to study the chapter on
the prepared environment and imagine the contrary.

This would only be the beginning of the troubles undergone
by my students. I would engage gigantic janitors whose sole
business was to hang around them, hampering and persecuting
them in all sorts of ways at every turn. Whatever they might
be doing—without warning, without compunction, and without explanation—these janitors would at times descend upon
them, banging them into silence and marshalling them into
immobility. At other times, as arbitrarily and suddenly, they
would bear down upon them and abruptly increase the tempo
of their life to a breathless and insupportable quickness. A
student, for instance, would be quietly putting on his coat when
one of these giants would snatch it out of his hands, and
unceremoniously hustle him into, accusing him all the while
for being so slow. Strong and irresistible arms would then
hoist him through the air and deposit him in an enormous
pram, where, after being strapped securely in, he would be
left for long and empty hours with nothing to contemplate
save a blank sky or a still blanker ceiling.

Or it might happen, during a mealtime and in the midst
of a quiet conversation, that the student would be abruptly
assailed by one of these inexorable beings, who would snatch
his spoon from his hand and begin violently shovelling food
down his oesophagus.

At the beginning of the last war I happened to be present
at nursery tea, where, because she did not at once swallow
what was in her mouth, a poor wee mite, not twelve months
old, was treated in just such a manner by her nanny. This

latter stretched the poor infant out flat on her back and forcibly held a table napkin over her tiny mouth until the morsel was swallowed. A lady who was present was so horrified by this barbarous treatment that she could not restrain the low comment to me: "Well, Janet at any rate will soon get used to wearing her gas mask!"

It is, or should be, a matter of perpetual astonishment that so many parents, who will go to no end of trouble and expense in selecting and maintaining a gardener to look after their flowers, fruit, and lawns, or a trainer for their horses, will not hesitate to place their children in the hands of nursemaids with little or no experience, and often nothing to recommend them except their honesty and their willingness to accept an almost nominal wage.

In my training college for parents the principle of making the punishment fit the crime would have endless applications. On those parents and nannies who did not respect the child's love of order and daily routine, I would retaliate by constantly changing the places of things in their bedroom or study, and also by perpetually upsetting their daily programme. A father would be standing wrapped in contemplation of a rose or a sunset, when, without even a by-your-leave, one of these janitors would rudely break in upon his reverie and drag him inexorably away. If a parent happened to be a geologist, and had just picked up a rare fossil which he had never seen before and was about to take home for further examination, his keeper would roughly snatch the treasured object out of his hands exclaiming "Nasty, dirty stone!" and would fling it away with disgust. Or if he were a golfer, and feeling in great form, and had in fact done the first fifteen holes in less than ever before, his janitor would forcibly seize his clubs, ejaculate impatiently, "How slow you are!" and exclaim "Here let me finish it for you!" Thereupon in spite of every protest he would complete the round himself. Should my "students," under the strain of this severe and penitential form of instruction, protest that they had erred through ignorance, I would remind them that the results were not less real and disastrous— just as a haystack is burnt down as inevitably by the cigarette dropped accidentally as by intention. I would also remind them of the many times *they* had punished children for faults which had been committed in ignorance, or in unconscious protest against wrong treatment. Further, I would make them realize—also by a corresponding experience—that the child, in his dealings with these overwhelming adults, has no court of appeal.

The Struggle in Later Stages of Development

Up to now we have been speaking of the (unintentional) oppression of the *small* child by the adult, and the consequences which ensue. But unfortunately this oppression and struggle does not end there. It often affects the secondary school; and at times even the university. My first experience in teaching—over thirty years ago—was in a secondary boarding school which had—and still has—the reputation of being a very good one of its kind. What astonished and perplexed me was the attitude of the boys, as a whole, towards the masters. I found myself at once involved, against my will, in a class war carried on with unrelenting severity. There was I eager to be helpful and friendly, and give the best that was in me; and yet I found that the boys turned on the young and inexperienced teacher like a pack of wolves. Not that there was any *personal* bitterness about it: it was simply a recognized rule that any master who did not know how to defend himself became their lawful and natural prey. The only way open to a new member of the staff was to accept the situation as it was, use his punitive powers, strike down ringleaders, and carry the war into the enemy's camp. Under that system friction was always potential in any group of boys under any new adult; but it was held as it were in solution by the master's disciplinary powers. Once that pressure was removed the potential warfare was precipitated into actuality, and the demons of ingenious ragging were let loose.

Later on I went, as a new member of the staff, to a boarding school in the north of Ireland. My bedroom was a cubicle in a corner of a large boys' dormitory. The first night the boys entertained themselves by banging at the window of my cubicle and throwing things over the top of the partition. (I sobered their enthusiasm—out of pure self defence—by making them all get up for several mornings half an hour before their usual time—to write lines!) Months afterwards, when I had got to know the boys well personally, and had introduced a measure of self-government into the running of the school, I remember asking one of them (now a teacher in the same school) why they had done it. His reply was most illuminating: "Well, you see, sir, we didn't know you then. *You were simply the new master!*" Why was it that the boys regarded every new master as a potential enemy? Obviously because there was something radically wrong with the relationship between the two elements—boys and staff.

So we are back again at the original theme of this chapter,

namely, that the fundamental problem in education is a social one—being the establishment of a new relationship between the adult on the one hand and the child in his various stages of development on the other.

Effects of the Struggle on Normality

In our efforts at educational reform therefore we must always keep before us this clear aim—to liberate at each stage the truly normal child—that is the child who has sloughed off his "deviations," revealing an integrated personality. The trouble however is, as we saw in Chapter X, that—as a consequence of this ubiquitous struggle (which *we* also took part in in our earlier years)—most of *us* too still bear what one might call "psychological scars," which will remain with us for the rest of our lives. In other words, very few adult persons have attained true normality. "Since this struggle between the child and the adult is almost universal, a psychically healthy adult is a rarity. The unsatified needs of the child leave their mark in the adult, in whom they come out as inhibitions preventing intellectual development, or deviations of moral character, or in countless other psychic anomalies." This blind struggle (it reminds one of Matthew Arnold's line —"Where ignorant armies clash by night") between the strong and weak tends, in effect, to produce a weakened man —inefficient, enslaved, stunted, and inharmonious—in short, a "diminished being."

How Is the Struggle To Be Ended?

How is the struggle to be ended? There is only one way. Not, as in most revolutions, by a raising up of the oppressed against their oppressors; not by the child "whose timid and uncertain voice finds no echo in the world." This "Last Revolution" will have to be organized and carried through by the oppressors themselves on behalf of those whom they persecute. This would indeed be an unlikely eventuality except for the unique circumstance that, in this case, the oppressors love those whom they keep in slavery.

The first step towards the liberation of these "enslaved masses" is the adoption of a new attitude of mind by the adult towards the child. An attitude more humble, more reverent, more full of faith in the inner God-given creative energies within him. We must do away with what Froebel used to call the "categorical, interfering way of dealing with the child."

Above all we must seek to find the limits of our help; and cease thinking, as we tend to do in our pride, that his progress depends entirely on us—and not just as much on those powers within him.

CHAPTER XVI THE PREPARED ENVIRONMENT OR THE NEW THIRD FACTOR IN EDUCATION

A number of educational authorities, both in Europe and America, maintain that children should not be taught reading, writing, and arithmetic until they are seven years of age. To anyone familiar with Dr. Montessori's work such a statement seems not only fantastic, but almost incredible. Only yesterday I spent the morning in a Montessori class in London[1] where the average age of the children was six to six and a half. Practically all the children over five could read and write. More than that, many of them could *express* themselves in writing, and were busy composing stories out of their heads. What might seem to some still more extraordinary was the fact that these children worked happily and spontaneously *all the morning from* 10 *a.m. to* 1 *p.m.,* and only stopped then because it was lunchtime.

How is it possible that two equally sincere groups of intelligent human beings should adopt such wholly contradictory points of view on a point so fundamental? The explanation lies in the fact that Montessori has taken into account two important factors which the others have neglected. These are: (*a*) the *absorbent mind* of the child, from birth to his sixth year; and (*b*) the educational importance of the *prepared environment*.

Anyone who thinks that the child's education in the three R's and other subjects, should not begin until he has reached his seventh year can never have realized that the child's mind, in the first epoch of its life (0-6 years) is of a *different kind* from that of an adult, and operates in a different way.

The Absorbent Mind

The child absorbs knowledge from his environment simply by living. As we said in Chapter VI, ". . . We adults

[1]The Gatehouse School, Dallington Street, London, E.C.1.

acquire knowledge with our intelligence, whilst the child absorbs with his whole psychic life . . . The impressions not only penetrate into his mind, they *form* it; they become incarnate." We may remind the reader of the example there given of the remarkable way the child's mind, unconsciously, absorbs his mother tongue—in all its complexity of grammar, syntax, and the most subtle nuances of pronunciation.

We are so accustomed to this and similar feats of mental construction accomplished spontaneously by the child that we take them for granted. Yet the great wonder of it remains nevertheless—the great miracle of how, without our help, little by little—passing through the vibrancy of one sensitive period after another—this tiny child, as the years pass, constructs his own personality. We see this small, helpless, inert, utterly dependent and incoherent morsel of humanity gradually passing from nothingness to power. We see him learn first how to raise his big head; then to sit; then to crawl; then to stand and to walk. We see him learning how to hold things in his tiny hands, at first unconsciously, soon with deliberate intent. Again, without being taught how or why, he selects certain sounds from the environment—just those that are concerned with language—while at the same time a psychic energy begins to inform the muscles of his mouth, tongue, larynx, lips. As a consequence he begins to babble, at first incoherently, then to make syllables; then separate words; and finally composes whole phrases and sentences in accordance with the laws of grammar—in this way expressing a whole new world that has been created within him. And, whilst all this has been happening, he has also been learning to orient himself in relation to his complicated environment in space, in time, and in society. His intelligence (working in conjunction with his hands) has been incessantly busy, as it were "stealing" from objects about him their names and their various qualities. By this means he learns to compare and classify them. Year by year his personality has grown, has unified itself, has become self-conscious. *Pari passu* with all this his imagination has acquired an immense store of images with which he is able to construct an imaginary world. And finally—as the light of reason dawns and waxes strong within him—behold! there he stands before us as he is about to enter his seventh year, a fully endowed, fully equipped, self-constructed personality.

What happens then? Just this. That we adults, who are responsible for his education, suddenly sit up and take notice —saying in effect: "Here is an individual who has an intelligence which can understand what we say to him; who has a will which can enable him to control himself sufficiently to make himself sit still and listen to *us* (whereas before we could never secure his volatile attention even with threats or cajolery): in short, he has arrived at a degree of development in which he is teachable. Very good, let us get to work! "So children, take your places; sit still and be good (always the old false synonyms—equating goodness with immobility) and listen to us, because now we are about to begin your education!"

How unreasonable is all this! How illogical, when one reflects for a moment on the gigantic strides which this same child has already made in his own "education" *all by himself*— a mental achievement which some modern psychologists have assured us is as great, by comparison, as what this same individual will accomplish later on by his *conscious* efforts in sixty years. How clearly this attitude of ours proves the truth of Montessori's oft-repeated saying that "One can pass quite close to the child and yet not see him."

In fact, up to the present time, there has always been (according to Montessori) a "blind spot" in our vision when we adults have looked at the child. We cannot see him as he really is because we unconsciously project on to him our own image and nature. We have always tended to look upon him as a miniature adult, instead of a being who exists in his own right; one who is, in his own way, as different from us— mentally—as a caterpillar differs in form from a butterfly.

Therefore, reverting to the theme of our opening paragraph, we can put the matter this way. Those persons who assert that we should not begin teaching the child until his seventh year are quite right *from their point of view*—that is, from the traditional point of view, in which the teacher addresses himself *directly* to the child's intelligence. But, nevertheless, they are wrong—tragically wrong—in concluding from this that the child's education should not begin long before that age. They are wrong because they have not taken into account the two important and correlated factors mentioned above: (1) The Absorbent Mind; and (2) The Function of the Prepared Environment. What Montessori has done is this: realizing the peculiarly absorbent nature of the child's mind, she has prepared for him a special environment; and, then, placing the child within it, has given him freedom to *live* in it, absorbing what he finds there.

We might illustrate the function and importance of the prepared environment in Montessori's approach to education, as compared with old-time methods, by the following diagrams.

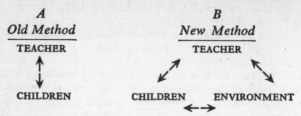

In Diagram A there are two main factors—the teacher and the children. In Diagram B we find a "new third factor" which is almost of equal importance as the other two—or at least as important as the teacher.

The old type of education was a simpler affair. The teacher taught and the children listened: and it was more or less a matter of indifference where this process took place. Teacher and class could migrate at a moment's notice to another room, or into the garden. But with the coming of the "new third factor" several fresh relationships are introduced. The teacher now not only has her relationship to the children but also to the environment. Similarly (from the children's point of view) they still have their relation to the teacher, but now also their relation to the environment. If the teacher and children all migrated to another room—leaving the prepared environment —these new relationships would vanish, and with them the inter-related function of the absorbent mind in the prepared environment.

Is a Prepared Environment Necessary?

The question is sometimes asked: Is it necessary to provide a specially prepared environment for children so young—two and a half plus? Why not leave them to run about freely and "absorb" what they find in home and garden? Montessori's answer to this is that firstly, only too often there is no garden; and secondly, the environment of the usual home is made for adults, and therefore adapted to the adult's needs and mode of living and not the child's. The general arrangements of the home, the daily programme, its "tempo or rhythm" are largely in conformity with adult necessities and habits.

It is true that in olden days (or even now in an agricultural community where life is still carried on in accordance with the unhurried rhythm of nature) the situation was better for the child. But the more complicated the civilization in which the adult is compelled to live the more necessary is it for children to have a prepared environment.

The Prepared Environment Is for Independence and Growth

The first aim of the prepared environment is, as far as it is possible, to render the growing child independent of the adult. That is, it is a place where he can do things for himself —live his own life—without the immediate help of adults.

Therefore the environment is a place where the children are to be increasingly active, the teacher increasingly passive. It is a place where the child more and more directs his own life; and, in doing so, becomes conscious of his own powers. As long as he is in a state of dependency on the adult he cannot grow as he should. But living in this way, freely in a prepared environment, the child enters into vital communication with this environment, and comes to love it. This love for the environment does not exclude his love for the adult; it excludes dependence. It is true that one adult—the directress— is in a sense a part of his environment, but the function of both directress and environment is to assist the child to reach perfection *through his own efforts.*

In this environment only those things are allowed to be present which will assist development. Out of it must be kept anything that would act as an obstacle—not least a too interfering adult. Even such things as are neutral or irrelevant should be rigorously excluded. The constructive psychic energy granted by nature to the child for building up his personality is limited; therefore we must do everything we can to see that it is not scattered in activities of the wrong kind.

An Environment of Protection

As Dr. Montessori frequently pointed out in her lectures the idea of a prepared environment, to assist the development of the immature, is no new thing. Nature has already thought of this idea and puts it into practice in many species. What, for instance, are the beehive, the birds' nest, the anthill, the placenta of the mammal, but just such carefully prepared environments to provide in advance for the needs of the developing young?

The child at birth is a very incomplete creature, physically. "The more people study it the more they realize how incomplete it is." [2] This is even more strikingly true when we con-

2*The Absorbent Mind,* p. 109.

sider the newborn child as a psychic entity. "The newborn
child does not possess developed psychic faculties, because he
has yet to create them." [3] That is why Montessori calls it the
Psychic Embryo. Now this psychic embryo needs protection
in order to develop properly—a calm, ordered environment
and the right mental nourishment. It should therefore be protected first from physical dangers. Therefore, although the
child is encouraged to live his own life freely in this environment, it is important from a practical point of view that the
whole of it, including the garden, should be within the purview
of the teacher's ever-vigilant eye.

An Environment for Activity

This prepared and protective environment must contain the mental food necessary for the development of this
psychic embryo. We need not labour again the point that this
environment is constructed for the child's activity. For we
have devoted many pages elsewhere to bringing out the fact
that—after the first year—the child builds up his mental life
through a twofold activity of mind and body. Therefore this
prepared environment will be rich in "motives of synthetic
activity."

A Beautiful Environment—But . . .

It goes without saying that we should make this prepared environment as beautiful as possible. "The best for the
smallest" was always Dr. Montessori's motto. A well-equipped
Montessori classroom is indeed a beautiful sight, with its
many low windows adorned with bright curtains, its gaily
painted tables and cupboards decorated with vases of flowers.
Even the materials themselves are beautiful: witness the colour
tablets with their sixty-three different shades, the ten different
colours in the bead stair (numbers 1–10), the shining golden
decimal system beads; the bright grammar symbols, and so on.
Colours are everywhere, bright and harmoniously blended; and
everything kept spotlessly clean and shining.

But in connection with this question of making the room
look beautiful Montessori sounds a warning note. The need
for providing the children with the right kind of activities
should override any purely aesthetic considerations, if they
should come into conflict. Thus, in Dr. Montessori's school in
Barcelona, some of her wealthy friends provided her with
low tables for the children with beautiful marble tops and

[3] Ibid.

decorative legs. Before long she scrapped the lot, replacing them by much simpler and more easily moved wooden tables, painted in light colours, because they were more adapted to the children's needs. They could be more easily transported by the children from place to place, and their light colours were quicker to reveal the presence of dust and dirt.

We do not propose in this chapter to enter into a detailed description of the prepared environment, but only to reiterate the point that *it should be constructed in proportion to the child and his needs.* This applies not only to the furniture—tables, chairs, cupboards, etc.—but to the whole building itself. Windows should be made so low down that the children sitting at work can easily look out of them; stairs, with shallow steps, easy of negotiation by short stumpy legs; door handles, cupboard doors, washbasins, lavatories, cloakroom, kitchenette—everything built down to Lilliputian dimensions. In short, it should be a *Casa dei Bambini*—a Children's *House*—which was Dr. Montessori's name for her first school. The details will of course vary according to locality, country, and civilization; but the principles which govern the preparation of the environment are the same everywhere; and it is upon these we shall concentrate in this chapter.

The Environment Must Liberate the Spirit

An environment built in proportion to the child's *physical* dimensions and needs, however perfect, would not by itself be sufficient. It would not of itself liberate the child's spirit—and "nothing is done if we do not liberate the spirit." An environment in which children are simply physically free to "run about and play" is not enough. "That," says Montessori, "is the kind of freedom we give to cats and lizards."

It is a general law in biology that any organism, in order to develop the potentialities within it, requires the presence of certain factors in its environment. Generally speaking, the simpler the organism the fewer the factors required. Thus a growing plant in order to sustain its life needs air, soil, moisture, and sunlight. An animal, however, such as a bird or a beaver, requires considerably more. It needs an environment in which it can move about freely to find its food, seek its mate, construct its home; and in general satisfy its many and various instincts. The child—this "son of man"—endowed with "capable and godlike reason," [4] has need of a very much richer environment to bring out *his* potentialities. He will require not only those things which will satisfy his vegetative and animal

[4]*Hamlet.*

requirements—food, light, air, opportunity for movement, etc. —but also those factors which will satisfy his intellectual, moral, and social needs. Finally, as a spiritual entity, he must also have that in his environment which will answer to his "immortal longings"—to his religious instincts. (Let us not be guilty of that most disastrous of all errors; of supposing that— because the young child has not yet attained the age of reason —he is therefore not susceptible to religious influences, nor capable of a deep, though intuitive, spiritual development.[5]

What the Prepared Environment Contains

It will be obvious then that the prepared environment will have to contain a great many more things than just the small tables and chairs, cupboards, lavatories, etc. We can group what is required under the following heads:

(1) The materials necessary for the carrying out of the exercises of practical life and similar occupations.
(2) The sensorial materials.
(3) The materials for the acquisition of culture—the Three Rs, history, geography, art, handwork, etc.
(4) Those things necessary for the development of his religious life.

It is outside the scope of this book to describe in detail the many and various materials which are subsumed under these four headings. We must confine ourselves to certain general principles which apply to them, and their proper use.

Order in the Environment

If there is one feature more than another which should characterize the prepared environment it is order. Order should pervade the Montessori classroom down to the smallest detail, being present wholly and completely in each part, as a spirit is present in every part of the body which it informs. This order expresses itself in many different ways, and on different mental levels, according to the degree of development of the children who are helped by it.

We have already spoken (Chapter VII) of the sensitive period for order in small children, which attains its maximum about the age of two, and continues for some years after. When the child comes to school, then, about the age of two and a half to three, the observance of the first law in a Mon-

[5]See *The Child in The Church* by Montessori.

tessori classroom—"A place for everything and everything in its place"—is no hardship to him. On the contrary, it gives these tiny creatures a deep sense of satisfaction. For to them— at this epoch—to be able to find things *in,* and return them *to,* their places responds to a need of their development. There is set up, therefore, between them and this ordered environment a reciprocal relationship which is the reverse of a vicious circle. The children (properly guided, of course) actually enjoy preserving this order which they find around them; whilst at the same time this same order, sinking into their souls, strengthens and fixes the disposition already there.

It is one of the main duties of the directress to maintain this order in the environment; and be ever on the watch lest it be impaired in the smallest degree. Every piece of the materials —down to the smallest cube in the pink tower, the points of the pencils, the accurate folding of the towels, the exact position of the materials in the cupboards, the correct tally of the words in the grammar boxes, the right number and order of the decimal system number cards, the soap in the soap dish, the shoe polish in the cleaning outfit—*everything* must be always and absolutely in its right place.

Order Prevents Waste of Energy

We must remember that these children are "working under their own steam" at all these various activities. But this spontaneous constructive mental energy in the child, as we remarked above, though exceedingly precious, is limited. This is why we must be especially careful lest any of this energy should be wasted owing to imperfections in the environment. For example, a child decides to make some coloured designs with the metal insets. He supplies himself with an inset and some coloured crayons; and then goes to where the specially cut paper is kept for this work, and finds—there isn't any! What happens then? He feels a sense of frustration. Perhaps he will go and seek the directress, who may be giving a lesson to another child. After a further wait he discovers she has forgotten to replenish the stock. Or again; another child goes and gets a little mat; a box of coloured beads, a box of tens, and a box of black and white beads (numbers 1–9) and sets to work with great gusto to do "the snake game." (This is a fascinating and quite complicated exercise in which a golden snake—made up of tens—with a black head, systematically devours a multicoloured snake of bead-bar units.) Suddenly in the middle of this long and intricate process he discovers that the 5 black bead-bar, which he now needs, is missing. As a consequence the whole work comes to a standstill. His entire being, intelligence, will, emotion, and bodily activity, is thrown into confusion as effectively as when the proverbial spanner is thrown into the works. His concentration is snapped clean across; his will frustrated; his energies dispersed and diverted into unfruitful, perhaps even disorderly channels.

The same sort of thing happens even with grown-ups. How many letters remain unwritten because of some little thing that is missing! Tired at the end of the day (that is with energies limited) one suddenly remembers and says, "Oh, I must write to so-and-so." With an effort of will one begins to gather the essential materials only to find, alas, that something is missing —either notepaper, or envelope, or stamps, or perhaps ink for an empty fountain pen.

It is hardly too much to say that on the way in which the directress preserves the order in the prepared environment— or not—will largely depend the success or failure of her class. Every Montessori directress might well take as her motto the saying of Saint Augustine, *Serva ordinem et ordo servabit te* (Serve order and order will serve you).

Rapport Between Children and Environment

When this principle of preserving the order in environment is understood and regularly practised by the children and directress, there springs up what Montessori calls a *rapport* between the children and their environment. So much has this love of order become part of themselves that, if anything upsets it, they immediately take steps to put it right.

Only last week, as I was observing in a Montessori class of forty (where the average age was under five), I watched a little boy of three and a half pouring rice from a jug into a cup. As he did so he spilt some of the grains on to the floor. Suddenly, as from nowhere, prompt as the fire brigade, a little girl of four and a half arrived on the scene with a miniature broom and began sweeping the fallen grains together. She had scarcely finished doing this when another child, even younger, appeared and gathered them into a tiny dustpan. Everything happened quite spontaneously. The teacher, who was at the other end of the room with her back turned, did not even know what was taking place.

Order and the Sensorial Materials

This order which pervades, or should pervade, every part of the environment, manifests itself on different mental levels. First of all, there is the general order and arrangement of the classroom as a whole. This concerns the miniature furniture, the cupboards containing all the domestic appliances for the exercises of practical life, and the various Montessori materials. In the case of the youngest children a great deal of their time is occupied simply in preserving this order in the environment—scrubbing, polishing, clearing out cupboards, tidying shelves, and so forth.

Next, there is the order to be found in the sensorial materials. Examine any one of the sensorial materials from this point of view, and you will see that it consists of a series of objects which have to be arranged in accordance with some principle of order latent within them. Thus the pink tower can only be constructed properly by finding and following amongst the various cubes an order which is based upon their size—from the biggest to the smallest. The colour tablets, on the other hand, have to be sorted and arranged on a principle of order in their colours—identity or gradation as the case may be. The long rods reveal an order based on the notion of length; whilst the bells must be arranged according to their musical pitch; and so on.

It goes without saying that one does not explain all this to the children. One simply shows them how to use various materials; and the less said the better. But at once, and intuitively, they grasp this idea of looking for a principle of order latent in each material; and as a result they become absorbed, not in each part of the material in isolation, but in the relation of each part to the rest of the series.

This is the stage when—in connection with the sensorial materials—the children are given those "naming lessons" mentioned above, which beget in the child's mind a new sense of the dignity, accuracy, and *order* of language.

Prepared Paths to Culture

But it is not only in the sensorial materials that the child's mind seeks—and finds—different kinds of order. The same may be said of the more advanced Montessori materials. Taken collectively these materials (which are sometimes called the didactic, or teaching, materials) form what one may describe as the "prepared paths to culture." Every subject—such as reading, writing, arithmetic, geography, geometry, grammar, history, and so forth—forms one of these prepared paths, which are waiting for the children to explore. They proceed along these paths spontaneously, each going at his own pace, making their own individual discoveries as they go.

Most of these paths, as the diagram shows,[6] radiate out from
the sensorial materials. In doing so they carry on, to higher
and more abstract levels, the various kinds of order revealed
in the particular sensorial materials from which they start. To
take arithmetic as an illustration. What is arithmetic but the
continuation, into ever more minute and detailed particulars,
of the study of the relationship of quantities *already begun
by the child in his work with the pink tower, broad stair and
long stair*. In fact the ten different rods in the number rods
(the first "number" material) are identical in length with those
of the long stair, which is still a purely sensorial exercise. The
only difference between these two series is that, in the case
of the number rods, the numerical divisions are marked, so
that each rod is treated as a particular number—three, five,
six, etc.—and not merely as a length.[7]

What again is the exercise of composing phonetic words
with the movable alphabet but a continuation of the sensorial
exercise of connecting certain sounds with certain shapes, as
was done previously with the sandpaper alphabet, but now on
a higher level of order—the order of sounds that make words?
Again, consider for a moment the study of geometry. The
more abstract study of geometric forms, their logical order
and relationships, follows on naturally from the child's previous sensory-motor activities with the wooden geometric insets. Similarly the study of grammar is nothing more than a
search for order in the relationship between words; either
between individual words (e.g. *un*do, *un*tie, *un*fold); or between words compared with each other according to their
functions as in the parts of speech; or in the relationship between phrases and sentences, as in grammatical analysis. (We
might mention, in passing, that the study of grammar is one
of the most popular subjects in a Montessori school owing
to the brilliant materials through which it is presented).

It will be seen, then—in actual practice—that as soon as
the child has absorbed what he can from the sensorial materials
he finds himself, without any break, but by a natural transition,
travelling joyfully along the various prepared paths to culture.
He is still the young explorer. But now he is concerned, not,
as in his first years, simply with the attributes and properties
of things, but with discoveries in such spheres as reading,
writing, and other school subjects. Along each of these paths

---

[6]P. 275.

[7]This is actually an immensely important difference from the psychological
point of view; for in working with the number rods the child is obliged to leave
the purely sensorial level and rise to the plane of the pure intellect, which com-
prehends abstract numbers. In fact one might say it corresponds to the difference between human and animal intelligence.

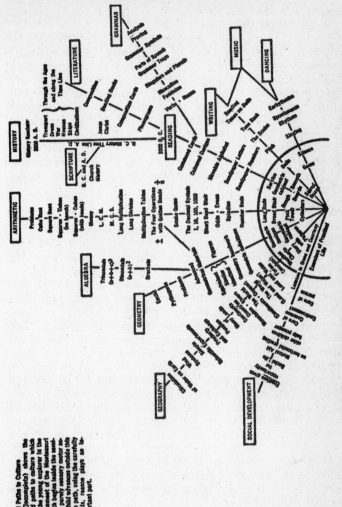

Prepared Paths to Culture (see page 273).

Prepared Paths to Culture

This diagram (incomplete) shows the various prepared paths to culture which are waiting for the young explorer in the prepared environment of the Montessori School. Each path begins inside the semicircle, i.e., with purely sensory motor activities. As the child advances outside this circle along each path, using the carefully graded materials, reason plays an increasingly important part.

he finds waiting for him a carefully graded series of interesting occupations so devised that, as he passes from one to another, he becomes progressively illuminated in the knowledge of that particular discipline.

Of course he is not left completely alone in his travels. All this presupposes the presence of the trained and sympathetic directress, who is always at hand—standing by like a guardian angel—to help and encourage at difficult moments. But, by and large, he does travel by himself. He is enabled to do this because the directress knows how to give him the least necessary assistance, the "minimum dose"—just enough for him to "make port under his own steam."

Thus we see that it is by means of the prepared environment that we are able to solve the problem of how to give culture to children without at the same time destroying their freedom and spontaneity.

The Directress and the Prepared Environment

Valuable and necessary as is the prepared environment, we must not make the mistake of overestimating its importance. To hear some people talk you would think that all you have to do is to get ready the prepared environment, and then let loose the children in it—like ponies in a meadow—and hey presto! all your educational problems are solved. They imagine there is a kind of magical efficiency in the Montessori materials, and the environment generally, which will automatically have an effect on the children—just as one chemical substance will react upon another. But the fact is that, without a trained directress, the prepared environment would be useless, one might almost say worse than useless. She it is who must make it alive. She is the "dynamic link" [8] between the children and the environment. It is her business, as we saw in Chapter XIV, to see that points of contact are established between it and the minds of the children. In other words she herself is an absolutely essential part of the child's environment, as essential as the "material" part of it which forms the subject of this chapter.

The Limitations of the Prepared Environment— The Question of Space and Numbers

Ideally a Montessori classroom should be part of a building specially constructed in every detail to form a "Chil-

[8] See Chapter XVIII.

dren's House." But happily there is no need, in order to start
a Montessori school, to wait for such ideal conditions. Some
of the best Montessori classes I have seen were in primary
schools under the L.C.C., and in the Borough of Acton. In
these the ordinary old type of infant class had been transformed into a Montessori class without reducing the number
of children on the register. It is true that a system of education
which gives so much freedom of movement, and requires at
the same time so much cupboard space, demands ideally more
room per child than the old system.

But lack of space need not be such an obstacle as one might
be inclined to think—for two reasons. Firstly, because Montessori children, who have been carefully directed through the
exercises of practical life, quickly learn to be very accurate
and disciplined in their movements. Secondly, because the
directress can let children who are working with those materials
which need a great deal of floor space (such as the thousand-
chain or the history time-line) [9] take their work into some adjoining corridor, hall, or verandah, where they can spread
out their materials without interfering with others, or being
interfered with themselves. Since the discipline in a good
Montessori class is self-discipline it operates outside the room
as well as in it.

Though it is true that the Montessori class requires more
space per child than the old type of infant school, Montessori
warns us against going to the opposite extreme. The room
should not be too big or it will lose its feeling of homeliness.

How many children can conveniently be taken at once in
a Montessori class by one directress? Many persons, including
sometimes even Montessori students, imagine that a method
in which children work individually must succeed best with
a small number of children—say not more than about a dozen.
But in actual practice it has been proved otherwise. Again and
again, in many different countries, experienced Montessori
directresses have said that they would prefer to work with a
class of thirty children rather than half that number. I myself
have seen many Montessori classrooms with an average of
forty under one teacher.

The reason for this rather unexpected preference is that,
in the free bustle and stir of a Montessori class, the children are
constantly learning from each other. It often happens that
children who are more or less at the same stage in a subject
will spontaneously form a group of two, three, or four, and
work together for an hour or so, perhaps the whole morning.
In such a partnership one child generally knows more than

[9] See illustration 9.

the others, and directs the operation. Or again, there is a type of child who likes to sit and quietly watch other children working with the materials. As long as he does this without interrupting them he should be allowed to do so. In such cases children often learn how to use the materials perfectly simply by watching. At other times a child, who has already been initiated by the directress into the use of a particular material, will pass on his knowledge by deliberately giving another child a real "presentation lesson." Or again, a child goes to ask something of the directress—how to read or spell a certain word for instance—and finds her already engaged. In such an emergency this same child, who may be in a fever to get on with her work, will often go and ask one of her more advanced companions. Sometimes, in fact, a younger child will migrate bodily with all his paraphernalia and settle down at a table beside an older one, just in order to make use of the latter's greater store of knowledge. The elder child usually takes this as a matter of course; and responds readily—often with an astonishing patience and generosity, since it involves a series of temporary suspensions from his or her own work. All this forms an excellent social training for all the ages concerned, and provides incidentally the answer to those critics who maintain that the Montessori system is too individualistic, and therefore anti-social.

Montessori regards forty as the outside number of children who can live and work happily together in one group under one directress. Beyond that, the little one would feel himself "as one lost in a crowd." "There should not be more children present than he can hold together in his little heart."

Limitations of the Prepared Environment in Time

Montessori sometimes used to speak of this prepared environment for children (two and a half to six or seven) as the *Luogo Chiuso* (the "enclosed space"). The enclosed space can be compared to a seed box or an egg, i.e., a place specially created with the purpose of assisting development. In these early years children tend to isolate themselves in their work—"like little hermits" (though of course not physically separated from each other). They have not yet developed into social beings in the fullest sense of the word. Such social life as they do spontaneously manifest is more a "society formed by cohesion," than one based on conscious unity of aim and division of labour.

The child's main aim in working at this stage is (as we have seen in Chapter VIII) more or less unconscious—to "construct himself." As Montessori puts it, "he is more interested to grow than to know." For these reasons he is beatifically happy within the limits of the enclosed space, and does not wish to go beyond it.

But this state of things will not last for ever. There will come a time when he no longer feels fully satisfied with this mode of life and this environment. As soon as we see the child's *joie de vivre* in any particular mode of life beginning to wane, we know that he is coming to the crossroads—that one stage of development is coming to an end and another about to begin. In this particular case we notice how the child now begins to look with wondering and eager eyes at the great world outside the enclosed space. New interests are awakening, and with them new needs. In fact a new sensitive period is being born; he stands on the threshold of the second period of childhood.

Adequately to respond to these new needs the prepared environment, as we have been describing it in this chapter, will no longer suffice. This does not mean that it will be needed no longer—far from it. For a long time to come it will still fulfil a necessary function; but it will not be all-sufficing as before. Along with the profound internal transformation that is taking place within him there will come, firstly, the need of wider social contacts and a more definite form of social life (organization of youth) and, secondly, the need of a more rational approach in the acquisition of knowledge.[10]

Stairs for the Spirit

Montessori compares the prepared environment, with its innumerable occupations, to "stairs leading upward towards a richer personality and a fuller life. The child is that indefatigable being who mounts continuously from step to step. His spirit finds support on the stairs, as he finds objects there which permit him to exercise himself with those mysterious energies which are in him, which oblige him to ascend continuously without pause—to became an adult."

Practical Rules for the Teacher in Relation to the Environment

(1) Scrupulous care of the environment: keep it clean, tidy, spick and span.

(2) Paint again, sew again, when necessary: beautify the house.

[10]See Chapter XXI, The Junior School, etc.

(3) Teach the use of objects; and show the way to do the exercises of practical life (this must be done calmly and graciously and exactly, so that all the children will do the same).

(4) Put the child in touch with the environment (active) and when this is achieved she becomes passive.

(5) Observe the children continuously so that she may not fail to see who needs support.

(6) Hasten when called.

(7) Listen and respond to the child's appeals.

(8) Respect and not interrupt the worker.

(9) Respect and never correct one who is making a mistake ("teach, teaching, not teach correcting").

(10) Respect one who is resting and watching the others work without disturbing him or obliging him to work . . .

(11) but she must be tireless in offering subjects again to those who have already refused them; and in teaching those who have not yet learnt, and still make mistakes.

(12) By her care and intent silence she must animate the environment: also by her gentle speech and presence—as one who loves.

(13) She must make her presence felt by those who are seeking; and hide from those who have already found.

(14) She becomes invisible to those who—having finished their work carried out by their own effort—are offering up their work as a spiritual thing.

CHAPTER XVII   LIBERTY IN EDUCATION—TRUE AND FALSE

Corruptio Optimi Pessima

The Montessori method has been defined as one which is based on "Freedom in a Prepared Environment"; and undoubtedly the idea of liberty is one of its most fundamental principles. At the same time, however, there is probably no aspect of Dr. Montessori's teaching which has been more widely misunderstood. You may still hear people say: "Montessori!—ah, that's the system in which children are allowed to do what they like! I don't want that for *my* child; *I* believe in discipline." So does Montessori—very much so. Yet still this misconception continues; largely due to the fact that many persons have set up so-called Montessori schools before they have really understood her basic principles. *Corruptio optimi pessima!* [1] Dr. Montessori told me, herself, that on one occasion when she reproved a disorderly child in a house where she was staying, the mother said, " 'But you shouldn't do that —it is against the Montessori principles!' As if I didn't know my own principles," she added with a wry smile.

Montessori is not alone in the value which she places on liberty in education—for the idea of freedom is in the air—but she stands apart in the clarity with which she realizes the essential nature of liberty, and the certainty with which she distinguishes true freedom from false. It is unfortunately only too true that there are many schools today which go in for what is called free discipline, in which however there is really no discipline at all. Of such schools one is tempted to exclaim, in the words of Madame Rolande on the way to the guillotine. "Oh liberty, how many crimes are committed in thy name!" With Montessori, however, liberty and discipline are insparable aspects of the same thing—like two sides of a single coin.

It is not just thinking what we like that makes us free. It is thinking what is true, according to the Biblical saying, "The truth shall make you free." Similarly doing what you like does not necessarily make you free, but doing what is right. Theologians tell us that it is impossible for the blessed in Heaven to commit sin; yet this circumstance does not destroy their freedom. It is both bad psychology and bad theology to assert that the possibility of doing wrong is essential to freedom. Montessori's point of view is well expressed by Goethe in his *Wilhelm Meister:* "I saw that the invaluable happiness of liberty consisted—not in doing what one pleases and what circumstances invite you to—but in being able, without hindrance or restraint, to do in the direct way what was right and proper."

Relation Between Liberty and Independence

Before we go on to consider, in its practical applications, the freedom granted by Dr. Montessori to her children, it will be well to say a few words as to the relation between freedom and independence. As Dr. Montessori uses it independence is a word with a wider connotation than freedom. It is possible, for example, for a creature to be independent without being free; but it is not possible to be truly free without having first achieved independence as a basis. With Montessori independence is a biological term. To possess it means

[1]"The best becomes the worst when corrupted."

that an organism is able to subsist and function without the immediate help of others. Thus a fledgling in the nest—and for as long as it remains in the nest—is dependent on its parents for its subsistence. But when it is able to fly away and fend for itself it becomes independent. Every degree of independence, in a developing organism, comes as the result of the acquisition of a new function—in the above instance, of the power to fly.

In human development the acquisition of successive grades of independence corresponds to such experiences as birth, being weaned, learning to talk, to walk, to reason, and so forth. No animal, however independent, can be free in the sense in which a man can achieve freedom; for true liberty of choice is bound up with the power to think and reason—every act of choice being necessarily preceded by an act of the intellect, i.e., a judgment.

Freedom or Slavery

"One who acts through a power outside himself," says the philosopher,[2] "is a slave." Now there exist two possibilities: (a) the child doing certain things by his own impulse, and (b) the child attaining certain external aims under the command of the teacher. For instance, you might see two children of the same age each doing a long division sum. Externally they would appear to be acting in the same way; but it need not be necessarily so at all. One boy might be doing it because he has been told to do so, and the other because he has freely chosen it. In the latter case it is the child's own personality which directs; in the former, that of the teacher. Following Montessori let us illustrate this point by a further example. We can have (a) a child walking and held by its mother and (b) a child walking alone and independently. In both cases we have "a child walking." But what a difference! They belong to two different epochs of the child's life. *What we must do, always, is to help the child to act alone, that is, independently.* We must act on the principle of the mother who, when her little child would only dare to walk clinging to her dress, unobtrusively substituted a piece of the child's own dress into its tiny hand. It then walked on alone; and discovered with joy that it was able to do so. The tendency of nature is to make the child wish to separate himself from the adult and act alone; but in order that he may be able to do so quickly and effectively we must give him the necessary assistance.

[2] St. Thomas Aquinas—following Aristotle.

In our schools you see little children who choose their occupations, and in carrying them out, execute continuously
many movements one after the other. If the child did not
choose this work himself but the teacher imposed it upon
him—guiding him along every step, saying—"move like this
and like this! Look and think as I tell you to!" then the
desired end would not be attained. For in this case the
child's personality would not be concentrated in one sole
unity, but wrenched and pulled apart by the teacher. So
vital is this independence that we see it is not a matter of
doing what he likes, but of doing it at all. It is a question
of acting or not as a separate entity—"to be or not to be."
This is the path of liberation; and I believe there is no other
way. Just as long as the teacher insists on interfering and
guiding the child directly, the personality of the latter cannot develop freely, but always acts through the influence of
another. So we see that this independence and free choice
is not simply a question of philosophy, but of life. For centuries educational reformers have recognized this principle
in theory—that the child grows by the unfolding of forces
latent within him, and should therefore be left as much as
possible to his spontaneous activities—but in practice, how
often do children still remain in "slavery" to an overwhelming and ever-dominating adult!

Freedom and the Prepared Environment

I have met persons who think that an open-air school
is very much the same thing as a Montessori school. Yet this
may be very far from the case. As Dr. Montessori says, "One
can be a slave and oppressed by an adult in the open air just
as much as in a school." It would be equally true to say that
a child could not be truly "free" if he were merely abandoned
by adults in an open space—let us say in a park—and left there
to his own devices. Such freedom would be suitable for "cats
and lizards," but not for children.

There is, as we saw in the last chapter, a definite relationship
between the nature of an organism, i.e., its position on the
scale of being, and the kind of environment which it needs
for its true development. Thus, an environment which contains fresh air, good soil, sunshine and moisture, etc., would
suffice for a plant; but it would be insufficient for an animal
such as a dog or monkey which has the power of movement
and the need to exercise that power. Similarly an environment
which might be quite adequate to meet the needs of an animal's
"freedom" would not suffice for the true and higher freedom
of the "rational animal"—man. He has other needs, far above

and beyond those of his vegetative and animal functions, needs which correspond to his rational, social, aesthetic, and religious possibilities. It is obvious therefore that in preparing an environment in which a child can act freely we must take into account these higher functions. In fact we could not give true freedom of choice to children without such a prepared environment—an environment which contains many motives for activities quite beyond the scope of even the highest animals. On the other hand it would be useless to place children in such a prepared environment unless, at the same time, we gave them independence, that is, the possibility of acting alone without direct adult assistance.

Montessori Liberty in Practice

Let us, for a while—leaving on one side all abstract definitions and theories—return to the schoolroom to observe for ourselves how this "liberty in the prepared environment" presents itself in action. It is the beginning of the morning, and the children are entering in twos and threes from the cloakroom to settle down to work. Here comes Johnny with smiling morning face (for he no longer "creeps like a snail unwillingly to school!"). Having first supplied himself with a little coloured rug, he goes to another cupboard and gets a box of movable letters and begins to compose words on the rug spread out on the floor. Janet gets a multiplication board with beads and settles down to work out for herself the "six–times table," writing it out as she goes along. Jeremy's choice hits upon a packet of reading slips. Having taken them to his table he proceeds, with gusto, to decipher them, faithfully carrying out the commands written on each of them. And so on with the others. Each selects some piece of apparatus and begins to work with it. One child however—Bridget— about five and a half, has selected a number frame, a sort of glorified abacus, and is taking it to a table. She has hardly reached her seat when we see the directress approach her; whereupon after a brief conversation we see Bridget returning to put the frame into its place, and choose the number rods instead. From time to time, whilst the other children are at work, we may observe the directress intervening in a similar manner. Now it may be to reprove Michael for deliberately putting his foot on the upturned lid of a box lying on the floor; now to separate John and Peter—for John is not at all advanced enough for such a partnership—now to stop Jimmy from building a house with the colour tablets (you may say

"Why not let him do so?"—a point which will be discussed later on).[3] And so on.

From our observation we conclude that—though for the most part the directress leaves the children alone to get on with the job they have chosen—there are, nevertheless, certain occasions when she steps in to put a limit on the free choice of their activities. The principle she acts on is this—to use Dr. Montessori's own words—"The directress should never be afraid of destroying what is evil; it is what is good she must fear to destroy—good being interpreted as any activity which leads to order, harmony, self-development and therefore to discipline; evil, being anything which leads to the dissipation of the child's creative energies, and therefore to disorder."

Limitation One: The Collective Interest

And so we get limitation one. "The liberty of the child should have as its limit the collective interest; as its form what we usually consider good breeding."

Limitation Two: Knowledge Must Precede Choice

No child is allowed to choose any piece of material unless he already knows how to use it. That is why Bridget (above) was not allowed to use the number frame, an apparatus beyond her present capacity to understand. This second limitation is very important, and illustrates how profound is Dr. Montessori's intuition with regard to the relation between cognition and volition. She says: "In voluntarily doing a thing we must first know what that thing is. This is a principle which runs all through my method, to be repeated for every spontaneous action. We cannot choose a thing without knowing it first"; or again, "Choice, even in a small child, presupposes a long series of experiences." This point is so fundamental that we will give yet another quotation:

The child spontaneously chooses amongst a great many stimuli: but he must-choose only those things he knows. For we must always consider the child's choice in relation to occupations which have already been presented to him. This is real choice. Of course a child might come into the room and pick up this or that material out of curiosity,[4] True choice is something from within. It is often said that it is curiosity which stimulates these researches with the material. But it is not curiosity which urges the child, because,

---

[3]Chapter XX, Montessori and Froebel—Differences.
[4]Curiosity is the expression of an instinct, true choice, of a reasonable being.

when he has understood a thing, he no longer has intellectual curiosity with regard to it. So it is just when curiosity is satisfied that there begins the real expansive activity of the child. He does not now act so that he may know, but that he may grow; because he has need of action to reenforce and expand his mind.

This is the "second stage" of learning a thing, of which we have spoken elsewhere. It is the long, continuous, serene and tranquil activity of the child who knows what he is doing; and is doing it because he likes it. "It is a form of love."

It is this kind of work, done at the rhythm of the child's own reason, at his own pace, and for as long a period as he wishes, which—often quite suddenly—leads to new discoveries, "Montessori Explosions." The light of the intellect, we must remember, is, in a last analysis, always an inner light. The teacher can present the truth or—better still—a teaching material which contains this truth latent within it; but the final understanding, the real illumination—that always comes from within. "She must guide the child leaving it free—this is the height and summit of liberty."

This second law or limitation—that the child may only choose from amongst materials he knows how to use—is in exact accordance with the philosopher's dictum that "every act of true choice is preceded by an act of judgment."

Limitation Three: Correct Use of Materials

The third limitation is this, that a child is allowed to occupy himself with any material only so long as he keeps on using it in the right way. Some critics have objected that this is an unwarrantable curtailment of the child's liberty! They say, for instance, that to prevent the child from playing trains with the cylinders is an arbitrary interference with his self-expression (see Chapter XX).

Liberty and Law Go Together

"On this question of liberty"—Dr. Montessori warns us—"we must not be frightened if we find ourselves coming up against certain contradictions at every step. You must not imagine that liberty is something without rule or law."

When we look into the question more deeply, we see that Dr. Montessori's insistence on the correct use of the materials has a sound basis in conformity with reason. For each of the Montessori occupations consists of a definite material, pre-

cisely determined to a particular use, the purpose of which
is the child's development; and this development comes
through a progress towards perfection which is attained precisely through this correct use of the materials. If the materials
were vague and indeterminate in their aim and structure they
would not lead to development. It is just their scientific precision which makes all the difference. It is comparable to the
difference between a vague statement such as—"The children
played in the street," and the more precise one—"The children played cricket in the street." If the children were allowed
to use the materials in the wrong way it would not bring about
that autoeducation through which development comes.[5]

Each Material a Means to an End

Each piece of material is designed to achieve a particular end; and—as the philosopher says—"Liberty is the
faculty of choosing means to the end desired." Take the pink
tower, for instance. "The cubes must be placed one upon the
other in the order of dimension. If our purpose were simply
for the child to move objects, any objects would do. But if
our purpose is more than just movement, namely, to stimulate a comparison between the sizes of the objects, then not
only must the material be precisely determined, but must be
used with a corresponding precision of movement."

Or again, "Many persons have seen the children playing with
the colour tablets which lend themselves to construction.
Nevertheless the directress should not let them use the material for this purpose.[6] In general the aim which is presented
by the material should never be left out of mind: in this case
it is that the child should learn to recognize and distinguish
colours with an increasing facility. Such limitations do not
represent a form of slavery but rather a help." Using a homely
simile to elucidate this point Montessori goes on: "In a large
family a child would not be allowed to take his father's shoes,
but his own. This is not tyranny. It is a help; for the purpose
of the shoes is to walk as well as possible in them."

Example: The Geometric Insets

Let us now take another example—the correct use of
the wooden geometric insets.

[5]It happens quite often that children discover new ways of using the materials
which are useful and constructive. Such innovations are incorporated into
general use.
[6]This point is further elaborated in Chapter XX.

There is first the general movement of the hand and arm in taking them out and fitting each one back into its proper socket. But this is not enough. We must teach the child to make a movement more determined, more accurate, more coordinated. So we teach it how to feel round the contour of the figures diligently with first two fingers of its right hand, slowly and accurately; and also round the contour of the corresponding socket into which it must fit. We must teach him thus to touch diligently; otherwise nothing is done. The reason for this is that the attention of the child should be made to fix itself on every particularity of the figure he is feeling, thus uniting the stereognostic to the visual sense.

The mind has to follow a line exactly; and for the little child this is very difficult. In fact we shall see him feeling round the inset and not touching it exactly. So we shall insist —not by force or violence or severity—but showing the child the more accurate way until he does it. This insistence means that we should repeat the presentation. So, instead of leaving the child (according to the supposed dogma of my method!) I persist. It is not punishment—or if it is—the punishment only consists in this persistence—whereas the child might be happier if left alone. The child may be surprised and ask why? and perhaps you will sympathize with him, but nevertheless I persist! In this case I am becoming "almost like an ordinary teacher." You may ask: Why not let the child do it as it can, or as it likes, and let him develop as he pleases? I reply that at the present moment, as we have seen, this little hand finds great difficulty in moving round the object. But this little hand— being the hand of a civilized person—will before long have to write. And to write means to follow certain determined movements not easy to make: and how will this little hand be able to do so, if it cannot even do this? So then it is an act of love towards this little hand to prepare it, at a distance, for a duty to come. And it is much easier now, with the insets, to touch contours already there. Finally we shall see that—once the child has mastered this technique—it becomes a pleasure to him to feel these outlines; for he is in a sensitive period for tactile impressions.

Canalizing the Energy

So we see that it is not just movement, but precision of movement that Montessori is aiming at; a precision which brings limitation; but it also brings progress. As Rabindranath Tagore says in one of his poems, "The river would never reach the sea were it not hemmed in by its banks."

One more example must suffice. We refer to the special
technique which is taught to the children, that they may know
how to make coloured designs with the metal insets and
crayons. They are taught to fill in the shapes with coloured
crayons; but in doing so they are taught to do this with parallel
lines.

If we were to allow any kind of scribbling the interest
would soon flag, and it would not lead to progress. But, by
following the rules laid down, these drawings represent a
gathering up of this instinct within determined limits. Thus
the instinct is enchannelled in an exercise which brings
great development. It is experience which has shown us
the necessity of these rules. When they are adhered to we
find the work goes on spontaneously and for a long time,
becoming more perfect as it goes. Furthermore it is just
by keeping to these rules that the children are able to
construct a great variety of designs, and in this way we are
enabled to see their individual differences (in design, col-
ouring, etc.) as it were coming to the surface.

Freedom and the Closed Circle

This precision makes something like a circle round the
child who is doing these exercises. He cannot do anything
by chance. *Anything* he can do in *any* place; but here we
give him a help, through this limitation, which he cannot
find elsewhere. We enclose him therefore in a circle which
is necessary for his needs.

We have then three forms of precision—first, in the object
(the particular material), then in the use of it as explained by
the teacher; and thirdly in the action of the child. Thus we
"weave a circle round him thrice," in which he must needs
act correctly and perfect himself by so doing.

To do this is not to enslave him; for these exercises are
conformable to his nature. If you tried to enclose a three-
year-old child in a circle not of his own making (that is, not
corresponding to his needs) you would never succeed. But,
as it is, he jumps into this "circle" as into a bath! Who could
force a child to repeat a thing again and again, thirty—fifty
—a hundred times, as he does—spontaneously? We grown-
ups would feel this circle restricting us. *We* could not stay
in it repeating and repeating the same exercises without
using up our strength and becoming fatigued. He, however,
has a purpose in this repetition, albeit an unconscious one—

the hidden urge of developing life. Work done with a purpose is less fatiguing than without purpose. To dig five holes in the ground for five trees is less fatiguing than to dig five holes simply to be filled up again.

So we find ourselves here in the presence of a general law that: Man needs for a time to enclose himself in a limited circle which is necessary for his development. Or to put it another way, we should say that—"Man's environment must have at times a definite limit, his actions being prescribed with precision, so that spiritually he may act within certain prescribed limits."

In such a circle the child encloses himself with joy because, by so doing, he fortifies himself. The real slavery would come if the teacher—under the illusion that she must help the child—should break into his circle and drag him out of it. The child is really free who is permitted to remain within that enclosed circle of activity (which he has chosen) without let or interference, and without even the obligation of explaining why he does so. If the teacher were to say, "What have you been doing, and why?," she would be obliging him to try and understand what even we cannot— to make crooked what he had straightened out, thus putting him into slavery. If he were made to stop and try and explain, the phenomenon of development which we are considering would *ipso facto* cease.

Liberty and Concentration

That astonishing concentration of which we have spoken elsewhere, a concentration so complete that the child does not notice any other stimuli around it—such as people, music, noises—is also bound up with, and arises from, the fact of this liberty of choice—combined with the nonintervention of the teacher. No teacher could enforce such close attention; but, alas! she is only too capable of destroying it by interrupting the child unnecessarily. This concentration, so fundamental for development, comes from within and has to be seen in order to be believed. "We often see children who seem to draw up their whole bodies, feet and all, into this concentration, as though everything was moving from a centre within, which works with a compelling force."

Freedom and the Inner Guide

"A child chooses one of the materials rather than another, but he could not tell us why. Neverthelesss this choice is significant. It is a form of self-expression, by means of which we can follow his development; for he expresses his needs better by choice than by words. It is not by chance or by a mere whim that he chooses this occupation today rather than that.' We touch here upon an important and somewhat mysterious factor. Montessori is quite definite on this point; and repeats it many times:—"The fact that the child chooses one object rather than another shows an orientation of his will dictated by an inner sensibility. Every 'voluntary' choice in this way is an exercise of an inner sensibility."

According to Montessori this faculty is not the same as conscious reasoning; it is more like an intuition. In whatever way we may try to explain it, the important practical point is that it exists, and that—the more we give opportunity to the child to exercise this inner sensibility the more sensitive will it become to his inner needs. This precious faculty which enables him to choose what is necessary for him is easily lost like a flame which can be extinguished. We grown-ups have largely lost it. It is true we still receive impressions from the environment with our senses—light, sound, etc.—but we have largely lost that sensibility which makes us able to choose what is necessary for our inner needs. Therefore all the more should the directress strive to keep alive in the child this "inner flame—as the Vestal Virgins strove to keep ever burning the sacred flame in the temple of Vesta."

The Inner Command

Why does the child choose today an object which he has passed very lightly many times? Who is this mysterious teacher who gives him his timetable? And why does he obey it with such fidelity? How *could* any teacher learn to guide this inner one?

We must therefore respect this inner voice and stand back making way for this very refined command which is so discriminating.

In this respect the child is a being who follows an inner command similar to that which prompted him to make those first vocal sounds preparatory to speech, or the first movements towards walking. It is clear that we have to do with one of those inner energies which are operative in the construction of man.

The more we render such choice easy, by presenting clear choice of stimuli, the more we are giving him the opportunity to develop this faculty and render it more discriminating and acute. For at the same time as the child—through his exercises with his materials—is refining his eyes, ears, touch, and reason, he is also developing this inner sensibility to choose, and apply what he chooses.

Freedom and the Cycle of Work

Work chosen by the children, and carried out without interference, has its own laws. It has its beginning and ending like a day, and it must be allowed to come full circle. The sun rises and sets and never becomes weary. No one comes and says to the sun, "You must stop working now or you will get too tired." These children show clearly that, if they are permitted without interruption to finish their cycle of work, they do not become tired. Scientists have studied how to reduce fatigue in the classroom. They say: "Shorten the hours of work; work half an hour then rest five minutes, or work an hour and rest twenty minutes," whereas in fact the children are only rendered more tired by these interruptions.

This inner guide has shown us that the only way to work without getting tired is to complete the cycle of work. These inner laws of development have their mysteries like all the other laws of life. We who try, in the scales of our logic, to weigh the balance between work and rest can never understand. This revelation on the part of the child has shown us that the best way to help is to stand on one side and not interrupt.

Limitation Four: In the Number of Materials in the Environment

There is one other limitation set to the free choice of the children which should be mentioned, especially as it is not a very obvious one. We refer to the fact that only certain occupations are allowed to find their way into the prepared environment. This involves a selection or choice made before the child comes to school at all. Yet in a sense, this choice *is* also made by the children themselves; for only those materials remain in the schoolroom that have previously stood the test of other children's interest and approval. They are occupations which, by experience, we have found to correspond to some activity the germ of which is in the child. A material might be prepared with much effort and good will and yet not be chosen by the children. It should therefore be eliminated. Those only are retained which bring about that concentrated self-activity which is the basis of all autoeducation.

Some Fruits of Freedom

Before going any further let us briefly review some of the results, or fruits of freedom, as we find them in the Montessori classroom.

First, freedom for individuality. Nature revels in diversity. She is like an artist who has such an immense creative fecundity that he never repeats himself. Just as no two human faces are alike, so each mind is a special creation and builds up a unique system of knowledge. Each has its own special capacities, its own affinities, its own emphasis, its own method of organizing its experience, its own flashes of illumination. Yet how often do these individual characteristics become blurred—not to say cancelled—by education, instead of being made ever more distinct? A modern writer says: "Children in their earlier years stand apart, each being a new personal life, a fresh centre or cell of indestructible free will, not entirely derived from any forces already existing in our world, a living immortal treasure cast into our midst from the creative hand of God. They are still more individual and unique in their nursery years than they will be later—say in their teens—or in full-grown life when fairly fitted into our conventional ways." [7]

The Montessori liberty is, par excellence, guardian of this individuality. Because of it the child's personality is always acting as a whole. All his faculties—intellect, sensations, memory, feeling, muscles and will, body and soul—are working together in the functional unity of one complete organism.

Such liberty works in a sort of beneficent circle to preserve and accentuate the child's individuality. First, because through his free choice the child expresses and strengthens his individuality. And secondly, because the directress—by observing these individual differences thus freely manifested—is able to take them into account; and therefore better able to respond to each child's needs accordingly, thus respecting and strengthening the individual traits of character.

The next fruit of freedom is discipline. "It was the children who taught us something very important—that freedom and discipline are two things that always go together; in fact they were aspects of the same thing. We have gone even further; and have taken it as a guide that—if discipline is lacking in the class—there must be some defect in the freedom."

Next, freedom reveals the capacity for that powerful spontaneous concentration which is the outward aspect of an inner development. It is freedom, too, which allows each child to go

[7] From *The Child at Prayer*, by Father A. Roche, S.J.

at its own pace, a varying factor in every child. In this way the fast worker is not held back by the slow, nor *vice versa*. The child's reason too has its own rhythm, which is not the same as an adult's. Its effective functioning largely depends upon the faithful carrying out of the commands of that inner guide spoken of above; and we have seen how essential liberty is for this.

Fourthly, freedom is also essential to the development of true obedience, i.e., a willed obedience; one which is freely chosen, not enforced. This brings us to the next point to be considered: freedom for the training of the will.

A common criticism of the Montessori method runs like this: "If the child is always allowed to do what he likes in school, will he not necessarily become wilful, self-indulgent, lacking in obedience and moral stamina? In every walk of life there is always a certain amount of drudgery to be faced; so to let the child always do what he likes is surely a very poor preparation for the uncongenial tasks of life." As we have noted already the child is not allowed to do "just anything he likes." In every case he is only free to choose something which is good and useful. But that is not a sufficient answer for objectors such as these, the more severe of whom hold the theory that the best way to make a child docile and diligent is to begin by "breaking his will"! (Like Mr. Murdstone in *David Copperfield*!) Actually, of course, what a child needs is not a broken will, but a strengthened will. "What would you think," says Dr. Montessori, "of a trainer who began the training of a young athlete committed to his charge by breaking his leg in order to make him a better runner!"

How does the will best develop? Like every other faculty it is strengthened and invigorated by methodical exercises. "When a child therefore completes a series of coordinated actions directed towards a given end; when he achieves some aim he has set out to do; when he repeats an exercise with great patience, he is training his will." Or again—"A child who is absorbed in some task inhibits all movements which do not conduce to the accomplishment of this work; he makes a selection amongst the muscular coordinations of which he is capable, persists in them, and thus begins to make such coordination permanent. A very different matter from the disorderly movement of a child giving way to uncoordinated impulses."

Or again: "When he begins to respect the work of others; when he waits patiently for an object he desires instead of snatching it from the hand of another; when he can walk about without knocking against his companions, or treading on their work spread out on the floor, or without overturning or disturbing the little tables—then he is organizing his powers of volition and bringing impulses and inhibitions into equilibrium. It would be impossible to bring about such a result by keeping children motionless, seated side by side."

The Question of Drudgery

"Ah but!" exclaimed the drudgery-school critics, "the child may be working, it is true, but he *likes* what he is doing; it interests him; it is not drudgery!" Well, after all why shouldn't he like what he is working at, so long as he *is* working. To begin with, it is much better for him physically. It is a well-established fact that "conscious effort to keep the attention concentrated induces fatigue more readily than when such effort is not necessary. Work done under compulsion, as from a sense of duty, results in fatigue more readily than when interest is the driving motive" (*Anatomy and Physiology*, by Kimber and Gray, p. 131).

There exists in some people's minds a confusion on this question of drudgery. There is nothing specifically valuable in drudgery itself. It is the "offering of it up" on the altar of some sacrifice, or better still to Almighty God in gratitude for his benefits, that transforms it into a virtue—"gilding it with heavenly alchemy." "No one will deny," says Dr. Quick in his *Educational Reformers,* "that as a rule the most successful men are those for whom their employment has the greatest attraction. We should be sorry to give ourselves up to the treatment of a doctor who thought the study of disease a mere drudgery, or to a dentist who felt a strong repugnance to operating on teeth."

Children Prefer Difficult Work

As a matter of fact those who have had most experience with regard to the work undertaken by "free children" know best that they prefer difficult work—something that they can get their teeth into, intellectually speaking. Nothing bores a child more quickly than having to work at something he finds too easy. I overheard the following conversation once in a Montessori class where I was visiting: "I am going to show you a new kind of sum today," said the directress to a little girl. Whereupon the latter replied "Are they difficult?" "Yes, they are rather," replied the directress. "Oh! hurrah!" exclaimed the child, clapping her hands. So convinced is Dr. Montessori that work is something natural to man that she says, somewhere, that man should be described not as *Homo Sapiens* but *Homo Laborans!*

Freedom and Obedience

The question of the training of the will through independent action is linked up closely with the question of obedience. It would be impossible to discuss the matter fully here; so a brief quotation must suffice. "For a small child obedience is a path, an achievement. To be able to obey, it is necessary to be a person who has obtained a certain maturity of development; and this a child can only form for himself, and by himself. If we do not permit the individual to develop himself, a person so undeveloped cannot possibly obey. A child must first learn to command himself before he can carry out the command of another." It would be quite useless to command a raw untrained recruit to shoulder arms, or carry out any complicated military order, unless he had acquired the necessary knowledge and skill to perform the movements required. Similarly it is useless to command a child to eat properly, blow his nose correctly, dress and undress himself, wash and dry his hands, and in general behave as you would have him behave, unless he first acquires the knowledge and the skill necessary to carry out such actions, together with the freedom to practice them.

Freedom for Social Life

Not the least important of the good results which accrue from the introduction of liberty in the classroom is that it enables the child to live as a free, independent, active member of a miniature but real society. He is presented with continued opportunities of practising that highest of all arts, the art of living together in right relations with one's fellow men. Right from the beginning the little ones are given those "lessons in grace and courtesy" which Dr. Montessori considers as important as anything else in her system. And because they are given at the sensititve period for fixing precise bodily movement, the children respond to them with alacrity. All day long and every day, in their free social contacts with each other and with the directress and with visitors, the children have innumerable opportunities of putting into practice those little social courtesies that oil the wheels of social life, until they become habitual. Without freedom the greater part of these little flowers of courtesy would never come into existence, but remain as ungerminated seeds in the rich soil of their generous little hearts.

A rather captious and sceptical visitor to a Montessori class once buttonholed one of the children—a little girl of seven —and said: "Is it true that in this school you are allowed to do anything you like?" "I don't know about *that*," replied the little maiden cautiously, "but I do know that we like what we do!" There was a world of wisdom in her reply. There was much wisdom, too, in the remark of the Superior of the St. Vincent de Paul Society in Spain, who, when lecturing on the Montessori method, wound up his discourse by saying: "Do not fear a method of liberty which counts the words in a teacher's mouth, and makes the children walk on a line on the floor!"

CHAPTER XVIII　THE MONTESSORI DIRECTRESS OR A NEW VOCATION FOR WOMEN

"The New Children" and "the New Teacher"

Anyone who has read through this book up to this point will have realized (I trust not to satiety!) that, in our belief, Montessori's real claim to our gratitude lies, not so much in the fact that she has invented a new method of education, as that she has revealed to us many and beautiful traits in "normalized children," traits so unexpected and so new that many writers have coined the phrase "the new children" in describing them. With equal justification we now claim that, along with the new children, Montessori has also brought into being a "new teacher." So true is this that Montessori has actually invented a new name for her—the directress. (This is because her primary function is not so much to teach as to direct a natural energy in the children.)

The new children and the new teacher unite to form inseparable parts of a single educational whole, which is a dynamic and continuous process of development for both of them. It would perhaps be more true to describe it as a single "social" whole rather than an "educational" one. In saying this we should only be restating, in different words, the truth elaborated in Chapter XV—that the fundamental problem in education is not an educational but a social one—the problem of the right relationship between those two great strata of society, children and adults. The Montessori directress may indeed be defined as one who understands this "new relationship" and carries it out faithfully into the smallest detail. Since this new relationship is the first thing to be aimed at in the training of a Montessori directress, it follows that Montessori's method of training teachers differs considerably from most others.

The Spiritual Training of the Teacher

To know how to direct the child's natural energies into those creative channels ordained by his Maker is no easy matter, and requires a very special preparation. The basis of this preparation consists in going through a fundamental change of outlook. The teacher needs to acquire a deeper sense of the dignity of the child as a human being; a new appreciation of the significance of his spontaneous activities; a wider and more thorough understanding of his needs; and a quicker reverence for him as the creator of the adult-to-be. How is this to be done?

Montessori makes it quite clear that is is not primarily a question of studying psychology, nor of the acquisition of certain items of culture. The first essential is that the teacher should go through an inner, spiritual preparation—"cultivate certain aptitudes in the moral order." This is the most difficult part of her training, without which all the rest is of no avail.

The idea that a moral preparation is necessary before one is fit to be entrusted with the care of children is a principle hitherto chiefly confined to members of religious orders. But according to Montessori such a preparation should be the first step in the training of every teacher whatever her nationality or creed. She must study how to purify her heart and render it burning with charity towards the child. She must "put on humility"; and, above all, learn how to serve. She must learn how to appreciate and gather in all those tiny and delicate manifestations of the opening life in the child's soul. Ability to do this can only be attained through a genuine inner effort towards self-perfection.

The first thing, then, the would-be teacher has to acquire is what one might call a "spiritual technique." And to attain it she will have to experience something akin to a religious conversion, for it will involve a "transvaluation of values."

Sin Blurs Our Vision of the Child

The crucial point in all this is the way in which the teacher regards the child. To see the child as he is, is made difficult for us adults on account of our own defects. "Between us and the baptised child lies the gulf created by our own sins." Because of this defective vision the adult is generally too much occupied in looking for defective tendencies also in the child, and seeking to correct them. We must first remove the beam from our own eyes, and then we shall see more clearly how to remove the mote in the child's. In this "removing the beam from her own eyes" consists the spiritual training of the teacher.

Of course this does not mean that we must all develop into saints overnight before we are fit to enter the schoolroom. In which case most schools would have to shut down, and stay shut. It means, rather, that the inner preparation required for the teacher is a specific one, being directed not to the acquisition of the whole gamut of virtues, but to those most needed in our relations with children.

Pride and Anger

There are two sins, in particular, which tend to distort our true vision of the child. They are pride and anger. Hence humility and patience—their opposites—are the virtues most needed by the would-be directress. If one reflects for a moment, one can readily see why it is specially easy for a teacher to become a prey to these two defects. The actions of an adult who lives amongst his equals, in an ordinary adult society, are constantly being reflected back to him. For instance, the man who gives way to anger arouses opposing anger in others; the proud person establishes an unpleasant reputation for being so, which sooner or later comes back to his own ears. In this way the extravagant growth of these defects tends, in some measure, to be kept in check by this "social control." Furthermore, being made aware of them is the first step towards overcoming them. As the Clown says in *Twelfth Night*, "My foes tell me plainly I am an ass, so that by my foes I profit in the knowledge of myself."

On the other hand the adult, who lives continually in the presence of small children, is without this social control. They are so young and inexperienced that they take everything the adult says and does for granted—having no standard of comparison. Thus they do not "reflect back" to the teacher his own defects. "It is therefore," says Dr. Montessori, "a real

relief to be able to mix with people who are incapable of
defending themselves or recognizing our shortcomings. Such
a situation naturally tends to develop a certain type of character. That is why Charles Lamb once said that 'a teacher is
a man amongst boys but a boy amongst men.' "

Small children have had so little experience that they will
even justify the teacher's actions at their own expense. They
will believe themselves to be in the wrong, when they are not
really so at all, just because the teacher has (unjustly) ac-
cused them; "even as, in the *Little Flowers of St. Francis,*
we read that Brother Juniper in his humility wept, thinking
he was a hypocrite, just because a priest told him so."

How the Tyrant is Formed

Now a person in a position of undisputed authority, free
from all criticism, is in great danger of becoming a tyrant.
The next stage will be that he comes to claim this undisputed authority *as his right;* and will regard any offence
against it—*ipso facto*—as a crime. Many teachers do, in
fact, unconsciously come to regard themselves and their
authority in this light; and claim dictatorial right over the
child. Respect is now paid by one side only, the weak to
the strong. Any offence on the part of the teacher is legitimate; he can judge the child unfavourably, speak ill of
him before others—even going so far as to strike him . . .
but any protest on the part of the child is an insubordina-
tion not to be tolerated.

No real progress in educational reform is possible, says Montessori, until this attitude on the part of the adult has been
changed. This does not mean that the teacher has to give up
her authority—far from it—but that she will exercise it in a
different way. (See p. 307.)

The first step, then, in the spiritual training of the teacher
is to purge herself of these defects of tyranny with which her
character is unconsciously encrusted. She must begin with an
act of humility—"just as the priest must say his *Confiteor*
before he is fit to approach the altar." From this humility will
be born a new respect for the soul of the child, that small
mysterious being "whose exterior semblance doth belie his
soul's immensity.' [1] She must come to see in the soul of the
child something so rich and pure, so delicate and precious
that it is a privilege to be with it. Instead, therefore, of trying
to bring the child down to her level she must endeavour to

[1] Wordsworth.

raise herself to his. For, in their innocence and purity, in their singleness of purpose, their simplicity, their humble and ready acceptance of truth, their undimmed faith in spiritual realities, their lack of pride, avarice, and other passions, children are higher than we—with souls "yet streaming from the waters of baptism.[2]

"As One That Serves"

Once the teacher has made this act of humility she will no longer look upon herself as someone whose duty it is to mould the growing personalities in her charge by the force of her own. Rather she must regard herself "as one that serves" —in the spirit of the gospel injunction—"He that would be the greatest amongst you, let him be as one that serves."

This idea of "serving the child" is a very urgent one with Dr. Montessori and she is tireless in finding metaphors to illustrate it. She compares the good directress, for instance, with the slave mentioned in the Bible who is waiting, and watching her mistress, ready and eager to anticipate her wishes. This is not the same thing (she says) as trying to understand all that is going on in the child's mind—that mysterious "centre" of its personality (see Chapter XIV)—"for the servant knoweth not what his master doeth."

Again Montessori compares the directress to a humble labourer who works at the task of building up the child's freedom. This is a lowly task requiring minute knowledge and patient attention. The child cannot attain to true freedom without the help of the teacher. Supposing (she says) a master had no servant. This would not make him free; rather he would be abandoned—a very different thing. Similarly, to leave the child by himself entirely to carry on by his own efforts, alone, would not make him free; it would be abandonment. The good servant prepares the dishes and places them on the table, but he does not take it upon himself to say to the master, "You must eat this and not that." Similarly the good teacher must make her preparations; but at the same time she must duly observe the limits of her interference by leaving the child free to choose his work (always of course within the restrictions described in the previous chapter). By doing this she will show her respect and devotion—and her faith.

An Act of Faith

It does definitely require an act of faith on the part of the directress to trust to this power of choice within the

[2]Francis Thompson.

child, and not always be taking upon herself to say, "do this—
and do not do that!" It is an act of faith which experience will
amply justify.

We must, however, make a distinction here. There is a
world of difference between trusting to the "inner sensibility" [8]
of a child who has been "normalized through work," and to
the capricious whims of a deviated newcomer.

"When the deviated child comes to school the directress has
before her—if one may use the phrase—a child who does
not yet exist. Teachers, who work in our schools, must therefore entertain a sort of faith in the revelation of a child who
has not yet appeared, but will appear one day—called into
being by concentration on work. The directress must not let
herself be troubled by the many different types, all more or less
deviated, who come to her in the beginning. In her mind's eyes
she sees before her in each of them, their true self—the
normalized child—who as yet exists only potentially on the
spiritual plane. She must hold on courageously to the belief
that, sooner or later, each will demonstrate his or her true
nature—as each in turn finds work to which he attaches himself with his whole personality."

A Transference of Activity

That there may be established this "right relationship"
between directress and children, not only has she to undergo
a change of character, but the children also. But here there
is an important difference. In the case of the adult, the change
is consciously willed and reached through conscious effort;
in the case of the child it is brought about unconsciously by
that process which we have called "normalization through
work." We saw in Chapter VIII that this "work" is nothing
less than the creation of the adult-to-be. Furthermore, as we
there pointed out, this work must be done by the child himself. No one, not even the best and most sympathetic teacher,
can do it for him. In still another chapter (XIV) it was made
clear that the very essence of this work of mental growth is
a twofold activity of hand and brain—a twofold rhythm of
activity between the periphery and the centre. Activity is the
keynote of all that is going on in a Montessori school.

In order that this essential and creative activity should come
into being, it is necessary that the directress should learn a
new approach to the child, and to the problem of teaching.
Usually, in the training of the teacher, emphasis is laid upon
equipping her with methods and matter for class instruction.

[8] See previous chapter.

She is taught how to arouse and hold the interest of her class; how to prepare her lessons; how to make the best use of the blackboard and other visual aids; how to maintain class discipline; how to draw up a timetable, and so forth. Such a training is based on the assumption that the teacher is still the more active partner, the children the more passive. The teacher is still regarded as the chief medium through which the children's growth in knowledge, culture, and character must be brought about, the main factor in their development; and above all the point of focus of the collective attention of the classs. It is the teacher who is free to move about at will, to talk or be silent as she chooses, to take the initiative and select the work to be done at any moment—whilst it is the part of the children to follow, to listen, to be still, to begin and stop working at the will of the teacher.

One of the first practical lessons to be learnt by the prospective Montessori directress is the necessity of reversing this arrangement. Not suddenly, of course, and never completely. But her ideal must be that the child should—ever increasingly —become the more active partner and herself the more passive. It is true that the Montessori directress will always have plenty to do in the way of instruction and guidance, more especially so at the beginning when the children are very small and have not yet been initiated into the many occupations which await them in the prepared environment. But the ideal, as well as the practice, is that—as time goes on—the child should become the ever more active partner and the teacher the more passive. Since her aim is to foster the child's independence, free choice and spontaneous activity, she will be successful only in so far as this transference of roles takes place.

In this connection Dr. Montessori often quoted the words of John the Baptist (spoken in reference to the Messiah): "He must increase and I must decrease." The directress rejoices when she finds the child progressing on his way alone. The most successful directress is the one who at times (though it will never be for long) sees all her tiny charges concentrating on their work independently of her. She knows well that, when they are working in this way, they are advancing more swiftly and more surely along the path of development than at any other time.

Not long ago—in a Montessori class—I was explaining to a child of seven how to use a certain arithmetical material. After a while—as soon as she had understood how to use it— she looked up at me, smiled, and said simply "You can go now!" A Montessori directress told me that one of the forty children in her class remarked to her one day, "You know,

Miss Willson, except to mark the register and see about the dinner-money there isn't really any need for you to come to school at all, as we do everything by ourselves." The directress took this, secretly and very rightly, as the highest compliment.

Stimulating the Motor-Ego

In the old type of school the teacher might be compared to someone who seizes the surface of the children's minds, as with a hook, and pulls them along with her altogether—just as Gulliver pulled the whole fleet of the Blefuscans after him. Montessori's conception of the teaching process is quite different—poles apart. It is based on the belief that there exists within the child a deep-seated urge for knowledge which seeks to expand of itself. This is a primordial energy which starts from within (from what Montessori calls the "motor-ego") and expresses itself through the choice and action of the whole personality. Unless we go down deep enough to set going this "motor-ego" the real process of learning has not really begun. "It is the difference between someone moving the hands of a clock from outside, and the same hands moving from a power which comes from within."

The Directress and the Environment

In Chapter XVI we spoke of the prepared environment as the new third factor in education; and we were right. Without it, this transference of activity, which is so essential, could never take place. We noticed in that chapter the various ways in which the presence of this new factor complicates the process of education. Besides their relations to each other both children and teacher have now also their relation to the prepared environment.

"The teacher," says Montessori, "should be the guardian of the prepared environment." But before she can be this the environment must first of all exist; and this is her very first task. No prepared environment, no Montessori school. The skill, care, and devotion with which the directress gets ready the environment is the very condition of the children's freedom. The simile mentioned above, of the servant preparing a meal for her master, is an inadequate one here. Rather, Montessori compares this preliminary task to the joyful affection and loving anticipation with which the bridegroom prepares a home for the bride. At other times she used to compare it to the work

of St. John the Baptist—the Forerunner—who goes in advance
"to level the hills, and make the rough places smooth."

In this prepared environment she will gather together many
gifts to bestow upon her little ones. Like the Father in Heaven
she knows what they have need of before they ask. Like Him
she must know when to present any particular gift, and when
on the other hand to hold it in abeyance until such time as the
growing intelligence can use it properly. Like Him, too, she
must insist on the proper use of the gift bestowed, since the
whole art of living well may be said to consist in making the
right use of those gifts with which the Creator has endowed us.
But the greatest of all gifts which she will bestow on them is
the gift of themselves—their true and normalized selves.

The Dynamic Link

Once the environment exists the directress will become
the link between it and the children. But this does not mean
that she will act as a sort of mechanical automatic coupling
between these two elements—far from it! Montessori always
insists that she must be a *dynamic* link. This requires a great
variety of qualities—knowledge, patience, observation, discrimination, tact, experience, sympathy—and above all charity. The science of being a Montessori directress consists in
knowing beforehand the general function of the prepared
environment and the nature and purpose of every piece of
material in it, and the age to which each is suited. The art
of being a directress lies in knowing how, and when, to give
any particular lesson to any particular child, or group of
children.

We need not repeat here what was said in Chapter XVI
concerning the paramount importance of the teacher's understanding and fulfilling her duties as guardian of the environment; but will only underline a few points. The first is that any
teacher who does not fulfil her duties in this respect can never
hope to be a successful Montessori directress. Her first care
must be to see to it that the environment is always kept in
order, down to the smallest detail—always beautiful and
shining and in perfect condition, so that nothing is wanting.

Appearance and Deportment

The directress should remember that, in a sense, she
herself is also a part of the environment—the most living part
of it, too. This means that she should always make herself
attractive and pleasing to the children by being tidy, well

dressed, serene, careful, and full of a quiet dignity. This care should precede all others. "If the environment be neglected, the furniture all covered with dust, the materials muddled and in disorder; and above all if the directress is slovenly and negligée in her appearance and manners, and not gracious and friendly with the children—then all the essential foundation of her work would be missing."

Silent Movement

The love and respect which the directress should feel for the children is not a mere sentiment; it is something which should pervade all her actions, even her bodily movements.

The directress should avoid being too energetic or angular in her movements. Interest and enthusiasm in what she is doing she should have, of course, but this should not prevent her from expressing it calmly and delicately. A directress may unconsciously distract or even repel a child in two ways: either by a rough movement on the one hand, or by being exaggeratedly silent on the other. What I call "silent movement" is just this—movement in which nothing stands out or jars. I do not mean merely a movement without noise. The directress should learn to move about silently, yet naturally, gracefully, spontaneously, economically—for it is always surplus and unnecessary movements which cause exaggeration.

On the other hand we must not turn ourselves into marionettes and become self-conscious; but acquire the art of moving naturally. [The directress should, as Hamlet said to the Players, "use all gently" and in everything she does "acquire and beget a temperance that may give it smoothness."]

This new type of teacher is a more attractive personality than the old, even as the "new child" is to be preferred to the deviated one. She no longer conforms to the typical "school ma'am." Gone are the strident tones, the domineering manner, the abrupt, not to say challenging, movements. We can say of her as was said of Cordelia, "Her voice is soft, gentle and low, an excellent thing in woman." It is seldom raised above a conversational level since she is usually speaking only to one or a small group of children. And when she does have something to say to the class as a whole they are so quick to respond that she seldom needs to speak loudly even then. At other times—as in the silence game—her voice is reduced still further, down to a tenuous whisper (see p. 227).

On the Giving of Lessons

Just because Montessori wishes the directress to be a *dynamic* link between the children and the environment she was always careful to avoid saying anything that would destroy the spontaneity and vivacity of the directress in her work. "I give very few lessons on how to give lessons, lest my suggestions—becoming stereotyped and parodied—should turn into obstacles instead of help. The directress is dealing with different personalities; and it therefore becomes more a question of how she should orient herself in what is for her a new world, rather than of any rigid or absolute rules."

Montessori does however lay down certain general principles with regard to the giving of lessons. One is that—in presenting the materials—the directress should say no more than is absolutely necessary. Whatever she adds beyond this tends to confuse and distract. The famous "three period presentation lesson" of Séguin is a model of efficiency in this respect; and Montessori recommends its use with small children, especially in the "naming" lessons. This is the manner of it (using the prisms):

PERIOD I. (Naming) "This is *thick*; this is *thin*."
PERIOD II. (Recognition) "Give me the *thick* one; give me the *thin* one."
PERIOD III. (Pronunciation of the word) "What is this?"

In general the directress should present the materials as objectively as possible, i.e., without obtruding her own personality. Further practical recommendations will be found in other parts of this chapter.

Once Again—True Freedom Involves Limitation

In Chapter XVII we saw that giving the child freedom does not mean that we allow him to do "anything he likes." So is it with the Montessori directress; her freedom, too, is not without its laws.

"Some people," says Montessori, "accuse me of tyrannizing over my teachers when I say you must present the materials in this way and not that. But this dogmatism does not come from me but from the very nature of the psychological facts. Take for instance the naming lessons. Each of you, in your own language, will present these lessons in the same way, using the same words. Why? Because I say so? No! But because they cannot be improved upon, nor made more perfectly adapted to the mind of the child. To keep to them simply means to profit by a long and useful experience."

To take another example. "If, in presenting the colours to a small child, we began by presenting the gradations first the child will not be interested. Therefore we begin with the matching of contrasting pairs, so that when he comes to the exercise on gradations his eyes have already been trained. Always in our presentation we must give something which does not exceed the child's powers, and yet at the same time calls forth effort."

These are not limitations of our making: they are inherent in the psychological nature of the case; and therefore to subject herself to them brings no curtailment of liberty either to directress or child. Such limitations form in fact the gateway to a wider life. Here, as in other realms of action, "realization often begins with renunciation instead of conquest."

Does the Child's Freedom Diminish the Teacher's Authority?

There are some who complain that Montessori, by giving so much freedom to the children, has diminished—not to say abrogated—the teacher's authority. She herself, however, emphatically denies this charge. "When the teacher says to the child [in the famous three period lesson of Séguin— see above]: "This is *red*! This is *blue*!" what is that but dogma, i.e., teaching on authority?"

In fact, far from taking away the teacher's authority, Montessori maintains that the general effect of her method is to enhance it. At the same time she admits, quite frankly, that there is a change both in the nature of the teacher's authority and in her manner of exercising it.

In the first place it is to be noted that a part of the teacher's authority has been taken over by the materials themselves. They are rightly called the didactic or teaching materials when properly used, because they impart knowledge to the children. But in many cases they do more than this: they also act as "a control of error." In this they exemplify a fundamental principle which goes right through the Montessori method, viz., that there should always be a "control of error" as a counterpart to the child's freedom. Furthermore, as far as possible, this control of error should operate independently of the teacher through the automatic action of the environment and the materials in it.

As a consequence of her being able thus to hand over much of this work to the effortless custody of the environment, the directress is set free to exercise her authority in higher and more subtle ways. The time and energy thus saved can be devoted to observing the children, and responding to their individual needs. She is more free, for example, to give her attention to any particular difficulty which may have cropped up in the course of this or that child's work; or to deal with some unexpected but necessary adjustment in the environment, or amongst the children. She has more time to pause—here— to give some words of encouragement, or—there—to correct some child who is not using a material correctly, either through ignorance or intention. The directress herself has often to act as a control of error, but on a higher and less automatic level than the environment.

To sum up then, we may say that the authority of the teacher is exercised as a "directing knowledge, strong in wisdom and sympathy," to which the children can appeal with assurance. It is in fact just the particular limitations of the teacher's authority, on the one hand, combined with new ways of exercising it, on the other, which give the special form and perfection to this new society.

The Teacher—The Sun—The Light-Giver

Montessori makes use of various similes to illustrate what she means by the teacher's being a dynamic link between the children and the environment. The directress must act as a "vivifying presence which awakens the sleeping soul of the child. Her role may be compared to that of the sun; for she is one who brings light, by means of which we are able to see distinctions which we could not see before. She also awakens that interest which comes from knowing better and more deeply what we knew before." (Like the sun, too, she must leave those she helps free to live their own lives.)

There are no dogmatic rules as to how she is to awaken this interest: but one thing is essential—the directress herself must be an enthusiast in the subject she is teaching. "If for example," said Montessori in one of her lectures, "you have no interest in nouns, you are not likely to arouse it in the children. You must remember to introduce the matter in an interesting way; an anecdote today, a little story tomorrow, or some imposing description. Such aids the teacher must have ready in her mind so as to impress the children with the solemnity and dignity of the subject in hand. Should she remain apart and silent, it would be to exaggerate the role of nonintervention. You yourselves must be filled with wonder; and when you've acquired that you are prepared." After which she went on— on that particular day—to give a model "stimulus lesson" on nouns such as I have never seen in any grammar textbook. It was brilliant, original, and fascinating, and touched upon such diverse aspects of the subject as Adam "naming" the animals; names for new inventions; new babies (baptism); the strange tenacity of such names as San Francisco, Los Angeles, Missouri, Colchester, which survive as "historical fossils," and a score of other such relevant but unusual facts.

The Teacher as the Encourager

The adult, both in the school and the home, should always be the person who encourages. Hers is the delicate work of protecting and encouraging the life-impulses. Therefore she must be quick to appreciate what the child says and does—not, as some adults do, pretending in a casual offhand way to see what the child has come to show, and at once brushing it aside for more important matters. Rather she must listen patiently, and follow it up if the child asks some question. We should remember that the child is weak and inexperienced, and therefore uncertain in his judgments. The world is still largely unknown to him. For this very reason he comes to the adult, seeking encouragement, approval, explanation or verification.

Hence it is the adult's duty to observe the child, not only in order to find the psychological moment to give it the necessary instruction along some new path, but also that she may be able to understand its tentative gropings, its doubts, its sudden discoveries (pp. 47; 247), its joyous wonderment; so that "nothing—no experience—which comes to the infant mind shall pass without bearing its fruit. . . . So that, on no road will it go astray because it has not understood the direction it is going in, or because it does not understand how to proceed further."

Not Too Much Praise

Though it is the teacher's duty to encourage the child and show an interest in his work, she must be careful not to "spoil the perfect dose" by going too far. She must not praise the child in such a way that it now wishes to work "so that it may obtain merit from her." This would be to give him an "external interest" of no value for his intellectual development. "If the child begins to work with the motive of obtaining praise from us he will begin to develop all sorts of tricks. . . . In this way we might waste that precious energy which is in him, which would escape as a liquid escapes through a small crack."

The Montessori Directress and the Principle of Nonintervention.

None of Dr. Montessori's idea has been more misunderstood nor more widely abused than that of the "nonintervention of the teacher," which is the complimentary principle to that of "the liberty of the child." Many so-called Montessori teachers have exaggerated it out of all reason. I heard Montessori once describe a "Montessori" (*sic*) school which she visited. "Pandemonium reigned there, but the directress did nothing to stop it. Instead she spent her time gliding like an ineffectual wraith from child to child whispering something— Heaven knows what—in their ears. That was her idea of carrying out my principle of nonintervention."

Another time I heard her relate how she was taken round another school in France, where they were supposed to be carrying out her principles. "We came to one room—it was the science room—not a soul was there except the master, nor for that matter had been for several days. When I enquired into his method of teaching the master airily replied that he did not teach; the children discovered! It appears he had placed a mysterious white mixture on the laboratory bench; and the children were supposed to ascertain the various substances it contained—'by discovery!' Considering," continued Montessori with a wry smile as she related this almost incredible story, "considering how few real discoveries are made by trained scientists in a lifetime, it was, to say the least, strange to expect inexperienced children, without knowledge, without method, without stimulus and therefore without interest, to make perpetual discoveries from day to day! No wonder the room was empty!"

Here, as so often happens, the truth lies in a balance between opposites. The right path for the teacher to take—the golden mean—lies, not in giving no instruction at all, but in giving just enough—no more—the "indispensable minimum," "the perfect dose." To give less would mean that the teacher had abandoned the child; to give more would destroy his spontaneity and diminish his interest.

The whole art of being a Montessori directress, one might almost say, lies in knowing when to intervene and when not to. The general rule is that the teacher should not intervene when she finds the child engaged in some spontaneous activity which is orderly and creative. She must respect what we have called the work of the child in the broadest sense (see Chapter VIII).

On the other hand she need have no qualms whatever about disturbing the child if he is not doing anything in particular; whilst if he is disturbing his neighbours it is her duty to intervene at once.

The Simile of the Poet

Supposing, she says, you have a friend who is a poet. You go to pay him a visit, and find him caught up in an inspiration, his whole soul concentrated on his work. You should not then interrupt him; but should discreetly efface yourself (not breaking in like that impatient butcher who interrupted—alas for ever!—the flow of Coleridge's *Kubla Khan*). If, on the other hand, you find your poetic friend with his feet on the chimneypiece reading the newspaper, you can cheerfully divert him from what he is doing and drag him out for a walk on the common. The teacher should "never be afraid to destroy what is evil. It is only the good that we must be careful not to destroy or damage."

To distinguish at a glance an activity which is creative from one that is unimportant is not always easy, especially for the beginner. Garden plants and weeds look so similar in their early stages that it needs a practised eye to distinguish them. A teacher had a most disorderly boy in her class who was always interfering with the others and upsetting their work. One day she saw him going round to the tables of the other children taking away the coloured crayons. She was just about to intervene when she noticed that he was moving only the blunt crayons and was replacing them by sharpened ones. It was the first helpful, spontaneous, orderly activity he had shown; and she very nearly nipped it in the bud through misunderstanding it. Similarly, it is not easy to distinguish genuine "slacking" from inattention due to indisposition, or lack of sleep, or to some "psychic barrier" set up at a previous school through wrong teaching.

Repression Is Much Easier than Encouragement

It is more easy to recognize the "deviated reactions" of a child than the constructive activities of its opening intelligence. This is because such deviated actions are, as a rule, clear, strong, violent and disorderly. It is often more difficult to recognize the delicate, positive manifestations of the child's mind towards growth. Yet these are just the ones that need most encouragement. The untrained adult may very easily be "like a blind person who passes close to a delicate flower without noticing it, which he crushes out of existence without meaning to, and even without knowing that he has done so."

Discreet and Indiscreet Correction

It is the teacher's duty to correct mistakes, even slight imperfections, but she must be very careful how and when she does this. Sometimes a child will make a mistake through sheer lack of capacity, as when he makes an error in grading the colours. It is useless then to point out the mistake. Further exercise with the material will so develop his power of colour discrimination that he will soon automatically do it correctly— without any intervention on the part of the teacher.

Again it would be a mistake to stop a child, in the full spate of some newly acquired activity, in order to draw his attention to some comparatively unimportant error. Supposing a child has just that morning discovered, with great joy, that he can express his thoughts to another in written symbols, and is full of the wonder of being able to write "commands" which another person can carry out without a word being said. We should be making a great mistake if just at that moment we kept on interfering to correct small spelling errors—"thus destroying this idyll between the soul of the child and the written symbol." There should, of course, be some adequate scheme for dealing with the vagaries of the English spelling in every school; and the children should be encouraged to work through it systematically. But, as the author of the Book of Wisdom says, there is a time to speak and a time to be silent. Montessori sums up the whole position in one of her apt maxims—"Teach, teaching, not correcting." [4]

Nonintervention MEANS Nonintervention

With children who have not yet become normalized— especially in the case of small children who are displaying their first real interest in the materials or the exercises of practical life—it is particularly important to observe the principle of nonintervention, because this new interest responds to natural laws and opens up a cycle of activity. "This début is so fragile, so delicate that the smallest thing suffices to make it disappear like a soap bubble, and with it at the same instant the beauty of its nature."

The directress must be very attentive to this point: not to intervene means not to intervene in any form. It is just here that many teachers go off the lines. The small child who,

[4] Cf. p. 312.

up to this point, has been so disturbed (*dérangé*), has now at last become concentrated in some work. If now the directress, in passing, should simply say "Good!" or "How nicely you are doing it!" this little thing would be enough to throw him back into his disorderly and silly actions. And perhaps for another week or two after this he will not show any further interest in any kind of work. Even if a child finds himself in some difficulty and the teacher intervenes in order to assist him, this may be sufficient to make him give up his work and go away from it. For the interest of the child arises not only from the work itself, but more often from the desire to overcome difficulties.

"If the teacher overcomes these difficulties instead of me it is she who is doing it; and I am no longer interested!" Thus if the child is carrying a heavy object and the teacher tries to help him he will leave the object with her and walk off. Unnecessary aid, or even a look, may be sufficient to destroy this activity; for—strange as it may seem—even the mere fact that the child becomes aware he is being looked at may stop his work altogther. (For that matter even we adults are sometimes put off our work if we feel that somebody is watching us.)

The great principle which leads to success is this: as soon as this concentration has arrived we must act as though the child no longer exists. Of course we must use common sense here, as everywhere else: it does not mean that one could not, and should not, take in what he is doing by a rapid glance without him being aware of it.

The ability to know when to intervene, and when not to, comes—along with other abilities—with practice. But it does not come so easily nor so quickly as with many others. It comes only with the attainment of a certain spiritual level. The true aid which the teacher can render to the child is not as a result of an impulse, but is derived from a disciplined charity exercised with discernment. Such charity brings as great a satisfaction to those who practice it as to those who benefit by it. Real charity is to succour those who have need of it without being discovered; or rather, it assumes the aspect, not of an assistance given, but of a spontaneous and natural gesture.

Obtaining the Consent of the Child

The essence of the "new relationship" is a mutual respect between the directress and the children. From this it naturally arises that each should consider as far as possible the wishes of the other party. Therefore, before giving a lesson, the directress should obtain the consent of the child. This is not only good manners but very sound psychology. "You know that it sometimes happens in life that an orator makes a great speech, but the speech loses much of its effect because the audience, for some reason or other, is not well disposed to listen to him. Some preparation is essential. Even if you are going to give someone a present you do not do so without first asking his or her consent. These flowers," Dr. Montessori went on, pointing to a bouquet on the table in front of her, which had been presented by one of the students before the lecture, "these flowers were not just simply flung down in front of me without my consent. No! The donor first approached me, then paused to prepare me for the event, and then said, 'Will you permit me to give you these flowers?' Even if we meet someone in difficulty we do not as a rule assist them without first saying 'May I help you,' or 'Can I be of any assistance?' "

Where there is consent all that is given falls on prepared soil *(terreno preparato)*. When we have obtained a person's consent we have taken down his defences. With a small child this is specially important, because it is very natural for a child to put up defences against the adult. Many children are, in fact, so sensitive to our approaches that they do not even like being touched physically. This is equally true of the spirit; so our manner of introducing a lesson should be "as an invitation to the spirit of the child."

The lesson, therefore, is not a thing to be thrown off *improviso,* dumped down willy-nilly upon an unprepared child. He should be made aware in advance that something important is coming to him; and the teacher should see to it that everything else is removed from the table except just the material required for the demonstration. She should see to it that she herself is prepared, even in her personal appearance, for the work of initiation, for if her hair is untidy or anything else in disorder the child's attention will be drawn to that and not to the materials. When all this *lavoro rispettoso* (respectful labour) is finished, then comes the actual invitation: "Would you like me to show you something?" To which the child as a rule responds with interest.

A Contrast in Point of View

Nothing perhaps could make more clear the difference between ordinary class teaching and running a Montessori class than to consider how each type of teacher contemplates her working day in advance. The former, as she takes her breakfast, might meditate something as follows: "Let me see, this is Wednesday, what lessons I wonder are on the curriculum today?—Ah!—Geography, History, Arithmetic, Nature Study, and Handwork" (or whatever it may be). Then she goes over in her mind what things she will require for the day. She will make sure that she has her lesson notes ready to fall back on in case of need, her books of reference, her maps and diagrams, the specimens for the nature-study period. Perhaps she decides to get to school a bit earlier in time to draw a special map for that geography lesson; or it may be to prepare her materials for the handwork period; nor must she forget those exercise books she brought home last night to correct. She knows quite well in advance what she and the children will be doing at any hour of the day.

The thoughts of the Montessori directress might run more on the following lines: "I sincerely hope the caretaker has found that 'six' number-rod which was missing at the end of the day yesterday. That reminds me, I must make sure that all the black-and-white bead bars are in order for the snake game, because I am going to start Johnny on that this morning—perhaps Janet too. I must get out a new box for the ten-bead bars as the one we have is falling to pieces with constant use; and I must not forget to replace the two names that were missing in the second box of the 'Singular and Plurals' series.

"I think I shall introduce Mabel today to the grammar boxes; and Michael could start on the grammar symbols. Valerie was not sure yesterday of the difference between 62 and 26, so I shall put her back again to doing 'the bird's-eye view of the decimal system.' (I might get Oliver to show her how to do it.) Then there's that little group who are so keen, just now, on doing their tables. I must remember to get them together and show them how to do the multiplication-pattern-game; and how to fill in the table of Pythagoras, as far as they have gone. If Robert wants to put out the thousand chain in the corridor I will let him; but not with Jimmy. It was a mistake to allow that partnership yesterday, for I could see that Jimmy did not really understand it (that was why he was inclined to fool about). He—Jimmy—might very well join Valerie in doing the 'bird's-eye view' again; for obviously he is not yet clear in his mind about the 'hierarchy of numbers.' I suppose Trevor will make a dash as usual for the history time chart to do 'transport through the ages.' Which reminds me he hasn't done any arithmetic for several days; I will tactfully remind him that there is such a subject! (That gives me an idea! I wonder if one could work out something in the way of a material for the history time line on the subject of 'Arithmetic through the Ages.' One could begin with a caveman trying to count the number of hares he has trapped; or how to divide a catch of twenty fishes between himself and two friends. You could bring in and teach Roman numerals *en passant* (I have often wondered how Caesar's quartermasters kept the accounts for their cohorts with those cumbersome symbols!)."

With the Montessori directress, one sees that her anticipatory meditations tend to revolve round the question of the prepared environment on the one hand, and the needs of individual children on the other.

Unlike the teacher who is tied to a curriculum she has no idea what either she or the children will be doing at any particular moment during the morning. This uncertainty, far from being a source of anxiety, is one of the most attractive features of her work. It turns each new day as it comes into a fresh adventure, both for her and for her children. To begin with, it is always a matter of interest to observe what particular materials the different children will choose to work with, and for how long. It is interesting, too, to see which children decide to work together in a group—for within certain limitations this is always permitted. Her first surprise, as she goes round the class that morning, might be to find that Johnny is already doing the snake game. It is a surprise because she knows she has never taught him. (Actually he learned it from Michael by sitting next to him and watching how he did it.) Later on she might get another similar surprise; for there is Clare, down on a rug on the floor, doing a division sum ($2,368 \div 3$) with the golden decimal system beads, and she never taught her that either.

For all she knows, that very morning, there might occur a genuine "Montessori explosion." Jimmy might suddenly discover he can write, or Nicholas run round telling everybody that "three eights are the same as eight threes" ("Nobody told me!"); or Florrie might start composing a story of her own for the first time. The best and most joyful surprise that could be in store for her that morning would be to find that that new boy—Fred who up to now has been such a "deviated nuisance" —has actually settled down to the work of grading the sixty-three colour tablets, and is doing it with such concentration that—wonder of wonders!—she had actually forgotten his existence.

It is of course quite possible that one of the unexpected events which might happen that morning would be that Robin, whilst washing a table, upsets a bucket of dirty water over Violet's painting; or Vivienne gets a piece of plasticine stuck in her hair; or that Sean gets a unit-bead stuck in his nostril ("nostrich" as one of my young friends called it in a similar emergency!); or it might even happen that Jack and Paul engage in a free fight. But these are comparatively rare occurrences; and, after all—in the little world of the Montessori classroom, as in the big world outside—one has to take the rough with the smooth. Happily the smooth far exceeds the rough, and steadily increases in proportion as the weeks pass.

Montessori was most apt when she described what goes on in a Montessori school as *una vita che si svolge*—"a life which unfolds itself." For that is exactly what it is, an individual and social life which goes on developing itself, from hour to hour, even from minute to minute, with all the glorious uncertainty of human freedom.

A Beautiful Relationship

It is a beautiful relationship which springs up between the directress and her little pupils as the weeks and months go by; and no one can appreciate it more fully than those who have passed from the old system to the new. Not that teachers under the old system were any less devoted to their children; nor any less willing to make sacrifices on their behalf. And of course it would be silly to deny that under that system there were very many happy classrooms; for the enthusiasm of the born teacher will overcome the most formidable obstacles. But we do maintain—and that categorically—that, in general, the relations between teacher and children were in the olden times not as happy, intimate, or fruitful as they might have been. The reason for this was that, under the old relationship, there existed—perforce—a certain amount of repression on the part of the teacher—albeit for the most part it was exercised unconsciously. Consequently a number of excellent qualities in the children (and teacher) were often suppressed, or rather nipped in the bud before they were allowed to see the light of day.

The role of the Montessori directress resembles more that of a guardian angel than a teacher of the old type. Or shall we say a combination of a guardian angel with an information bureau! It is her lot to watch with humble reverence, day by day, the spontaneous unfolding of the children's lives; seeking always to remove obstacles, both internal and external, from their path, whilst she guides with science and sympathy the irrepressible energies of life.

To live day by day, month by month, in such a joyous company—for joy is the keynote; to be surrounded constantly by so much innocence and charm, by such engaging candour; to see her children's characters deepen, as they acquire more and more the admirable traits of "normality"—all this makes the vocation of the Montessori directress a singularly enviable one.

The Best Reward

What gives to the directress her deepest joy is to feel that she is becoming, in an ever-increasing degree, the personal friend and confidante of all these small but intensely human beings. Not that she sets out, or should set out, deliberately to win their affection. That would be to obtrude her personality on theirs; to drag them out of the natural orbit of their lives into hers. She is, as we have so often emphasized, the link between them and the prepared environment. She must be ever ready to efface herself when once that link has been established. She must not resent it when the children choose the materials and concentrate upon them rather than upon herself, even to the extent of seeming to forget her very existence. She should be glad when they prefer to go on working by themselves, in this way, rather than hanging on her lips listening spellbound to one of her thrilling stories.[5] In this respect she must exercise a patient reticence not unlike that of the Creator to his creatures. How many persons—not to mention the whole animal creation—receive innumerable benefits, daily, without giving a passing thought to Him who has so bountifully provided for them—provided them not only with their own individual lives and talents, but also with the "prepared environment" of the universe in which they live.

But the day will come—which will probably be a different one for each child—when the little ones will come to realize who it is who has so carefully prepared the way for them; guided them along such interesting paths; lived with them, and for them; given herself so unstintingly; served them so patiently, asking nothing in return. "On that day—with the freedom which is the keynote of the whole method—the little ones will choose not this or that piece of material in the environment, but the directress herself, the living key to its treasures." This is the teacher's highest reward! Has earth anything more precious to offer than the grateful affection of a child?

Yet for some there is a reward still higher; but it is not of this world, but rather "a treasure laid up in Heaven." For— "Inasmuch as ye have done it to the least of these my little ones ye have done it unto Me."

[5]Stories of course—especially Scripture stories—should have their proper place in a Montessori class. But here, as always, the directress should aim at that "transference of activity" which weans the children from her; and enables them to nourish themselves directly at the fountainheads of literature.

Montessori and Froebel

NOTE: Quotations from Froebel in this section of the book (Part Five) are all taken from his *Education of Man*, unless otherwise stated.

CHAPTER XIX   MONTESSORI AND FROEBEL: SIMILARITIES

The question is often asked: What is the relation between Montessori and Froebel and their respective systems? Is it one of antagonism? or even of incompatibility? Is it a case of having to choose between two masters so that if you cleave to one you can no longer serve the other? Perhaps the best answer to this query is that given by Rusk in his *History of Infant Schools,* where he sums up the matter as follows: "That the doctrines of Montessori and Froebel are incompatible is a common, but unfortunate assumption in this country, whereas were Froebel alive today he would doubtless be the first to acknowledge that the Montessori system, both philosophically and pedagogically, is a natural development of his own system."

This does not mean that the two systems are in agreement on all points. On the contrary, as we shall see in the next chapter, there are certain differences—more in practice but also in theory—which go very deep. It is rather when one compares the spirit of Froebel with that of Montessori that one realizes their profound affinity. It is in their attitude of love and reverence for the child as a spiritual being that they are in complete unity—not in the details of their system nor in their philosophy of life.

This unity of spirit doubtless explains why so many of the best Montessori directresses have started off as disciples of Froebel, and have found in her doctrines and practice the fulfilment of their aims. Such was the author's own experience. Thirty years ago, at the outset of my teaching career, I began by being an enthusiastic admirer of Froebel; and scoured the country to visit all the Kindergartens I could find. More than a quarter of a century's collaboration with Montessori, however, has not lessened one whit my admiration—not to say affection —for Friedrich Froebel. Because Montessori is a genius does not make Froebel any less one; for, as the apostle tells us, "One star differs from another in glory": but both are glorious. It cannot be doubted that Froebel's spiritual approach to childhood and the emphasis he laid on training in infancy prepared the soil in which later Montessori's ideas were to take root and flourish.

In attempting a detailed comparison between the two systems, as they exist today, we have come upon a rather unexpected difficulty. Whereas the Montessori system still holds together in a harmonious and inter-related whole, like an organic unity, a Froebelian system of education as such no longer exists. In its latest pamphlet the National Froebel Institute admits that "there is no longer a Froebel System."

Nevertheless, by going back to the fountainhead in each case, it is possible to compare principles and practice of these two great educators. It is a task well worth doing because it is at once interesting and illuminating.

Both Discovered Their Vocations by Accident

It is a curious but noteworthy fact that the two individuals who have most profoundly influenced education in the past century and a half discovered their vocations as it were by accident. The young Froebel was studying architecture at Frankfort-on-Main when he was persuaded by a friend, who was fired by the enthusiasm of Pestalozzi, to give up architecture and take a post in a school. "The very first time," says Froebel, "that I found myself before thirty or forty boys I felt thoroughly at home. In fact I perceived that I had at last found my long-missed life element. I was as well pleased as a fish in water. I was inexpressibly happy." We have already noticed (Chapter II) by what indirect and unexpected bypaths Dr. Montessori was led until she finally found herself, at the age of forty, standing amazed amidst the revelations of her first *Casa dei Bambini*.

The Affinities of Genius

There is always something mysterious and inexplicable about the operations of genius in any sphere. Every genius is born with a secret affinity for the work he is destined to perform, and for everything connected with it. This was so in

the case of both Froebel and Montessori, both of whom were
sent into the world to illuminate unseen depths in the soul
of the little child. Right from the beginning—before each had
discovered his mission in life—we can catch glimpses, here
and there, of a deep subconscious undercurrent which was
bearing them irresistibly towards their destined goal. Such
incidents as the following, taken from the early life of Froebel,
can be compared with the similar signpost that we have noted
in Montessori's case (p. 25).

In 1813, Froebel was returning from the front. (He fought
in the Napoleonic wars). "During the long march home," he
writes, "my soul was filled with an unceasing, inexplicable,
restless longing. We passed through many a beautiful land-
scape and many a fair garden, but my soul was left unsatisfied. It chanced that in F—— I went into a small garden
decked with many gay and beautiful flowers. I gazed at all
that vigorous growth with its display of fresh blossoms but
not one of the flowers brought my soul any ease. All the
flowers seemed to present themselves in my soul at one moment; and as they did so, it struck me as most remarkable
that there was no lily amongst them. So I enquired of the
owner if he had any lilies in his garden. He replied in the
negative, adding (rather querulously but with justifiable self-
defence) that 'nobody had missed them either.'

"Then I realized that what I was seeking under the form
of the still pure lily was my own heart's ease, my soul's
peace—unity and clarity of soul. That garden with all its
manifold variety, but without any lilies, seemed to symbolize
my life so full of incident and variety and yet without unity."

Froebel then goes on to describe how, on another day,
still on the homeward march, he saw some lilies in the
garden of a country house, but separated from him by a
fence, which however he surmounted. Then follows the
most illuminating sentence of all: "One thing I must mention, and that is that, in the place where I was looking for
the lilies, there was in the garden a three-year-old boy
who looked at me and smiled with an expression of especial
trust and confidence."

In these days of depth psychology we are all aware of the
power of the subconscious to create thought-symbols:[1] and
while it makes us more ready to believe the story it happily
does not destroy its beauty. We see how something in this
young man's soul—an intuition too deep for words—had already related the unity and purpose which his life had hitherto

[1] The *Puer Aeternus* is a well-known psychological archetype, as Jung has shown
us.

lacked with the trusting confidence and mute appeal of child-hood. In that moment—of the vision of the child in the garden of lilies—there was already contained, by implication, the Garden of Children ("Kindergarten") of later years.[2]

The Child the Active Factor

All through this book we have emphasized the point that—according to Montessori—the vital thing in a true educational method is the activity of the child, and that the function of the teacher is to direct the child's spontaneous energies. This is also Froebel's fundamental maxim; "Education, in instruction and training and in its first principles, should necessarily be a passive following—only guarding and protecting—not prescriptive, categorical, interfering." Again, "All prescriptive categorical interfering must necessarily hinder and destroy." As Dr. Montessori so succinctly phrases it, "Every useless aid arrests development."

Use of Teaching Materials

Because Froebel and Montessori both realized the vital importance of self-activity (*Selbst-Tätigkeit*) in education they both saw the necessity of devising special occupations to arouse and sustain it—the "Froebelian Gifts" on the one hand, and the "Montessori Materials" on the other. But they differed considerably as to the principles on which these materials were constructed. As the Board of Education's report on infant and nursery schools says: "Madame Montessori, like Froebel, stands for the right of the child to unfettered growth; but while Froebel approached problems of education from the stand-point of theology and metaphysics, Madame Montessori has approached them from the standpoint of modern physiology and psychology."

Froebel's "gifts" are credited with a mystical and symbolic significance which has no real relation to the child's reactions. "In a wholly unwarrantable fashion Froebel assumes that the play objects symbolize to the child highly complicated processes and have even a deep metaphysical significance. (E.g., *Der Ball ist ein Bild des All*—Rusk)."

On the other hand Montessori's didactic materials—both sensorial and advanced—are based on clearly defined psychological principles such as identity, contrast, gradation, isolation of stimulus, the "concrete materialization" of ideas,

<hr>

[2]These incidents are taken from an article *Froebel and die Gegenwart* by Herman Nohl printed in *Die Erziehung*, November 1929.

"the point of contact" (see p. 239) and so forth. The German writer, Gerhards, in fact goes to some pains to demonstrate that Montessori's sensory materials exemplify the principles of the Gestalt psychology.[8]

The Child as Soft Wax

Montessori often uses the simile that the child's soul can be compared to soft wax; while at the same time she inveighs against the notion, once so prevalent, that the teacher must make use of this delicate plasticity in order to mould it. On the contrary she maintains that just because it is so sensitive we must be extra careful not to obliterate the first delicate tracings made on this infantile intelligence by destroying its spontaneous activity. Froebel uses this same simile:

We grant space and time to young plants and animals because we know that, in accordance with the laws that live in them, they will develop properly and grow well. Young plants and animals are left in peace; and arbitrary interference with their growth is avoided so as not to disturb their pure unfolding and sound development. But the young human being is looked upon as a piece of wax which man can mould into what he pleases, instead of being allowed to unfold in beauty and all-sided harmonious development.

The Metamorphoses of the Developing Child

In Chapter VI we saw how Dr. Montessori compares the child's mental development to a series of metamorphoses; and insists that the important thing is that, at each stage, the child should have what it needs *at that stage* without thinking of the future. "Each plane must be lived through in order that the individual may pass from one plane to the next." Otherwise there may be arrested development, for "those who have not lived through any plane fully may return to it later: for example the young man who has lacked maternal love may find satisfaction by marrying an older woman. . . . The child's work is to create the man that is to be, and we cannot hurry it. The adult will be a fully harmonious individual only if he has been able at each preceding stage to live as Nature intended him to."

This is exactly Froebel's idea, which he repeats again and again in many different forms. "The child," he says, "the boy, the man, should know no other endeavour but to be at every

[8]*Zur Beurteilung der Montessori-Pedagogik*, Karl Gerhards.

stage of development wholly what that stage calls for. Then will each successive stage spring like a new shoot from a healthy bud, for only the adequate development of man at each preceding stage can effect and bring about adequate development at each succeeding stage." Or again, "The boy has not become a boy, nor has the youth become a youth, by reaching a certain age, but only by having lived through childhood, and further on through boyhood, true to the requirements of his mind, his feelings and his body. Similarly the adult man has not become an adult simply by reaching a certain age, but only by faithfully satisfying the requirements of his childhood, boyhood and youth." "Rousseau has ascribed all the defects of body and mind in pupils to the 'desire to make men of them before their time.'"

"Dropped Stitches" in Our Mental Life

Just in so far as the individual in his growth and development has *not* been able to live himself out to the full in each successive stage as it comes, there will be something lacking in his mental equipment—some defect which Dr. Montessori aptly compares to "dropped stitches" in his mental development (see Chapter VII). Froebel insists on this same principle.

In general whatever of human education and development has been neglected in boyhood will never be retrieved. . . . Shall we, men and fathers and perhaps mothers, too, not at last be frank, and cease to conceal from ourselves the never-healing wounds and permanently callous places in our dispositions, the dark spots left in our souls by the ruthless extermination of noble and elevating thoughts and feelings in the days of our misguided boyhood and youth? Shall we never see that noble germs were at that time broken and withered, nay killed in our souls? And shall we not take notice of all this for our children's sake?

Sensitive Periods or "Budding Points"

In Chapter VII we have seen too how these various stages through which the developing child passes are each characterized by special sensibilities and corresponding interests. Froebel, too, in a general sense was aware of these periods of special sensibility, though they were never so clearly demarcated by him as with Montessori. (Indeed some of the most important of them—as for instance the sensitive period for order and that of the absorbent mind—he does not even mention.) But he does speak in general of these special periods as "budding points." "We should," he says, "in all instruction start from a certain want or need in the boy. Indeed, to a certain extent, such a want is indispensable if the boy is to be taught with profit and success." Froebel realizes too the danger of letting these periods go by without making full use of the special aptitudes which come with them. Thus, for instance, he laments the fact the sufficient use is not made out of the exploring activities of small children. "In that way," he says, "they could be taught many things almost without effort"—things which have to be taught them later by the teacher at a time when their minds should be busy with other matters. "Every phase of development, however beautiful and proper in its place, must vanish and perish wherever a higher phase is to appear. The sheltering bud-scales must fall when the young branch or fragrant blossom is to unfold, the blossom in its turn make room for the fruit; the fruit decay that the young tree may sprout."

These budding points are certainly related to Dr. Montessori's idea of sensitive periods though Froebel never actually uses the phrase. He goes on: "For the purpose of a life-giving, life-stirring instruction it is most important to note the moment, the proper place, for the introduction of a new branch of instruction. In fact the distinctive factor of a dynamic education consists in finding and fixing these points. For when found the subject for instruction grows independently in accordance with its own living law. Therefore the whole attention of the teacher must be directed to these 'budding-points' of new branches of instruction."

The Child as an Explorer

Dr. Montessori constantly refers to the small child in her lectures as—the explorer. And as we have shown (Chapter V) she sees in the child's never-ending interest in stones, flowers, coloured objects, sticks—anything he can get hold of—an activity of the highest importance—corresponding to the researches of the scientist into the mysteries of matter and energy. So also does Froebel, who says:

Behold the child laboriously stooping and slowly going forward on the ground under the eaves of the roof. The force of the rain has washed out of the sand, small, smooth, bright pebbles, and the ever-observant child gathers them as building stones as it were, as material for future building. And is he wrong? Does not the child in truth collect material for his future life-building? Like things must be ranged together, unlike separated. . . .

The child would know all the properties of things, their innermost nature. . . . For this reason he examines the object on all its sides: for this reason he breaks it: for this reason he puts it in his mouth and bites it. We reprove the child for his naughtiness and foolishness; and yet he is wiser than we who reprove him.

Both Froebel and Montessori emphasize the importance of assisting this "little explorer" in his researches. With the former this is to be accomplished by the direct help of the adult; with the latter more indirectly by means of a "prepared environment" so simplified and set in order that the objects in it easily and systematically reveal their qualities to the enquiring mind of the little scientist.

Yet even here Froebel is one in principle with Dr. Montessori, if not so successful in practice: for he says—"To have found one-fourth of the answer to his own question by his own effort is of more value to the child than to hear it all, half-understood, from another; for this causes mental indolence. Do not therefore answer your children's questions directly at once, but *as soon as they have gathered sufficient strength and experience furnish them with the means of finding an answer in the sphere of their own knowledge.*" This is indeed the very principle on which the Montessori environment has been built up; and one of the chief differences between the Montessori school and the Froebel Kindergarten lies just in the fact that Montessori has been more successful in finding and placing at the child's disposal "the means to find the answer in the sphere of his own knowledge" by himself. For as we have seen the function of the Montessori directress is not so much to teach directly as to act as a "link" between the child and this prepared and instructing environment. The environment should be *par excellence* a place where the little explorer can carry on his researches under the most helpful and stimulating circumstances.

Macrocosm and Microcosm

By means of his constant researches amidst the objects and persons which he finds about him the child is striving to create within his mind an orderly system of knowledge corresponding to the world without. Dr. Montessori is never tired of comparing this process of creating an inner world to the story of the Creation of the world as told in the Book of Genesis. It is interesting to note that the same simile occurred to Froebel. "In the mind of man, in the history of his mental development, in the growth of his consciousness, in the experience of every child . . . there is repeated the history of the creation and development of all things, as the holy books relate it." [1] But here again we find the Dottoressa goes further and gets more out of the simile—pointing out that, as in the general Creation so in the child's mind, there comes first the creation of the rough or main divisions, and after that, and on the basis of it, the finer and ever more detailed forms of being.

Normality and Deviation

In Chapter X, we have shown how many of the disagreeable traits of children—their caprices, fears, lying, timidity, etc.—are generally caused by a deviation of the child's vital energies from their normal constructive channels. Froebel too realizes this; but again in a more vague and general way. "The child's life accords with the destiny or mission of humanity" (i.e., the 'norm of the species') "but we know it not. We not only fail to guard, nurse and develop the inner germs of life but allow them to be stifled and crushed . . . or to find vent on some weaker side in unnaturalness. We see the same phenomenon which in the plant we called a wild-shoot—a misdirection of energies—in the misdirection of the desires and instincts of the child."

Where Montessori diverges from Froebel is in her belief that the cure for deviations lies not in play but in "normalization through work." (For what she means by "work" see Chapter VIII.)

The Child Relives the Cultural Achievements of Humanity in the Past

The normalized child, Dr. Montessori insists, is a higher and more elevated being than we have hitherto reckoned it to be—capable of loftier sentiments and higher flights. For this reason, in presenting him with the cultural achievements of the race, we must not do so in a dead manner but rather in such a way that the child can relive, reexperience in his own life the wonder and excitement which must have accompanied the various steps in the onward march of civilization. Thus for instance in teaching reading we must do it in such a way

[1] As the late Margaret Drummond said, "In each child the world begins anew." *The Dawn of Mind.*

that the child relives the stupendous wonder of the written word. Froebel, too, teaches that "Man should, at least mentally, repeat the achievements of mankind"; though he does not furnish us with the wealth of practical suggestions that we find in Montessori.

Just a sentence here to prevent a misunderstanding. When we say that, according to Dr. Montessori, we should try and arrange things so that the child is able to "recapture something of the surprise and wonder which marked the important steps forward in the cultural development of the race," it does not mean that she subscribes to what she calls "the materialistic idea now discredited that 'ontogenesis sums up philogenesis' ": i.e., the life of the individual reproduces the life of the species. Nor must we conclude that "the child, like the savage, is attracted by the fantastic, and the unreal"—a point which will be further elaborated in considering the differences between Froebel and Montessori.

The Exercises in Practical Life

We have referred in many places in this book (especially Chapter XIII) to the exercises in practical life which form so important and indispensable a part of the training of small children. And we have shown too how the main object of these exercises is to assist the "progressive incarnation" of the child—i.e., the attainment of a more complete harmony between soul and body, so that the latter becomes the ever more perfect instrument of the former. Froebel realizes that in childhood: "the will, as such, does not yet control the body at all times; therefore we should aim at enabling the body to obey the mind implicitly at all times, as in the case of a musical composer." Froebel also points out that this happy relationship between the mind and its instrument cannot be obtained "by continual admonitions to act properly." He also says that "the occasional cultivation of the body in domestic occupations may do much to remedy this" (i.e., the discrepancy between the will and its power to carry out a bodily action). But it is quite clear from the use of the word "occasional" that Froebel never understood the profound significance of the exercises of practical life, as Dr. Montessori uses them, especially in conjunction with the introduction into them of the "motive of perfection" and the principle of the "control of error in the environment." Froebel is more inclined to look to special "drilling lessons" to supply this coordination and refinement of the muscular system—a procedure which Dr. Montessori thinks inadvisable for chil-

dren, except in so far as this term might be made to include
spontaneous exercises in balance and rhythm.

Autoeducation and Liberty

As we saw at the outset of this comparison, Froebel
stood firmly for autoeducation as a first principle. "To stir
up, to animate, to awaken and to strengthen the pleasure and
power of the human being to labour uninterruptedly at his
own education has become and always will remain the fundamental principle of my educational work." Realizing too, that
the will can be strengthened only by voluntary activity he sees
the importance of liberty in the schoolroom; and that this freedom "can only come by self-activity." We have noted elsewhere how much further Dr. Montessori has gone in actually
achieving this liberty for the child *in practice*. But here we
are only concerned to point out how vividly Froebel realized
the importance of freedom. With him, too, as with Dr. Montessori, freedom was not to be confused with licence; and
for him, too, "only freedom within the law was to be regarded
as true freedom."

Montessori and Froebel Were Both Idealists

Montessori and Froebel resemble each other in relating
their educational aims to ultimate religious values as they saw
them. In this sense they can be both called idealists. On this
point Rusk makes an interesting comment: "The background
of Montessori's thought and work is a spiritual realism or a
modern realism; and from what we can infer of Froebel's
thought we are convinced that he would have seen in this
new philosophy the logical outcome of his own views." Rusk
may or may not be right: for our part we have often found
it so hard to find out exactly what Froebel did think that we
would hesitate to hazard definite views as to what he *would
have* thought.

The difficulty about Froebel is that he never seems to be
able to see where exact science leaves off and mystical insight
begins. Montessori has the advantage of him in this respect,
since as a doctor of medicine and a university professor of
anthropology, she had a long and rigorous training in scientific
method before she entered the sphere of education. Froebel's
teaching is hard to absorb (as the Board of Education Report
points out) because of the way in which it was presented.
"Froebel," it continues, "was a mystic and a sentimentalist,

and mysticism and sentimentality for long interposed a fog between the teacher and her children."

Nevertheless, in spite of these differences of expression, Montessori and Froebel are both at one in having a spiritual or religious aim in their educational systems; and both are equally opposed to purely utilitarian or materialistic conceptions of education.

There are still other points of similarity between Montessori and Froebel which could be mentioned [5]; but we have already said enough to make it clear on how many important points they are in fundamental agreement, and how absurd is the view of those who maintain that there is, as it were, a great gulf unbridgeably fixed between them.

CHAPTER XX   MONTESSORI AND FROEBEL: DIFFERENCES

Having considered some of the many resemblances between Montessori and Froebel, what about the differences? Looking on the matter in the broadest outline we should express the situation thus: both Froebel and Montessori are aiming at the same thing—the education of the child through self-activity—but Montessori has been more successful in obtaining it.

The Teaching Unit of Each System Compared

Coming now to differences in detail let us first look at the sphere of practice. All who have had experience both of Montessori schools and Froebelian kindergartens are in agreement as to one fundamental practical difference. It relates to what one might call the Teaching Unit. In her attractive little book, *Learning and Teaching in the Infant School,* Miss Hume states the matter succinctly as follows: "In the Froebelian school the unit of teaching is the group of eight to ten children; in the Montessori school the unit of teaching is the individual child." In the paragraph preceding this statement Miss Hume has asked the pertinent question, "Why should the Froebelian ideas, which were not understood by the great body of teachers of young children in the nineteenth century, have been accepted with enthusiasm when expounded by Mon-

[5] See Chapter XXI.

tessori?" And she finds the answer "principally in the fact that Montessori was able to demonstrate how her principles could be applied, in some measure at least, to our large infant classes."

This statement is borne out, from another point of view, by the Board of Education *Report on Infant and Nursery Schools* in a discussion on the "Individual Work System." "With the discovery," it says, "that children were ready and eager to work by themselves and profited by doing so, what was popularly known as individual work became a feature of the infant school: its rapid spread owes much to the teaching and practice of Madame Montessori."

Some years ago a questionnaire was circulated to a number of Montessori directresses in different countries, making the enquiry—amongst others—as to what they regarded as the ideal number of children for a Montessori class (all working individually of course). From this emerged the rather surprising fact that most preferred a larger class to a smaller one. Not too large a class of course; but most of them said they would prefer a class of some thirty to thirty-five children to one of twelve to fifteen. This is an important practical point in favour of the Montessori system. But what interests us, at the moment, is that it is also a clear indication that there must be certain factors in the Montessori system which make it possible for *each individual* child to carry on his work freely as a separate unit—factors which admittedly (at least by implication) are not present in the Froebelian kindergarten. We believe this latter state of things is what Froebel himself would have preferred, since as the Board of Education Report points out, it was Froebel's aim that "each child should have liberty to grow in its own way and to learn by doing."

Montessori Has a Deeper Faith in Spontaneity

If we look deeper for the root of this difference in the unit of teaching we shall find it in the fact that Montessori has more faith in the spontaneous intellectual and social powers of the child; and is consequently not afraid to trust the running of the school to these inner energies. In a word, the Froebelian teacher is still a teacher whereas the Montessori teacher has been changed into a directress.

Thus, to take one point as an example. In the Montessori class, when the child is tired of one occupation, it is not the teacher but the child himself who chooses the next piece of work, guided by the "inner sensibility" of which we spoke in Chapter XVII. Whereas in the kindergarten, according to

one of its leading exponents, "it is the teacher's part to suggest
a change when the child's interest is beginning to wane and
to encourage the children to undertake new duties." [1] What
Mrs. Fisher wrote twenty years ago in her *Montessori Mother*
is not without application at the present day:

> The first thing Montessori requires of a directress in her
> school is a complete avoidance of the centre of the stage,
> a self-annihilation, the very desirability (not to mention the
> possibility) of which has never occurred to the kindergarten
> teacher, whose usual position is in the middle of a ring
> of children with every eye on her, with every sensitive,
> budding personality receiving the strongest possible im-
> pressions from her own adult individuality.
>
> The average American kindergarten teacher needs the
> calming and quieting lesson taught by the great Italian
> educator's reverent awe for the spontaneous, ever upward,
> irresistible thrust of the miraculous principle of growth.
>
> In spite of the horticultural name of her school the or-
> dinary kindergarten teacher has never learned the whole-
> hearted, patient faith in the long, slow processes of nature
> which characterizes the true gardener. She is not penetrated
> by the realization of the vastness of the forces of the human
> soul, she is not subdued and consoled by a calm certainty
> of the rightness of natural development. She is far gayer
> with her children than the Montessori teacher, but she
> is really less happy with them because, in her heart of hearts,
> she trusts them less. She feels a restless sense of respon-
> sibility for each action of each child. It is doubtless this
> difference in mental attitude which accounts for the physical
> difference of aspect between our pretty, smiling, ever-active,
> always beckoning, nervously conscientious kindergarten
> teacher, always on exhibition, and the calm unhurried tran-
> quility of the Montessori directress, always unobtrusively
> in the background. [2]
>
> The latter is but moving about from one little river of
> life to another, lifting a sluice-gate here for a sluggish
> nature, constructing a dam there to help a too impetuous
> nature to concentrate its forces, and much of the time
> occupied in quietly observing, quite at her leisure, the
> direction of the channels being constructed by the different
> streams. The kindergarten teacher tries to do this, but she
> seems obsessed with the idea, unconscious for the most
> part, that it is, after all, her duty to manage somehow to
> increase the flow of the little rivers by pouring into them
> some of her own superabundant vital force.

[1] *Froebel To-day*, Priestman.
[2] Cf. the description of "Silent Movement," p. 306.

The Prepared Environment—The Counterpart of Spontaneity

If we look still deeper, and ask ourselves the question: How is it that the Montessori directress has such confidence in trusting the running of her class to the spontaneous energies of growth rather than to her own efforts, we shall find that the secret of her confidence, as of her success, lies not only in giving the children freedom to choose their occupations, and the length of time they may wish to work at them, but—just as much or even more—in the careful forethought which she has put into the creation of the prepared environment.

Play or Work

Unless the prepared environment is there with all its special occupations, and unless there is a teacher who knows how to be the dynamic link between it and the children, one would see all sorts of activity going on (for free children are always active) but one would not be likely to see that special, creative, spontaneous activity which Montessori calls "*work*."

If such work is not going on, and the children are quite free—what will you see then? You will almost certainly see them playing in one way or other, but not working in the special sense in which Montessori defines that activity. Here we find ourselves coming up against an important point of divergence between Montessori and Froebel (or rather between Montessori and the followers of Froebel—which is not always the same thing). With Montessori the child's highest and noblest form of self-expression is work, in the sense that it has been often defined in previous chapters—especially VIII and X—that is, in that spontaneous activity by which the child creates himself.

With the Froebelians the child's highest form of spontaneous self-activity is *play*. This is usually a make-belief activity in an environment which is no longer treated as an objective reality, but transmuted by the child's imagination into something else. To this contrast we shall return later on by a rather long and circuitous route. Meanwhile let us turn to an allied subject— the vexed question of Montessori and the teaching of fairy tales.

The Question of Fairy Tales

There has got abroad a firm conviction that Dr. Montessori is a bitter and implacable opponent of fairy tales. The writer was once giving a course of lectures to elementary schoolteachers in a town in Yorkshire and the chair was taken by one of His Majesty's Inspectors. This gentleman, in the course of his opening remarks, referred to one of his predecessors who had gone down to history under the nickname of "Fairy-Tale-Brown." It appears that over thirty years ago this Mr. Brown had organized a violent anti-Montessori campaign, basing his whole attack on Dr. Montessori's "prohibition of fairy tales for children."

"Fairy-Tale-Brown" had got hold of the wrong end of the stick. If he had only taken the trouble to read Dr. Montessori's own books attentively he would have discovered the exaggeration of his outlook. He would have then seen that—in giving a description of the literature which she caused to be read aloud in her *Casa dei Bambini* whilst the children were busy filling in their coloured designs—Dr. Montessori herself places the fairy tales of Hans Andersen first on the list. (*Advanced Montessori Method,* Vol. II, p. 191.)

Nevertheless, since there can be no smoke without a fire, there must be *something* in Dr. Montessori's point of view which has given rise to so widespread an opinion.

The Right Age for Fairy Tales?

The whole question depends upon the age of the child to whom the fairy tales are told. If fairy tales are read for what they are—as literature, as fiction—there is no harm done. On the contrary much good lies buried in the fairy story like precious metal in a rich ore. As G. K. Chesterton says:[3] "There is the chivalrous lesson of Jack the Giant-killer that giants should be killed because they are giants; there is the lesson of Cinderella which is the same as that of the Magnificat, *exaltavit humile.* There is the great lesson of *Beauty and the Beast* that a thing must be loved *before* it is lovable." In many a fairy tale, too, there is clearly taught what Chesterton "for the pleasure of pedantry" calls the doctrine of conditional joy—a doctrine which goes to the very roots of our moral existence. "For"—he continues—"in the fairy tale an incomprehensible happiness rests on an incomprehensible condition. A box is opened and all the evils fly out. A word is forgotten and cities perish, a lamp is lit and love flies away. A flower is plucked and human lives are forfeited: an apple is eaten and the hope of God is gone."

But whilst a child of seven or eight would read these stories with profit, it is quite different with a child of two, three, or

[3]Chapter IV, *Orthodoxy.*

even four years of age. At this age, according to Dr. Montessori, you may be doing the child serious and even permanent injury by relating such stories.

We Must Not Handicap "The Young Explorer"

It is fatally easy for us to forget and thoughtlessly take advantage of the small child's extremely limited experience. In other parts of this book (Chapter V) we have drawn attention to the colossal task which is laid upon every infant from the moment it comes into the world—no less a task than the building up, out of a primordial chaos, an orderly scheme of things; a world truly related in all its parts—in short a cosmos. And further, we have seen that the child of three—although he has already single-handed made an immense progress—still "carries around within himself a heavy chaos." [4] His experience is so limited that the commonest sights and sounds are to him full of mystery and wonder. Small children have therefore no need of "tales of mystery and the imagination." G. K. Chesterton again hits the nail on the head: "When we are very young," he says, "we do not need fairy tales. Mere life in interesting enough. A child of seven is excited by being told that Tommy opened the door and saw a dragon. But a child of three is excited by being told that Tommy opened a door. Boys like romantic tales but babies like realistic tales because they find them romantic." [5]

At this early stage of his existence then, the child has plenty to do, in all conscience, in trying to piece together this funny old jigsaw puzzle of a universe without having it made still more difficult for him by our arbitrary introduction of fairies, witches, dragons and goblins, etc., which do not even exist. We must remember that at this stage the child will accept all these things as objective realities, and will (G.K.C. again) "just as readily believe there is a dragon round the corner as a dragoon." This means that sooner or later, if we tell him about such things, he will enter a period of confusion, not to say disillusionment. He will be obliged to waste part of his mental energies in sorting out "fay" from "fact"—energies which are needed early in life for more constructive purposes.

Sometimes, indeed, we may even expose the child to physical dangers as well as mental. A small girl of two to three years, after seeing *Peter Pan*, thought that she would fly too; and, on returning home, jumped from an upper window and was killed. The writer once mentioned this incident at a lecture; and at the

[4] Cf. p. 101.
[5] *Ibid.*

end of it a lady said, "I was very interested in what you said about the little girl who tried to fly, because, last summer, my own little girl jumped down from a bedroom window into the garden. Providentially she was not seriously injured as there happened to be a flower bed below. When I asked her why ever she had done such a thing, she replied simply, 'Well, Goldilocks did it too!' "

Imaginary Beings as Realities

It may be urged that these are exceptional cases; but it is undoubtedly true that the untimely introduction of make-belief may expose the child to other dangers almost as serious though perhaps less obvious. Imaginary fears (of witches and giants, etc.) may be set up, the influence of which may persist, subconsciously, to a much later age. I once knew a boy who, after having heard the story of Conan Doyle's *Lost World*, was haunted (even at the age of ten years) by a desperate fear of pterodactyls. By day, his reason convinced him that his fears were imaginary; but twilight always brought with it the terror of those ponderous leathern wings and crocodile teeth. I also knew a girl who had been brought up to believe in fairies, elementals, pixies, and a whole world of imaginary beings. At the age of sixteen she still not only believed in fairies but actually maintained that she saw them. I never doubted her sincerity, but her whole training had been one in which the boundaries between reality and make-belief, between believing and the wish-to-believe, had been so deliberately blurred that a certain amount of self-deception had become an unconscious habit. How easy such self-deception might be, to an imaginative person, is well illustrated in the following quotation from Francis Thompson's *Essay on Shelley:*

On a day when the skirts of a prolonged darkness were drawing off from him he (the poet is speaking of himself) walked in the garden, inhaling the keenly languorous relief of mental and bodily convalescence: the body sensitized by suffering. Pausing in reverie before an arum, he was suddenly aware of a minute white-stoled child sitting on the lily. For a second he viewed her with a surprised delight, but no wonder: then, returning to consciousness, he recognized the hallucination in the moment of vanishing. The apparition had no connection with his reverie; and though perhaps not so strongly visual as to deceive an alert mind, suggests the possibility of such deception.

It is much easier, at this early stage, to lead the child away from reality than to bring him back into it at a later one. "The way of Truth is difficult through the crust of imagination which is fixed without being first constructed upon a basis of truth." (Montessori.)

The Development of the Imagination

"But what about the development of the imagination? Do away with fairy stories, and how will the child develop this precious faculty? Your Montessori school is too realistic! There is not enough make-believe in it! Is not the child's natural tendency to prefer an imaginary world to a real one? As they themselves say—Let's Pretend! Will not all this preoccupation with reality stunt the child's imaginative growth and make him prematurely prosaic?"

We are now approaching a vital issue between the Montessorians and Froebelians of which this perennial discussion about fairy tales is but one expression. Let us state the matter in Dr. Montessori's own words:

> It is a common belief that the young child is characterized by a vivid imagination, and therefore a special education should be adopted to cultivate this gift of nature. His mentality differs from ours: he escapes from our strongly marked and restricted limits to wander in the fascinating worlds of unreality, a tendency which is also characteristic of savage peoples.
>
> There are other forms of imperfect development in the child which have their parallel in the savage; but we do not deliberately encourage these—such as for instance poverty of expression in language, the existence of concrete terms, and generalization of words by means of which a single word is used to indicate several purposes or objects: the absence of inflections causing the child to use only the infinitive is another example.

It would however be quite wrong to argue from this that Montessori does not consider the imagination an important faculty, or that she is not interested in its full development. On the contrary, in her *Advanced Montessori Method,* Vol. I, she treats of the subject to the tune of some 120 pages. We cannot do more here than summarize some of the main points.

Imagination Has a Sensory Basis

In the first place, far from wishing to suppress the imagination, she is anxious that the child should be able to develop it to the best advantage, and therefore she provides means to that end. Imagination, as the name implies, has to do with images. But whence are these images derived? In the first place from the external world. If it is true, as Aristotle maintained, that there is nothing in the intellect which was not first in the senses, it is equally and more obviously true of the imagination. As Dr. Montessori says:

> Imagination can have only a sensory basis. The sensory education which prepares for the accurate perception of the different details in the qualities of things, is therefore the foundation of the observation of things and of the phenomena which present themselves to our senses; and with this it helps us to collect from the external world the material for the imagination.
>
> Imaginative creation has no mere vague sensory support; that is to say, it is not the unbridled divagation of the fancy among images of light and colour, sounds and impressions; but it is a construction firmly allied to reality; *and the more it holds fast to the forms of the external created world, the loftier will the value of its internal creations be.* Even in imagining an unreal and superhuman world the imagination must be contained within the limits which recall those of reality. Man creates, but on the model of that divine creation in which he is materially and spiritually immersed. (*Advanced Montessori Method,* Vol. I, p. 248.) The creative imagination cannot work *in vacuo.* The mind that works by itself, independently of truth, works in a void.

Creative Imagination Is Saturated With Reality—Examples

Take any great work of the creative imagination and examine it from this point of view, and you will be struck immediately with the justice of these remarks. Take, for example, Shakespeare's *Midsummer Night's Dream* (a work of the creative imagination if ever there was one) and examine his fairies. You will see that, wonderful and ethereal as they are, as though belonging to another world, they are nevertheless impregnated with the reality of this. His description of them is based on the most accurate observation of *real* things. "Monsieur Cobweb, slay me a *red-hipped bumble bee on the top of a thistle!*" Or the tasks on which Titania sends the fairies for "the third part of a minute"—"some to war with reremice for their leathern wings to make my small elves coats." Where in nature could one find a material more suited to the making of "leathern jerkins for small elves" than the frail membrane of a bat's wing? Or take the opening lines of Keats' *Hyperion,* describing "that vale far sunken from the healthy breath of morn."

> No stir of air was there,
> Not so much life as on a summer's day
> Robs not one light seed from the feathered grass,
> But where the dead leaf fell, there did it rest.

Marvellous creations of the imagination these, and such as these, yet see how impregnated they are with reality! Shakespeare himself says that

> The lunatic the lover and the poet
> Are of imagination all compact;

but goes on to add that

> Lovers and madmen have such seething brains,
> Such shaping fantasies, that apprehend
> More than cool reason apprehends.

In them imagination is out of touch with reality and therefore not creative. But in the imagination of the poet there is so much latent or dissolved reality that he is able "to give to airy nothing a local habitation and a name," and thus create something which outlasts the marble monuments of kings. In this connection one might recall, as an illustration, a story of the young Leonardo da Vinci when he wished to create a dragon. This he did by carefully studying all sorts of fearsome reptiles and insects, which he kept alive in captivity, getting inspirations from each—an eye from this, a limb from that, a scale from the other. The resulting "fabulous monster" was so realistic, that it sent his frightened servant screaming out of the house!

Reality or Make-Believe

The question then boils itself down to this. What is the best way, at this stage, of helping the small child to build up a strong creative imagination? Are we, by trading on his immaturity and inexperience, to lead him by suggestion into a world of make-believe entities and unreal activities? Or are we to keep him in a real world, with real activities, real problems, real decisions?

Dr. Montessori is unhesitating in her reply: she is all for a real world, an objective world, a world of things seen, felt, moved, experienced. The best way we can help the child to develop his imagination, then, is to put him in relation with an environment so prepared that he can lay up a store of accurate images by means of his spontaneous observation in it.[6]

"Ah, but," exclaim Montessori's objectors, "that is going in flat contradiction to the nature of the child. You claim her method is based on the observation of the child; yet everyone knows that the child left to itself prefers to escape from reality into a world of make-believe and play."

Does it?

That is the whole point.

It is true, says Dr. Montessori, that the child often does escape from the real world into a world of make-believe and "let's pretend." *But from* WHAT *real world?*

From a world which adults have made for themselves. A world with adult proportions, adult standards, adult aims, a world with an adult tempo (cf. the rhythm of childhood, Chapter VIII), a world where the child is looked upon as *il disturbatore*—a disturber of the adult peace; a world from which the child is therefore relegated, if possible, to the nursery or schoolroom, so as not to be in the way, until he is ready to reenter it as a useful member of society. Remember, too, that in these places of relegation, the nursery and the school, he is still under adult domination.

Dolls' House or Children's House

No wonder the child seeks to escape from a reality such as that into a make-believe one of his own which he can control and dominate. But again the objectors exclaim: "But the facts, the facts—look at the facts! You cannot escape from the logic of the facts! Look at that child, there, with her dolls and dolls' house, setting out a dolls' tea party, pouring out cup after cup of imaginary tea, arranging the dolls' furniture, *pretending* to wash up the dolls' crockery after an *imaginary* meal! What has Dr. Montessori to say to that?"

Dr. Montessori has a great deal to say to this; and what she says is ingenious and original. She begins by noticing that of late years there has been a tendency for children's dolls to get bigger and bigger. And with this increase in their size there has naturally been a corresponding increase in the size of the dolls' chairs, tables, and appurtenances generally. "Now," says Dr. Montessori, "supposing this process goes on

[6]Cf. *Keys to the Universe*, pp. 27 and 144.

until the child's doll becomes as big as the child, with all the dolls' furniture proportionally enlarged, what will be the result? You will see that this same child, who amused itself perforce by playing in an imaginary dolls' world, living by proxy in the unreal world of the dolls' house, now takes the place of the doll, and lives his or her own life, actively in a real world which corresponds to it. You will see this same child who—before—was laying a dolls' table for an imaginary dolls' party, now laying a real table, with real cups and knives and forks, for the children's own meal. And you will see the children wait upon one another at table, with real victuals; and clear away and wash up afterwards. You will see these tiny mites, not so very much bigger than a big doll, dusting and sweeping and scrubbing, washing tables, arranging flower vases; and in a score of other ways earnestly keeping their own real house in order." Let us not forget the name of the first Montessori school was *Casa dei Bambini*. That was its name, and that was—and is—its nature, The Children's House, not the Dolls' House. Thus we see—to put it in a nutshell—the child has passed from a make-believe world to a real world—and much prefers it.

Furthermore, with this transition from a make-believe world to a real world, where the child can "work," there comes about a great change in his character and behaviour. I remember once in a conversation with Dr. Ballard (the well-known L.C.C. Inspector and author of many valuable books on education) that he made the following observation. He told me that he had that morning just visited two nursery schools in the same district. In one, the children had been provided with nothing but toys of various kinds; in the other, Montessori and similar didactic materials. The difference in the general atmosphere of the two schools, he said, was quite remarkable. In the former there was continual crying and quarrelling and disturbance; in the latter an atmosphere of tranquility, order, and joy.

An Interminable Discussion or the Two Forms of Intelligence

Speaking generally, I think it would be true to say that the Froebelians, as a whole, tend to regard the Montessori system as too rigidly intellectual, not giving enough scope to the child's spontaneous play and make-belief. On the other hand, the point of view of the average Montessorian is that the Froebelians have never realized—*because they have never seen*—the child's passion for intellectual work. The Froebel-

ians, they would say, treat the child as something lower than
he really is; and this because they have never seen what Montessori calls "the soul of the awakened child."

Which is right?

Montessori once gave a lecture on "The Two Forms of
Intelligence," which bore directly on this discussion.

We are constantly coming across certain contrasting ideas
with regard to the nature of the child's mind. On the one
hand there are many who think that in small children (from
three plus) the imagination should be encouraged; and
that in general children should develop along the imaginative side rather than along the exact lines which characterize our method. We, on the other hand, maintain that
children should be given exact occupations, and that they
should be allowed to continue at these as long as they like—
which in fact they do for so long a time that we have
called it "work."

The discussion between these two groups has been going
on for nearly thirty years, *and it will go on for ever*. Indeed
one might say that over this matter there will always hang
a note of interrogation. *They* say, imagination, make-belief,
play. *We* say, reality, exactitude, work. We did not start
out with any preconceived ideas on the subject, but were
led to it through observation; and our point of view rests
on a long experience.

Supposing that we were to put our different points of
view before a judge, what would happen? He would say
that we were both right; and we should be just where we
were before. What is the explanation of this anomaly?
Generally speaking, when we find two contrasting points of
view stubbornly continuing to exist, we shall find that each
has a reason for existence. It is so in this case. We are
forced to the conclusion that there are "two forms of
intelligence" in each individual. One of these—the imagination—has no need of special means external to the
individual to cause it to reveal itself. But the other—this
aptitude for spontaneous intellectual work—*has* need of
special means to bring it to light—just as a microscope is
needed to reveal certain things which have always been
there but were unsuspected without its aid.

Everything, says Montessori, which is an expression of the
human mind needs a special exactness which we call "technique." The difference between Montessori and her predecessors Froebel and Pestalozzi is that she has discovered
the technique by which this latent capacity in childhood is

made to reveal itself. As a consequence she has made it clear beyond all doubt that, when children are placed in certain circumstances (briefly, with freedom in a prepared environment with established "points of contact") they reveal an astonishing love of order, exactitude, an immense concentration on intellectual work, and all the other characteristics of "normalization." There is no gainsaying this, any more than it can be denied that children under other conditions love to play or eat sweets.

In the lecture from which these extracts were taken Montessori went on to say: "So truly is this the case that—under these circumstances—children display a universal love of mathematics, which is *par excellence* the science of precision, order and intelligence." [7] In all his experience of thirty years the writer has never met, or even heard of, a child brought up on the Montessori system from the beginning who disliked arithmetic. In fact, Montessori asserts quite roundly that her experience has convinced her of the truth of Blaise Pascal's dictum that the "human mind is by its nature mathematical." But, having said this, she goes on at once to add (with Pascal) that it is only one form of our intelligence; and that "life is full of mysteries, and the sphere of these mysteries is not suited to the mathematical mind."

"There is," she says, "the Divine Mind behind the Cosmos which differs from the mind of man in extent, substance, and nature. We cannot penetrate this mind but we can come in contact with it. When you have arrived at the point where you can say your intelligence can go no further, just there it touches the Beyond. This experience does not form an obstacle to the intelligence, it is a contact. The mind of man must work and work until in the end it arrives at this contact, the contact of the created intelligence with the Uncreated."

It is interesting to notice that the operation of our mind, which leads to this contact with the Beyond, according to her takes as its starting place the study of the world of reality, not of imagination or make-belief. It is a passage from Reality to more Reality, and not, as in the case of the girl mentioned on page 337, from one form of unreality to another.

What Is the Difference Between Work and Play?

Without going into the various theories as to the nature of play, we may note that Dr. Montessori maintains that play is something which satisfies only a part of one's nature, but

[7]Absence of any aptitude for number is generally regarded as one of the signs of a deficient intelligence. See also *The Myth of the Unmathematical Mind* C. A. Claremont.

that work goes deeper and brings a satisfaction to one's whole being. The child prefers work because it satisfies the subconscious longing of his nature to grow and develop into a harmonious personality. Every moment is precious to him as representing a passage from a slightly inferior stage to a higher one. Children need recreation, of course, just as adults do, and they enjoy it as we do. "Chess and bridge are pleasant enough for our leisure moments; but they would no longer be so if we were forced to do nothing else all our lives." Or, as Shakespeare says: "If all the week were holiday to play would be as tedious as to work." [8]

Perhaps no part of Dr. Montessori's doctrine has aroused more opposition than her belief that the child prefers work to play. Not only prefers work; but—as we have shown—never really comes to himself until he has had the opportunity of "becoming normalized through work." [9]

There are some persons so obsessed with the idea that play is the chief characteristic of childhood that—when they are confronted with the undeniable spontaneous activities of children in a Montessori classroom—still insist on calling the Montessori method a method of "teaching through play." Against such a point of view Dr. Montessori protests vigorously. "I have to defend my method," she says, "from those who say it is a method of play. Such people do not understand that work is natural to man . . . that man builds himself up through work."

On this question of work or play—or to put it another way, reality or make-belief—we come to a real divergence between Froebel and Montessori. "Play," says Froebel, "is the purest, most spiritual activity of man at this stage, and at the same time typical of human life as a whole." Dr. Montessori says: "The child's aptitude for work represents a vital instinct, and it is by work (not play—*sic*) that the child organizes his personality." To her it is work, not play which is typical of humanity—*Homo Laborans* should be man's title even more than *Homo Sapiens*.

Freedom to Work—A New Thing

No doubt many a reader will object to this, and exclaim that the consensus of mankind, from Plato down to Froebel —and beyond—is against this theory. To all these Montessori replies that it is no use arguing over the question. It is not one

[8] It is interesting in this connection to note that the children themselves often call their work with the Montessori materials play, even when they are doing quite difficult sums. It is partly therefore a matter of definition.
[9] Chapter X.

which can be decided *a priori*. It is a scientific matter which does not depend on us, but can only be decided by experiment and observation. "The person who will have the last word is the child." Dr. Montessori, as we have seen, believes that much of the child's preoccupation with play and make-believe is a "deviation," an escape from a reality not suitable to it. It largely depends upon the circumstance that the child usually has no opportunities to do *real* things, of the right kind, in a *real* world corresponding to his needs. Up to the present generation such a world has not existed for children: they have lived in a world made primarily for adults. Even in the school they were not free to choose their work. Indeed up till now we have not considered the child as being *free to work*. Freedom for the child has nearly always been connected in our minds with freedom to *play*. But given the right kind of environment, with the right kind of work in it—along with freedom to choose—the child reveals itself as one who prefers work to play, reality to make-believe.

We are well aware that this must seem a very heretical doctrine; but the only persons who are in a position to speak authoritatively upon it are those who have taken the trouble to prepare this real world suitable to the child's needs, and have observed the reactions of free children within it. And if the child prefers to use the longest number rod as 10, instead of bestriding it and galloping about on it, as on a horse, it is no good the play enthusiasts wringing their hands and crying (with Hamlet!) "For oh and for oh, the hobby-horse is forgot!" I have heard Montessori say on many occasions: "It is not I who propagate the method which has been named after me: it is the children themselves."

The Prepared Environment an Essential Difference Between Montessori and Froebel

The key then to this problem of the child's preference between work and play is the prepared environment; or, what Dr. Montessori often called the *Ambiente Rivelatore*—i.e., the *"Revealing* Environment," just because it *reveals* these unsuspected capacities. At this point, too, we lay our finger on another divergence between Montessori and Froebel. Our ordinary social environment has been made for adults, and is not suitable for the creative activities of the child. The child's energies are irrepressible; and if they find no outlet in a real world, they are diverted into make-believe activities. Give the child a real environment which corresponds to his needs and we find he occupies himself with real things, taking them for what they are (not what he imagines them to be). We must remember this prepared environment is a simplified world. The ordinary world of the adults is too big for the child, too complicated, too incomprehensible, and therefore beyond the reach of his capacity to dominate and bring within the scope of his immature intellect.

The Relation Between the Little World of the Prepared Environment and the Big World Outside

Dr. Montessori is quite content to leave the child in the limited circle of this prepared environment, this world within the world, i.e., during these early years. The child who occupies himself with the various occupations is developing his faculties. He is preparing himself for the time when he will burst through the chrysalis case of this prepared environment—this *Luogo Chiuso* (enclosed space) and enter into a larger and wider world without.[10] Dr. Montessori leaves the child, in this prepared environment, to occupy itself spontaneously with the real activites he finds there, without bothering at this stage to try and make it understand the big world outside. This point is well brought out by Professor Gerhards:[11]

The difference in the educational aims of Montessori and her opponents can be made clear when we take as a starting point the contrast between the large world of the adults and the small world in which the child's existence is carried on. . . .

From this little world the child looks out, now and then, with wondering eyes, into that other big grown-up world: but he is not yet developed enough to appreciate its reality. For a long time to come this reality must still remain unknown to him and outside his range—making no appreciable demand on his responsibility and action.

The child can only take part in this world of grown-ups in so far as he is able to represent it in imaginary play. Now Spranger and Muchow (the chief German opponents of Montessori) make it their chief aim to stimulate this imaginary representation, so that the child takes the big world into his own little one in a specifically childish and illusionary way.

Montessori, on the other hand, makes it her aim to create round the child a real and sensible world; and to do it in such a way that the child can act and work in this world independently of the adult; and in a manner proportionate

[10]See Chapter XVI.
[11]*Op. cit.*

to his needs—carrying out real activities with real responsibilities. In short the child will be able to take a part in *his* world just as really and seriously as the grown-up does in his.

Play Has its Place of Course

It would however be quite a mistake to conclude that Montessori would like us to *suppress* make-believe activities in the child. Rather, we must make sure that they are not due to (1) a lack of suitable opportunities given to the child to expend its energies in *real* activities, or (2) that they arise from the suggestion of adults.

Dr. Helen Helming, one of Montessori's ablest supporters in Germany, and principal of a training college for Montessori teachers, very rightly says:

> The danger comes when play, which should arise spontaneously from the child as occasion demands, is deliberately and consciously introduced into that little world which we have prepared for the child, *at the suggestion of the adult.* . . .
>
> Perhaps, just because in the Montessori kindergarten the adult has placed at the child's disposal a material able to give it clear and systematic help in its development, in those times when the child is *not* using the material, play may once more find its real place and opportunity in the kindergarten—the natural spontaneous play of the child, which under the hand of the adult so easily becomes forced and superficial.

We would agree, then, with Sir Percy Nunn's criticism that "the Froebelian practice errs when it introduces make-belief gratuitously, i.e., when the child's spontaneity does not need this aid," [12] On the other hand the present writer, for his part, would protest against being included amongst "those Montessorians who would refuse its aid, even when it would serve to widen the child's range of serious interests and achievements." This is in fact quite in accordance with Montessori's practice. Thus for instance, when they are working through the Montessori reading slips, the children have to act out little "stories"—such as "The doctor looked at his watch while he felt the patient's pulse." (CF. p. 193.) And again—for example—in Dr. Montessori's school at Barcelona the children acted some scenes from Dante's *Divine Comedy,* produced under her own personal direction. At other times a group of

[12] *Data and Ethics of Education.*

children will join together spontaneously to act together a scene from history or literature which they have been reading.

Objective or Subjective Approach?
"To Make Anything out of Anything"

What we have said so far in this chapter may be summed up by saying that Montessori and Froebel differ in their attitude or approach to reality. Montessori's approach is more objective while Froebel's is more subjective. In the Montessori system the child takes things (selected things) for what they are, instead of turning them by imagination into something else. The Montessori child is subject to the discipline of reality, to the persuasion of truth as revealed in sensible objects, and in their relations one to another. On the other hand the most ardent supporters of Froebel, such as the German Professor Hessen, maintain that it is the teacher's business to exploit the child's immaturity; and deliberately to encourage his tendency *aus allem alles zu machen* ("to make anything out of anything"). This is why such Froebelians as he protest against the Montessori principle that the child must use each piece of material for the purpose for which it was intended, and not otherwise. He would allow the child, for instance, to use the bells as silver toadstools for fairy dolls to sit on; the five-cube-chain to be used as a necklace; and encourage the child to hang out the contents of the box of fabrics along the 1000-bead-chain in an imaginary washing day. Montessori would say: If the child wants to wash something—let him do so by all means. Let him wash out the dusters and hang them on a real line in the garden.[13] If the child wants to build a house or a bridge [14] let him use some materials specially kept and made for this purpose. If he wants to make a necklace let him use the proper beads kept for that purpose; *but not those which are dedicated to some special problem in number*.

The insistence on the right use of the material is not—as we have pointed out elsewhere—an infringement of the child's liberty: it is the very means to it. The world of reality is more full of wonder and interest than anything the immature mind of the child can create for itself. (This indeed should be true for all of us, but it is especially so for the child who has not lost the sense of wonder.)

It is the sense of wonder which is the driving force which impels the child to progress along the prepared paths to culture described in Chapter XVI. The point emphasized here is

[13]See illustration 3.
[14]See *Spanning Space*, by C. A. Claremont.

that these wonder-stimulating lines of research are paths in *reality* and not make-believe. It is quite certain that the child would not make the same progress along them were he allowed to misuse the apparatus by "turning anything into anything" according to the momentary whims of his fancy.

The Difference in Weltanschauung

In conclusion there is one more point of divergence between Montessori and Froebel which ought to be mentioned. It is so fundamental that it is perhaps the cause of all the rest. We refer to the profound difference in what the Germans call the *Weltanschauung* "world view" held by Montessori and Froebel. Froebel's religious philosophy was very largely pantheistic and Nordic; whereas Montessori's is Catholic and Latin. It is not difficult to see how their differing philosophies affect—albeit unconsciously—their two systems. It is interesting to note, also, that Spranger, Hessen and Muchow, the German defenders of Froebel against the Montessori system, support their statements by appealing to a pantheistic philosophy. Thus Spranger sees in the play of the child a sign that—"he finds himself in many-sided and living unity with the divine current and rhythm of the world"—his life "being filled with divine fullness and unity." And Muchow says "that the child through his imagination is capable of living essentially and primarily as part of the whole—able to see life in everything, a faculty grown-ups have unhappily lost" (except primitive savages at the animistic stage!). Hessen, as we have seen, speaks of the child's power of "making everything out of everything." Again Spranger speaks of the "meaning of Life at all stages which is to allow the inner movements of our small and limited souls to beat in time with the vast and mighty Rhythm of the Law of Life—*as Froebel taught.*"

We do not pretend to follow exactly what all this signifies; but one thing is clear—it is pure pantheism. It is the breaking down of all distinctions and forms, the flowing together of everything in the universe—soul, body, matter, spirit, you and I, God and man—in one great whole. As opposed to this view historical Christianity presents a universe with definite and abiding forms, eternally distinct, and distinct from its Creator. The dogmatic teaching of traditional Christianity, with its doctrine of the Incarnation, of the visible Church with its Sacramental system, of Heaven and Hell, of Spirit and Matter, and many others—all combine to form an objective body of truth, external to the individual, hard as adamant, to be taken for what it is or not at all. The Gospel is essentially the "good news," and news is something which comes from the *outside,* to be accepted and believed—or rejected.

Making the Outer Inner

Readers of Froebel are aware how often he speaks of the importance in education of "making the inner the outer." This is well enough in so far as it refers to the importance of creative self-expression; but it does not sufficiently realize the importance of also *making the outer the inner,* especially in early childhood. After all, it is the Macrocosm which has to be reflected in the Microcosm—and not *vice versa.*

The German writer Dr. Helming, already referred to, quite independently from the present writer, emphasized this same point, in the following passage:

> The Montessori occupations have been prepared as the result of long observation of the child, and correspond to his needs. The child works with them as long as he wishes to do so. The Montessori material does not enter the child's life as a hard and forbidding task to be accomplished; but rather as a door through which he enters a fuller life.
>
> It is just the definite limits of the material which form a further help to the child. More than is the case with other playthings they are proof against the arbitrary whims of the child, and so lead him towards reality. Out of an ordinary piece of wood the child can make anything he likes, and even a doll is subject to the child's arbitrary decision. But the Montessori material stands solidly there, an invitation to something definite, not to be changed by the child's arbitrary whim, something which teaches obedience with freedom.
>
> That world, which is not the child's self, reports itself there and draws the child towards it. Here we see the difference between the Catholicity of Montessori and the philosophy of Froebel, which leaves the child shut up in itself *(in geschlossener Einheit).*
>
> The soul of the child is awakened by the material. By its resistance to the child's own still very limited and short existence it stirs within it the presentiment that it stands at the threshold of two worlds—within and without—and thereby wins readier access to that freedom which is his human birthright. [15]

[15] From *Die Kristliche Frau.*

The Transition to the Second Period of Childhood

In this book our main concern has been with Montessori principles, and in particular with their application to infant or primary education. But since the question is often asked: "After the Montessori school—what then?" it will not be out of place to devote a chapter to Montessori's ideas on junior education, especially as it will enable us to carry our comparison between Montessori and Froebel a stage further.

In Chapter VI it was pointed out that—according to Montessori—the first stage of childhood is characterized by the possession of a type of mind which she calls the "Absorbent Mind." This type of mentality is different from that of the adult in that it "absorbs" an immense amount of knowledge from the environment, spontaneously and without conscious effort, "simply by living in it." It is interesting to note that Froebel makes a somewhat similar observation when he says, "The period of childhood is predominantly that of life for the mere sake of living."

We saw, too, in Chapter XVI how Montessori would have us respond to this remarkable trait by placing the child in a specially prepared environment, into which we have put the things we wish his mind to absorb. Montessori's long and varied experience all over the world made her believe without a shadow of doubt that, when children are so treated, and allowed freedom of choice to follow the guidance of their sensitive periods, they make astonishing progress. "Within the child there is a very scrupulous and exacting teacher, who even adheres to a timetable; and at three years has produced a being whose acquisitions are already such that—as psychologists assure us—it would take an adult sixty years of hard work to achieve as much." Again it is interesting to note in this connection that Froebel quotes, with approval, a contemporary German writer who said that "there is a greater advance from the infant to the speaking child than there is from the schoolboy to a Newton."

As we noted in Chapter XVI, the child in the first period of childhood is "beatifically happy," living and working in his prepared environment with his materials for development, and his little group of thirty to forty companions. His happiness is primarily the joy of self-creation: for this, *par excellence,* is the epoch in which he is constructing his individuality. As Montessori puts it, "He is more interested in growing than in knowing," that is, in the self-conscious acquisition of culture (cf. Chapter VIII).

With the approach of the second period of childhood—as was pointed out in Chapter XVI—the child feels no longer completely satisfied with his life in the *Luogo Chiuso*—the enclosed space of the prepared environment. This has now become too limited to furnish him with all he needs for what Montessori calls "the valorization of his personality"—i.e., for full and harmonious development in every direction—physically, mentally, socially, and spiritually. New sensitive periods are coming to birth, and with them new needs that must be satisfied in new ways. As soon as we observe that the child's *joie de vivre* is beginning to fade, and his spontaneous concentration to diminish, then we know that a fresh phase of development is dawning.

The Young Explorer Again—But on a Higher Level

The age at which these changes begin to show themselves varies naturally with individuals; but generally speaking, by the time the child has reached his (or her) ninth or tenth year, these new tendencies will have begun to reveal themselves. We now find him looking with an awakened interest and longing eyes on that wider world beyond his Montessori classroom. Then begins the time characterized—as Froebel says—by "the daring and venturesome feats of boyhood; the exploration of caves and ravines; the climbing of trees and mountains; the searching of the heights and depths; the roaming through fields and forests." Happy those children who live in the country and have the opportunity to explore in this way.

This is the period, says Montessori, when a good many boys start playing truant from school—going off, it may be, on birds' nesting expeditions, or hunting for "tiddlers"; or "messing about" with running water—damming streams and making canals. At this age too we find them forming themselves into gangs and secret societies, which—for lack of proper direction—may even come into conflict with civic authorities. Such escapades are frequently put down to a moral badness, which the adult feels it is his duty to punish severely—thus widening the gulf of misunderstanding and sharpening the struggle between them. "Escapade" is really the right word to use; for there is a genuine element of "escape" in these exploits—escape from a manner of life which in some ways has become intolerably dull and restricted. They are, one might say, unconscious protests against a certain void in their environment. In general it is true that at every stage whenever some factor is missing from the child's environment which is necessary for his full development, there will result some such "deviations from the normal." The real root of the matter is that these young people have arrived at the psychological moment when they feel a strong instinctive need to widen their contacts with the world outside.

Education as a Preparation for Going Out

Here, as always in the child's development, we must make use of his natural urges. But in this case how are we to do it? We cannot simply throw wide open the door of the school and let the children go out into the world. "That," says Montessori, "would be more like flight; and they would run the risk of getting lost—like Hansel and Gretel." The world outside is still in many ways too complicated and too dangerous. The prepared environment in which they have been *freely* living up to now is, by the very fact of its preparation, simplified and safe; its very scope is the protection of growth, like the embryonic placenta. "What we have to realize now," says Montessori, "is the important and practical fact that *this going out into the world requires a preparation.* This is our cue, our signpost, or at least one of them." She tells us that "Séguin erected a whole system of education on this conception of a preparation for going out into the world."

The idea of relating the activities of the junior school to the wider life of the community is one of the main educational arguments of our time. To take an example, at random, we might mention a little book entitled *Actuality in the School* which came into our hands recently. In it the author describes how, in a certain school, various representative persons—such as the postman, the milkman, the dustman—were invited to come to the school to talk with the children about their respective jobs, and to answer questions. This of course is excellent in its way; but it is more like bringing the world into the school than sending the children out into the world. A still more important criticism would be that it does not consciously set out to harness the child's eagerness to explore the world to the perfecting of capacities and talents in himself; which would enable him to move about in that world with greater confidence and independence. In the same way class excursions (*en masse*) directed by the teacher to museums and other places of interest—though good in themselves—do not from our point of view achieve the end we are seeking.

The Boy Scout Movement

The educational movement which comes nearest to fulfilling Montessori's idea of "Education as a Preparation for Going Out" is the Boy Scout Organization. One has only to look at the *Boy Scout Manual* and note the various tests which the scout is invited to pass, to see how all these, in effect, come under the heading of helping the boy to act efficiently and independently in the world outside the school. How to tell the points of the compass by the sun and the stars; how to find your way across country with only these or a compass to guide you; how to follow the rules of traffic; how to render first aid; how to defend yourself and others; how to look after one's clothes, mend them and keep them tidy; how to make a fire and cook a meal; how to pitch a tent and run a camp; how to read a map; how to construct a bridge over a stream; how to signal a message by semaphore—what are all these and many more besides but "preparations for going out"?

The chief limitation that besets the scout movement, as Montessori points out, is that—as a general rule—its activities are generally not linked up with those of the school. As a consequence the enthusiastic scout or girl guide tends to live a sort of double life—as a member of the school on the one hand, and as a member of the scout organization on the other. This is to be regretted because the child is himself a unity, and his life should be a unity too as much as possible. It would be better if the sort of studies which the scout or guide undertakes, in order to pass their tests, were in some way a part of the school curriculum. I have in fact known some teachers, who were also scout masters, do this with great success; and recently heard of some schools where the incorporation of scout activities as an organic part of the school life is their avowed policy.

Froebel, I am sure, would have been in sympathy with any such method of vitalizing the school curriculum. Already at the outset of his teaching career he was doing something similar—*though it was nearly 150 years ago*—as the following description by a contemporary shows.

That his (Froebel's) pupils had carefully studied the plants, animals, hills, rivers, mountain streams, rocks and other features of the country round Frankfort was evident; and that the facts thus discovered by themselves were utilized for their benefit in the schoolroom was equally evident. Froebel placed the blackboard on the floor, and with the help of the boys traced upon it the course of the River Main. The position of Frankfort being determined, he traced round it a line limiting the area to be taken in the lesson. From this starting point the boys proceeded to fill in the features of the locality which had come under their direct observation—roads, hills, streams, buildings, etc. When the picture was complete it was set up, and the boys were allowed to copy what they themselves had put together. (*The Kindergarten System*, Hanschmann, English Translation, pp. 31-32.)

Moral Training Through the "Organized Group"

It would be a mistake if we were to think of this notion of "Education as a Preparation for Going Out" as something which merely aimed at preparing boys and girls to orient themselves in the *physical* world beyond the school walls. Montessori is even more concerned that they should know how to move with certitude and independence in the *moral* world outside. In that, too, there exist many problems and dangers which had been eliminated from the specially prepared environment of the earlier stage.

Successfully to achieve this moral preparation we must also make use of two other characteristic traits which reveal themselves about this time. The first is an increased sensibility towards, and interest in, the rightness and wrongness of actions. Montessori describes this as "the child's exploration in the moral field—the discrimination between good and evil." She explains it psychologically thus—"The child is no longer receptive, passively absorbing impressions with ease, but wants to understand for himself; and is no longer content with merely accepting facts. As moral activity develops he wants to use his own judgment . . . An inner change has taken place: nature now arouses in him not only a hunger for knowledge and understanding, but also a claim to mental independence, a desire to distinguish good and evil *by his own powers*. In the field of morality the child now stands in need of his own inner light." (*To Educate the Human Potential*, pp. 6–7.)

The second trait which appears about this time, and of which we must also make use, is what is usually called the herd instinct. But it is more than a mere instinct. Montessori describes it as "the child's need to associate himself with others, not merely for the sake of company, but in some sort of *organized activity.* He likes to mix with others in a group wherein each has a different status. A leader is chosen, and is obeyed, and a strong group is formed. This is a natural tendency, through which mankind becomes organized."

What is required, then, at this stage is a special form of organization of youth which will, at one and the same time, give satisfaction to this heightened social instinct and to the quickened interest in discriminating between right and wrong; together with that longing for wider horizons spoken of above. This organization of youth should take the form then of a *"moral union of boys (or girls) who have consented to form part of a society which has a moral aim, and which requires its members to live up to a certain moral level."*

It should be noted carefully that this is not a question of numbers—of belonging to a crowd. The mere coming into contact with a greater number of individuals outside the social environment of the school—or even in it—will not attain the end which we are seeking. The important factor is that of the boy or girl being bound up together with other persons, inside and outside the school, *who have consented to follow the same moral aim.* The limits of the group are not formed by the walls of any institution but by the moral obligations undertaken. As Montessori puts it:

> Our point of departure at this stage is to present to the children new actions which, on account of the effort required to carry them out, would often be considered beyond their capacity. In general children should be called to a harder and more effortful life which corresponds to that strength and stability which is characteristic of this period.

That Froebel also realized the effectiveness of the group as a practical means of inculcating moral virtues is clear from such passages as the following. Discussing the effect of such games as running, boxing, wrestling, ball games, racing, games of hunting and war and so forth, he writes:

> It is by no means only the physical power that is fed and strengthened by these games: intellectual and moral power too is definitely and steadily acquired. Indeed a comparison between the relative gains of the mental and physical would scarce yield the palm to the body. Justice, moderation, self-control, truthfulness, loyalty, brotherly love and again strict impartiality—who, when he approaches a group of boys engaged in such games, could fail to catch the fragrance of these delicious blossomings of the heart and

mind and of a firm will? Other such "blossoms," springing from the same sources, are courage, perseverance, resolution, prudence; together with forbearance, sympathy and encouragement for the weaker.

While Montessori also recognizes the moral value of games she reminds us that after all they *are* games; and as such are not grounded on the most fundamental realities of life. Here again, in her opinion, it is the scout organization that is moving in the right direction. She asserts that its universal appeal to boys and girls in all lands arises from the fact that it responds—amongst others—to these special moral needs. For what is the scout movement if it is not a voluntary association of boys with a moral purpose, summoning them to a higher and more strenuous life both physically and morally? This is obvious to anyone who knows the scout law of which the following are some of the rules:

A scout's honour is to be trusted; a scout is loyal to King, country, his officers, parents etc.; a scout's duty is to be useful and help others. Other laws bind him to be courteous, kind to animals, cheerful under difficulties, thrifty and "clean in thought, word and deed." Note, too, that the scout organization is quite voluntary; it is a matter of free choice: the scout promise being "On my honour I *promise . . .*"

But here again the scout organization is subject to the same form of criticism as that mentioned above—that it tends to be carried on in a sphere separate from that of the school, which is often run on different and even contrary principles. There is no adaptation of the general organization of the school life and its curriculum to take into account the new sensibilities which are stirring in the child's soul. Lord Baden-Powell himself was aware of this. In his preface to *Scouting for Boys,* after remarking that scouting has justly been called a revolution in education, he goes on as follows:

> The fact is true that scouting aims for a different point of view than is possible in the average school training. It aims to teach boys how to live, not merely how to make a living. There lies a certain danger in inculcating in the individual the ambition to win prizes and scholarships, and holding up to him as success the securing of pay, position and power, unless there is a corresponding instruction in service for others.

The manner in which Montessori's idea of a "moral union" of boys and girls—pledging themselves to membership in a group with a definite moral aim—would be organized would of course vary according to country, religion, and civilization. The important thing to realize is that this is the age at which it should be formed, and that in doing so we answer an urgent need of development.

The Age of Reason

The most characteristic of all the mental traits which make their appearance with the transition from childhood to boyhood (or to what Montessori calls the second stage of childhood) is the marked development of the reasoning power. As the first period was one of more or less unconscious absorption from the environment, this succeeding one seems to have been ordained by nature for the acquisition of culture. Montessori describes this stage as follows:

We are confronted with a considerable development of consciousness that has already taken place, but *now* that consciousness is thrown outwards, intelligence being extraverted; and there is an unusual demand on the part of the child to know the reasons of things . . . All other factors sink into insignificance beside the importance of feeding the hungry intelligence and of opening up vast fields of knowledge to eager exploration.

Froebel is in entire agreement with Montessori on this point— though as so often happens with him—his manner of expressing himself is less clear and scientific. He says, "As the preceding period of human development was predominately that of life for the sake of living . . . so the period of boyhood is predominately the period for learning . . ." (*Education of Man,* p. 95.)

Reason the "Motor"—the Dominant Factor

In the old type of infant school there was what we might call a starvation of the small child's imperative need for bodily activity. With the introduction of such occupations as the exercises of practical life, and the sensorial and other materials to be manipulated—along with freedom of choice—there has been brought about a restoration of the child's mental balance, with the result that his psyche can now function in its entirety. A similar restoration of mental balance must now be brought about in the junior school. In the past, educational methods applied at this age did not usually take sufficiently into account this great increase in the power of reasoning. As a consequence there was an undue emphasis upon memory. The balance must be restored by giving a much greater prominence to the reason, which now becomes the driving power in the child's mental progress, the focus of all his activities. "We trust too little," said Froebel, "to the energetic and uniting power (i.e., the reason) in the boy."

How do we know, enquires Montessori, that we are right in placing such an emphasis on the reason? And she replies, "By observation." "When the child's mind—which has arrived at this degree of maturity—sees a group of facts related together in the light of reason, it experiences a sense of satisfaction, an inner harmony, a state of repose." (This reminds one of Emerson's words: "Generalization is an influx of divinity into the mind—*hence the thrill that attends*.")

Montessori warns us that we must not be misled by the above phrase—"a state of repose"—into thinking that we have here to do with a *passive* state of mind. It is much more comparable to the repose of a spinning top; for this sense of satisfaction is the deep joy which attends the right use of a faculty.

Since reason always tries to find the underlying causes of things, Froebel speaks of this new stage of development in the following terms: "It is the leaving of the outer superficial view of things on the part of a child, and his entrance upon an inner view leading to knowledge, insight and consciousness—this transition from the domestic order to the higher cosmic order of things—that makes the boy a scholar, and constitutes the essence of the school." Or again, "The school endeavours to render the scholar fully conscious of the nature of the inner life of things, and of himself—to teach him, that is, the inner relations of things one to another." These "inner relations" of which Froebel speaks so constantly, what are they but the deeper vision of phenomena *as seen in the luminous bonds of reason*?

The intellect by its very nature is always seeing the relations between things—whether those things are objects of sense, or ideas in judgments. In the earlier stage of development—that of sensorial-motor activities—the child's intelligence is largely concerned with the external and superficial relations between *material* objects and their qualities—relations of space, size, form, position, colour, weight, and so forth (see Chapter IX). Incidentally, that is the reason why the Montessori sensorial materials are presented to the children in groups or sets which form a whole,[1] such as the *ten* diminishing cubes which form the Pink Tower, or the *ten* red rods in the Long Stair. The children, as they work with the materials day after day, become ever more clearly cognizant of these relationships revealed to them through *sensorial* gradations and contrasts.

But when we come to this higher stage we have to change our tactics. It is true that, here also, we have to present the child with a "Whole"—what Montessori calls an *insieme di conoscenza* ("a number of things known together"); but *now* this whole is not something which has to be apprehended primarily through the senses; it is a *logical whole,* and its several parts are seen to be related by the "*bonds of reason*"— or by Froebel's "inner connections."

Centre of Interest and Radial Lines of Research

Still applying ourselves to the practical importance in method of this newly awakened faculty, the reason, we must now go a step further. The reason is an appetite which grows by what it feeds on. It is insatiable in its desire for unity and system. In fact—ultimately—nothing but the *universe* can satisfy it. That state of intellectual satisfaction and joy, noted above, which comes to an intelligence which beholds a series of phenomena united in a logical whole *does not end in itself.* It becomes at the same time "a plane for further conquest." Or to put it in another way: any such discovery of a logical unity, combining a multiplicity of separate details (as for instance the law of gravity, or the law that "the carrying power of running water varies with its speed") tends to act as a stimulus to further research.[2] The Reason resembles those pilgrims in Elroy Flecker's *Hassan*—"We are those that seek to go always a little further." Or, as Froebel puts it, "The spiritual eye [by which he means the intellect] in thoughtful search seeks and finds the common bond among the nearest particulars; and *proceeds from every new-found unity to a higher.*" (p. 165.)

These considerations, rightly appreciated, indicate the lines along which we should proceed in our task of presenting the vast field of culture to the junior school child. In every subject which lends itself to such a treatment, we must present—not isolated facts—but groups of facts related together in a logical

---

[1] Several psychologists have pointed out that—contrary to what is often maintained—Montessori's psychology has in this respect a marked affinity with the Gestalt Theory.

[2] "Every ultimate fact," says Emerson, "is only the first of a new series. Every general law is only a particular fact of some more general law presently to disclose itself."

whole or unity. These in their turn will form "centres of interest," from which will lead out "rays of interest"—radial lines of research, along which the reasoning mind will travel further, spontaneously, discovering as it does so fresh details and new problems.

The Project Method

It will be seen that Montessori's suggestion of "incandescent centres of interest with radial lines of research"— which she put forward more than twenty-five years ago—bears a certain resemblance to the "Project Method" of which we hear so much nowadays. Yet it is not really the same thing, though they have elements in common. The project method, as it is usually applied, would be regarded by Montessori as too casual and sporadic, too dependent on the whim of the teacher, or other local circumstances. Its chief danger is that an undue proportion of time and energy may be squandered on a few comparatively unimportant subjects, whilst other much more necessary matters are neglected or even omitted.

A Cosmic Curriculum

Granted then that the method must be the one we have just outlined—(i.e., in which "reason is the motor"), and assuming that the project system as usually understood is too indefinite, the problem still remains—*What* and *How* are we to teach these junior school children? Montessori's answer, though expressed in different terms and arrived at independently, is remarkably similar to what Froebel said over a century ago. As we have already seen, Froebel tells us that the boy who has left the kindergarten for the school proper has passed "from the domestic order of things to *the higher cosmic order.*" "The essential business of the school," he goes on, "is not so much to teach and communicate a variety and multiplicity of things as to give prominence to that *ever-living unity that is in all things.*" (*Education of Man,* pp. 134–5.)

In one of her latest books published in India, with the rather strange title *To Educate the Human Potential,* Montessori in discussing this problem says:

Let us give the child a vision of the whole Universe. . . . The Universe is an imposing reality, and an answer to all questions. We shall walk together on this path of life; for all things are a part of the Universe, and are connected with each other to form one whole unity. This idea helps the mind of the child to become fixed, to stop wandering in an aimless quest for knowledge. He is satisfied, having found the universal centre of himself with all things. (P. 10.)

At this point I can well imagine an exasperated reader—especially if he or she is a teacher—saying, "Of course that *sounds* very nice—very lofty and inspiring and all that—but it does not give me, as a teacher, anything very practical to work on. Exactly how am I supposed to bring the 'whole universe' into my classroom at 9.30 a.m. next Monday morning! Have either of these philosophical idealists any *practical* suggestions to offer?" Montessori certainly has—plenty—and doubtless Froebel would have had, too, were he living at the present day, and had had the advantage of acquainting himself with the immense progress in the sciences since his day. Those who wish to acquaint themselves with the details of Montessori's scheme for "Cosmic Education" are recommended to consult her books, especially the one just referred to: or better still—if feasible—attend a lecture course on her "Advanced Method." All we can do here is to touch on some general principles.

Sowing the Seeds of Culture

In the first place, it must be made clear that Montessori has no notion of presenting children at this age with a closely reasoned and systematic scheme of universal knowledge. She has no intention either, of turning the teacher into a walking encyclopedia.

To appreciate the practicability of Montessori's approach to this problem, we have to remember that she is speaking in the light of thirty years' experience with regard to the scholastic attainments of Montessori children, i.e., children who have already lived and worked freely in a prepared environment. She found that these children—if they begin their education at an early age (certainly not later than four)—by the time they have arrived at the age we are discussing, are different from other children. They are what she calls "awakened souls." Already they have not only learned to read, and write, and express themselves in writing, and know the "four operations" in arithmetic, but have also made genuine progress in history, geography, biology, literature, and the beginnings of geometry and algebra. They are in fact "individuals who have already acquired the basis of culture, and are anxious to build on it—to learn to penetrate deeper into any matter of interest." She goes on to compare the child who has arrived at this stage to a "fertile field ready to receive what will germinate into culture." It is an easy task therefore to introduce them to further knowledge.

There is no question, however, at this stage, of expecting children to master whole branches of knowledge organized in watertight compartments—as "subjects." Rather the teacher must think of this epoch as one in which the seeds of everything can be sown. At this age all items of culture are received with enthusiasm in the form of seeds which will later germinate into real culture. If you were to ask her how many such seeds should be sown in this epoch, Montessori would answer, "As many as possible."

Individual Activity (Selbst-Tätigkeit) Still Essential

To give the *whole* of modern culture has, in any case, become an impossibility; so what we need is a special method whereby "all factors of culture can be introduced, not as a syllabus imposed on him with exactitude of detail, but by the broadcasting of a maximum number of seeds of interest." "These will be held lightly in the mind but will be capable of later germination as the will becomes more directive" (that is, as the lines of research become more and more freely chosen individual affairs).

It is clear already that Montessori's idea is not the same as that of a whole class being led (or dragged) along, *en masse* and willy-nilly, in the wake of an arbitrarily chosen "project." This becomes clearer still when we are reminded that:

(1) The child must learn by his own activity.
(2) He must be granted a mental freedom to take what he needs; and—
(3) He must not be questioned in his choice—since the "teacher should answer the mental needs of the child, not dictate them."

Development Always Our First Aim

Even at this age, which is *par excellence* the time for storing up information, the question of *what* he is learning—important though it is—is secondary to that of mental development. "Just as the small child cannot sit still because he is in need of coordinating his movements, so the older child, who seems troublesomely curious over the what, why, and wherefore of everything he sees, *is building himself up by this*

his mental activity; and for this reason must be given a wide field of culture on which to feed."

Even *were* our primary aim the acquisition of culture, we should still be obliged to put development first. For what is the difference between a man of culture and a man who is simply a mine of unrelated information—like a dictionary? The fundamental difference lies in the way in which that knowledge has been built up. In the case of the former it has been through a vital mental process, coming from within from the "centre" (see Chapter XIV), set going, and kept going by a living interest. That is why the man of culture possesses a vitality organized, ever-expanding system of knowledge—all parts of which are united. They are united because they are presided over by an intelligence which informs and vitalizes each part, as well as the whole—just as the soul informs, vitalizes and unifies the body. On the other hand the content of the mind of the uncultured man is simply a compendium of unrelated facts—like a sack full of potatoes; and is so because his knowledge has been acquired mechanically (just as you might drop potatoes into a sack) and not by a process of integrating growth.

Freedom of Choice Must Still Be Based on Knowledge

It is just because it is so important that the process of acquiring knowledge should be a vital one that Montessori reminds us once again, as before (Chapter XVII) that the freedom of choice insisted on, just above, must be real freedom. This means, too, that whatever the child chooses to work at, at this stage, must be related to what he already knows—to knowledge already assimilated. Only thus can we be sure that the new will be vitally assimilated to the old.

Some of the new educationists—says Montessori—in a reaction against the old system of forcing children to learn by rote a tangled skein of uninteresting facts, go to the opposite extreme, and advocate giving the child "freedom to learn what he likes but *without any previous preparation of interest. . . .* This is a plan for building without a basis, akin to the political methods that today offer freedom of speech and a vote, without education—granting the right to express thought where there are no thoughts to express, and no power of thinking! What is required for the child, as for society, is help towards the building up of mental faculties, interest being of necessity the first to be enlisted, so that there may be natural growth in freedom."

Here, as always, the child's liberty consists in being free to choose from a basis of real knowledge, and not out of mere curiosity. He is free to take up which of the "radial lines of research" appeals to him, but not to choose "anything he likes" *in vacuo*. It must be based on a real centre of *interest*, and therefore motivated by what Montessori calls "intellectual love."

The teacher's task in all this, Montessori admits, is no small and easy one. "He has to prepare a large amount of knowledge to satisfy the children's mental hunger; for he is not like the old teacher limited by a syllabus prescribing just so much of every subject to be imparted within a set time, and on no account to be exceeded. The needs of the children are clearly more difficult to answer in this system; and the teacher can no longer defend himself behind syllabus and timetable. He will need to acquire a reasonable acquaintance with every subject." If on reading this any teacher's heart should sink, Montessori quickly adds, "but let him take courage, for he will not be without help, and without a scientifically tested plan."

As already said above, it does not come within the scope of this book even to outline this "scientifically tested plan of cosmic education," which Montessori first explained—as the foundation stone of her Advanced Method—at a course given in London in 1935. "Since then," she says, "it has already proved itself to be the only path on which our feet can firmly tread in further educational research."

Montessori does not claim that her plan is complete. On the contrary she asserts that the problem is such a vast one that it can only be solved completely as the result of large-scale experiments carried out over long periods, involving the collaboration of many workers. Nevertheless a start has been made; and already there is a solid basis of experience to work on. There still remain however many collateral fields of research awaiting and inviting the enthusiastic collaborator.

The Right Use of the Imagination

Of more importance than the details of this plan is the comprehension of the general aim and spirit in which the work has to be carried out. For that reason we ought not to close this chapter without mentioning one other principle which Montessori considers of supreme importance at this stage—viz., the right use of the imagination. Amongst the criticisms which are often levelled at Montessori's ideas nothing is more common than the accusation that she neglects and even starves the imagination, thus frustrating its normal development (see Chapter XX). It may perhaps surprise such critics to learn that—in presenting this scheme of cosmic education to the junior school children—she goes so far as to say:

> We do nothing if we do not set on fire this wonderful faculty. Human consciousness comes into the world as a flaming ball of imagination. Everything invented by man, physical and mental, is the fruit of someone's imagination. In the study of history and geography we are helpless without it; and when we propose to introduce the Universe to the child what but imagination can be of use to us? I consider it a crime to present such subjects, as are noble and creative aids to the imaginative faculty, in such a manner as to deny its use.
>
> The secret of good teaching is to regard the child's intelligence as a fertile field in which seeds may be sown, to grow under the heat of flaming imagination. Our aim therefore is, not merely to make the child understand, and still less to force him to memorize, but so touch his imagination as to inflame his enthusiasm to the inmost core. It is along the path of the higher realities, which can be grasped by the imagination, that the child at this age (8–12) is to be led.

Here too, as in the earlier stage, she warns us against the dangers of cultivating the imagination in separation from the intelligence. Many modern educationists are, she says, "vivisectionists of the personality." Just as there are still many who would separate the activities of brain and hand, so there are others who teach the "dry facts" of reality on the one hand; and on the other, cultivate the imagination separately, by fairy tales in an imaginary world which is full of marvels, but is not the world in which we live. "By offering the child the story of the universe, we give him something a thousand times more wonderful and mysterious to grasp with his imagination, in a cosmic drama no fable can rival."

L'Envoi: *Life Is Wider Than Logic*

In her later years Dr. Montessori used to sum up the aim of education, as she saw it, as "An Aid to Life." In this volume it has not been possible to give a full and complete account of the ways she would have us accomplish this. Our emphasis has been laid upon how we can best assist the individual's development in his earlier years (0–12 years). And within this limitation we have set ourselves a still further one,

in so far as we have concentrated more on the child's intellectual development than any other aspect.

We have done this—since choice was inevitable—because
after all the intellect is the highest faculty we possess; and
is in a sense the basis of all. There is no need to repeat here our
eulogistic comments on the sovereignty of human reason, and
the vital part it plays in our lives, as given on page 204.
We propose, in fact, to close on rather a different note.

A few paragraphs above we referred to Montessori's warning against the danger of cultivating the imagination in separation from the intelligence. Similarly, since life is wider than
logic, there is an analogous danger in cultivating the reason in
separation from a still higher faculty. "How can you say that?"
the reader might exclaim, "since you have just stated that reason is our highest endowment?" The answer to that is that
reason is our highest *natural* endowment. But there is a realm
of reality which yields up its secrets neither to deductive nor
inductive reasoning—neither to the syllogism nor to scientific
research—but rather to what one might describe as the total
functioning of the whole personality—including the obedient
will. This is the realm of revealed truth; of which it was said
by Him who knew it best that "he that doeth the Will shall
know of the doctrine. . . ."

Montessori was well aware that Faith is a *super*-natural
endowment, and does not belong to us by nature as do the
gifts of the senses, instinct, emotion, reason, and will. She
was aware too (like our first parents) of the meaning behind
those lines in Byron's *Manfred:*

> they who know the most
> Must mourn the deepest o'er the fatal truth—
> The Tree of Knowledge is not that of Life

And therefore—to complete the picture of Montessori's idea
of "Education as an Aid to Life"—we ought to have three
more volumes. The first would deal with what Montessori used
to call "Valorization of Personality." This would include such
matters as—the progressive adjustment of the child to his
ever-expanding social environment; the acquisition of culture
through spontaneous mental expansion; self-expression through
the arts; the reform of secondary education; and much else
besides.[3] The second would be devoted to the manner in which
Montessori would have us apply her vitalizing principles to the
teaching and practice of religion.[4] And finally there should be

---

[3]Such a book already exists in manuscript form.
[4]See footnote p. 69. Cf. pp. 80–82.

a third volume dealing with what is perhaps the most urgent of all subjects—what Montessori herself described as "Education as the Armament of Peace."

The Two Dependencies

It is impossible to explain in a few paragraphs what, in Montessori's philosophy, lies behind this last phrase—*Education as the Armament of Peace*. On pages 77–82 and 154 we have given a few inadequate hints; and at this stage we can only add a few more by way of conclusion.

In a lecture on *The Child and Civilization* Montessori once made the interesting and original comment that, whereas the Old Testament begins with an adult (Adam) the New Testament begins with a child; or, to be more precise, with a child and his mother. Between two luminous figures—the Madonna and her Child—there exists a wonderful and beautiful relationship, which has been a perennial source of inspiration to Christian art. It is the relationship of a mysterious and mutual interdependence. The tiny Infant, who lies helpless in His Mother's arms, at the same time supports the great globe and all that it inherits, including His Mother. The Child as He grows up learns from His Mother; but the Mother no less learns from the Child, who is Divine Wisdom incarnate. The Child reverences and obeys the Mother, who in her turn bows down and worships the fruit of her womb. Nay more, we can go further and say that though this Mother created her Child, as every mother does, this Child also created His Mother —"for without Him was not anything made that was made."

Now all these things are a symbol—indeed more than a symbol—of a great truth that Montessori was always trying to bring home to us. She was tireless in urging us to recognize what she used to call "The Two Dependencies" and their immense importance. How often, and in how many different ways did she impress upon us that childhood is not merely a stage which has to be passed through in order to become an adult. No! childhood is an entity in itself; it is in fact "The Other Pole of Humanity." For in a very real sense (Chapter VIII) the child creates the adult, as truly as the adult creates the child. His "work" is, in fact, nothing less than the tremendous task of creating the man-that-is-to-be.

The genius of Montessori has not only showed us the inner significance of the child's work, but the conditions necessary for its accomplishment. Further, she has proved beyond doubt that, given these conditions, the "awakened" child develops a higher type of personality—more mentally alert, more capable of concentration, more socially adaptable, more independent and at the same time more disciplined and obedient —in a word a complete being—a ready foundation for the building up of a normalized adult.

This is Montessori's great achievement, the "discovery of the child." This, in the realm of the human spirit, can be set over against the discovery of those terrible energies latent in the atom. And just as these physical energies are being used to prepare the armaments of war between the nations, so should these newly released spiritual energies be used to create the Armament of Peace. What a splendid hope for the future is the growth of these natural virtues in the child—precious preparation for those supernatural virtues that transform each individual into the likeness of Christ!

It is along this path that the nations of the world will progress most surely towards that harmony foretold by the prophet, when "the wolf shall dwell with the lamb, and the leopard lie down with the kid, and the calf and the young lion and the fatling together—*and a little child shall lead them.*"

Appendix

BIBLIOGRAPHY

BOOKS BY MARIA MONTESSORI

The Absorbent Mind. New York, Dell Publishing Co., 1967.

The Child in the Church. London, Sands & Co., 1930.

The Discovery of the Child. New York, Ballantine Books, 1983.

To Educate the Human Potential. Madras (India), Kalakshetra, 1973.

Education for a New World. Madras (India), Kalakshetra, 1948.

The Formation of Man. Madras (India), The Theosophical Publishing House, 1971.

From Childhood to Adolescence. New York, Schocken Books, 1976.

The Mass Explained to Children. London, Sheed & Ward, 1932.

The Montessori Elementary Material. New York, Schocken Books, 1973.

The Montessori Method. Tr. by Anne E. George, first published in English in 1912. New York, Schocken Books, 1964.

Dr. Montessori's Own Handbook. New York, Schocken Books, 1965.

Peace and Education. Geneva, International Bureau of Education, 1932.

Pedagogical Anthropology. New York, F.A. Stokes Company, Inc., 1913; London. W. Heinemann, 1914.

The Reform of Education During and After Adolescence. Amsterdam, Association Montessori Internationale (AMI), 1939.

The Secret of Childhood. New York, Ballantine Books, 1981.

Spontaneous Activity in Education: The Advanced Montessori Method. New York, Schocken Books, 1965.

What You Should Know About Your Child. Colombo (Ceylon), Bennet & Co., 1948.

BOOKS ABOUT THE MONTESSORI METHOD

Educazione religioso liturgia a metodo Montessori, by Sofia Cavallette and Gianna Gobbi. Rome, Edizioni Paoline, n.d.

Montessori Matters, by Sister Mary Ellen Carinato, et al., Cincinnati, Ohio, Sisters of Notre Dame de Namur, 1983.

The Montessori Principles and Practice, by Edward Parnell Culverwell. London, G. Bell & Sons, Ltd., n.d.

Montessori on a Limited Budget, by Elvira Farrow and Carol Hill. Los Angeles, California, Education Systems Publisher, 1984.

A Montessori Mother, by Dorothea Frances (Canfield) Fisher. New York, H. Holt & Co., 1912.

The Montessori Approach to Special Education, by Lena Gitter. Johnstown, Pennsylvania, Mafex Associates, Inc., 1971.

The Essential Montessori, by Elizabeth G. Hainstock. New York, New American Library, 1978.

Teaching Montessori in the Home: Preschool Years, by Elizabeth G. Hainstock. New York, New American Library, 1976.

Teaching Montessori in the Home: School Years, by Elizabeth G. Hainstock. New York, New American Library, 1978.

Montessori: A Modern Approach, by Paula Polk Lillard. New York, Schocken Books, 1973.

A True Romance: Doctor Maria Montessori as I Knew Her, by Anna M. Maccheroni. Edinburgh, 1946.

Montessori and Your Child, by Terry Malloy. New York, Schocken Books, 1974.

Montessori Matters—A Language Manual, by Sister Mary Motz. Cincinnati, Ohio, Sisters of Notre Dame de Namur, 1982.

Maria Montessori: Methods, Schools and Materials, As Described in the Famous McClure's Magazine Articles, Edited by Reg Orem. Alvin, Texas, George Chyka Productions, 1978.

The Montessori System in Theory and Practice, by Theodate Louise Smith. New York, Harper & Bros., 1912.

The Montessori Revolution in Education, by E.M. Standing. New York, Schocken Books, 1966.

A Guide to the Montessori Method, by Ellen Yale Stevens, New York, F. A. Stokes Company, 1913.

Montessori Schools as Seen in the Early Summer of 1913, by Jessie White. Birmingham, Cornish Bros., Ltd., 1914.

A Parent's Guide to the Montessori Classroom, by Aline D. Wolf. Altoona, Pennsylvania, Parent Child Press, 1980.

MONTESSORI PERIODICALS

Communications of the Association Montessori Internationale (AMI), 161 Koninginneweg, Amsterdam, Holland. Four issues a year (for members).

Montessori Observer, newsletter of the International Montessori Society (IMS), 8 issues per year (for members).

Montessori Opvoeding, magazine of the Dutch Montessori Society, ten issues a year (for members).

Mitteilungen der Deutsche Montessori Gesellschaft, four issues a year (for members).

Vita dell Infanzia, monthly magazine of the Ente Opera Montessori (Rome).

Bulletin of the Association Montessori de France, four issues a year.

Bulletin of the Montessori Society in England, four issues a year.

Around the Child, annual journal published by the Association of Montessorians in India (Calcutta).

Those who wish to order any of these magazines and news letters should write to the Secretary of the Montessori Society concerned. The addresses are given in the following list.

MONTESSORI SOCIETIES

Association Montessori Internationale, Koninginneweg, 161, Amsterdam, Holland.

Nederlandse Montessori Vereniging, same address as above.

The American Montessori Society, 175 Fifth Avenue, New York, New York 10010, U.S.A.

The All-Ceylon Montessori Association, 9, Nimalka Gardens, Kollupithya, Colombo 3, Ceylon.

The Chilean Montessori Society, Avenida El Bosque 56, Santiago de Chile, Chile.

The Danish Montessori Society, Hellerupgardvej 13, Hellerup, Denmark.

The Deutsche Montessori Gesellschaft, Anna Schmidt Schule, Fellnerstrasse 1, Frankfurt a. Main, Germany.

The English Montessori Society, 25a, St. Edmund's Terrace, London, N.W. 8, England.

Association Montessori de France, Rue Henri Cloppert 5, Le Visinet (S. el O.), France.

The Indian Montessori Society, Brila Montessori High School, Pilani (Rajasthan), India. (There are also groups of Montessorians in Delhi and Hyderabad, but the addresses of these are not available.)

The International Montessori Society, 912 Thayer Ave., Silver Spring, Maryland 20910 U.S.A.

The Irish Montessori Society, Rosemount Terrace, Booterstown, Co. Dublin, Ireland.

Ente "Opera Montessori," 116, Via Vittorio Emanuele, Rome, Italy.

MONTESSORI TRAINING COURSES

Montessori training courses are offered by many institutions and organizations throughout the world. In general, a certificate or diploma is issued upon completion.* The following list indicates some of these courses:

Ceylon Montessori Training Course, 9, Nimalha Gardens, Kollupithya, Colombo 3, Ceylon.

Good Shepherd Maria Montessori Training Center, Colombo 13, Ceylon.

Nordisk Montessori Kursus, Hellerupgardvej 13, Hellerup, Denmark,.

Courses organized by the Deutsche Montessori Gesellschaft, Fellnerstrasse 1, Frankfurt aM., Germany.

Arbeitskreis Berlin of the Deutsche Montessori Geselleschaft, Friedrich Wilhelmstrasse 72-74, Berlin-Templehof, Germany.

Centre Montessori de France, 22, rue Eugène Flachat, Paris 17e, France.

Indian Montessori Training Courses in various towns of India. Applications should be addressed: c/o Messrs. Bhaidas Cursondas, Postbox 764, Bombay, India.

Montessori Training Center for village schools: Yeotmal, Midhya, Pradesh, India.

Courses organized by the International Montessori Society, 912 Thayer Ave., Silver Spring, Maryland 20910, U.S.A.

Courses organized by the Ente Opera Montessori, Corso Vittorio Emanuel 166, Rome, Italy.

Training courses organized by the Dutch Montessori Society, Secretariat, 161 Koninginneweg, Amsterdam, Holland.

Training course of the Municipal Training Center, Amsterdam, Nieuwe Prinsengracht 89, Amsterdam-C, Holland.

Roman Catholic Montessori Training Center, Oude Stadsgracht 32, Nijmegan, Holland.

Roman Catholic Training Center "Sint Lucia," Aert Van Nesstraat 29, Rotterdam, Holland.

*Note: Since about 1967, the term "Montessori" has been considered to have a "generic and/or descriptive significance" and is therefore now available for free public use in the United States. See *American Montessori Society, Inc. v. Association Montessori Internationale*, 155 U.S.P.Q. 591, 592 (1967). There may be significant distinctions as to nature, content and format of training among the various organizations which issue certificates or diplomas for completion of their particular type of Montessori training course. Such distinctions generally revolve around the question, "What is 'Montessori?' "

FIRMS SELLING MONTESSORI TEACHING MATERIALS

Holland: A. Nienhuis Montessori, Industriepark 14, Postbus 16, Zelham.

India: Kaybee International, 75-B, Patharia Palace, Ground Floor, Mohamedali Rd., Bombay 400 003.

Italy: Organizzazione per il Materiale Montessori, Via Marchetti 19, Rome.

France: For details apply to French Montessori Society, 22 rue Eugène Flachat, Paris (17e).

U.S.A.:

Educational Teaching Aids, 159 W. Kinzie St., Chicago, Illinois 60610.

El Paso Montessori Suppliers, 3109 Dyer St., El Paso, Texas 79930.

Kaybee Montessori, c/o Toni Sinopoli, 4717 Chesapeake NW, Washington, D.C.

Nienhuis Montessori U.S.A., 320 Pioneer Way, Mountain View, California 94041.

Yankee Montessori Manufacturing, 8655 South Amin St., Los Angeles, California 90003-3499.

Specialized Materials:

Albanesi Educational Center, 4331 Allencrest Lane, Dallas, Texas 75234. (Cultural Subjects)

Montessori Matters, 701 East Columbia Ave., Cincinnati, Ohio 45215 (Language)

Montessori Services, 816 King St., Santa Rosa, California 95404. (Practical Life)

Southwest Montessori Training Center, P.O. Box 13466— North Texas Station, Denton, Texas 76203. (Cultural Subjects)

Note: Parents and teachers are warned that the Montessori materials are of comparatively little value without previous training in the technique of presenting and using them.

MONTESSORI FILMS

With the Montessori method, seeing is believing. The following films were taken in The Gatehouse Montessori School Dallington Street, London E.C. 1, under the direction of Mrs. Phyllis Wallbank, the principal. They have been found useful in universities, training colleges, parent-teacher associations, psychological societies, and also, with the aim of arousing interest, by those who wish to start a Montessori class in a new neighborhood.

The first two films deal with the activities of children under five. Each lasts about twenty minutes and is furnished with full explanatory captions. They are:

1. *The Exercises of Practical Life:* This film shows how children who are still in the sensitive period for order, are given opportunities to carry out a variety of domestic activities such as sweeping, scrubbing, polishing, dusting, and dishwashing. The more remote purpose of these activities is to help the children acquire better muscular coordination, a deeper love of order, and self-discipline.

2. *The Montessori Sensorial Materials:* In this film the children manipulate the various sensorial materials. The aim is to help them to explore the various qualities of objects in their environment, such as colors, sounds, the sizes of objects, their forms (e.g., geometric and leaf forms), and musical pitch.

The purpose of these sensorial materials is not primarily to provide new sensations, but to bring order and system to the sensations the children have already spontaneously acquired from their home and school environment.

3. *The Young Scientists:* Children from an early stage are wide-eyed with wonder at the many mysterious things they see around them—living animals, floating and sinking objects, elements of magnetism and electricity, the swing of a pendulum, the magic of running water, and air currents. This film shows the young scientists making individual researches into these mysteries by means of specially devised apparatus. The children are still too young (from three to ten years) for a systematic study of the sciences, but Montessori believes in "sowing the seeds of the sciences" in an informal manner at this early age. Length: About forty minutes.

4. *A Montessori Arithmetic Film Strip:* 35 mm. Thirty-two frames may be purchased for about $2.

WHERE TO GET THE FILMS:

Films 1 and 2 may be purchased from Mrs. Phyllis Wallbank, Gatehouse Montessori School, Dallington Street, London E.C.1, England. Film 3 is available from the Education Supply Association, High Holbourn, London W.C., England. Film 4 may be bought from the English Montessori Society, 24a, St. Edmund's Terrace, London, N.W. 8, England.

Index